Praise for *Natural Curiosity* 2nd Edition

Natural Curiosity 2*nd Edition* is an excellent resource for educators seeking to act as co-inquirers with their students and share the learning spirit while fostering relationship with our natural kin and relations. With a newly expanded lens on Indigenous perspectives and worldviews, this resource encourages teachers with philosophies, rationales, tools and activities to help them grow ecological and social justice citizens. A timely resource and highly recommended.
— **Jean-Paul Restoule**, Ph.D., Professor and Chair,
Department of Indigenous Education, University of Victoria

Natural Curiosity is a great gift not only to North American educators, but to people around the world. As this good book makes clear, the often-Eurocentric deconstruction of reality does not represent reality. The point of natural curiosity is not to study a *thing*, but to inquire into the connections and relationships of all things and spirit, seen and unseen. This book is an inspiration, a doorway into a web of life and truth.
— **Richard Louv**, Author of "Last Child in the Woods" and "The Nature Principle"

Perhaps the greatest strength of this edition is the care taken to ensure that Indigenous peoples, along with their knowledges and pedagogies, are understood as contemporary, and that they have important contributions to make to environmental education ... This text is remarkable in that it takes theory, including Indigenous knowledge, and applies it through storytelling from both an educator's and child's perspective ... *Natural Curiosity* takes the important step of highlighting broader societal obligations such as those laid out by the Truth and Reconciliation Commission ... The pedagogy employed offers a sensitive and respectful way to present challenging topics. I much enjoyed the stories by educators and children alike and how art and creative expressions were used to convey profound teachings.
— **Deborah McGregor**, Associate Professor, Osgoode Hall Law, School & Faculty of Environmental Studies, Canada Research Chair, Indigenous Environmental Justice, York University

In *Natural Curiosity* 2*nd Edition*, Western ways of relating to nature intermingle with Indigenous ways. The book respects the integrity of both coexisting cultural perspectives. By understanding both, readers and their students will gain greater curiosity and deeper insights to make sense of the world around them or to solve problems.
— **Dr. Glen S. Aikenhead**, Emeritus Professor, Aboriginal Education Research Centre, College of Education, University of Saskatchewan

I must admit to having a case of Canadian envy, and the second edition of *Natural Curiosity* is a good example of why I feel this way. There aren't any education resources like *Natural Curiosity* in the United States. The wedding of theory and practice, the case studies of real live classroom curriculum, the vibrancy of childrens' and teachers' voices about their environmental work--it's compelling and exciting. And the integration of Indigenous perspectives as part of the warp of the fabric of environmental inquiry makes the whole endeavor deeply equitable and just. If I teach my Place-based Education course again, this book will play a leading role.
— **David Sobel**, Senior Faculty, Education Department,
Antioch University New England

The second edition of *Natural Curiosity* from Indigenous perspectives gives educators practices and pedagogies for helping learners develop a much needed deeper sense of place. We are at a significant moment in time where we need more sustainable and ecologically just ways of being in this world. This resource provides rich possibilities for all of us to achieve shared commitments to reconciling our relationships with land, people, and place.
— **Dr. Jan Hare**, Associate Dean for Indigenous Education,
University of British Columbia, Unceded Musqueam Territory

My students and I found the first edition of this text book to be very engaging and accessible ... With the incorporation of Indigenous perspectives, the 2nd edition is an even better fit! The text is an excellent balance of theoretical perspectives illustrated with practical examples from a range of classrooms. I particularly enjoyed drawing on the actual transcripts from teachers and students as they engaged in knowledge building discourse and explored students' questions. The content also complements education transformation that is occurring in British Columbia right now.
— **Rachel Moll**, PhD, Chair, Graduate Programs and Professor,
Faculty of Education, Vancouver Island University, BC

The second edition of *Natural Curiosity* is an excellent resource for educators wanting to include Indigenous perspectives in their environmental inquiry with learners of all ages. More than a "how to guide", this text engages educators in learning from Indigenous thought.
— **Susan D. Dion**, PhD, Associate Professor, Indigenous Education,
Faculty of Education, York University

This book should be held close to the heart of all educators in Ontario. It synthesizes the breadth of current theory and provides a wide variety of critical perspectives. The 2nd Edition of *Natural Curiosity* acts as a beacon, lighting the path along which we should and must selectively and collectively evolve. It should be embraced by all and will, no doubt, stand as a substantial part of the foundation upon which the future of education in Canada can be built.
— **Matt Brundle**, Assistant Coordinator/Site Supervisor,
Toronto Urban Studies Centre, TDSB

Natural Curiosity 2nd Edition is a resource that should be used in every classroom across Canada ... Stories that include the importance of reciprocity, spirituality and place-based learning will support exemplary educators with a land-based teaching practice further connect with their students to the natural world. Through living in harmony, mutual sustainability and heightened environmental consciousness, it is what many Indigenous people and Indigenous nations around the world have already believed and practiced on a daily basis through prayer, meditation and thanksgiving since time immemorial. Quite simply, it is called "all my relations."
— **Stephanie Roy**, M.A., OCT, Executive Director,
Kenjgewin Teg Educational Institute

This timely and useful resource supports the increasing recognition of the importance of embodied learning in nature. Challenging Euro-Western child-centered pedagogies common in nature and environmental programs, it acknowledges and honours Indigenous ways of knowing and being and the pedagogical significance of connectedness and relations with place, materials, plants, animals, land, water and weather.

— **Louise Zimanyi**, Professor, School of Health Sciences, Early Childhood Education, Humber College

This second edition of *Natural Curiosity* feels like an invitation and a gift. The text invites me to respect the relationships and ways of knowing that Indigenous peoples have had with this land since time immemorial. It is also an invitation to deeply understand that as a guest on Turtle Island, my role is to listen and learn. The gift is that of responsibility – now that this knowledge has been shared with me, how will I take it up with my students? From its first pages, this resource invites non-Indigenous teachers to welcome these understandings into our teaching with humility. Thank you to Doug and the entire team for this important work.

— **Angela Nardozi**, PhD, OCT, Author Listen & Learn newsletter, Sessional Lecturer, Ontario Institute for Studies in Education

At ALCDSB we have been on the integrated environmental inquiry journey since 2011 when the first *Natural Curiosity* resource came out. Since that time we have embraced more deeply student voice in the learning process and have benefited greatly as a result. The second edition of *Natural Curiosity* comes at an important time for us as it nurtures another voice, the voice of the land through an Indigenous perspective. It is through this perspective that we become more fully aware that as human beings we are "of the land" not separate from it. When we educators begin working with our students in this way a much different learning journey begins, one that reinforces our collective call to care for the sacred gift of creation.

— **Mike Bibby**, Outdoor and Environmental Education, Special Assignment Teacher, Algonquin & Lakeshore Catholic DSB

Natural Curiosity (First Edition) opened a door and inspired many educators, including myself, to engage in and shift to an environmental inquiry stance – outside! The professional development and conversations I was involved with repeatedly left educators wanting MORE. After the anticipation of this second edition, I am confident it has met its objective to go deeper. This is not a resource that will sit on a shelf, rather it will be weathered and folded from being used to align what was always meant to be connected: environmental inquiry and Indigenous ways of knowing. Congratulations on yet another outstanding resource that will set the stage for future caring environmental citizens.

— **Tanya Murray**, OCT, Ontario Environmental Educator, York Region Nature Collaborative, Child and Nature Alliance of Canada

Natural Curiosity 2nd Edition is a welcome, practical and vital evolution of the original edition of this resource that first appeared in 2011 with such promise. Where the first version was successful in promoting meaningful inquiry in outdoor natural space, the second edition will do that and more. For education, the practice of recognizing and applying indigenous ways of learning will inspire educators in rich new ways of teaching, and students in deep personal learning. For society, delivering on our collective commitment to reconcile Indigenous and non-Indigenous cultures to move into a future with greater hope, understanding and partnership is crucial. In short, the sacred educational ground of this important new resource needs to be an honoured path on which all educators tread.

— **Bill Kilburn**, Program Manager, Back To Nature Network

The Laboratory School
Dr. Eric Jackman Institute of Child Study
UNIVERSITY OF TORONTO

Natural Curiosity 2nd Edition

A Resource for Educators

The Importance of Indigenous Perspectives in Children's Environmental Inquiry

Doug Anderson, Julie Comay, and Lorraine Chiarotto

www.naturalcuriosity.ca

NATURAL CURIOSITY 2nd Edition: A Resource for Educators.
The Importance of Indigenous Perspectives in Children's Environmental Inquiry
Copyright © 2017. The Laboratory School at the Dr. Eric Jackman Institute of Child Study.
All rights reserved.

Funded by TD Friends of the Environment, the Norman and Marian Robertson Charitable Foundation, and private donors.
An online, digital version will be available at www.naturalcuriosity.ca.

No part of this book nor its affiliated website, www.naturalcuriosity.ca, may be reproduced in any manner without written permission except in the case of brief quotations embodied and properly cited in critical articles and reviews.

This book has been printed on 100% recycled paper, approved by the Forest Stewardship Council (FSC). The FSC is an international, non-profit organization that supports the responsible management of the world's forests in terms of environmental, social, and economic viability.

Printed in Canada by Marquis Book Printing, 350 des Entrepreneurs, Montmagny, Québec G5V 4T1

For information please write:
The Laboratory School at the Dr. Eric Jackman Institute of Child Study
Ontario Institute for Studies in Education, University of Toronto
45 Walmer Road, Toronto, Ontario M5R 2X2, Canada

SECOND EDITION

Managing Editor – Haley Higdon

Written by Doug Anderson, Julie Comay, and Lorraine Chiarotto
Edited by Glen Aikenhead, Christine Higdon, & Tracy Pryce
Designed by Dino Roussetos & Doug Baines
Indigenous Artwork created by Invert Media Inc.

Library and Archives Canada Cataloguing in Publication
ISBN (Print): 978-0-7727-2643-8
ISBN (Electronic): 978-0-7727-2644-5

Contents

Acknowledgements i

Introduction to the Second Edition 1

Part 1: A Pedagogical Framework 4

Preface *An Indigenous Lens on Natural Curiosity* 5

Branch I: Inquiry and Engagement *Nurturing a Sense of Wonder* 11
    Theoretical Underpinnings 11
        Curiosity Is Natural 11
        Sustaining and Cultivating Curiosity 11
        What Is Inquiry-based Learning? 12
        Why Take the Leap? The Benefits of Inquiry-based Learning 14
        Inquiry and Knowledge Building 14
        What Is Knowledge Building (KB) Discourse? 15
        Key Principles of Knowledge Building 18
        How Does Knowledge Building Progress? 19
        Children's Preconceptions 25
    Putting It into Practice 26
        Space and Time: What Might an Inquiry-based Classroom Look Like? 26
        Cultivating Curiosity: Starting the Environmental Inquiry Process 29
        What Is the Role of the Educator? 33
    Inquiry and Assessment: Why, How, and for Whom? 37
    Thinking About Different Learners 53
    Summary of Chapter 55

Lighting the Fire: The Spirit of Learning *Indigenous Lens on Branch I* 57

Branch II: Experiential Learning *Building a Sense of Place* 65
    Theoretical Underpinnings 65
        What Is Experiential Learning? 65
        Inquiry and Experiential Learning: Experience and Reflection 65
        Why Is Outdoor Experiential Learning Essential for Children? 66
        Why Is Outdoor Experiential Learning Essential for the Planet? 66
        Nature as a Complex Environment 67
    Putting It into Practice 70
        Take Your Students Outside 70
        Bringing Children into Nature 70
        Explore the Local Community and You'll Find the Curriculum 74
        'Unnatural' Outdoor Spaces: Why They Count 76
        Informal Learning 78

    A Place for Solitude 79
    Summary of Chapter 79

Sending out Roots: Grounding Learning in Place *Indigenous Lens on Branch II* 81

Branch III: Integrated Learning *Making Connections and Broadening Perspectives* 88
    Theoretical Underpinnings 88
        What Is Integrated Learning? 88
        Some Benefits of Integrated Learning 88
        Building an Integrated Learning Program 89
        Putting the Pieces Together 92
    Putting It into Practice 92
        Getting Started 92
        Student Questions and Big Ideas 92
        Building Connections, Planning for Possibilities 100
        Broadening Perspectives 101
    Summary of Chapter 102

The Flow of Knowledge: Everything is Related *Indigenous Lens on Branch III* 103

Branch IV: Moving Toward Sustainability *Living and Acting in the World* 109
    Theoretical Underpinnings 109
        Situating Ourselves in Nature 109
        Fostering Environmental Responsibility 111
    Putting It into Practice 114
        Fostering Environmental Agency 114
        Structuring Outdoor Time 115
        Linking Sustainable Action to Classroom Learning 116
        Environmental Consciousness and Social Justice: Building Connections 119
        Thinking Developmentally 122
        How Do Children Understand Environmental Sustainability? 123
        Children Reflect on Their Connections with Nature 124
    Looking Forward: Building Communities of Sustainable Practice 130
        Tracy's Story – A Parent's Perspective 130

Breathing with the World:
Applied Learning through Reciprocity *Indigenous Lens on Branch IV* 133

Part 2: Environmental Inquiry in Action – The Educators' Stories 140

The Early Years
    Stephanie's Story (Fraser Mustard Learning Academy) 142
    Marge, Sara, Glenda, and Gail's Story (Mine Centre School) 150
    Beverly's Story (Elmdale Public School) 160
    Carol's Story (Lab School) 168
    Hopi's Story (McMurrich Junior Public School) 178

Grades One and Two
    Zoe's Story (Lab School) 187
    Ellie's Story (The Grove Community School) 194
    Cindy's Story (Lab School) 204

Grades Three and Four
    Velvet's Story (The Grove Community School) 211
    Lisa's Story (Lab School) 219
    Marlo's Story (Johnny Therriault School) 226
    Robin's Story (Lab School) 234

Grades Five and Six
    Mike's Story (Lab School) 251
    Murray's Story (Rideau Heights Public School) 262
    Janice's Story (Belfountain Public School) 271

Acknowledgements

The Laboratory School at the Dr. Eric Jackman Institute of Child Study is grateful to the many individuals and organizations who contributed to the development of this resource and to the larger initiative of sharing environmental inquiry with educators across Canada.

In 2014, members of the Laboratory School's Environmental Education Initiative team realized, through conversations with educators from Johnny Therriault School on Aroland First Nation, how much there still was to learn about situating Indigenous perspectives into Canadian curricula. Thank you to the Elders and educators of Johnny Therriault School for starting us on this journey, and for motivating us to find support for the second edition.

Our sincerest thanks to our donors; without you it would not have been possible to write this resource. The second edition of *Natural Curiosity* was produced with funding from TD Friends of the Environment, The Norman and Marian Robertson Foundation, and private donors.

Chi Meegwetch (a big thank you) to the following key advisors on the Indigenous Lens in this edition: to Glen Aikenhead, for consultation, review, contributions and revisions; to Vernon Douglas (Biidaabun), Anishinaabe, for review, consultation and advice; to Christine Luza, Anishinaabe, for consultation, review and contributions; and, to Jennifer Wemigwans for her consultation on design and conceptions that are rooted in Indigenous worldviews and understandings.

Thanks are also in order to the following people for diverse advice, consultation, review, and helpful contributions to various aspects of the Indigenous lens on this edition: Cliff Abbott, Beverly Caswell, Donna Chief, Eileen (Sam) Conroy (Wahgeh Giizhigo Migizi Kwe), Debra Cormier, Katherine Hensel, Jason Jones, Shelly Jones, Angela Mainville, Deborah McGregor, Sharla MacKinnon, Angela Nardozi, Jean-Paul Restoule, Rowan Sky and Sandra Styres.

This resource has grown out of the professional insights and experiences of the educators at the Lab School, whose input was essential to the creation of this document. These teachers include Norah L'Espérance, Raadiyah Nazeem, Carol Stephenson, Zoe Donoahue, Cindy Halewood, Sarah Luongo, Lisa Sherman, Robin Shaw, Michael Martins, Julia Murray, Benjamin Peebles, Christel Durand, Judith Kimel, Nick Song, Tara Rousseau, Renée Smith, and Krista Spence.

Richard Reeve has been instrumental, first as a classroom teacher then as a researcher, in the development of computer-based knowledge building practices at the Lab School and elsewhere. We thank him for his contribution to this edition.

The following educators courageously and openly shared their stories of environmental inquiry, allowing all of us to learn and benefit from their experiences: Stephanie Hammond, Beverly Papove, Marge Hale, Sara Empey, Glenda Potson, Gail Jones, Hopi Martin, Carol Stephenson, Zoe Donoahue, Ellie Clin, Cindy Halewood, Velvet Lacasse, Lisa Sherman, Marlo Sobush, Robin Shaw, Michael Martins, Murray Dee, and Janice Haines.

The Lab School is especially grateful to Tracy Pryce for her invaluable support, not only in her capacity as a skilled and thoughtful editor, but as an individual with unlimited energy and commitment to the project. We are also very grateful to Christine Higdon for her timely and incisive editing. Thank you to Casey Dabiet and Ron Gurfinkel for helping us to navigate the world of book distributors, and to Cindy Hall at University of Toronto Press for her support with the distribution process. Thank you to Alessandra Sanchez and Deepta Rayner for joining our think tank and sharing their marketing advice, and to Sheri Allain for providing inspiring strategy leadership. Thanks also to Zach Pedersen for his wonderful photos and to Dino Roussetos & Doug Baines for their design expertise. And a very special thank you to Invert Media for their consultation and beautiful and original Indigenous artwork.

Deep appreciation is extended to the Lab School's Environmental Education Team: current Project Lead Haley Higdon, former Project Leads Andrea Russell and Lorraine Chiarotto, Vice Principal Chriss Bogert, Principal Richard Messina, and former Principal Elizabeth Morley. Their leadership and keen vision for sharing environmental inquiry with the broader educational community is what made this project possible. Many thanks to past project coordinators, Becky Stewart, Camila Miki and Nikki Fletcher, and work study students Anna Silverstein and Mariah Martin. A special thank you is owed to Amanda Santos, current project coordinator, whose skill and dedication have been integral in pulling together the administrative pieces of this resource.

Finally, we owe our deepest thanks to all the children in the classrooms represented here for joining us on this journey. Without their willingness to follow their curiosity, try things out, and wholeheartedly embrace their teachers' experimentations with environmental inquiry, there would be no resource.

The Dr. Eric Jackman Institute of Child Study Lab School is grateful to the writers and contributors to this resource. Julie Comay so beautifully revised and enriched our first edition, after extensive research, reading, and carefully interviewing Lab School teachers, to express our pedagogy as we currently understand it. Lorraine Chiarotto created the visionary first edition of this resource, upon which this revised edition is built. Ed Burtynsky has shown unwavering support and encouragement. Andrea Russell has been dedicated to growing Natural Curiosity into a transformative professional learning program and laying the groundwork to make this edition possible. Haley Higdon's passionate commitment to environmental sustainability and nature-based learning has been an inspiration as she masterminded the creation and production of this resource. Finally we thank Doug Anderson for his powerful, thought-provoking prose which unfolded from two years of heartfelt discussion and reflection. His writing is an immense gift to us all.

Richard Messina Chriss Bogert
Principal   Vice Principal

Introduction to the Second Edition

When the first edition of *Natural Curiosity* came out in 2011, its goal was to introduce an inquiry-based approach to environmental education. This approach was situated within a longstanding tradition of progressive schooling that places children at the centre of their learning, responds to their lead as they construct meaning through engagement with the world, and supports the emergence of a community of learners.

In 2009, a key document issued by the Ontario Ministry of Education (*Acting Today, Shaping Tomorrow*) called upon educators to mobilize their teaching around issues of environmental education. In response, the first edition of *Natural Curiosity* set out to demonstrate how an inquiry-based approach could enable educators to meet Ministry expectations as students absorbed themselves in learning shaped by their own questions and ideas. *Natural Curiosity* offered educators a four-branched framework that included Inquiry-based Learning, Experiential Learning, Integrated Learning, and Environmental Stewardship. The second part of the resource brought these theoretical orientations vividly to life as teachers described how they embraced the possibilities offered by this approach and, with their students, found new ways to meaningfully and joyfully engage with the natural world.

About the Dr. Eric Jackman Institute of Child Study Laboratory School

Natural Curiosity was developed by the Laboratory School at the Dr. Eric Jackman Institute of Child Study, which is part of the Ontario Institute for Studies in Education (OISE) at the University of Toronto. Established under the leadership of Dr. William Blatz in 1925, the Laboratory School is a Nursery to Grade 6 elementary school dedicated to exploring what is possible in education, operating in conjunction with an MA in Child Study and Education teacher certification program and the Dr. R.G.N. Laidlaw Centre for multidisciplinary research in child development. The Lab School philosophy emerged from three foundations: an understanding of the unique development of children; Dr. Blatz's theories about the critical role of security in children's education; and John Dewey's ideas for child-centred inquiry. Today at the Lab School, these beliefs remain central to our program, while we continue to expand our understanding of what these guiding principles might mean for school communities in this century.

Impact of the First Edition

Since its initial launch, *Natural Curiosity* has gained widespread implementation in schools, school boards, and ministries of education across the country and internationally. As environmental education becomes a priority for schools everywhere, the resource continues to be in high demand. *Natural Curiosity*'s message has been disseminated through partnerships with schools, communities, and faculties of education, professional development workshops, and by word of mouth among enthused practitioners. In addition to high rates of electronic downloads of both French and English versions, more than 20,000 paper copies of the book have been printed and sold to date.

Since teachers first began to incorporate environmental inquiry into their practice, the word "inquiry" has become commonplace in educational settings. At the Lab School, addressing teachers' questions and encountering myriad interpretations of the concept in action have forced us to reflect upon what inquiry-based learning does and does not mean to us. One important feature that characterizes our approach to learning is the use of community knowledge building practices. We also find ourselves frequently returning to Dr. Blatz's prescient ideas about the importance of children's security or emotional well-being to their learning. This foundational concept continues to inform our understanding of inquiry and *Natural Curiosity*'s other three branches through all their permutations.

Rationale for a Second Edition

The driving motivation for a second edition was the burning need, in the wake of strong and unequivocal recommendations by the Truth and Reconciliation Commission (2015), to bring Indigenous perspectives into the heart of Canadian educational settings and curricula, most notably in connection with environmental issues. Momentum gathered as points of convergence (as well as discontinuities) between *Natural Curiosity*'s approach and certain Indigenous perspectives were identified. Doug Anderson, who has thought long and deeply about such matters, agreed to articulate these perspectives in this edition; other experts offered their insights, and a project was launched. Looking back at the first edition, Lab School educators realized that it was not enough to simply layer an Indigenous perspective on our own fixed way of doing things. We began to see our values and practices through other eyes, and this triggered a process of rethinking or refining what was most important about our philosophy and practice. We had never intended to freeze our approach; our beliefs and practices remain living, breathing, dynamic processes that are inevitably and repeatedly revised, as our school, like all schools, builds relationships with changing communities in changing times.

Organization of the Second Edition

We have preserved the structure of the first edition, in which a theoretical section is followed by teachers' voices. The four branches continue to provide the framework for our approach, with intriguing and substantive links to the views expressed so eloquently through the Indigenous lens. This lens illuminates both marked continuities and evident disjunctions with *Natural Curiosity*'s approach to environmental inquiry. One beautiful connection lies in the high value placed on what Indigenous cultures regard as "learning from the heart" and what we think of as "curiosity-driven learning"; despite telling differences in terminology, at their core, both descriptions see worthwhile learning as coming from what matters most deeply to the child.

While they provide a useful analytic scheme, the four branches outlined in *Natural Curiosity* are deeply entangled. We see interweaving threads in each branch – with an emphasis on agency in inquiry-based learning, on place and real-world experience in experiential learning, on the holism and interconnectedness of integrated learning. Though both editions begin with a chapter on inquiry – for one must start somewhere – any branch could have equally well served as a starting point. Each circles back to the others. Especially because we are aspiring to education with implications for living in an increasingly unsustainable world, the Indigenous lens offers an invaluable counterpoint to the more "evidence-based" practices of mainstream Euro-Canadian schooling, and recalls David Orr's caution that "the skills, aptitudes, and attitudes necessary to industrialize the earth are not necessarily the same as those that will be needed to heal the earth or to build durable economies and good communities" (2004, p. 27).

Part 1: The Branches

The resource consists of two parts. Part 1 describes the four branches of environmental inquiry. These branches appear under chapter headings that have been slightly amended from the first edition to reflect our current shifts in emphasis: Inquiry and Engagement, Experiential Learning, Integrated Learning, and Moving Toward Sustainability. Each chapter presents a theoretical background followed by ideas for putting the theory into practice. Each branch is considered first from a Lab School perspective, then through an Indigenous lens.

Part 2: Educators' Stories

Part 2 describes the experiences of educators who have integrated environmental inquiry into their practice. Whereas all of the classroom stories in the first edition were written by the author of the resource (Lorraine Chiarotto) after interviewing teachers, the current stories have been written by the teachers themselves. What may have been lost in uniformity of presentation is wonderfully replaced by the multiplicity of voices we encounter. From diverse backgrounds and teaching situations, some new to this approach and some highly experienced, the educators represent the variegated social and educational landscape of Ontario. They write from schools in rural northwestern Ontario, in downtown Toronto, in Caledon, Kingston and Ottawa. They teach at alternative schools, inner-city public schools, a First Nation school, and our university lab school. Taken together, the educators' stories powerfully illustrate some of the unique ways that environmental inquiry comes to life in classrooms.

As we think about strengthening environmental inquiry with Indigenous perspectives, these stories from teachers reflect the beginning of a journey rather than a destination. It is hoped that they will motivate meaningful dialogue about the links between environmental education and Indigenous thinking as we move forward on this path together.

While only a few of the educators explicitly address Indigenous perspectives or content, aspects of the perspectives highlighted in the Indigenous lens surface through all the stories. As teachers everywhere begin to build Indigenous content and perspectives into learning experiences for their students – an emerging and challenging area for many – stories such as these provide a starting point for a continuing conversation.

Changing Terminology in the Second Edition

The words we use sometimes have unintended connotations. For that reason, we have revised our use of two common terms in this edition.

Teachers or educators?
There are many who support the learning of others, including classroom teachers, early childhood educators, Indigenous Elders, community educators, school administrators, professors, camp counsellors, parents, and caregivers. Though many of the voices in this book reflect the experiences of elementary school teachers, we hope that the relevance of this resource will extend beyond the school context. We have therefore used the broader term "educator" in the title, and referred to "educators" and "teachers" interchangeably throughout the resource.

Stewardship or sustainability?
Thinking about the ultimate purposes of environmental education, we use the term "sustainability" to represent a broader and more meaningful goal than "stewardship", while continuing to acknowledge a place for concepts of stewardship or caretaking in children's environmental learning. Details of this thinking can be found in the introduction to Branch IV.

Looking Ahead

Natural Curiosity was never intended as a "how-to" manual for teachers. It offers an approach and framework that encourages educators to find their own ways to connect their students with the natural world. Nor is it the intent of the second edition to provide a step-by-step method for implementing Indigenous pedagogy in classrooms. At this early stage of our learning, that would be presumptuous. What we offer instead is an encounter with Indigenous perspectives on some of our own ideas about children and their learning. The Indigenous lens opens our eyes to transformative possibilities for practice. Working with Doug Anderson and his colleagues has brought the Lab School into a conversation that has initiated us into acting in reconciliatory ways.

This edition represents only one leg of an unfinished journey. We are grateful to Doug Anderson for offering, within an Indigenous framework, this thoughtful response to some of our ideas and practices in environmental inquiry. The next step is up to all of us, creators and readers of this second edition, as we work out ways to respond to the challenges revealed by that lens and actively bring Indigenous perspectives into our classrooms. Sharing our stories is essential to this process.

Preface to the Second Edition:
An Indigenous Lens on Natural Curiosity

The approach to environmental inquiry in both editions of the *Natural Curiosity* resource finds common ground with Indigenous values in some important ways, and reflects an emerging sense of respect for Indigenous knowledge among educators. One Anishinaabe Elder and retired elementary teacher said of the first edition, "I cried when I read it. I said to myself, they're finally starting to get it!"[1]

The second edition of *Natural Curiosity* supports a stronger basic awareness of Indigenous perspectives and their importance to environmental education. Over time such awareness can support better understanding of Indigenous knowledge through relationships with Indigenous people. This awareness and understanding can serve, in turn, as the basis for the application of Indigenous perspectives in modern learning contexts.

Indigenous perspectives cannot be deeply reflected in a written document or outside of their cultural contexts. All that can be provided here are some indications of how such perspectives can inform environmental inquiry. The living and moving spirits of students, educators, and communities are needed for transforming awareness over time into understanding, knowledge and, eventually, wisdom.

The Indigenous lens in this edition represents a cross-cultural encounter supporting what can become an ongoing dialogue and evolution of practice in environmental inquiry. Some important questions are raised that challenge us to think in very different ways about things as fundamental as the meaning of knowledge. We hope this lens inspires educators to explore learning in relation to these challenging questions.

If we begin to understand and appreciate Indigenous wisdom traditions, and work ethically with Indigenous people to bring those traditions to bear on how we learn, we can improve any education system. This edition provides some examples of how Indigenous perspectives confirm and deepen principles and practices laid out in both editions of *Natural Curiosity*. We begin to ask: How do Indigenous perspectives relate to environmental education? How might they enhance educators' understanding over time as they explore environmental inquiry? What Indigenous perspectives and principles apply to all of us, and can these be supported ethically in any learning environment?

These questions need to be approached with humility and a recognition that exploring them will take time and involve the development of meaningful relationships with Indigenous people. The Indigenous lens in this edition provides a glimpse of what such a process and relationship might mean. Exploring these perspectives, in partnership with Indigenous communities and educators, should be the work of all educators.

We have consulted with Indigenous teachers and academics in both Indigenous and mainstream learning contexts, as well as non-Indigenous educators and scholars.[2] We hope this edition advances discussion on how learning takes place in the classroom, around the school, and in relation to the places we live.

Why an Indigenous Lens?

Canadian education systems have begun to acknowledge the importance of building Indigenous perspectives into curricula to support learning *about* Indigenous histories and cultures. The need for reconciliation is also pressing and, as we move through the 21st century, making it a priority is long overdue. This adds to the urgency of addressing Indigenous issues and content, but these are not the most compelling reasons for exploring Indigenous perspectives in education. The greatest opportunities lie beyond cross-cultural awareness of issues and content, and involve profound challenges to *how we learn*, and *how we live*.

---

[1] From a conversation in 2013 with Wahgeh Giizhigo Migizi Kwe (Eileen "Sam" Conroy). The Anishinaabek (plural of Anishinaabe) include the peoples of the Three Fires Confederacy (Odawa, Potawatomi, and Ojibwe) surrounding the Great Lakes region, and the term is also applied to closely related peoples, such as the Algonquin in eastern Ontario and Quebec, or the Saulteaux in the west, for example.

[2] Contributors to this edition are listed in the acknowledgements section.

Indigenous knowledge and processes related to learning and life in general, and to environmental education in particular, are useful everywhere – for anyone.

For example, one Indigenous principle we would all do well to consider is the idea of thinking seven generations into the future. Another would be the idea that a living Spirit resides in everything, and that for this reason, everything around us, whether seen or unseen, deserves respect. Such ideas have enormous implications for how children learn to think about and relate to the world. Indigenous wisdom traditions challenge us all, regardless of our background, to directly address the most difficult and pressing questions about learning, being, knowledge, love, death, and our purpose and survival in Mother Earth.[3]

The World Commission on Environment and Development, the United Nations Declaration on the Rights of Indigenous Peoples, and the Convention on Biological Diversity all recognize the significance of Indigenous knowledge to all peoples (McGregor, 2014). Indigenous ways of thinking involve "an understanding that has *endured* for a *reason*" (Meyer, 2013, p. 98). Indigenous people have not struggled, against all odds, to maintain their cultural traditions simply because it is their right to do so. These cultural traditions have survival value in themselves. They express a deeply felt *responsibility*. Indigenous cultures point out important factors in our very survival, factors that are generally neglected today.

While distinct in many ways from popular conceptions of the world in recent history, Indigenous perspectives belong in *all times*, and are contemporary in ways that extend far beyond "cultural content" for schools. There are not just *Indigenous perspectives on science*, for example; there is *Indigenous science*, offering clear remedies to the narrowness and blind spots of what most people consider science in the 21st century (Cajete, 2000).

[3] Saskatchewan Cree and Dene Elders believe the common expression "on Mother Earth" continues the subtle colonization they experience from Anglophones. The expression "in Mother Earth" is closer to their Indigenous meaning. Similarly, the phrase "on the land" becomes "in the land."

Indigenous perspectives also inform good teaching practice, are applicable to all educators and students, and are increasingly relevant to mainstream education systems as we struggle with 21st century realities (Aikenhead & Michell, 2011; Metallic & Seiler, 2009).

This edition of *Natural Curiosity* is not about improving outcomes for Indigenous learners, or adding Indigenous content in classrooms, although it can and should connect with these critical aims. This edition is about beginning to consider how an Indigenous lens *informs learning, in ways that address our present and future, by improving our relationship with the world around us*. This is where the approaches taken in both editions of *Natural Curiosity* begin to intersect with Indigenous perspectives. It is a humble beginning that holds great promise for all people.

What Are "Indigenous Perspectives?"

There are many Indigenous perspectives, rooted in complex, dynamic knowledge systems, and grounded in the long-standing cultural worldviews of Indigenous peoples. These perspectives reflect Indigenous processes, principles, and wisdom that are alive today. This edition of *Natural Curiosity* draws on Indigenous perspectives of the Americas, whose cultures (while never static) have existed for millennia and continue to have profound implications for the present and the future. Because the Dr. Eric Jackman Institute of Child Study Laboratory School is in Toronto, this edition mostly considers Indigenous sources in Ontario and the surrounding provinces and states (although sources as far as Saskatchewan, British Columbia, and Hawai'i are also considered).

Not all genetically Indigenous people should be stereotyped as holding Indigenous cultural perspectives, which have been under assault for generations. This genocidal assault has included widespread, systematic attempts at the intellectual colonization of Indigenous peoples and the eradication of Indigenous cultures. As a result, many Indigenous people have an extremely disrupted experience of their own cultures.

Reducing Indigenous perspectives to simplistic terms is problematic; even leading Indigenous Elders, scholars, and knowledge keepers cannot be expected to always agree on particulars. However, with this in mind, commonly agreed on qualities of most, if not all, Indigenous perspectives include:

- a strong sense of spirituality
- a deeply rooted sense of place
- a recognition that everything is related
- an emphasis on reciprocity

These qualities, and the genius and importance of Indigenous perspectives, are grounded in what are sometimes referred to as "Original Instructions," or various levels of "law" – from Sacred laws to natural laws – which, in turn, define (or should define) customary human laws.[4] These "Original Instructions" apply to all nations, but have become increasingly forsaken around the world in modern times.

The four qualities listed above are not a comprehensive summary of Indigenous perspectives. However, they do correspond in important ways with the four branches of the *Natural Curiosity* approach, and help frame the Indigenous lens to the second edition. They are explained and explored further on in this edition, in relation to those branches.

How Do Indigenous Perspectives Relate to the Four Branches?

It is impossible here to give comprehensive examples of the implications of Indigenous perspectives for environmental education. However, aspects of Indigenous perspectives certainly correspond with best practices promoted in the *Natural Curiosity* resources, and can deepen our understanding and practice of environmental education as it evolves.

Ideas that relate to the cultural principles, practices, and communication styles found in diverse Indigenous cultures are found in many parts of the *Natural Curiosity* resource. An Indigenous lens placed on any page would enlighten and add value, but this edition cannot contain and analyze all the places we might apply an Indigenous lens; to do so would be to write another, much larger book. Rather, each of the qualities of Indigenous perspectives outlined above is placed in relation to *Natural Curiosity* as a reflection at the end of each branch in this edition:

[4] These English terms are inadequate to convey the full meaning of the ideas. For example, some connotations of the English word "law" conflict with certain Indigenous values.

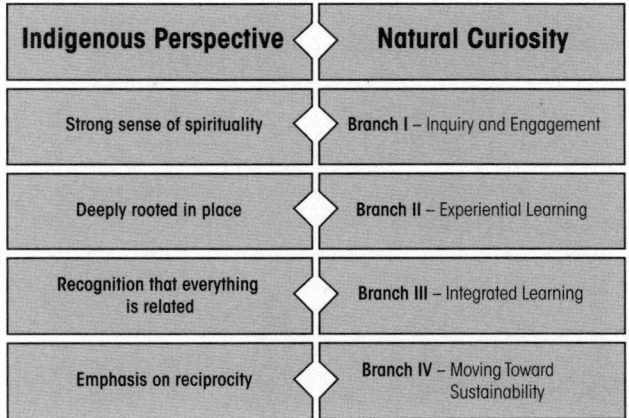

Table 1: Relating Indigenous Perspectives to Natural Curiosity

Indigenous Perspective	Natural Curiosity
Strong sense of spirituality	Branch I – Inquiry and Engagement
Deeply rooted in place	Branch II – Experiential Learning
Recognition that everything is related	Branch III – Integrated Learning
Emphasis on reciprocity	Branch IV – Moving Toward Sustainability

These Indigenous perspectives often, but do not always, correspond with the perspectives that have informed much of the *Natural Curiosity* resource. This correspondence is not rigid, and any of the qualities of Indigenous perspectives may relate to any of the branches.

"But I'm Not Aboriginal!"

Many educators want to address and build Indigenous perspectives into their classrooms, but feel hesitant about how to do so. This is actually a good sign. Teachers in earlier decades often presented highly misinformed views on Indigenous people and cultures as fact. While greater understanding generally exists today, the stereotypes and misconceptions[5] held by that earlier generation of teachers still exist and will take time to more fully address.

The inevitable persistence of misconceptions should not stop us from trying to provide learning environments informed by Indigenous perspectives. Many Indigenous Elders are happy with educators trying their best and learning from their mistakes. It is better to innovate with Indigenous perspectives in steps that fit actual learning contexts, than to try to implement many aspects of the ideas being shared here all at once.

This second edition of *Natural Curiosity* does not assume significant knowledge of Indigenous cultures and peoples beyond the general knowledge most Canadian teachers are already likely to hold. For educators with this basic awareness, the suggestions below can be helpful in trying to build Indigenous perspectives into learning.

[5] Stereotypes can be positive and negative; idealizing or romanticizing Indigenous people and cultures in general can be as misleading as casting them as savages.

Table 2: Suggestions for Building Indigenous Perspectives into Learning

- Work wherever possible with Indigenous resource people
- Be up front about what we do and don't know
- Be clear that Indigenous people, cultures, and knowledge are contemporary
- Respect Indigenous knowledge as a precious heritage
- Be aware of the complexities of real Indigenous people

Work wherever possible with Indigenous resource people

Many educators may not have access to or awareness of keepers of Indigenous cultural knowledge. Elders with a lot of cultural knowledge are generally busy and hard to reach. However, local Friendship Centres (urban Indigenous community centres) or nearby reserves may be able to help educators find appropriate resource people. While Elders may not be available, a younger generation of Indigenous people is working to ethically bring Indigenous perspectives into learning environments.

Be up front about what we do and don't know

As we explore Indigenous issues, knowledge, and practices as important ways to inform environmental inquiry, we must recognize that we are doing so not as experts, but as a community of educators and learners who are involved in our own lifelong learning process.

Be clear that Indigenous people, cultures, and knowledge are contemporary

It is insulting to many Indigenous people when they are considered only in the context of "how they used to live." Exploring the history of Indigenous life and cultures is important, but it is critical for learners to understand that Indigenous people and their worldviews are both traditional and contemporary. They exist and survive today.

Respect Indigenous knowledge as a precious heritage

Many keepers of Indigenous cultural knowledge have legitimate concerns about protecting their knowledge from misuse, misappropriation, or exploitation. Indigenous peoples wish to maintain ownership over their knowledge, even when they choose to share it with others. This is best achieved through collaboration (McGregor, 2014).

Be aware of the complexities of real Indigenous people

Maintain a distinction between traditional ideals of Indigenous cultural values and wisdom and the present-day realities of individual Indigenous people. Avoid romanticizing Indigenous people, who are as diverse and complex as any other broad category of people. Canadian cultural genocide has had the effect of dislocating many Indigenous people from land, culture, and language. Before inviting Indigenous students to share information about their culture, it is important to establish a relationship with them, and to gain a sense of their nature as individuals, as well as their comfort level with sharing such information.

Challenging Dominant Worldviews

For centuries, increasingly dominant modern Eurocentric modes of knowing have too often been assumed to be the final intellectual framework, and the only road to the truth. In reality, there are a variety of worldviews supporting diverse paths to the truth, and Indigenous worldviews represent important and essential aspects of the human intellectual tapestry. Indigenous ways of knowing are in many ways inherently better adapted for the future than modern Eurocentric intellectual frameworks which, for all their strengths, appear to have some fatal flaws.

The Indigenous lens in this edition of *Natural Curiosity* challenges us to shift from a Eurocentric perspective (which usually considers Indigenous cultures only at the level of a topic to be studied), and to rethink some of the assumptions of modern Eurocentric thought. Of course, the degree to which we meet this challenge is left to individuals. Perhaps the most important thing to remember is that knowledge and perspective are not stagnant, and never have been, and that some of the assumptions many of us now have and consider unassailable may well come to be seen as dead ends by future generations.

At the same time, Indigenous and Eurocentric ways of knowing are not simply opposed or incompatible. The two can be complementary *and* incompatible. While there are areas where divergences are wide, the Indigenous lens in this book is an attempt to see how Indigenous perspectives can inform and relate in good ways with non-Indigenous learning contexts and systems.

Our Common Ground

The contribution of Indigenous perspectives and approaches is about much more than cultural diversity, much more than learning some unique cultural knowledge about animals or plants, or about how to have a "talking circle." These kinds of opportunities may happen in a good way in certain contexts. More than this, however, Indigenous cultural ways enrich what it means to be human in relation to the world around us. We are challenged to ask not just what we need to learn, but what kind of people we need to *become*.

How do we effectively set the broadest possible parameters for our children's learning? How can the process become more holistic, seamless, meaningful, and less institutionalized? How can we involve families and communities; connect outside of school with parents or play, *in the land, as part of it*; link with our food and our future; think and feel deeply about our ancestors and our great, great, great grandchildren? How are the solutions for survival in the 21st and 22nd centuries social and spiritual and not merely technocratic? Are we raising nations of people who can work together and define how technology and resources are applied for common and deeply ethical purposes? Or, are we preparing our children to become increasingly atomistic, isolated, and defined by technology, anxiety, and money?

While these challenging questions are deeply informed by Indigenous cultural values and wisdom, they are not for Indigenous peoples alone. They are the most pressing issues of our time.

Reconciliation

We cannot make this journey without reconciling with Indigenous people, without a transformation of Canada's encounter with Indigenous peoples. A respectful conversation can and must emerge that meets all our needs, and educators are critical helpers in facilitating that conversation, not working alone as educational experts, but also as reflective practitioners who hopefully have the safety to grow and learn and feel joy with their students in the process.

None of this should be considered in isolation, without a sense of history. Nor should the hard facts of colonization – a colonization which is both historical and also expresses itself today – be avoided. Perhaps what is needed is a "reconciliation pedagogy," a recovery of relationship, an encounter that brings us all together as co-creators of our children's survival. After all, reconciliation with Indigenous people cannot really take place in a vacuum, apart from the big questions of mutual concern, a point that has been emphasized in the Truth and Reconciliation Commission's final report (2015).

> Reconciliation between Aboriginal and non-Aboriginal Canadians, from an Aboriginal perspective, also requires reconciliation with the natural world. If human beings resolve problems between themselves but continue to destroy the natural world, then reconciliation remains incomplete. This is a perspective that we as Commissioners have repeatedly heard: that reconciliation will never occur unless we are also reconciled with the Earth. Mi'kmaq and other Indigenous laws stress that humans must journey through life in conversation and negotiation with all creation. Reciprocity and mutual respect help sustain our survival. It is this kind of healing and survival that is needed in moving forward from the residential school experience.
>
> *– Honouring the Truth, Reconciling for the Future: Summary of the Final Report of the Truth and Reconciliation Commission of Canada*

The most vital reason for educators to understand Indigenous perspectives is this: it already is – and increasingly will be – Indigenous peoples around the world who are the first and most effective in standing up to prevent our current wholesale destruction of life in Mother Earth. The perspectives driving this broad trend need to be understood and supported by our children and youth. And we have to move fast.

We all need to work together towards Mino-Bimaadiziwin ("living in a good way" in Anishinaabemowin) – a vision that we hope can come about over seven generations as our children and grandchildren succeed us. This is something we must plan for and act on urgently. It is the job of educators today to process the reflections provided through Indigenous perspectives, and to act, deepening a mutual encounter with Indigenous people and perspectives in our work.

> Respect is more than tolerance and inclusion. It requires dialogue and collaboration.
>
> – *8 Ways: Aboriginal Pedagogy from Western New South Wales*

Branch I: Inquiry and Engagement
Nurturing a Sense of Wonder

> I should ask that a gift to each child in the world be a sense of wonder so indestructible that it would last throughout life, as an unfailing antidote against the boredom and disenchantments of later years, the sterile preoccupation with things that are artificial, the alienation from the sources of our strength ... If a child is to keep alive his inborn sense of wonder, he needs the companionship of at least one adult who can share it, rediscovering with him the joy, excitement, and mystery of the world we live in.
>
> – Rachel Carson, *The Sense of Wonder* (1998)

Theoretical Underpinnings

Curiosity Is Natural

Humans are curious beings. From birth, they behave in ways that demonstrate a drive to figure things out, a natural capacity and desire to learn about their world (Worth, 2001). Babies rely upon their senses as they explore the concrete, observable aspects of their immediate surroundings. Their world is full of wonder and newness. They gaze at faces, put objects into their mouths, respond to voices and sounds – all to gain more experience and information (Thornton, 2003, as cited in Ogu & Schmidt, 2009).

As children acquire language, they build upon this foundation of sensory exploration. They begin reflecting on and asking questions about the many things they notice in their environment, both material and social. Their curiosity seems insatiable, the process of learning self-propelled and unstoppable. One analysis of four young children's questions over a four-year period (starting at 14 months) revealed a total of 24,741 questions in 229 hours of conversation, averaging to about 107 questions *per hour* (Chouinard, 2007, as cited in Engel, 2015).

As children grow and develop, the nature and expression of their curiosity changes. To the very young child, not fully aware of regularities in their world, many events are surprising and evoke the drive to make sense of them (Kagan, 2002). As experiences become more familiar, this kind of all-encompassing curiosity often shifts into a narrower, more targeted mode linked to specific interests; what is lost in breadth gains depth and focus. This kind of curiosity provides a perfect starting point for school learning.

However, as Rachel Carson notes, a child's sense of wonder can be lost or diminished, and with it, the desire to learn (1998). Through an inquiry-based learning approach, educators have the opportunity to build upon students' natural curiosity and nurture their ability to be fully engaged learners throughout their lives.

Sustaining and Cultivating Curiosity

> Inquiry does not bubble up just because the child is intrinsically curious. Nor does it simply erupt when something in the environment is particularly intriguing. Whether the child has the impulse, day in and day out, to find out more, ebbs and flows as a result of the adults who surround her.
>
> – Susan Engel, *The Hungry Mind* (2015)

It has often been noted that curious children learn more easily, and teaching students how to harness and pursue their curiosity provides them with a powerful learning tool. Yet an oft-cited study of children's conversations by Tizard and Hughes (1984) showed a marked decline in the number of "why" questions posed by children as they moved from home to school. Developmental psychologist Susan Engel (2015) similarly observed little evidence of curiosity in the classrooms she visited. She noted that even in rich learning environments it tended to be actively discouraged through statements such as "I'll give you time to experiment at recess. This is time for science" (p. 162).

Engel (2015) suggests some simple ways to sustain and nurture children's curiosity at school. First, refrain from oversimplifying: children are attracted to complexity and ambiguity, intrigued by the possibility of the unexpected. A rethinking or defamiliarization of the everyday can also trigger the desire to find out more. Rather than aiming for the perfect clarity of a textbook, information requiring interpretive work tends to be more interesting; one study showed children's comprehension of complex writing to be significantly higher than their understanding of more straightforward and transparent texts (Garner, Brown, Sanders and Menke,1992, as cited in Engel, 2015). Beyond textual information, the natural world right outside our doors is probably the most perfect example of a highly complex environment.

Second, educators need to follow their own curiosity, to welcome not-knowing as an opportunity to learn more. Ideally, an educator's curiosity will encompass questions about curriculum or content, about children, and about pedagogy. Admitting ignorance as a starting point for an investigation can offer to students one of the best possible models of curiosity and its satisfaction. Setting up a learning program that leaves room for the unexpected will also make classroom life infinitely more interesting for both educators and students.

Finally, make the cultivation of curiosity a priority – perhaps *the* priority – throughout your teaching day. Start to notice where your students show curiosity, and how they show it, verbally or nonverbally. What happens after they ask a question or demonstrate an interest? And where is curiosity not happening? As you focus on it, it will start to happen more. Refrain from rushing to completion in any subject; encourage students to decide if they are satisfied with an answer. And remember – it is the promise of a satisfying answer to a pressing question that drives real learning. While an educator may be most interested in the *process* by which students approach a question, it is the burning desire to find something out that motivates students to wholeheartedly pursue their curiosity.

In all, this focus on curiosity will form a solid ground for launching inquiry-based learning in children's lives.

What Is Inquiry-based Learning?

Inquiry-based learning is a dynamic and emergent process that builds on students' natural curiosity about the world in which they live. It places their questions and ideas at the centre of the learning experience. While the educator may offer the big idea that becomes the focus, it is the students' own responsive questions and ideas that drive the learning forward. Educators using an inquiry-based approach encourage students to pursue their own questions about the world. They support student learning by providing tools, resources, instruction, and experiences that enable learners to rigorously investigate, reflect upon, and discuss potential solutions to their own questions about a shared topic of study.

Inquiry gains richness from its situation within an interrelated and reciprocal learning community of questioners, hypothesizers, and observers, all with different kinds of expertise, perspectives, interests, and priorities. Both the educator and the students work together as learners and thinkers within this community. The sense of community is both what makes classroom inquiry possible in the first place and what emerges out of the multiplicity of voices that come together to move an inquiry forward.

Jerome Bruner once famously remarked, "You can no more teacher-proof a curriculum than you can parent-proof a family" (1996, p. 84). An inquiry-based approach is not a rigid methodology or set of procedures that, blindly followed, will yield consistent results. Rather, it entails an overall orientation that pervades classroom life to foster a culture of collaborative learning and idea improvement. Within this classroom culture, educators encourage students to contribute their ideas and engage in critical problem-solving processes in a variety of contexts, both curricular and social.

For the educator, the focus tends to be more on the process of student learning than on curriculum coverage for its own sake. By actively engaging in their own learning, students deepen their understanding of content knowledge in a manner relevant to their interests and stage of development. To this end, an educator might respond to a child's question with an open-ended question of their own: "What a great question. How can we find that out?" Knowing the value of struggle in coming to truly own an idea, the educator will also allow students time to grapple with problems, and may suggest, "Why don't you tell us more about this after you have had some time to think about it?"

Over the course of a single inquiry, a class will move back and forth along a continuum of structure and openness, depending on the balance of student-driven and teacher-directed learning. Both openness and structure have important places in inquiry-based pedagogy, depending upon many aspects of the learning context (including the topic of study, the social dynamics, and the specific learning goals). Indeed, an implicit structure inheres in even the most open-ended learning situation, with clear expectations for learning and engagement that have been explicitly taught to and internalized by the students. These may include developmentally appropriate expectations of focus, of industry, of kindness, of intellectual rigour, of persistence, of respectful contribution to group knowledge. Though curiosity may be natural, inquiry in a school setting is neither natural nor easy; it must be learned and worked at.

Many educators invest effort in helping children to independently navigate more open-ended forms of inquiry. Making the decision to do this may require what some have described as a "leap of faith," a trust that this way of thinking and acting in the pursuit of meaningful questions will enhance learning for their students.

Figure 1: Defining Characteristics of Inquiry-based Learning at The Laboratory School

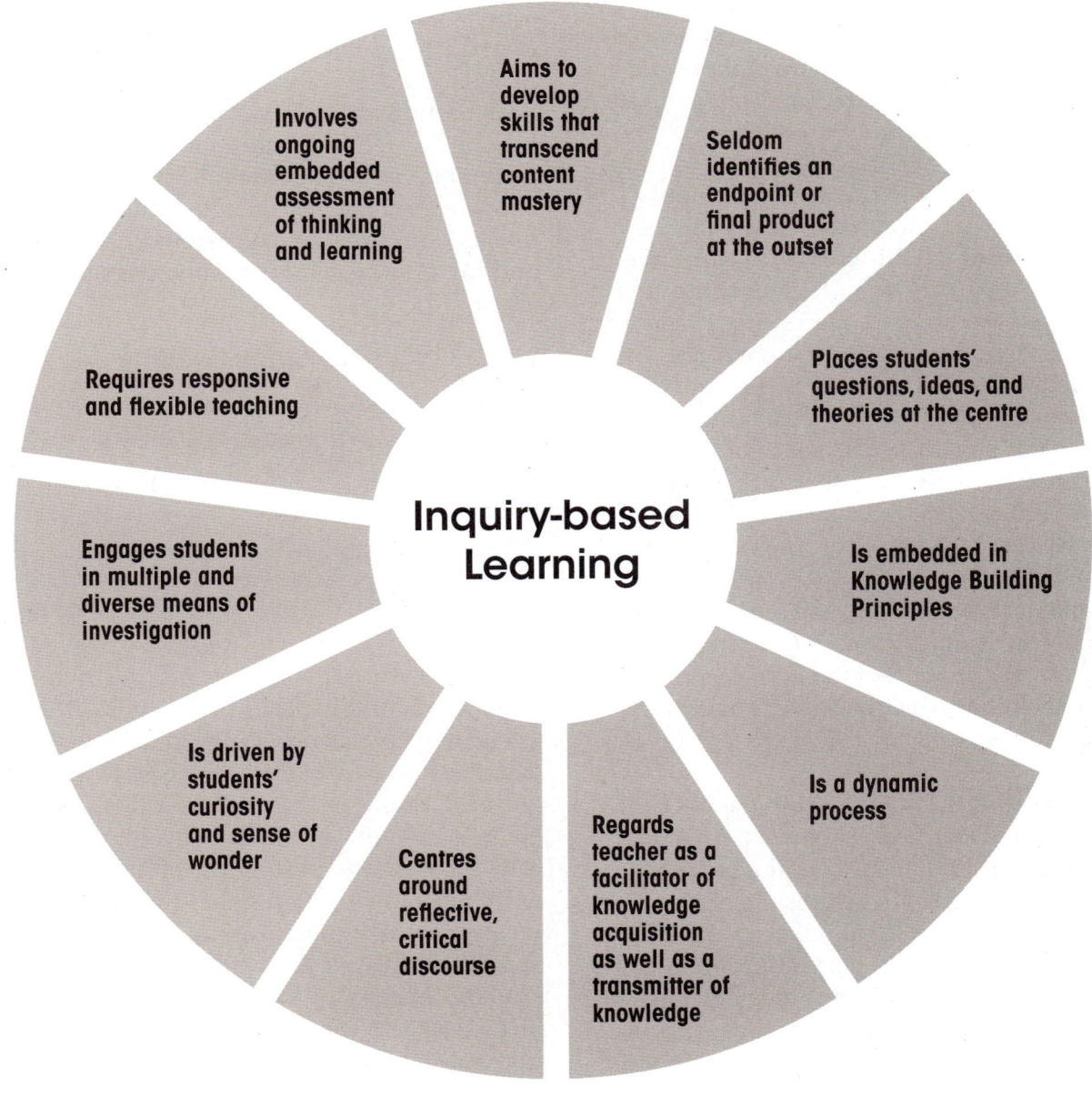

Why Take the Leap? The Benefits of Inquiry-based Learning

Whether they have been teaching through inquiry for several years or several months, most educators agree that inquiry-based learning offers far-reaching benefits for students. Some of the major benefits include the following:

1. Honouring interests and questions related to a common focus or big idea leads to higher levels of engagement, improved understanding, and a love of learning. Genuine questions from students both provide their teacher with information about what they want to know and reveal their understanding. A student's degree of interest profoundly affects their attentional and retrieval processes, acquisition of knowledge, and expenditure of effort. When students engage deeply with the content because it interests them, their learning is deeper and more complex; they use more elaboration strategies, seek more information, and reflect more on the material (Hidi, 1990).

2. Inquiry stimulates and focuses students' curiosity, leading to progressively deeper questions and a habit of critical thinking. By fostering a culture of inquiry, educators help students become more discerning observers, deeper thinkers, and more innovative problem-solvers. Curiosity is cultivated and preserved — and for good reason. As David Orr (2004) cautions, "the sense of wonder is fragile; once crushed, it rarely blossoms again" (p. 24). The consequences can be dire. Students eventually stop noticing and asking questions about their world, at least at school. They may instead opt to disengage completely from classroom learning, or else resort to the 'game' of education, figuring out what the teacher wants to hear or what will be on the test.

3. Inquiry builds lifelong learning skills that go beyond content mastery. We live in an age of information overload and rapidly changing technologies. Access to content knowledge is literally at our fingertips. However, information accumulation in itself should not be the primary objective of education. Students in the 21st century need to build skills for dealing with complexity, interpreting and connecting information as they assess its utility in the light of their current learning goals.

4. Engaging in inquiry encourages perspective-taking, collaborative problem solving, and communal knowledge building. In learning to relate their own hypotheses and knowledge to the knowledge of others, students begin to see themselves as integral members of a learning community.

Through practicing inquiry, students wholeheartedly bring many aspects of their lived experience into the learning environment. They develop and apply skills across content areas and grade levels. As they reflect on the purpose, meaning, and process of their information gathering, they interpret information in relation to their own beliefs and experiences. Working with others to build understanding, they learn the need to articulate ideas clearly, pose focused questions to clarify a point of view, and respect the diverse contributions of individuals within a collaborative community ("Partnership for 21st Century Learning," n.d.). A powerful culture of communal knowledge construction both emerges from this process and provides a framework that supports and furthers student learning, engagement, and agency.

Inquiry and Knowledge Building

> The goal of Knowledge Building is not simply to create life long learners, but rather, life long contributors.
>
> – Carl Bereiter, Co-founder, Institute of Knowledge Innovation and Technology, University of Toronto

Inquiry provides an opportunity for rich knowledge building talk to flourish within a learning community. Knowledge building pedagogy is a unique approach to teaching and learning that aims to improve the ideas of the entire learning community beyond those of individual learners. It emphasizes collaborative exchanges in which students publicly negotiate ideas with each other. In placing ideas, rather than activities, skills, or facts, at the centre of student learning, a knowledge building approach prioritizes the widening perspective and deepening understanding that develops as children question, argue with, and begin to incorporate each other's divergent views into their own thinking. Knowledge building is an essentially metacognitive process; for students, the knowledge that they co-construct through ongoing mutual discussion becomes the most significant artifact of their thinking.

For more than 20 years, Marlene Scardamalia and Carl Bereiter at the Ontario Institute for Studies in Education (OISE/UT) have worked in consultation with teachers to refine principles and procedures that will most effectively guide and support students as they engage in knowledge building. Central to this process is the conscious use of knowledge building discourse within the classroom community. Encompassing quite specific ways of communicating and reflecting upon understanding, knowledge building discourse is a specialized form of idea exchange which can uniquely support inquiry in the classroom. The following section spells out (in limited detail) a few of its most basic features.

What Is Knowledge Building (KB) Discourse?

Through oral and written knowledge building exchanges, learners come together to pose questions and posit theories. They revisit, negotiate, and refine their thinking with the shared goal of idea improvement. Knowledge building discourse "serves to identify shared problems and gaps in understanding and to advance the understanding beyond the level of the most knowledgeable individual" (Scardamalia, 2002, p. 12). While the content of these exchanges remains very open, educators in knowledge building classrooms often offer particular linguistic forms to scaffold student exchanges and highlight the processes by which collective knowledge is constructed.

Knowledge building discourse focuses on deepening understanding through encounters with the diverse perspectives and ideas of classmates. These conversations occur both informally and within more structured "Knowledge Building Circles (KBCs)" that are designed specifically to facilitate the group exploration of emergent questions and ideas. The resulting questions and theories then serve as entry points for further investigations and discussions.

Knowledge building discourse differs from other forms of class discussion in several important ways as outlined in Table 3.

Table 3: The Unique Role of Knowledge Building Discourse in Inquiry-based Learning

Student discourse shapes the learning. Students are encouraged to frame their contributions with metacognitive phrases that support mutual respect and foster awareness of how ideas interrelate. Examples are: • I want to build on to Nigel's idea ... • I think ... because • I think something different ... because • Something I still don't understand is ... • I wonder if ... • My theory is ... • I need to know ...
The teacher is unlikely to know in advance all of the questions and ideas that will emerge from student discussion.
The teacher nurtures student engagement through open-ended questions such as: "Did anyone notice/read/find out something that might help us better understand our question?"
Students work to reconcile their own theories and ideas with new pieces of information. Teachers support them in this process by asking questions: • How does that information support your theory? • Have you changed or added to your theory? • How has your thinking changed since we started learning about this? • Is there a theory that can make sense of both Anna's and Sophia's ideas?
The teacher models and prompts multi-directional dialogue to help students internalize and practice using it themselves. "Would anyone like to build on to Fatima's idea?"

There are many possible ways to support knowledge building discourse, depending on factors ranging from the available physical space to the developmental readiness of the children. Within this variation, there are certain protocols for KB discussions which help to support idea-centred discourse and reinforce the guiding values of a knowledge building culture. Especially with students who are new to this discussion format, an educator will take time to introduce and model some behavioural and linguistic protocols for ensuring mutual respect.

Most educators find that taking the time to teach explicit procedures for engaging in knowledge building discourse is a worthwhile investment of effort. Overall, they have learned that when students become accustomed to the process, and are engaged in dialogue about a topic that is important to them, classroom management issues tend to diminish.

With younger students, the circle configuration is often used for KB discussions for some of the following reasons:

- Sitting in a circle with classmates builds children's sense of themselves as part of a community.
- Circles support attentive communication and face-to-face dialogue. Attentive body language – a physical sign of respect and active listening – is more visibly apparent. An educator will often help to build children's awareness of the tacit meaning of the verbal and nonverbal signals they observe and transmit.
- Circles are non-hierarchical. Both students and educators enjoy equal places in a circle; no one takes precedence and teachers position themselves as co-learners within the circle. As members of an egalitarian knowledge building community, all members learn from each other's understanding. Students build self-regulation as they wait for their turn to speak.
- Learning how to communicate respectfully with others is a critical aspect of children's social development. It is also integral to developing respect for all living things. Respect and care for close members of one's community become the basis for building a respectful, caring relationship with the world at large.

Within the general KB format, there are many effective structures for promoting discussions. In classes new to knowledge building, the educator may help to manage the conversation by selecting who will speak next (ensuring that all willing students have a chance to participate). As children grow older and more experienced, they may sometimes take responsibility for selecting the next person who wishes to speak once they have had their turn. As these procedures become automatic, an educator may encourage students to try conversing without raised hands, as they learn to interpret a speaker's cues and jump into the discussion without interrupting. However, the educator is always watching closely to make sure that the process remains democratic and that sufficient focus is maintained for the learning to move forward. Sometimes, a child's body language may suggest they have something to contribute, even in the absence of an overt signal that they would like to speak; noticing this, an attentive educator will offer the possibility of participation.

In KB discussions, students learn to take a step back from their immediate thoughts and impulses as they develop a public voice. They listen respectfully to others and build on to their ideas in a way that takes seriously the enterprise of building knowledge together. They learn that others cannot read their mind, that they need to convey their meaning precisely to be fully understood. They become aware of the need to recognize the perspectives of other participants in order to voice ideas that are relevant and available to everyone. None of this learning happens overnight, and the educator plays a key role in facilitating its development.

Of course, the circle is not the only grouping format an educator will use. In most classrooms, there are likely to be times – such as picture book read-alouds – in which students clump together to focus on the book rather than on each other. And there will likely be other times during which everyone finds a private space in which to comfortably focus on individual projects. But to sustain democratic and egalitarian discussions, especially among children just learning how to engage in this kind of talk, there is value in a format that reinforces their ongoing awareness of one another.

As literacy develops, knowledge building discourse need not be limited to oral discussions and conversations. Sorting and connecting movable sticky notes on a board is one concrete way to represent and keep track of the shifting interconnections that emerge in group knowledge building. At a more sophisticated level, there are a number of web-based databases that lend themselves well to dynamic representations of individual and group thinking, deepening understanding even as they provide a means for archiving and returning to it. An example of computer-based knowledge building on a networked database called "Knowledge Forum" appears in "Mike's Story" (Part 2, p. 251). For more information, see "In the Ground Beneath the Trees" on p. 20.

Key Principles of Knowledge Building

A knowledge building approach to environmental inquiry follows a number of key guiding principles, summarized in Table 4.

Table 4: Some Principles of Knowledge Building within an Environmental Inquiry (from Scardamalia, 2002)

- Students work with authentic problems and real ideas
- All ideas are improvable
- A diversity of ideas is valued
- Students exercise epistemic agency
- All members assume collective responsibility for community knowledge

Students work with authentic problems and real ideas

Genuine knowledge problems arise from a learner's authentic efforts to better understand the world and their place within it. Problems that students genuinely care about drive their learning very differently than the decontextualized problems posed by many textbooks. Further, the ideas that students create or develop are as real and important as any other artifacts of their learning. Ideas can be expressed in many ways, not only in explicit verbal or concept-heavy communication, but also in action and more concrete manifestations. It is the educator's job to notice and interpret the many ways in which a child's ideas begin to emerge.

All ideas are improvable

The history of science provides convincing evidence for the improvability of ideas. Even the most sophisticated theory expresses a partial or provisional understanding with the potential to deepen and change through reflection, negotiation, and empirical testing. Participants in a knowledge building community work together to improve the coherence, complexity, and utility of their ideas. Such a culture relies on a safe setting that encourages risk-taking, the possible pursuit of blind alleys, and the acceptance of ignorance or error as integral to idea improvement. High value is placed on rethinking a belief in the light of new evidence. Only through voicing and working through misconceptions is it possible to eventually move beyond them to a more nuanced or accurate view.

A diversity of ideas is valued

Idea diversity is essential to knowledge advancement. To fully understand an idea requires a grasp of how it relates to ideas that surround it, both related or supporting ideas and those that stand in contrast. As learners encounter and struggle to accommodate other perspectives, their own perspective broadens and their original beliefs gain complexity, coherence, and objectivity. An environment that welcomes diverse perspectives enables new and more refined ideas to emerge.

Students exercise epistemic agency

Students who develop epistemic agency take control of the process of creating and working with knowledge. As they negotiate their ideas about meaningful questions in the light of other views they encounter, they take responsibility for important aspects of their own learning, including goal-setting, prioritizing, assessment, and planning. This sense of agency can empower children to go far beyond typical grade expectations as they, along with peers, take ownership of their learning process. The resulting sense of autonomy has strong implications for the development of environmental concern and action.

All members share collective responsibility for community knowledge

As learners trade ideas of value on an ongoing basis, they share the responsibility for furthering the knowledge of the entire learning community. Each student understands that they are responsible for the overall advancement of the community's knowledge in addition to advancing their own knowledge. Though students may exercise different roles in the knowledge building process, every student understands their obligation to play a part in contributing to communal learning.

Other knowledge building principles

Grounded in discourse practices that promote the exchange and refinement of ideas, knowledge building is a continuous process that pervades all aspects of classroom life. Beyond the five principles detailed above, it embodies a number of other guiding values, including the understanding that within knowledge building communities there is a clear role for more authoritative sources of knowledge – such as books or expert testimony – which are received and interpreted critically and reflectively. The community makes ongoing efforts to synthesize or "rise above" individual or conflicting ideas to see the bigger picture. Within such a knowledge building community, assessment is embedded, concurrent and transformative.

How Does Knowledge Building Progress?

During the course of an inquiry, a mix of hands-on exploration and KB discourse will begin to permeate the classroom. Through discussion and argumentation, students learn to become critically mindful of their investigations, guarding against making cursory observations, drawing hasty conclusions, or reading information perfunctorily. As students become accustomed to reporting back and thinking through ideas with the group, they develop a sense of responsibility for their learning and a desire to make meaningful contributions to the collective community. In the process, critical thinking and self-reflection become habitual modes of inquiry. Figure 2 shows one possible example of a knowledge building progression.

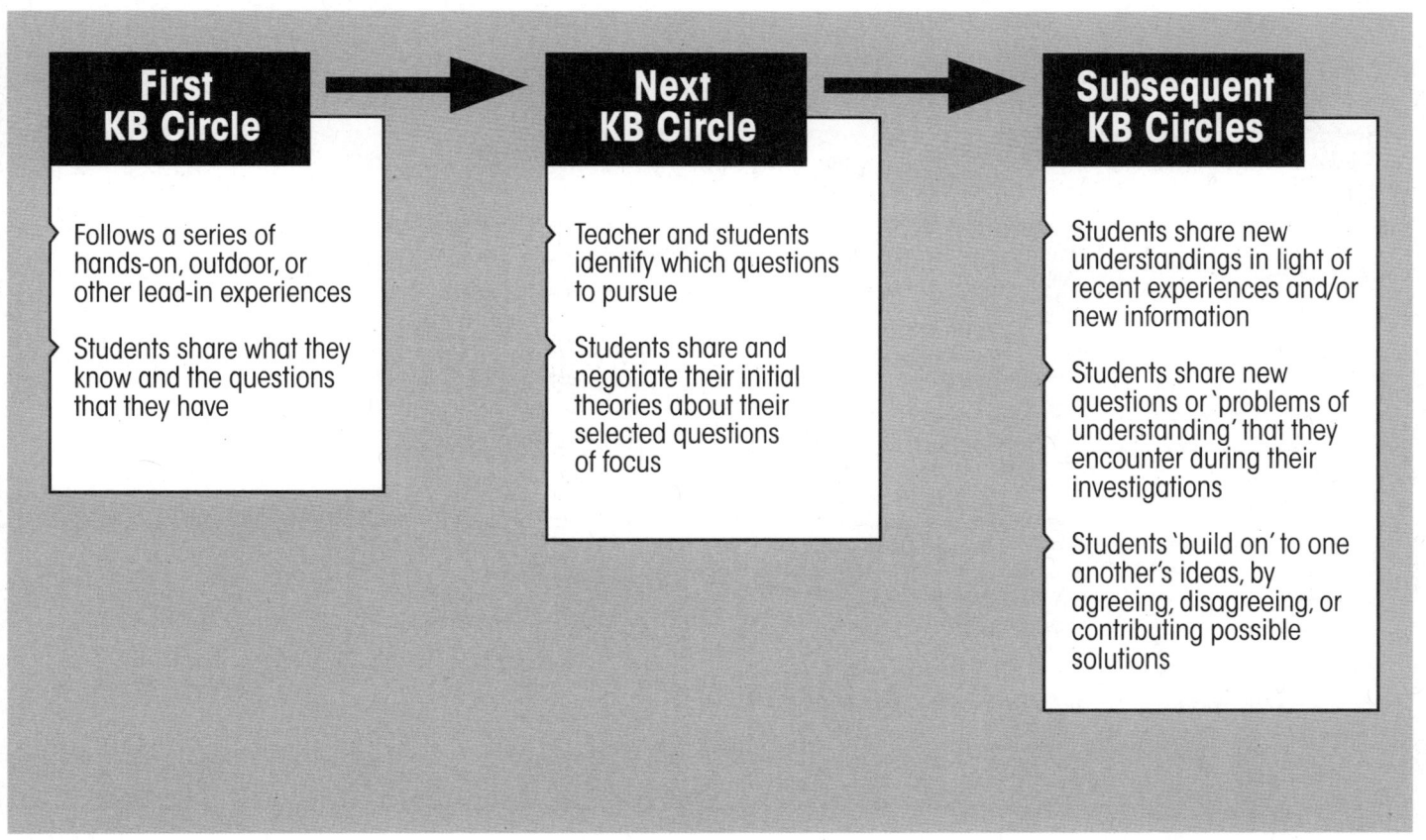

Figure 2: Example of How Knowledge Building Discourse Unfolds

Knowledge Forum:
In the Ground Beneath the Trees

By Richard Reeve

Knowledge building is an approach to education that places knowledge creation at the centre of student activity in classrooms. Throughout the history of its development, including a 20-year partnership between educators at the Dr. Eric Jackman Institute of Child Study Lab School and researchers from the Institute for Knowledge Innovation and Technology (IKIT) at the Ontario Institute for Studies in Education, University of Toronto, knowledge building has involved the construction of student-generated online databases. My goal in this short section is to describe the technology that has been most closely associated with knowledge building and to show how this technology coordinates with environmental inquiry.

Carl Bereiter and Marlene Scardamalia initiated the development of knowledge building through research into expert writing and collaborative writing tools. Subsequently, they focused on theory development in various disciplines (Bereiter & Scardamalia, 2012). Since the Lab School adopted a knowledge building approach in 1995, at the dawn of the use of the internet in schools, the software designed to support knowledge building has been an online database called Knowledge Forum (KF). Community participants use this software to collaboratively build knowledge.

Knowledge Forum View Showing All Student Contributions (Original Grammar Maintained)

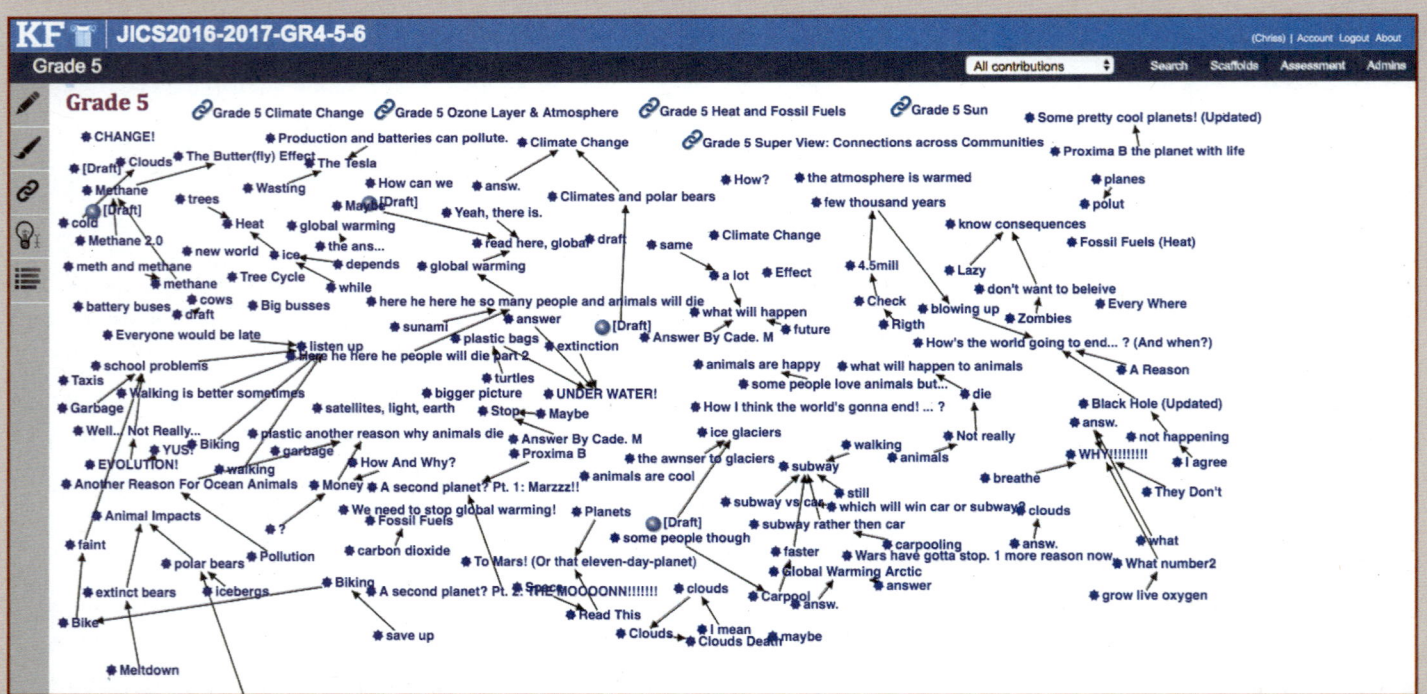

Example of View Showing Selected Student Contributions (Original Grammar Maintained)

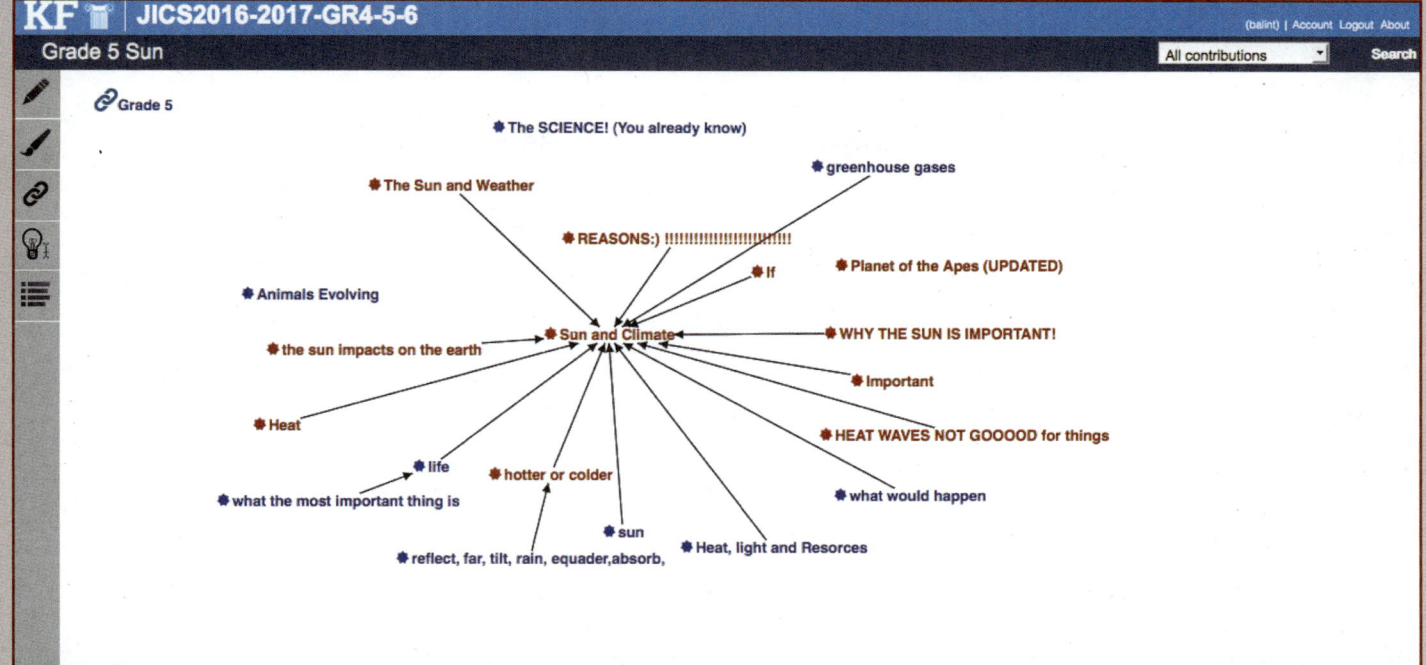

KF functions as an infinitely malleable space where students can work collaboratively on ideas of interest. Basic functions include the ability to contribute notes, draw pictures, attach resources, read the notes of others, build onto the notes of others, and arrange notes within and across views related to the knowledge being developed. Scaffolds in the form of sentence starters are provided to support student writing and sharing of ideas and knowledge. A "super note" and its supporting scaffolds allow students to document their journey of thinking and synthesize understanding in order to share with other KB communities, while a "rise-above" note helps a community of learners to take their knowledge to the next level together. The overall intention of KF is to support the community as it builds knowledge within and between domains.

Example of Student A's Theory of Greenhouse Gases (Original Grammar Maintained)

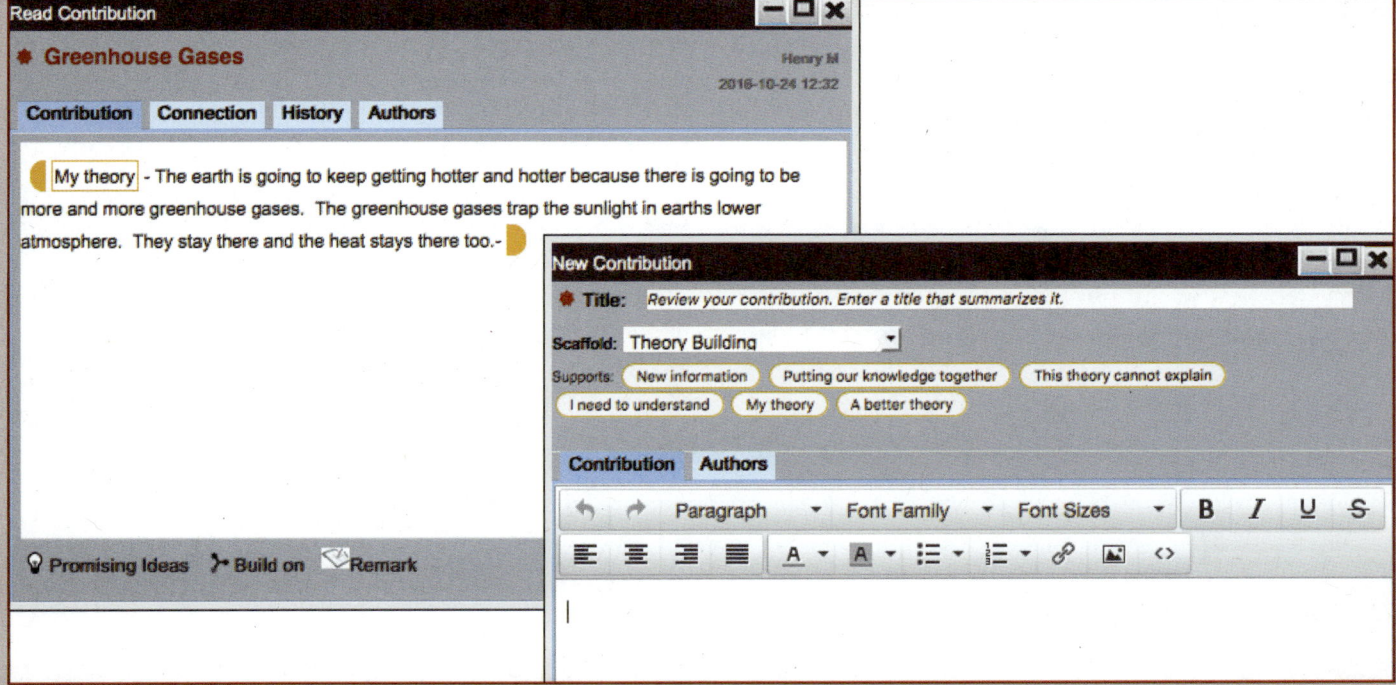

Branch I: Inquiry and Engagement

Example of Student B's Response to Student A's Theory (Original Grammar Maintained)

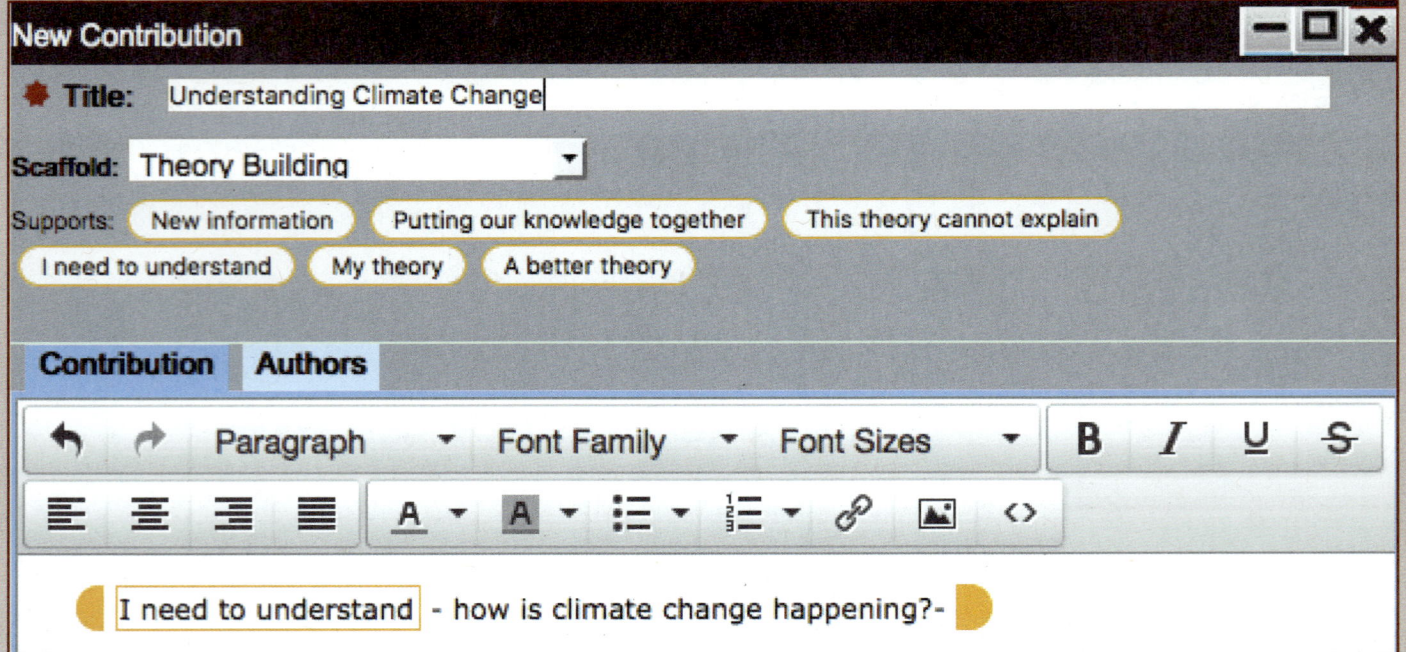

Readers may recognize the basic functions of KF as resembling a number of social networking tools that have become part of our daily digital lives. However, a key difference between KF and other environments intended to support the social sharing of knowledge (e.g., learning management systems or social media platforms) is that KF was specifically designed to support a knowledge building approach. There are 12 principles associated with KB, but two pairings (four principles) that I feel the KF environment is particularly well-suited to support are highlighted here:

- **Embedded Transformative Assessment and Knowledge Building Discourse**
  Through contributing, reading, and building onto KF notes, students begin to make judgements about the knowledge being developed. Discourse in the KF database often overlaps with what is put forward in the KB Circles with one key difference – the KF work is available for repeated review and continuous revision. Assessments of the ideas in the notes are ongoing and this form of KB discourse lends itself to idea refinement.

- **Improvable Ideas and Rise-Above**
  The KF system provides spaces for similar ideas to be worked on, in the form of views of notes, but a key KB principle and KF feature that is often overlooked is the concept of "rise-above". The database offers the option of creating a "rise-above" note that students can use to figuratively pull together their thinking and literally pull together their notes. An effective rise-above note does justice to the ideas it subsumes and also creates a new plateau from which to continue the work.

Examples of Super Notes Which Illustrate Development in Thinking (Original Grammar Maintained)

Read Contribution

Supernote: Why are glaciers melting a critical problem?

Nicola P
2016-11-10 14:02

Contribution | Connection | History | Authors

We used to think that the only affects of glaciers melting was polar bears dying and some places being flooded. Yes, those are effects that it has, but they may not be the worst ones.

Most of the freshwater in the world is locked up in glaciers, and we can't drink saline (salt) water, also glaciers can completely stop the flow of the gulf of Mexico and if the arctic goes above 0° then it can really change the world for the worse. Also, polar bears need the glaciers for homes and food and the world may get flooded. Finally glaciers reflect so much heat away from the surface of the earth so if they melt the world will get hotter. More water means more heat is stored away.

We want to research everything to do with this topic.

💡 Promising Ideas   ⤳ Build on   ✉ Remark

Read Contribution

climate vs weather effects

Lauren K
2016-11-10 14:00

Contribution | Connection | History | Authors

Topic: The difference between climate change and weather

We used to think: that climate and weather were the same thing. we also didn't know much about climate and climate change.

What we know now: We know now that there is a pretty big difference between them both. Climate its a long term weather effect. And weather is a short term effect of weather. Like summer is a climate, and one weather effect to another.

We have to research more about: Learning a bit more about climate change and what causes it to happen. we also need to know how can weather change so quickly like from hot to cold.

💡 Promising Ideas   ⤳ Build on   ✉ Remark   ✏ Edit

An ecological metaphor may help here. After being asked to contribute to this edition, and seeing the tree image on the cover, I did some research into trees and forests. My basic question was, how does the KB/KF aspect fit with this image? This search led me to the popular 2016 book by Peter Wohlleben – *The Hidden Life of Trees* – and then to groundbreaking work by Canadian researcher Suzanne Simard. Simard, a forest ecologist, along with colleagues at the University of British Columbia, published a paper in the international science journal, *Nature*, about their discovery of carbon transfer between tree species through a shared (ectomycorrhizal) fungi network (Simard et al., 1997). Coined the "wood wide web" by writers at the journal, Simard recently described her discovery:

In pulling back the forest floor ... I discovered that the vast belowground mycelial network was a bustling community of mycorrhizal fungi species ... [that] connect the trees with the soil in a market exchange of carbon and nutrients and link the roots of paper birches and Douglas firs in a busy, cooperative Internet (Simard, 2016, p. 248).

Research into these underground networks has continued, with findings clearly demonstrating that trees cooperate and "share their sugar" when nearby neighbours are in need (Wohlleben, 2016). As Wohlleben states, "these fungi operate like fibre-optic Internet cables. Over centuries a single fungus can cover many square miles and network an entire forest ... helping to exchange news about insects, drought and other dangers" (2016, p. 10). In short, trees communicate in an attempt to help support the survival of their forest community.

In many ways the metaphor of a fungus network, a sharing system designed to support community development and survival, represents well the way in which students in a KB community use KF. They share their knowledge with each other in a bid to strengthen the community's understanding of the topic at hand. The applicability of the fungus metaphor falls short only in that production of these valuable community resources, for trees, appears to be developed outside this communication system, while KF can function as a place where community knowledge is developed. The KF "sugar-sharing" network is one effective way, amongst many, for teachers and students to share their knowledge in an effort to strengthen their inquiry communities.

Please refer to the *Natural Curiosity* website, in the Resources section, for more information on knowledge building and Knowledge Forum.

Children's Preconceptions

> The theories children build, whether they are right or wrong, are not capricious. They are often logical and rational, and firmly based in evidence and experience.
>
> – Karen Worth, "The Power of Children's Thinking" in *Inquiry: Thoughts, Views, and Strategies for the K-5 Classroom* (2001)

Children do not come to school as blank slates waiting to receive instruction. With strong instincts for making meaning out of experience, they come full of knowledge and ideas about the world that they have either heard, figured out, or intuited through observation. While some of these preconceptions will easily support the learning they encounter in the classroom, others may be fundamentally incompatible with some of the knowledge they encounter in school, impeding their ability to assimilate certain concepts. Teachers must therefore make it a priority to find out what prior knowledge their students are bringing into the classroom (Gelman & Lucariello, 2002).

Joan Lucariello and David Naff distinguish between "anchoring conceptions" that are consistent with curricular concepts and conceptions that tend to work against them (n.d.). Straightforward misconceptions based in lack of information are relatively easy to address, and exposure to the correct facts usually suffices to rectify the false belief. However, some misconceptions take the form of strongly entrenched intuitive or common-sense theories which have served the child reasonably well in their day-to-day efforts to make sense of their world. Held tenaciously by both children and adults, these theories can be extraordinarily difficult to counter. They are often unarticulated and unconscious, yet observations are made and new information interpreted within the framework of the misconception just as it would be through any theoretical lens. Since modifying these intuitive theories can require radical cognitive reorganization, just telling the child otherwise is unlikely to have much effect.

Everyone who lives or works with children encounters dozens of such misconceptions. A kindergarten teacher gives the example of the child who refused to put on a coat on the coldest day of winter because the sun was out and the day must therefore be hot. Many children of that age also insist that height is totally dependent on age, people get visibly taller on their birthday, everything in the ground, including a rock, grows, or that bigger things fall faster.

Sometimes, as theories become more entrenched, children seem to lose the common sense of an earlier age. A telling example is provided by Pine, Messer, and St. John (2001), who showed that most six- and seven-year-olds were unable to balance a weighted rod on a fulcrum, claiming that for something to balance it needed to be placed on its midpoint (despite the proprioceptive feedback that told them otherwise). The four-year-olds, on the other hand, had no problem with the task, because they hadn't yet built a generalizing theory that got in the way. As the authors of that study ask, "if the child ignores information from his or her own senses, will he or she find it difficult to assimilate evidence that is counter to the center theory from a teacher?" (Pine et al., 2001, p. 81)

Children also work hard to find ways of incorporating new information into a preexisting naïve theory. For example, they may struggle to reconcile their physical sense that the Earth is flat with the received information that it is spherical, developing a variety of compromise theories, such as the idea of a flattened sphere, or the belief that the flat world in which we live is located inside a larger spherical Earth. Unless we know that the child is thinking this way, we are talking at cross-purposes when they and we both agree that the Earth is spherical. Similarly, we cannot assume that a child means the same thing that we do when they parrot the common wisdom that humans are animals.

Inquiry and knowledge building processes encourage students to explore the ramifications of all their preconceptions. Sometimes, a well-timed and aptly designed experiment will provide counter-evidence that sows the first seeds of doubt. Sometimes, encountering other viewpoints in books or KB discussions begins, bit by bit, to turn thinking in another direction or at least widen its scope. It has also been found that greater pedagogic diversity – in teaching strategies, in available perspectives, in modes of expression – encourages the uncovering and working through of deep-seated student beliefs (Hayes, Goodhew,

Heit, & Gillan, 2003). However, this process can be long and drawn out, with a strong tendency to revert to old beliefs in times of uncertainty. Along these lines, Mike describes what he calls "sticky misconceptions" in his fifth graders (p. 254).

It is therefore unrealistic to expect that every student will fully grasp abstract or counterintuitive concepts by the end of an inquiry. Bringing an implicit theory to awareness and watching it begin to shift may be considered a strong measure of success for many students. This process can take weeks, months, or even years.

In his work *The Unschooled Mind* (1991), Howard Gardner writes: "For the most part, early science education need not directly address the students' misconceptions. Such a confrontation … should await the time when the child has been thoroughly immersed in the phenomena … and has taken her intuitive theories as far as they can go" (p. 213).

It is also important to distinguish between children's misconceptions, often developmental, which reveal some kind of error in their thinking, from other kinds of beliefs they may hold. This includes other cultural or spiritual ways of parsing the world. These are not something to overcome but have the potential, in their distinctly different purposes, to broaden or transform understanding. In these instances, the aim is not for children to reorganize existing conceptual structures. Rather, we can help them to become aware of the varied purposes different knowledge structures can serve and to consider the contexts in which different kinds of theories might be useful.

Putting It into Practice

Space and Time: What Might an Inquiry-based Classroom Look Like?

> For educators it may be important to realize that classrooms and the things in them are cultural things, things that not only reflect cultural assumptions but may also have effects on how students see themselves in relation to school, communities, and nature itself. This observation represents both a challenge and an opportunity.
>
> – Megan Bang and Douglas Medin, "Culture in the Classroom" in *Phi Delta Kappan* (2013)

In designing a classroom that will support inquiry, there are a multitude of possibilities. While physical classroom design alone cannot guarantee high-level learning, inquiry-oriented educators take seriously the idea of the physical learning environment as a "third teacher" (as described by Reggio Emilio educators), forming the "bones of the curriculum" (Curtis & Carter, 2008, p. 54). Most decisions that educators make, from the wall displays to the layout of workspaces to the selection and organization of materials, will reflect the value they place on fundamental principles of inquiry and knowledge building. Educators, therefore, work to balance practicality with the following considerations:

- Is this classroom conducive to learning in which students' ideas and thinking are at the centre?
- How can I provide long periods of time for students to delve deeply into a topic?
- What values about learning does the physical classroom convey? For example, does the displayed work show a range of skills and levels of thinking, including errors and beginning ideas?
- Can all students find themselves represented in the materials and learning tools of this classroom?
- Have I ensured that each student's thinking is visible in some way?
- Does the classroom set-up encourage students to connect their ideas with those that have gone before (e.g., through archived discussions

or the choice of books)?
- Are materials presented in an undistracting, inviting, and aesthetically pleasing way that awakens curiosity?
- Are materials organized so as to encourage agency, independence, and resourcefulness in students?
- (in an environmental inquiry) How can we bring "the outdoors in," maintaining strong connections between classroom practices and the natural environment that is our focus?

The physical classroom

At the start of the school year, the walls of an inquiry-based classroom will often be quite bare. Few, if any, pre-purchased teaching visuals are on display. Educators want their students to understand that the classroom belongs to everyone. The walls serve as blank canvases to be filled with students' questions, ideas, and expressions of understanding.

As the year proceeds, diverse representations of student learning – in art, writing, building, action photographs, curated collections, and so on – are displayed throughout the classroom. When useful, an area may highlight the questions, ideas, and theories that have emerged from knowledge building discussions. The purpose of these displays is not to highlight the most accomplished work, but to archive ideas – including the less accurate or developed – as they emerge and play off each other. This approach makes explicit the growth of understanding over time.

Such egalitarianism reinforces respect for different ideas, and creates a culture of psychological safety which is essential for genuine learning. Students are more likely to "feel safe taking risks, asking questions, revealing ignorance, voicing half-baked notions, and giving and receiving criticism" (Scardamalia, 2002, p. 9). They come to understand the value of questioning, thinking critically, and testing ideas. They learn that a correct answer or nice-looking end product is not the full measure of learning success. By extension, they come to appreciate their own value as learners.

In this kind of classroom, students often return to use their archived questions or theories as reference points for rethinking existing ideas and triggering new questions. The visible documentation of learning naturally invites conversation with people from outside the classroom, such as family members or other students. As new people are drawn into the learning community, fresh perspectives inevitably emerge.

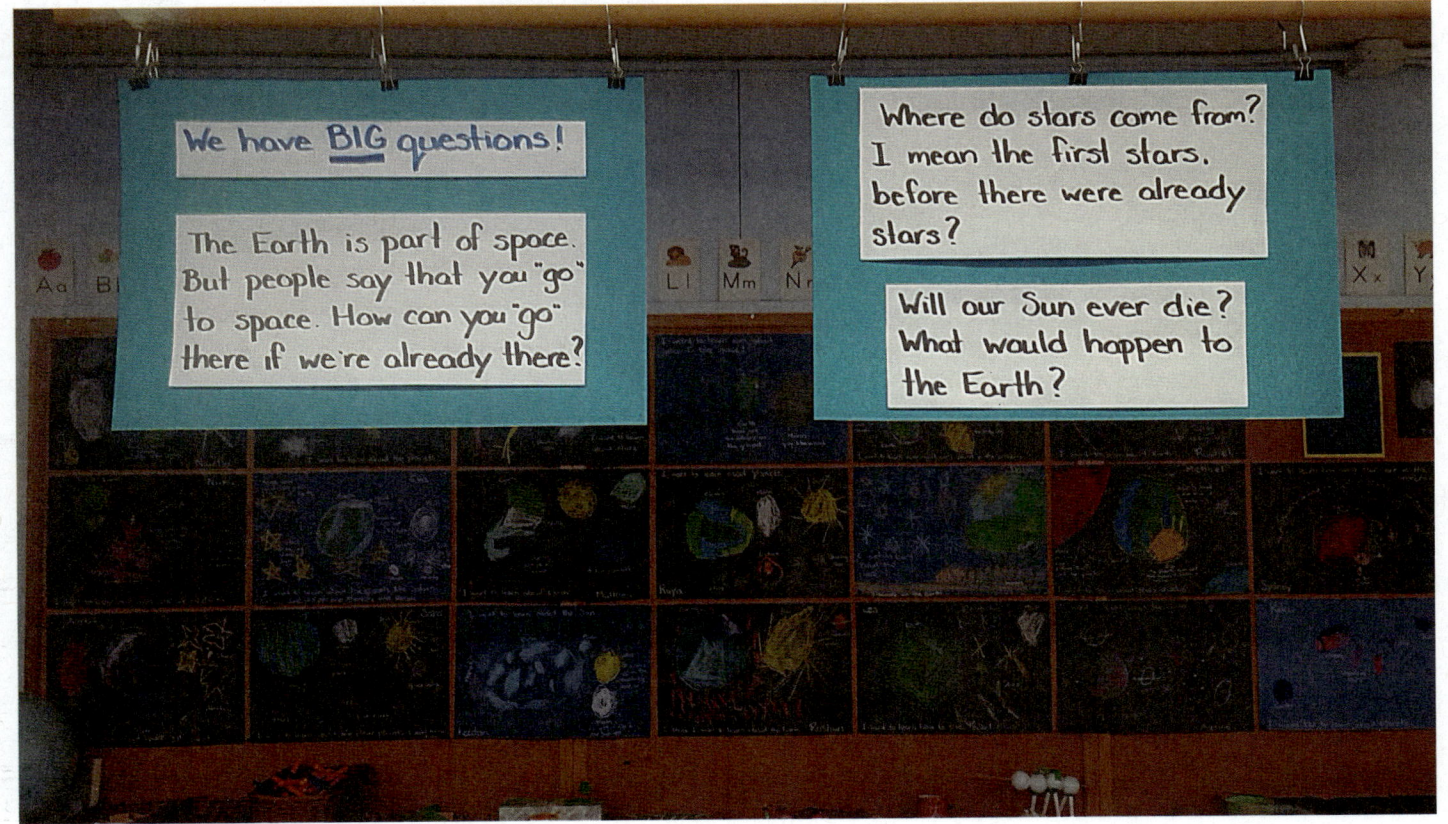

Given the importance of these physical markers of thinking in the ongoing inquiry process, they need to be made readily accessible to all the students. For example, in classrooms with young children, educators ensure that student work is placed at a child's eye level, not high up where only adults can see it.

When there is room, evidence of student questions and theories may remain on display even after the class has moved on to another topic. This encourages students to build connections among topics and reinforces the notion that individual learning about a particular subject can continue even if the overall focus has shifted to another curriculum area.

Configuration of workspaces

In an inquiry-based classroom, desks or tables are often arranged so that students can interact face-to-face as they work. This encourages students to exchange ideas, learn from one another, and solve problems of understanding together. In contrast, desks arranged in rows and facing the teacher's desk at the front of the room create a narrow path of communication that hinders knowledge building and signals to students that learning occurs solely through the teacher.

At the same time, a program that recognizes different personalities and learning needs will also make it a priority to provide opportunities for children to find private spaces for themselves in the very public setting of most classrooms.

Materials

Beyond displaying ongoing learning, we want our classrooms to be places that curious children will find intriguing, places in which they encounter possibilities that trigger the desire to find out more. The public library is a great place for an educator to start. Books of all kinds, from rich, enticing stories to fascinating factual accounts, along with field guides, maps, and other repositories of information, well-organized and readily accessible, will inevitably draw students into new worlds. It is quite amazing to see the intent focus with which even pre-literate kindergarteners pull meaning from well-designed graphics, or to watch a pair of children animatedly discussing the information they are encountering. Along with large collections of books on topics under study, relevant to the developmental range of students, there should be enough other books readily at hand to intrigue every kind of learner, from dinosaur- or bird-lovers to mythology mavens or bridge builders, reflecting the wide spectrum of both development and interests in any classroom. Watching children freely engage with books of their choice often provides the first indication of their passions.

An inquiry-focused classroom will also have a range of open-ended materials available for play and experimentation, at all levels of development. There are many games or building materials, for example, that offer limitless possibilities for children of all ages.

In keeping with the values of student independence, resourcefulness, and agency, classroom materials will be organized for children to manage as independently as possible, as they purposefully carry out plans for exploring their ideas.

What might the classroom sound like?

Inquiry-oriented classrooms are often pervaded with a buzz of conversation and interaction, sometimes loud and excited, sometimes quieter

and more focused. Some people find it easier than others to work in the midst of so much activity, and each educator will find a balance that works for them and for the individuals in their classroom.

How is time organized?

True learning takes time. The expectation of constant interruption precludes focus and engagement. If we want students to become deeply engaged, we need to give them time to do this. Educators will therefore work, within the non-negotiable limits of their schedules, to ensure long blocks of time for students to immerse themselves in investigating, reading, writing, thinking, discussing, browsing and all the other facets of an inquiry-based program. There needs to be time for exploration at a child's own pace as well as for teacher-planned use of time. Only through genuine and repeated opportunities to manage their own time do children build the kinds of self-regulation skills that have been repeatedly shown to make key differences to their success in school (and in life).

If educators or children believe that time is short, there will be little room for the kind of messing about with ideas and materials and following of false leads that lead to true insight. It also takes time for children to build sufficient familiarity with objects or ideas to know what is worth asking about them.

Cultivating Curiosity: Starting the Environmental Inquiry Process

As educators set up their classrooms to support environmental inquiry, they are also thinking in concrete and specific terms about where to begin. How will they provoke the kind of curiosity that leads to and sustains a focused inquiry? How can they find out what their students are thinking – what intrigues them, what they wonder, and what they would like to know more about? Do they just wait in the hope that something will emerge? Above all, how can they make plans without taking over the students' learning?

While open to the many directions an inquiry may take, an educator usually gives considerable thought to a topic before launching a study. Whether it arises organically, out of observed student interests, or externally, from designated curriculum expectations, or from a mix of both, the educator considers beforehand how to give a topic sufficient scope to engage all learners. They also give thought to identifying some key "big ideas" or the main purpose that makes the topic meaningful and worth studying. They research potentially useful materials and resources and gain content knowledge that will help them to maintain focus through the diversity of pathways that students may follow. Though they may or may not have a specific endpoint in mind (compare, for example, Lisa's and Carol's stories in Part 2), they usually begin with an overall (albeit flexible) idea about what directions student learning will take, as well as key concepts with which they consider it important for students to engage.

There is no single way to begin an inquiry. Students have diverse personalities, skills, talents, and interests. As a result, educators may use a variety of strategies to stimulate interest and engage students in common experiences before asking them to share their questions about a topic. Table 5 lists a few strategies that educators have found effective. Each strategy is then discussed in more detail in the section that follows.

Table 5: Cultivating Curiosity

- Help students connect a topic to their lives
- Take your class outside
- Elicit prior knowledge
- Read to children
- Provide opportunities for children to build community in their own way
- Provide opportunities for children to observe natural phenomena
- Pay attention to spontaneous questions
- Provide hands-on experiences
- Start with simple questions
- Revisit related questions or topics from previous inquiries

Help students connect a topic to their lives

> It is the affective elements – the subjective experience and observations, the communal relationships, the artistic and mythical dimensions, the ritual and ceremony, the sacred ecology, the psychological and spiritual orientations that have characterized and formed Indigenous education since time immemorial.
>
> – Gregory Cajete, *Look to the Mountain: An Ecology of Indigenous Education* (1994)

Students are especially keen to explore a topic when they appreciate its relevance to their own experience. To help them make this connection, educators in an inquiry-based learning environment may ask their students to bring in an object related to the current topic and connect it to aspects of their own lives. This invites the whole child, personal experiences and all, into the learning process.

For example, a Grade 1 teacher started the year by asking her students to bring in all the seeds they could find (see "Zoe's Story" in Part 2, p. 187). The children's excitement around the topic quickly grew as the classroom collection built momentum.

The strength of this strategy lay in its utter simplicity – this was a project that every child could manage on their own, on the way to school, on the playground, munching on an apple. Looking everywhere for seeds, they began to see the world in a new way. Everyone's sample immediately found a place within the classroom collection, which led to a strong sense of belonging and investment in the learning for every member of the classroom community.

Take your class outside

The essence of environmental inquiry lies in its connection with the world outside the classroom walls. This means spending significant amounts of time in the natural environment – fall or winter, rain or shine – to fully appreciate its wonders and forge lasting bonds. Students need meaningful opportunities to explore their environment. This need not involve an excursion to a distant forest or river. A short walk around the school neighbourhood or to the local park, encouraging students to investigate their surroundings using all of their senses, can awaken curiosity and spark questions. Children are avid collectors, and analyzing their collections from outdoor ventures is a wonderful beginning to an inquiry. Many of the teachers' stories in Part 2, as well as the chapter on experiential learning, convey the richness of outdoor learning in more detail.

Elicit prior knowledge

Questions often emerge as students describe what they already know about a topic. This may first occur on either an individual or a group level. Educators sometimes begin an inquiry by asking students to draw or write about what they know about the topic. Once each child has documented his or her ideas, the educator might bring the entire class together in a Knowledge Building Circle. At that point, the educator might ask, "What are you interested in learning more about?" Conversely, a KB discussion might provide the first encounter with a topic, followed by individual reflections.

Read to children

Reading a story or information book to the class is a powerful way to trigger curiosity and knowledge about a topic. For example, in "Marlo's Story" (Part 2, p. 226), a simple picture book launches an extensive investigation into rocks and their place in the community. "Carol's Story" (Part 2, p. 168) recounts how a retelling of a Haida creation tale stimulates children's thoughts about their place in the universe. Books serve both as a catalyst for thinking and as a source of information. When presenting informational texts, an educator may read only a couple of pages before a flood of ideas and questions pour forth. At other times, especially in more narrative contexts, there may be value in asking children to hold their thoughts until they have heard the whole story. In all cases, it is remarkable to see how even students new to the English language can glean meaning (and rapidly build vocabulary) from a series of engaging books.

The profound value of story in making sense of the world is common across most cultures. Grounding learning in stories and storytelling offers a point of connection between Indigenous ways of learning and more school-based approaches.

Provide opportunities for children to build community in their own way

Especially in the early years, as children are just becoming aware of what it means to be in school, it can be challenging to find a topic that everyone will immediately connect with. Opportunities for engaging in common but unforced experiences, often through sustained and purposeful social play, can be an important step in developing a classroom culture of shared learning. In "Stephanie's Story" (Part 2), the first inklings of a kindergarten learning community appear as the class comes together in a freely chosen construction project. Later on, the experience of nature and pursuit of shared questions further cement and enrich this early sense of community.

Provide opportunities for children to observe natural phenomena

Children become deeply engrossed in witnessing natural processes. Whether they are tracing the path of an ant or watching a bird take off in flight, observing pumpkins rot or waiting for a butterfly to emerge from its chrysalis, these mysteries of life always generate myriad questions. Introducing living examples of natural change usually provides an immediate and compelling common focus for a class, in which almost every student is sure to find something that intrigues them.

Pay attention to spontaneous questions

Many children's questions come up spontaneously when you least expect them. Such questions arise in all kinds of situations, ranging from overheard observations in play to sudden insights during discussions.

Unprompted student questions are often the most genuine instances of curiosity. Even if they seem vague or initially difficult to fathom, and whether or not they take the form of classic questions, children's spontaneous wonderings provide educators with valuable clues about their thinking processes and interests. This is especially true in the very early years, when four-year-olds, for example, may still be learning what a question is and how to ask it. Rather than interrupt what is happening at the time, an educator might note these questions as they come up and bring them later to the group for consideration, supporting or even initiating a full-scale inquiry in this way.

At times, a spontaneous observation elicits immediate interest that generates a more sustained look. For example, a Junior Kindergarten boy at the Lab School approached his teacher in the schoolyard, remarking, "There's something very weird happening. The sun and the moon are both out at the same time." Before long, a crowd of children had gathered to puzzle over this strange occurence – thinking about why it was surprising, how to make sense of the phenomenon, how it meshed with what they thought they knew, and so on. Their ideas, imaginings, and theories formed the basis for a prolonged investigation into day, night, and the solar system.

In another kindergarten playground, a child summoned his teacher to watch rainwater disappearing down a drain. "Where is the water's real home?" he wondered. Within a short time, his question had become the focus for a class-wide study of the water cycle (Stephanie Hammond, personal communication).

Sometimes, spontaneous discussions in one curriculum area can open up unexpected possibilities in another. A group of Grade 4 students at the Lab School were comparing the contemporary staging of a recently attended Shakespearean play with their understanding of staging in Shakespeare's day. A girl commented that in Elizabethan times, the theatre would have lacked a roof "because there was less light then." This intriguing comment evoked widespread interest in the curriculum topic of "Light," and a study was launched on the spot (Richard Messina, personal communication).

Provide hands-on experiences

Many children need to physically engage with materials to really think about them. Hands-on experiences such as planting, digging through soil to deconstruct its composition, or holding a worm can be deeply engrossing to children and inspire many observations and questions.

Start with simple questions

The simplest questions have rich potential to provoke students into seeing the familiar anew. One class began a study of plants by sorting a motley collection of objects (amassed on an outdoor excursion) into "living" and "non-living" categories. It soon became clear that the boundaries between living and non-living things were much fuzzier than originally assumed, awakening speculations, arguments, and theories about the meaning of these terms (literally, the meaning of "life") that turned a fairly mundane exercise into a profound philosophical investigation that drove inquiry for many months.

A focus on children's questions does not preclude an important role for educator questions as well, especially questions that probe the implications of a theory or cast new light on a topic or problem.

Revisit related questions or topics from previous inquiries

Questions posed in a previous inquiry sometimes relate closely to a current area of study. Revisiting points of interest from past learning can create helpful entry points for further questioning in a related topic.

Sometimes, starting with a longstanding question that people have pondered for millennia (such as what matter consists of) helps students to connect their own thinking with past ideas and situate their own speculations within an ongoing historical process of knowledge construction.

What Is the Role of the Educator?

One practitioner of inquiry-based learning has described the educator's role as that of an "expert learner" alongside less experienced learners. In modelling expert learning, an educator's passion for (and resulting knowledge about) a topic can be quite inspiring for children (see "Cindy's Story" in Part 2, p. 204). As the students move forward with their questions and theories about the world, the educator proceeds with unanswered questions of their own, not only about the topic under study but also about the students and how they relate to the topic, to each other, and to their own learning.

Figure 3 suggests the complexity of an educator's multifaceted role within an inquiry-based learning environment. Depending on their degree of experience in this mode, an educator may exercise only a few of the roles described in Figure 3. For example, many educators already "provide opportunities for students to express what they know in multiple ways," but may have less experience "documenting and reflecting on student questions" to inform subsequent planning. As educators become more comfortable moving from a teacher-directed to a student-centred classroom, they gradually build more roles into their instructional repertoire.

In many classrooms, the teacher remains the keeper and arbiter of knowledge, who transmits information through sequenced lessons organized to cover predetermined curriculum expectations. In contrast, an overall examination of Figure 3 suggests that the primary role of an educator in an inquiry-based learning environment is to "facilitate knowledge building among participants in a setting dominated by interactions among students" (Kozak & Elliot, 2014, p. 90).

However, "facilitation" in the narrow sense is not the only role that an educator will play during the course of an inquiry. There will be times where more teacher-directed instruction becomes appropriate to the topic, question, or learning needs of the class. Every educator will encounter moments at which the momentum of student-driven inquiry stalls in circular speculations that go nowhere. At such impasses, they must decide whether (or for how long) it is productive to leave the students struggling, and to decide when teaching a specific skill or offering a piece of pertinent new information is the best way to move things forward.

This kind of direct instruction in no way detracts from the children's sense of autonomy as they pursue their learning, but rather serves to support them in achieving learning goals they have come to care about. Using judgement to decide when and how much teacher direction is appropriate is part of what is involved in the facilitation process. Similar judgements may be called for in deciding when to introduce other kinds of more "authoritative" knowledge found in books or other repositories of expertise.

Figure 3: The Educator's Role in an Inquiry-based Learning Environment

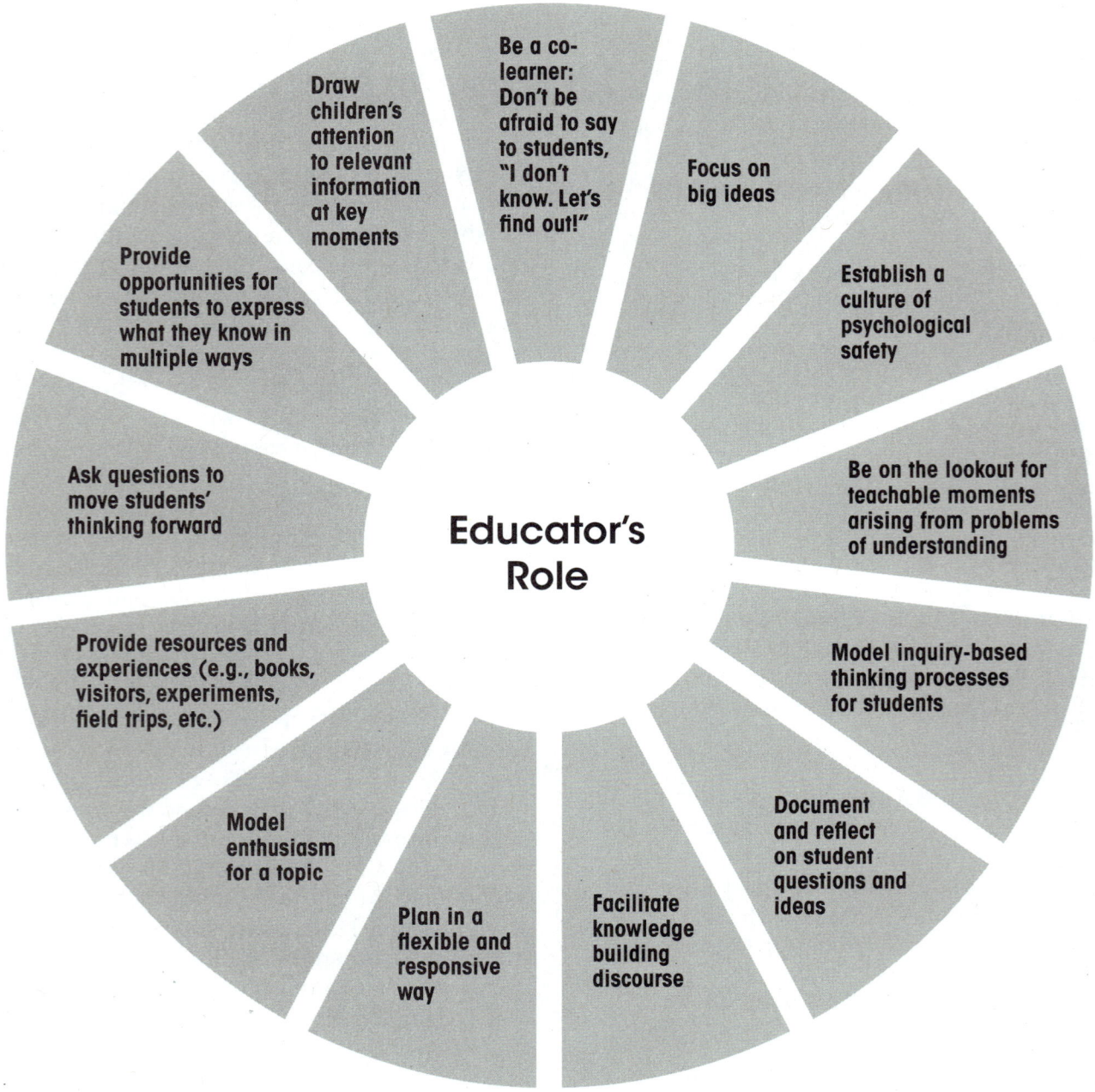

Some of the roles in Figure 3 are self-explanatory. Others, such as modelling inquiry-based thinking processes and flexible planning, may be less obvious to educators who are new to this kind of learning.

Modelling inquiry-based thinking processes for students

Educators model inquiry-based thinking processes when they pose the kinds of open-ended questions that help students become independent problem-solvers. As Scardamalia notes, "By serving as a model of expert learning, the educator helps students gain insight into the executive processes by which learners take charge of their understanding" (2000, p. 6). Examples of these kinds of questions often include the use of metacognitive language:

- "What do you **notice**?"
- "What do you **think** might happen if …?"
- "Does this **remind** you of anything?"
- "I **wonder** why your plant grew shorter than Samira's?"
- "What can we do to **find out**?"

- "**Why do you think** that happened?"
- "How has your **thinking** changed?"
- "What **evidence** supports your **idea**?"

Along with this kind of metacognitive modelling, an educator's own demonstration of lively curiosity and enthusiasm for a topic makes an enormous difference to how wholeheartedly students will plunge into the learning.

Planning in a flexible, dynamic, and responsive way

Rigid adherence to a predetermined sequence of lessons in a unit plan rarely accomplishes the fundamental goals of inquiry-based learning and knowledge building. When learners are offered opportunities to explore and satisfy their curiosity, their pursuit of their own questions often leads them down exciting and unexpected pathways. In an inquiry-oriented environment, educators allow students' questions, ideas, and conceptions to chart the course of their learning and influence the direction of planning. But how do educators do this?

Table 6 provides examples of lead-in actions that educators might use. It illustrates the dynamic interplay between students' questions and educators' responsive planning.

Table 6: A Sample Sequence of Lessons

Key Actions	Example
Choose a key concept related to curriculum	Soil Ecosystems
Brainstorm all possible directions it can go, how it might connect to big ideas in the curriculum, and to other strands or areas of the curriculum.	Rocks and minerals; planting, worms, food, composting, agriculture, insects, habitats, archaeology, geology, subways and tunnels
Brainstorm initial supporting resources that may be useful.	Magnifying glasses; information and story books; field trips; guest speakers; soil samples; multi-media resources
Decide what the first lead-in experience(s) will be.	Take students outside to collect soil
Gather together in a Knowledge Building Circle to talk about the first lead-in experience, in order to assess what students know and want to know.	Document questions and theories that arise in discussion "What did you notice? What do you know about soil? What do you wonder?"
Reflect on the students' shared questions and ideas and how they could be used to inform subsequent planning.	"Hmm. Many of the children posed questions about worms and how they help soil. We might benefit from seeing some worms in a terrarium or even a vermicomposter."
Decide if students will be exploring questions individually, in small groups, or as a whole group.	Students who are not yet skilled readers and writers may need more adult support to pursue questions. Kindergarten students may initially engage more easily in small group settings with fewer self-regulation demands. Students in older grades are generally more able to branch out into groups to independently investigate different questions.

Look for teachable moments and problems of understanding

Students don't always know how to move forward with their questions. As they begin to gather information from expert sources, as well as through observation and experimentation, they are likely at some point to come to a roadblock in their understanding. For example, they may be unable to find age-appropriate reading materials relating to their questions. Educators need to identify such moments and be prepared to support their students using some of these strategies:

- Guiding a student to reformulate their question to make it more precise and answerable
- Encouraging students to bring problems of understanding to a Knowledge Building Circle in the hope that other students can help to clarify the problem
- Directing students to helpful resources; the educator may need to rewrite, read aloud, or paraphrase a difficult text
- Teaching a mini-lesson to clarify the problem of understanding, especially if others have reached a similar impasse

> As the teacher engaged in this kind of learning process, it's about knowing that the kids will be heading down a particular road, and that they may need to know certain things in order to reach their destination. If they need to know x in order to learn y and z, then I need to be aware of that and somehow find a way to show them x.
>
> – Ben Peebles, Grade 5/6 Teacher, The Laboratory School

Focus on the big ideas in the overall curriculum expectations

Lab School Principal, Richard Messina (2001), notes, "In coverage-oriented instruction, topics are merely checked off and students move on whether there is understanding or not" (p. 21). However, when teachers focus on the larger overarching ideas and key concepts, they discover that students' questions are more likely to connect with or exceed curriculum expectations. This was the case for teachers in the Toronto and York Catholic District School Boards who piloted environmental inquiry in the first edition. At the end of the school year, they reviewed the content that had been covered and realized that their classes had addressed all of the required curriculum expectations and more!

Establish a culture of psychological safety

According to Dr. William Blatz, the first director of the original Institute of Child Study Laboratory School, a child's sense of security within a learning setting provides a necessary foundation for their learning to flourish (Blatz, E. Bott & H. Bott, 2010). This fundamental sense of security allows them to take intellectual risks, ask genuine questions, and posit half-formed theories. They need to feel confident that they will neither be judged nor ridiculed and that their contributions needn't always be correct or sophisticated.

To create a culture of psychological security, educators pay close attention to the social and emotional lives of their students. Building relationships is a priority, both with and among students, as well as with their families. An educator is careful not to skew a child's offerings through undue praise or criticism. Instead they are careful to model patience and neutrality through a variety of techniques:

- Encourage children to take time to think before giving an answer. Tell them to close their eyes and think about a question for a few moments before answering (Ogu & Schmidt, 2009).
- Receive children's ideas in a neutral manner, perhaps paraphrasing what they say without judgement. Summarizing a child's contribution before throwing it back to the group makes their ideas available for reflection and encourages children to think for themselves instead of seeking teacher validation. "Paolo thinks that sand comes from rocks and Andrea says it is dirt from the ocean. What do you think? Where does sand come from?" (Ogu & Schmidt, 2009, p. 15). When paraphrasing what a student has said, it is important to check in with them to ensure you have conveyed their intended meaning ("I think I heard Tibor say X. Is that what you meant, Tibor?") Resist the temptation to interpret a less-than-clear offering in terms of your own wishes.

- Be a co-learner. Don't be afraid to say, "I don't know. Let's find out!" When an educator acknowledges their own lack of knowledge, students are more likely to admit their own uncertainties. On occasion, the educator may also refrain from answering in order to encourage students to problem-solve: "That's a great question! How can we try to figure it out? Where can we look?"

Inquiry and Assessment: Why, How, and for Whom?

> A vision of schools in which the purpose is deep understanding of ideas and concepts requires a dramatic change in the assumptions underlying education and it requires a different view of schools, schooling, teachers, teaching, and, particularly, assessment.
>
> – Lorna M. Earl, *Teaching for Deep Understanding* (2004)

New paradigms of learning such as inquiry will necessitate new paradigms for assessing the learning. The open-ended nature of the inquiry process can lead to the common misconception that inquiry is somehow incompatible with assessment. If all ideas are both embraced and improvable, how can we begin to adjudicate among them? In reality, it is almost impossible to speak of inquiry without speaking of assessment. Every aspect of student involvement – every piece of work, every expressed idea – both advances their learning and provides essential information about them as learners. As an example, a careful drawing of what they see both reveals a child's understanding and helps them to further develop this understanding.

Ongoing and productive, a great deal of assessment in an inquiry-based classroom can be characterized in terms of reflective questioning. The child's ongoing assessments drive their inquiry: Is this the best question to ask? Will this help me figure out an answer? Is this answer fully satisfying? How am I fitting into the learning community? The educator's ongoing assessments drive their teaching: How can I help this student become fully engaged? What skills do I need to teach to whom? How can I best move thinking forward? This last question involves a complex and multi-layered piece of reflection. It encompasses an educator's self-assessment, questions about children, and questions about the topic and its key ideas.

Students continually assess the quality and utility of their ideas and situate them in the broader social and intellectual class context. Educators assess the growth of student ideas, skills, learning strengths, and emotional investment both as a group and individually. The entire learning community assesses where the inquiry is going and how to best achieve its purposes. In line with the idea that "virtually all classroom activities, whether formal or informal, provide teachers with information that can be used to monitor learning progress" (Fostaty-Young, & Wilson, 2000, p. 13), assessment is an ongoing process inextricably embedded in everyday classroom life throughout an inquiry.

Why assessment?

Like all assessment, inquiry-based assessment can be considered *as* learning, *for* learning, or *of* learning (Ontario Ministry of Education, 2010).

> **As** Learning: Assessment gives educators a window into a child's thinking and understanding. This informs their next steps in developing a responsive curriculum and providing appropriate supports.
>
> **For** Learning: Assessment allows educators to provide meaningful, explicit, and actionable feedback to students. This allows them to identify areas for growth and participate in targeting areas that need attention.
>
> **Of** Learning: Assessment provides concrete and accessible information to parents and other educators. This demonstrates the growth of a child's understanding and skills as well as indicating how they engage and apply those skills.

While a piece of assessment will frequently serve more than one purpose, not every function will be covered in every instance of assessment. In an inquiry-based classroom, assessment as and for learning tend to be prioritized. Along with informing the teaching and learning process, these modes of assessment provide crucial information that can be used for reporting purposes.

In assessment as and for learning, timely feedback can help the child understand what is going well in terms of their skills, learning process, and content knowledge. They can then make authentic use of this knowledge, not as an exercise in self-improvement, but because it will help them to find out what they want to know and convey what they have learned. Working with a student in this area, the aim is for the child to develop the ability to reflect upon their own thinking and thereby assume increasing responsibility for their own learning.

How does assessment apply to inquiry?

At the heart of assessing a student's engagement in inquiry is the question of what it means to know an individual child, both as a unique learner and as a member of a learning community. How do the two roles interact and support each other for that child? Inquiry provides a lens through which to view a child's thinking, questioning, and application of skills in the pursuit of meaningful knowledge and real-world problem solving.

Because inquiry requires an ongoing synthesis of ideas, many skills will be assessed in an embedded way as they are used for real purposes. Getting to know a child in this way takes time – as Robin Shaw, Lab School teacher, described it, "We are looking for things that grow over time. It takes a whole unit, or year, to form a profile for a particular child." Such an expansive view allows an educator time to watch the slow growth of complexity, sophistication, and depth of thinking in learners. It also recognizes that children (like adults) may be very different kinds of learners in different situations, depending on the area of study, their perceived place in the social fabric of the classroom, and the kinds of activities and projects undertaken. It is therefore a educator's responsibility to ensure sufficient diversity of topics and learning over the year to build a multi-dimensional portrait of an individual.

What might assessment of inquiry look like?

In creating a full picture of a learner, the assessment of students in an inquiry-based setting will take many different forms, depending on its purpose.

- Embedded or Decontextualized? Though often embedded in a learning activity, there are times where an educator might structure a more explicit assessment to gain a clearer picture of certain aspects of their students' learning. For example, they may ask targeted questions to find out what a child understands about a given concept.
- Individual or Group? An assessment may be individualized or it may ask a question common to all. A wide range of individual responses will be both expected and appropriate.
- Explicit or Implicit? Children may or may not realize that they are being assessed in some way. But they will always understand that the purpose is to help the educator know them better in order to better support their learning and well-being at school.
- Multiple Sources of Assessment: Individually or in a group, assessment may involve speaking, writing, art, math, building, digital creations, or imaginative play, to name just a few possibilities.
- Multiple Purposes for Assessment: The intention may be to elicit prior knowledge, document the growth of understanding, or to elicit reflection upon changes in understanding. An educator may also be assessing narrower skills that will help the child pursue their questions or express their understanding.

It is less likely that inquiry-based assessment will

- take the form of a multiple-choice test
- require one-phrase answers
- hope to elicit the same response in everyone
- only occur at the end of a unit

What do we look for?

Throughout the grades, beyond subject-specific expectations, there are significant markers of engagement and learning approaches that educators look for. They ask whether (or how) the child

- demonstrates curiosity
- shows focus
- persists in the face of difficulty
- works hard to achieve goals
- sustains interest in a topic
- shows excitement or pleasure in learning new things
- closely observes the world
- is organized
- shows flexibility
- is open to other ideas
- clearly communicates ideas and understanding
- asks rich questions
- revises a theory in the face of counter-evidence
- makes predictions
- reasons logically
- builds arguments and counter-arguments

There are also a host of relevant social skills to be considered, including the ability to listen attentively or collaborate respectfully and productively with others.

Understanding common developmental trajectories in key areas provides a useful framework for assessing many aspects of a child's involvement in the inquiry process. As children get older, the expectations change. Once established, each area remains important throughout a child's schooling as they spiral back to old issues at new levels of maturity. Table 7 provides a developmentally informed summary of learning criteria that can guide what a teacher might watch or listen for at various stages of the inquiry process.

Table 7: Summary of Developmentally Informed Learning Criteria in Inquiry

Grade Level	Knowledge Building Discourse	Experimentation and Theory Building	Exploration and Research	Depth and Expression of Content Knowledge
Early Years Children are just learning how to engage in ideas as a community as they begin to realize that others have viewpoints of their own. They are becoming aware of the interests of others and starting to find common interests with peers. Developmental differences mean that expectations are still strongly individualized.	**How does the child ...** Participate actively: offering questions, ideas, theories? Participate as an onlooker: watching and listening to peers? Make connections? Take turns? Respectfully agree or disagree with ideas regardless of who offers them?	**How does the child ...** Observe and describe phenomena? Ask focused questions? Offer predictions? Identify outcomes? Note (mis)match between prediction and outcome? Show causal thinking?	**How does the child ...** Engage in hands-on exploration? Show curiosity? Explore books, photos, or other sources of information? Listen attentively to information? Connect new information with pre-existing knowledge or personal experience?	**How does the child ...** Express understanding in diverse ways? Retain and convey information? Apply new concepts in different contexts? Change ideas in response to new information?
Primary Incorporating and building upon the learning assessed in the Early Years, children more intentionally engage as members of a learning community. Though individual responses remain varied, group expectations become more generalized.	**How does the child ...** Share knowledge, experiences, and theories? Engage in topic-centered discussion? Listen to and build on to the ideas of others? Show appreciation for other ideas? Justify ideas? Suggest next steps?	**How does the child ...** Organize and record observations? Ask productive questions? Reason logically? Think causally? Build simple explanatory theories? Test theories experimentally?	**How does the child ...** Express and pursue interests? Independently access resources? Identify relevant information? Make connections to previous learning or experience?	**How does the child ...** Show depth of understanding in a variety of ways? Reflect on own understanding? Reflect on community understanding? Convey ideas orally and in writing? Explain their thinking so that it makes sense to others?
Junior Children are encouraged to pursue their own interests within the broader community, while bringing this knowledge back to the group to deepen collective understanding.	**How does the child ...** Contribute to group knowledge building? Identify and offer productive ideas? Identify problems of understanding? Develop and refine promising questions? Incorporate conflicting ideas into a higher level theory?	**How does the child ...** Develop testable hypotheses? Design experiments to answer questions? Draw and justify conclusions? Create models and analogies? Build complex theories? Test theories against observations? Revise theories in face of counter-evidence?	**How does the child ...** Rigorously investigate questions? Find relevant information for building personal and community understanding? Summarize and synthesize information? Critically analyze information, including assessing credibility of source?	**How does the child ...** Reflect on growth of personal understanding? Reflect on growth of community understanding? Apply knowledge to real-world phenomena? Summarize knowledge clearly and engagingly for an outside audience?

How do you assess students in an inquiry-based learning environment?

Inquiry-based assessment, evaluation, and reporting is as student-centred as the inquiry-based learning process itself, and can be characterized as follows:

- It focuses on the growth of each student over time, rather than comparing them to other students or to a statistical average.
- It makes thinking processes explicit.
- It embeds assessment into everyday classroom life throughout the inquiry.
- It focuses on learning skills and higher-order thinking skills as well as the accumulation of information.
- It aims to be helpful and transparent for students and families as well as for the educator.
- It is based on ongoing and varied sources of student expression.
- It supports the development of "students' self-assessment skills to enable them to assess their own learning, set specific goals, and plan next steps …" (Ontario Ministry of Education, 2010, p. 6).

In an inquiry-based classroom, the educator assesses student progress on a continuous basis throughout the school year, collecting and using a wide range of information to provide an informed and comprehensive picture of the students' learning. As well as helping each student situate themselves in the learning, using multiple sources of evidence "increases the reliability and validity of the evaluation of student learning" (Ontario Ministry of Education, 2010).

Some examples of authentic assessment sources include

- student questions
- inquiry lab books
- portfolios
- visual art
- anecdotal observations
- transcripts of KB discussions
- culminating projects

Some strategies for working with each of these sources for assessment are described in the section that follows.

Student questions

Even as they move an inquiry forward, students' questions also provide an educator with invaluable information about how they understand a topic. Through recording questions that arise during Knowledge Building Circles and in other conversations, it often becomes possible to trace the growth of children's thinking.

A key aspect of a teacher's role is to help children refine their own initial questions – as scientists do – to make them more answerable, thinking about what they are really asking and how to best ask it. Students ask many different kinds of questions, ranging from simple factual queries to causal questions to questions that deeply probe the implications of a theory or attempt to make sense of inconsistencies. And some questions – the more philosophical "wonderings" – go beyond the scientific to probe fundamental assumptions about the world and how it works. Each type of question has an important place in inquiry – we need the details as well as the big picture – and the diverse kinds of questions offered by different students enrich the learning process for everyone.

Determining the scope of a question is not always straightforward. Word choice or grammar do not always signal a question's purpose or function; sometimes a pertinent factual or statistical question serves to probe a much deeper idea. While identifying a child's preferred mode of questioning provides valuable information for an educator, it is also important to see how and whether the range and scope of their questions broaden over time. As an inquiry proceeds, educators can profitably draw students' attention to the way in which certain types of well-timed questions may be especially valuable in extending and deepening group understanding, while others (perhaps more simply answered through a Google search) may do less to advance the overall course of the inquiry. Table 8 offers suggestions for assessing students' questions.

Table 8: Assessing the Content and Quality of Students' Questions

Assessment Considerations Arising from…	
…the <u>content</u> of a student's question	…the <u>quality</u> of a student's question
What does this question tell me about this student's interests and curiosity?	Is this question formulated precisely enough to be answerable?
What does this question reveal in terms of gaps in this student's content knowledge?	Does this question represent this student's ability to make connections among ideas?
What evidence of existing content knowledge does this student's question reveal?	Does this student tend to ask questions that are fact-based, higher-order in nature, or a combination?
Does this question build on recently learned information or experiences, revealing a consolidation of learning?	Has this student shown growth in the questions that they ask?
Does this question show an understanding of what information will help the group to move forward?	Does this question play a valuable role in advancing group knowledge?

Inquiry lab books and portfolios

Inquiry lab books are notebooks in which learners record all kinds of information related to their inquiry, including their

- initial questions
- causal theories
- observational sketches and diagrams
- reflections on experiments
- notes on research from books, internet sources, and guest speakers
- notes and/or drawings from field experiences
- new questions and theories

With each entry dated, the lab book archives a learner's ideas and research over time and provides a window into the evolution of their thinking. By contrast, a more conventional test reveals a slice of their knowledge as it manifests itself at one particular moment in time.

> If you are paying any attention whatsoever during this inquiry process you will have a really fine-grained understanding of what the child understands; and a much more fine-grained understanding than if you were only to rely on a series of tests. Even a really well-written test only reveals what a student happens to recall or output on a particular day. But with inquiry, they have multiple ways of demonstrating their understanding over time. So you see their developing understanding, as opposed to a snapshot in one moment.
>
> – Ben Peebles, Grade 5/6 Teacher, The Laboratory School

Drawings and other forms of visual art

New insights into how children understand the world, that don't always come out in verbal exchanges or written communication, sometimes emerge through drawings and other visual modes of expression. Especially with English language learners or the less verbally forthcoming, art offers educators another window into what a child notices and how they connect their observations of phenomena.

In Junior Kindergarten, students were studying the development of a chicken, from egg to hatchling and beyond. Notice the knowledge and vocabulary that was revealed through this JK student's drawing of a chicken's development from "a little dot" to "growed up," including the suggestion of a new life cycle beginning (Photo 1).

Photo 1: JK Drawing and Scribed Reflection, Example 1

The drawings in Photos 2 and 3 show quite different focuses and kinds of understanding. Through such comparisons an educator builds context for their own understanding of the different ways children have been thinking about the process.

Photo 2: JK Drawing and Scribed Reflection, Example 2

Photo 3: JK Drawing and Scribed Reflection, Example 3

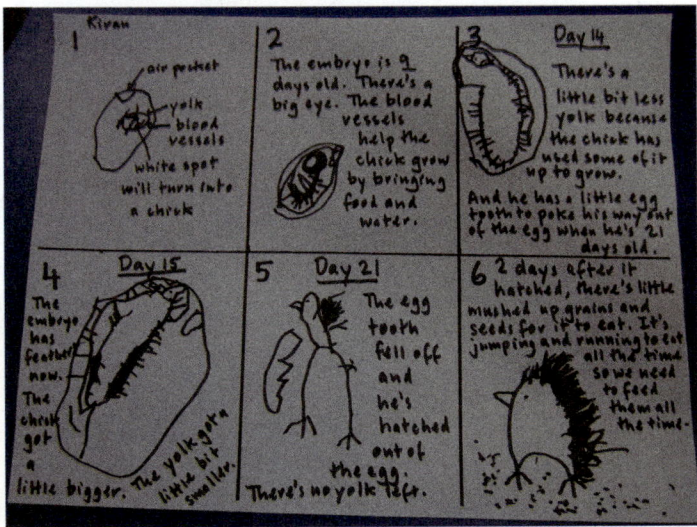

Drawings illuminate a student's perspective and allow the educator to consider their attention to detail. By noting what is included or excluded, an educator may identify which elements of an experiment or observation a student finds most relevant or memorable, as well as what they might be overlooking. Analyzing and interpreting evidence of student learning in this manner is an essential step in the assessment process (Ontario Ministry of Education, 2010). Figure 4 shows in more detail how comparisons of student responses can inform a teacher's understanding.

At the same time, not all students are comfortable representing ideas in drawing, and a cursory scribble needs to be probed further. Often the true value of the drawing lies in the ideas that emerge when an educator engages with the child to discuss their work.

Branch I: Inquiry and Engagement

Figure 4: Opportunities for Assessment through Inquiry

The four examples below were created in response to a child-designed experiment during a study of bees. Identical little metal balls were to be dropped simultaneously into four different kinds of honey. Each student made a prediction as to which metal ball they thought would sink the fastest (a test of viscosity!). They then considered the results.

In this example the child reports that her prediction was correct, and makes an observation that one ball never made it all the way to the bottom – a fairly straightforward observation, but notice how the drawing clearly shows the balls sinking at different rates.

In the second example, the student has not only made a prediction but has also offered a plausible theory to support her thinking. The drawing effectively illustrates the uniformity of the jars and balls being used – proper scientific method.

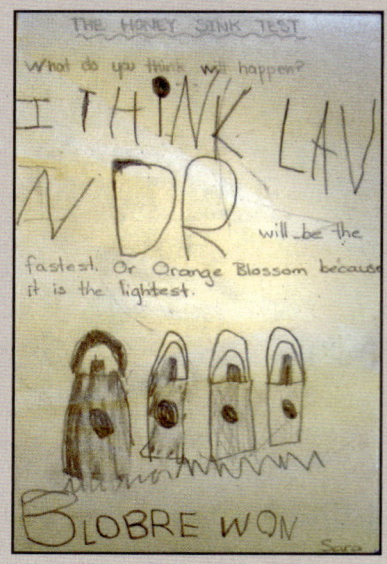

In this example, the student has offered a prediction and makes a close observation of the results, implicitly reflecting upon her expectation that the balls would have sunk to the bottom more quickly. Despite the more rudimentary drawing, this student's illustration carefully notes the variable colours of the honeys. Note that the student does not seem to consider being "right" in her prediction of particular importance.

In the fourth example, the student actively reflects upon his prior assumption of what would happen (very meta-cognitive). He goes on to offer a theory for why the balls, particularly the one pictured, seem to be sinking so slowly. Again, note that the student does not bother to add that he was correct in his prediction. He seems much more interested in understanding what happened!

Each of these responses highlights different ways of seeing and thinking about the world. Rather than comparing them on a hierarchical scale, the teacher can use these artifacts to better understand and communicate each student's thinking to others.

Documenting observations

Student-to-student small-group interactions

When students work collaboratively, it is sometimes difficult to precisely determine the accomplishments and learning of individuals. Yet the interactions that occur among students during small-group work can significantly reveal their developing understanding. Once students have developed the maturity and independence to independently investigate their questions in pairs or small groups, an educator can casually walk around the class to observe and listen to student interactions, while informally recording notable remarks, questions, or observations. In this way, the educator can assess the extent to which a student has internalized newly acquired concepts. The way in which a student spontaneously extends or applies newly acquired concepts within the group may offer the clearest sign of their understanding or misunderstanding.

Mini-conferences

Holding mini-conferences with individuals or research groups as they investigate problems of understanding offers another assessment opportunity. Touching base with each group can provide a detailed sense of each student's level of understanding, as well as highlighting the learning skills and work habits that are instrumental in student success.

Table 9 offers some suggestions from the Ontario Ministry of Education for assessing learning skills and work habits.

Table 9: Learning Skills and Work Habits in Grades 1 – 12*

Learning Skills and Work Habits	Sample Behaviours
Responsibility	The Student: • fulfils responsibilities and commitments within the learning environment; • completes and submits class work, homework, and assignments according to agreed-upon timelines; • takes responsibility for and manages own behaviour.
Organization	The Student: • devises and follows a plan and process for completing work and tasks; • establishes priorities and manages time to complete tasks and achieve goals; • identifies, gathers, evaluates, and uses information, technology, and resources to complete tasks.
Independent Work	The Student: • independently monitors, assesses, and revises plans to complete tasks and meet goals; • uses class time appropriately to complete tasks; • follows instructions with minimal supervision.
Collaboration	The Student: • accepts various roles and an equitable share of work in a group; • responds positively to the ideas, opinions, values, and traditions of others; • builds healthy peer-to-peer relationships through personal and media-assisted interactions; • shares information, resources, and expertise and promotes critical thinking to solve problems and make decisions.
Initiative	The Student: • looks for and acts on new ideas and opportunities for learning; • demonstrate the capacity for innovation and a willingness to take risks; • demonstrates curiosity and interest in learning; • approaches new tasks with a positive attitude; • recognizes and advocates appropriately for the rights of self and others.
Self-regulation	The Student: • sets own individual goals and monitors progress towards achieving them; • seeks clarification or assistance when needed; • assesses and reflects critically on own strengths, needs, and interests; • identifies learning opportunities, choices, and strategies to meet personal needs and achieve goals; • perseveres and makes an effort when responding to challenges.

*Source: Ontario Ministry of Education (2010)

Hands-on activities

Insights into students' conceptual understanding abound as children immerse themselves in focused experiential explorations.

Table 10 provides an example of one teacher's observations during a class inquiry on structures. As the students worked with a variety of building materials, she walked around and conversed with them about their structures.

The simple act of jotting down students' actions and comments can provide educators with worthwhile information. As an inquiry progresses, the teacher might periodically revisit an activity to reflect on how a student's structures and understanding are developing over time. However, the timing of these conversations is important, and an educator should be sensitive to when it is appropriate or useful to move in with their own observations and thought-provoking questions. There is a delicate balance between extending learning in this way and interrupting a child's focused absorption in an investigation. Fortunately, the child's response to your questioning will usually let you know how welcome or productive it is in the moment.

Branch I: Inquiry and Engagement

Table 10: Example of a Teacher's Assessment Notes for a Grade 2/3 Inquiry about Structures

Teacher Question	Student Response	Indication of Initial Understanding
"Why do you think this tower won't stand?"	"The skinny tower won't stand because is doesn't have a big base."	• Importance of form to a structure's stability
"Why do you think the tower fell over?"	"My tower fell over when I put this block on top because it is heavier than the ones underneath it."	• Importance of form to a structure's stability and strength
"Do you think this tower will stand?"	"This tower will not fall over because the pieces [unifix cubes] stick together. If they didn't stick together, we could probably just breathe on it and it could fall over."	• Importance of the type of materials to the strength of a structure • The action of external forces can affect a structure's stability

Knowledge building discourse

When a student contributes an idea to help the group tackle a question or problem of understanding, they provide the educator with knowledge about how they engage in the learning, how they express their thinking, and their depth of understanding. During a KB discussion, an educator may consider these areas:

- Language and communication: Does the student convey thoughts in a clear and coherent manner that allows their classmates to understand and respond?
- Ability to interact with diverse ideas and perspectives: Does the student listen to other students' ideas? Do they productively agree or disagree?
- Contribution to community knowledge: Does the student make connections and build upon other ideas?
- Ability to use authoritative sources constructively: Is the student's understanding deepened by information they receive from a variety of sources?
- Understanding of key concepts: Has the student revealed a misconception?
- Flexibility of ideas: Does the student modify their ideas in the face of counter-arguments or counter-evidence?
- Providing supporting explanation: Does the student provide a logical argument or empirical evidence for ideas?
- Participation: What role does the student play in the discourse? (e.g., asking questions, offering facts or theories, listening carefully and summarizing/synthesizing what they have heard)

There are various methods for recording the questions, ideas, and theories in KB discussions that make this information readily available for assessment purposes. For example

- Write down the main question(s) being discussed and record students' ideas underneath for later reflection and analysis.
- Grade 1 teacher Zoe Donoahue often uses a tally chart for categorizing student comments, such as the one shown in Figure 5.

Figure 5: Knowledge Building Discourse Tally Chart

Knowledge Building Discourse				
Date:				
Student	Theory	Supporting Evidence	Question	Build-on

Revisiting questions

Revisiting questions at points throughout an inquiry is a common way to gauge the growth of student learning. This allows educators to ascertain the growth of learning over time, to determine whether students are incorporating new information into their developing understanding, and to identify what they are learning and how they are learning it.

This strategy offers opportunities for self-assessment, making the assessment process transparent for the student. When students revisit earlier work, they see concrete evidence of their own growth, regardless of where they stand among their classmates (Fostaty-Young, & Wilson, 2000). They are encouraged to critically reflect upon their own learning.

Consider Photos 4 and 5: two drawings made by the same child in Carol Stephenson's SK class. The drawing in Photo 4 was created on September 14, when Carol asked the class to draw everything they knew about bees. This initial drawing revealed this child's preliminary knowledge about bees, as Carol scribed his words. The drawing in Photo 5, created on October 10, revealed clear growth in this child's anatomical understanding of bees. His fine-motor control had not improved significantly, but he had a different focus and awareness of what might be important to communicate in a drawing. We also see here how the attentive act of drawing not only reveals knowledge but can lead to new questions (lower-left corner).

Photo 4: What Do You Know about Bees?*

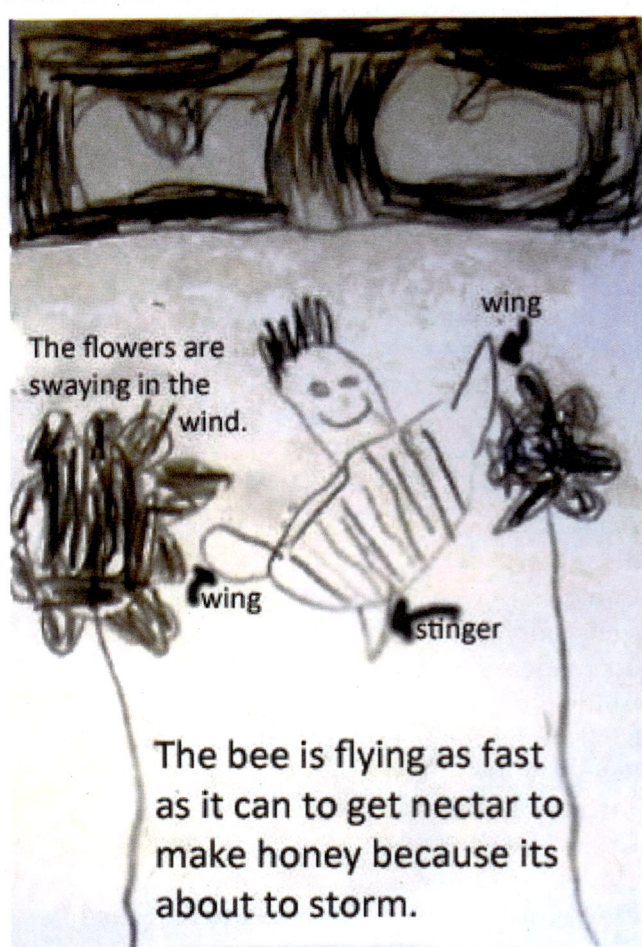

*Text enhanced to ensure legibility. Original grammar has been maintained.

Photo 5: Revisiting the Same Question*

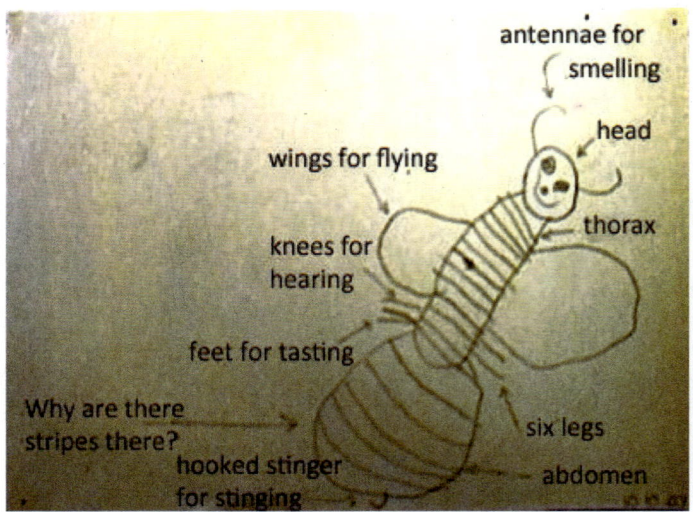

*Text enhanced to ensure legibility. Original grammar has been maintained.

Culminating activities

Despite the pedagogic stress on the *process* of developing understanding in inquiry-based learning, the creation of summative projects that summarize and communicate learning can provide new and compelling motivation for students at certain stages of their investigations. Such culminating activities require students to organize the wide array of ideas and information they have encountered and provide them with confirmation that their many questions have led to some answers. In designing projects that effectively share learning with an audience (whether classmates, families, or other classes in the school), students are forced to confront their own problems of understanding as they clarify their ideas for someone who may be unfamiliar with the topic. Sometimes, this sharing prompts new questions and knowledge building among classmates. At other times, it provides the deep satisfaction of closure (for the time being, anyway), affirming for students that the inquiry had purpose, that learning has taken place, and that certain goals have been met.

Culminating projects take a variety of forms, on many scales. They can be the work of groups or individuals. As well as offering motivation and a sense of closure to students, they provide educators with yet another lens on learners – how they organize and communicate information to an outside audience, for instance. They can play a significant role in developing critical skills, such as learning to categorize and rank information in terms of its overall importance. Students learn to communicate succinctly as they extract key points and synthesize their findings for an audience in an engaging and informative fashion.

Figure 6 provides an example of a teacher-created summative assignment in Ben Peebles' Grade 6. This carefully structured project asks students to develop culminating demonstrations through an explicit process in which reflection on earlier knowledge building generates new questions, research and information. Finally, students are asked to find a way to tie their learning together and communicate their overall understanding to an audience. The stress placed on the importance of conveying ideas to people outside the immediate learning community shows how deeply connected understanding, reflection, and communication can be. Another noteworthy aspect of this assignment is that the ongoing project work occurs in class where learning support and monitoring are ongoing. This presents a very different model than the typical science fair project in which students bring in home-created artifacts that can be quite starkly detached from their classroom learning.

A few other recent examples of student-created projects include

- constructions (e.g., Biodomes in "Lisa's Story," Part 2, p. 219)
- environmental documentaries
- environmental raps (shared with the school at an assembly)
- murals or 3-D models
- an in-class science fair, with experiments demonstrated to other classes in the school
- Grade 3 students teaching Grade 2s all they have learned about worms
- individual books about self-chosen topics (shared in a gathering with parents)
- environmental action projects (see "Murray's Story" and "Mike's Story," Part 2, p. 262 and p. 251)
- powerpoint presentations (shared in class)
- books on topics written for and shared with younger children in the school

Student participation in assessment

Knowledge Building calls for embedded, concurrent, and transformative assessment in the inquiry process. This suggests that students can play an important role in assessing their own progress and that of the entire learning community. The beauty of inquiry is that, from the beginning, students' questions define their goals. For example, when a student asks, "Do all plants need sun to live and grow?" that student is shaping a learning goal.

As a class builds knowledge over time, an educator will often identify points at which it is important to pause and consider questions such as: "What do you think are some of the most important things that we have learned about so far? What do we still not understand or need to know about?" Student participation in this kind of discourse serves as an authentic form of self-assessment. With teacher guidance, their ideas may help to form the basis for different kinds of learning tasks or assessment tools such as rubrics, surveys, homework assignments, group projects, etc.

Figure 6: Example of a Grade 6 Culminating Activity

STEM Fair Project

As a class we have built our knowledge about electricity, and our thinking has expanded into considering a wide range of topics that are related to our original thinking about circuits. For the next couple weeks, you will have the chance to explore a topic in depth, to research it in detail, and to share your new understanding by creating an artifact, experiment or display for a STEM fair in our classroom.

This project will have 3 parts: Knowledge Building, deeper research, and sharing in our STEM fair. I don't need to remind your that we have limited time left this school year, so you will have to be efficient to finish on time. You will not have time to waste time!

Part One: Knowledge Building

We have explored several topics so far as a class. In this part of the project, you will review everything we have learned as a community about your chosen topic, and create a special Knowledge Forum note detailing where we are now in our knowledge. You will use what we already know to decide what more you need to research about your chosen topic.

- Carefully read all the notes related to this topic in our Knowledge Forum view.
- Build on or add a new note with any information that you researched last time, but didn't yet have a chance to contribute.
- When you are ready, go to the Super Note View, and create a Super Note for your chosen topic. The purpose of this note is to summarize what we know about this as a community, and to decide what more we ought to learn. You will also have the chance to look at the knowledge built by other groups of students from past years.
- Read as many other Super Notes as you can, and look for ways your topic connects with others.
- Use the "We Need Deeper Research" scaffold to decide on the main research questions you will pursue in the next section.

Part Two: Research

In this part of the project, you will research and learn more, to deepen the knowledge that we built as a class.

PRINT a copy of your Super Note, paying special attention to what you wrote under the "deeper research" scaffold.
Using your computer or pencil and paper, take detailed notes from books and online sources. You should use at least 3 different sources.
Check in with Ben for feedback!

Part Three: STEM Fair Sharing!

In the final part of the project, you will create an artifact, demonstration, experiment, or display that will help others understand what you have learned about your chosen topic in your research. I am open to your ideas and creativity about what form this could take. Be inventive!

- Come up with an idea for how you could share some of what you know.
- Ask yourself:
    - Will my idea really help others understand this topic deeply?
    - Is it feasible to complete in the limited time we have?
- Run your idea by Ben, and get approval and some feedback.
- Make it happen!

Our STEM Fair will take place on June 2nd... make sure you use your time wisely.

Thinking About Different Learners

There are many different ways that students come to inquiry and knowledge building. Any approach that prioritizes communal processes of knowledge construction needs to be especially careful not to lose sight of individuals in the exciting momentum of group learning. It cannot always be assumed that communal knowledge advancement has necessarily reached every student. While it is often (though not always) clear who is thriving in a class inquiry, it is also crucial to consider the outliers, who may need thoughtfully tailored opportunities that allow them access to the knowledge under construction. There are many reasons for differences in engagement and understanding – development, culture, brain processes, family life, gender, personality, and so on – and to give the topic its due is well beyond the scope of this book. Apart from the obvious implications for assessment, respecting differences among learners lies at the heart of all responsive teaching.

Developmental considerations

A large body of research has documented children's developing ability to recognize that others do not see the world exactly as they do, coming to realize that human beliefs and actions only make sense in the light of a point of view. This ability to explicitly recognize other perspectives, or what is commonly called a "theory of mind" (e.g., Wellman, 1990), starts to emerge in the preschool and kindergarten years as four- and five-year-olds begin to reliably appreciate that other people have opinions and feelings different from their own. It continues to grow in refinement and complexity into adulthood.

These developmental considerations have implications for knowledge building in the early years. While conversations that expose children to different points of view are an important means for building this awareness of other minds, an educator cannot assume that young children will fully understand the idea of a perspective, nor that knowledge building talk among four-year-olds will in any way resemble that of fifth graders. With this in mind, a significant portion of early years education (as laid out in the most recent Ontario Kindergarten curriculum document) is designed to further the ability to see the world through someone else's eyes, largely through conversation, social and imaginative play, and exposure to the inner lives of characters in stories.

Kindergarteners are only beginning to build the self-regulation skills needed to wait their turn and listen attentively in group settings. More accustomed to responsive one-on-one dialogue with an accommodating adult, they are just developing the social awareness and control to stay on topic, make themselves clear for a less accommodating peer, or interpret a peer's less-than-clear verbal messages. For these reasons, educators of this age group often find it useful to introduce initial KB talks quite informally, in very small groups, so that viewpoints can be exchanged without the management issues that frustrate children and educators alike.

As children become more familiar with knowledge building exchanges, gradually enlarging the group size can increase the scope of the students' thinking. But even after children gain a basic awareness of other perspectives, there is still a long developmental trajectory in their growing capacity for group knowledge building. How they understand the nature of knowledge will affect the way they pursue it, and it takes many years before the staunch realism of preschoolers gives way to the more nuanced belief that knowledge is humanly constructed and that conflicting ideas can legitimately co-exist but are also subject to evaluation (Kuhn, Cheney, & Weinstock, 2000; Kuhn, 2010). It also takes time before a child learns to evaluate an idea on its own merits, independently of who proposes it, or to realize that friendship is not a reason for blanket agreement.

Cultural considerations

Of course, development will look very different in different cultural settings, and a child's beliefs about school and knowledge will often reflect deep-seated intellectual beliefs and values in their broader cultural milieu. It is therefore essential for an educator to keep in mind the powerful cultural influences that students will bring to their learning. To be motivated and engaged at school, children need recognition of and appreciation for these values, even when they may not mesh fully with an educator's own assumptions about optimal ways to learn. While appreciation for diverse ideas can be a strength of inquiry-based learning, it is still worth reflecting upon our unexamined cultural assumptions and expectations for the way this might look in a Canadian classroom.

For example, direct questioning may not be everyone's way of showing curiosity. It is important to start with the working assumption that every child will be interested in something and observe your students closely to find out how different children reveal that interest. Asking questions is only one possibility. Spending long periods studying things is another. Also consider what kinds of questions are important to them. For some children, mastering vast bodies of facts may be their preferred route to understanding, and one that can involve considerable conceptual creativity if you look for it. For others, it might be the deep pondering of metaphysical mysteries. Such different approaches are often both individual and cultural; either way, all types of questions have a valuable role to play in building understanding.

There are likewise a multitude of cultural and individual ways of listening attentively, and demands for strong eye contact may confuse a child who has learned more indirect ways of showing respect and paying attention.

Thinking about Indigenous learners, Doug Anderson has identified tensions between the technology-driven endeavours of European science and the more holistic, relational views that saturate many Indigenous cultures. These disjunctions may have an impact on how some Indigenous students relate to mainstream curriculum. Another discontinuity between the cultures has been identified by Barbara Rogoff and her colleagues (e.g., Rogoff, Paradise, Mejía Arauz, Correa-Chávez, & Angelillo, 2003; Paradise & Rogoff, 2009), who describe "observation and pitching in" (or "Learning through Intent Community Participation") as a fundamental participatory mode of learning for many Indigenous and Mexican-American children. These observations remind us that "active learning" can take many forms, and serves as a warning to not underestimate the learning of the child who quietly watches and listens to what others say and do.

Students who are new to the English language need equal opportunities to show curiosity and ask questions at school. "Inviting students to [share their questions] in their first language as well as in English enables them to draw on their strengths, including their existing academic, linguistic, and cultural knowledge. This approach also enriches the class environment by exposing English-speaking students to the advantages of knowing more than one language and of cultural diversity in general" (Ontario Ministry of Education, 2005a, p. 15). Finding ways to forge links with non-English-speaking family members, communicating through interpreters, siblings, body language, or showing the child's work, will go a long way toward making school a more meaningful place for the student.

Considering individual differences

Entangled with, but not limited to development and culture, are as many ways of learning and engagement as there are learners, each with its own strengths and liabilities. Some children are risk-takers, plunging with enthusiasm into whatever is on offer; others are naturally cautious, watching and biding their time until they have fully assessed what is going on. For some students, verbal expression is their primary mode of coming to know (and showing what they know); others learn and show their learning differently. Some children are highly social, embracing with enthusiasm the possibilities of group work; others are introverted and more comfortable with solitude. It is important that the values accorded to risk-taking, verbal negotiation of ideas, and community processes in knowledge building environments do not end up relegating some children to the margins.

In any inquiry, educators are often aware of an imbalance in the amount that students contribute. They wonder how best to support children who appear less engaged in the learning or fail to grasp concepts that others have moved forward with. Students at both ends of the learning spectrum can pose challenges to sustaining an inclusive, democratic classroom. A student with unusually advanced understanding of a topic needs opportunities to explore further at their own level without either being constrained by the less formed ideas of the group or shutting down conversation with their confident answers to still-emergent questions. What to do with the most dominant voices – whether advanced or not – can be a conundrum, and some have found that allowing many opportunities for individual and small-group work can help to mitigate their outsized influence.

To ensure that she doesn't lose sight of individuals, one Grade 4 teacher, Robin Shaw, gives each child a notebook for recording their thoughts (in drawing or writing, sometimes scribed by the teacher). "Each time we started a new concept, each child answered open-ended questions so I could understand where each child was coming from before the able kids immediately started putting ideas out. I also had kids individually reflect following each activity, then [I] put these [thoughts] into the [Knowledge Forum] database – this way I could make accessible to everyone ideas that would not have otherwise appeared in the database." Over the course of the inquiry, children returned periodically to their notebooks see how their thinking had developed. In this process, Robin was sometimes surprised by what she learned. Some children who had appeared less knowledgeable or engaged showed themselves to have thought deeply and productively about concepts, while for others, the frequency and articulateness of their verbal communications had obscured some significant areas of confusion.

Summary of Chapter

Over the past 50 years or more, the work of educational practitioners and theoreticians has demonstrated a broad range of interpretations of "inquiry-based learning." It has not been our intent in this section to provide a definitive interpretation, but rather to lay out some features that in our experience help to create rich, focused, and engaging problem-centred environments and to show a range of possibilities for the environmental learning offered by this approach. Put simply, children's curiosity is key – both the starting point and endpoint of all inquiry work. We do not feel that releasing all decision-making to the students provides for useful learning, but instead favour thinking about classrooms in which educators use their understanding of children, learning, and subject matter to thoughtfully guide students as they explore questions they care about with growing skill, rigour, and persistence. Our vision of inquiry highly values structured processes of group knowledge building that benefit the classroom learning community; navigating the productive tensions between individual and group learning is both the challenge and the great reward of this approach.

Lighting the Fire: The Spirit of Learning
Indigenous Lens on Branch I

Lighting the Fire

Learning from the Heart

Inquiry-based learning reflects a simple, profound truth: learning is most powerful when rooted in the heart. The heart is our connection to Spirit, which in turn is what unifies all things. The heart is the seat of the fire igniting our whole being. We gain understanding and knowledge most meaningfully in relation to the inner spark that lights the fire of learning, rather than when learning is externally imposed. Externally imposed learning separates knowledge into artificial categories – as if the world were merely a huge *machine* with *no spirit* – and makes it harder to place anything in relation to broader contexts. And so, we learn best when we feel a strong, inner, *spiritual* connection with everything around us. This truth is deeply reflected through Indigenous worldviews.

Indigenous worldviews emphasize the spiritual source of our world, without separating Spirit from matter and nature. Matter, which Eurocentric thought tends to see as reality, is more like an immanent *symbol* of Spirit to Indigenous thinking. *This is a complete reversal of the usual modern worldview*, where symbols are seen as abstract, even fanciful, representations of material realities. Indigenous perspectives ultimately see Spirit as the greater reality, preceding matter in the creative order. This creative order transcends time, so Spirit and matter co-exist constantly in the process of Creation. Everything is always *coming into being* from a spiritual source. In a way, this is obvious: the origin of all things is unseen, beyond even the most microscopic forms, and ultimately beyond space and time. The origin of all things is a Great Mystery.

The emphasis on Spirit as the basis of the world has far-reaching implications. In some ways, this emphasis corresponds with the principles of inquiry-based learning.

Wonder

It is an immutable law that all growth proceeds from within, from the unseen. A child is not constructed from her disparate parts but is rather *brought into being*, emerging from what ultimately appears to be a vanishing point. In the same way, learning proceeds from within the child, which corresponds to the sense of wonder emphasized in inquiry-based learning. Wonder is innate and sacred, and cannot be imposed from without. While all beings are sacred, children are especially so because they are closer to their spiritual source than adults. As different children are given different gifts, they are drawn in wonder to the world in unique ways; they bring their unique gifts with them on their learning journey.

This does not mean we all have to "be spiritual." Many people are motivated more by materialistic concerns. But our worldly motivations arise from inner *emotional* or heartfelt attachment to those external motives. Learning is born from that which is pregnant with *inner meaning*.

And so we learn best *from the inside out*. Even rote learning is best done with a high level of inner motivation. Each person has his or her own intuitive way of growing into his or her relationship with the world. This does not mean educators should abandon all "worldly" learning agendas. It *does* mean we need to respect and connect with children's inner lives, through strategies that bring them closer to the knowledge they need. Invite, and see. Invite in another way, and see – until the spark is lit. Rather than impose learning paths, we tell a story,[1] or go somewhere with purpose, or show something fun or new, and the path is taken up by learners. The late Anishinaabe Elder, Art Solomon (1990), elegantly described how we nurture our innate sense of wonder:

> The traditional way of education was by example, experience, and storytelling. The first principle involved was total respect and acceptance of the one to be taught, and that learning was a continuous process from birth to death. It was total continuity without interruption. Its nature was like a fountain that gives many colours and flavours of water and that whoever chose could drink as much or as little as they wanted to whenever they wished. The teaching strictly adhered to the sacredness of life whether of humans, animals or plants.

This way of learning is for educators as much as for students. To paraphrase from the first edition of *Natural Curiosity*, when a student's heart and spirit are engaged, learning naturally blossoms. When the same happens for the educator, practice is transformed. Rather than feeling worried about what might happen if we move away from a learning path prescribed by adults, we need to feel a kind of freedom in approaching children. They will lead the learning in the way it needs to happen for them.

Coming to Know

Because we learn from the inside out, learning is a journey of emergence from Spirit into a relationship with knowledge. Indigenous thought sees knowledge as an active process (like a verb) in which we develop a way of living and being in relation to what is learned. This is different from the Eurocentric emphasis on knowledge as a *thing* (a noun) that can generally be grasped by those who have the aptitude to do so. Indigenous ways of learning respect the emerging *personal connection* of each learner to what is being learned, through her inner voice and heart.

"Coming to know" (Cajete, 2000)[2] is a way of describing distinct Indigenous views on the process of learning via more intuitively connected pathways. Indigenous ways of coming to know respect the individual's relationship with and responsibility for what is being learned, and explore stories and other diverse approaches to the subject at hand, learning pathways that appeal to diverse learning styles in non-prescriptive ways. Coming to know ultimately invites us to *explore* our emergent learning process as part of our own journey, rather than challenging us to enter into externally imposed, isolated theme areas.

---

[1] Stories are essential vehicles for connecting with Spirit. Rather than having mere amusement as their main purpose, stories in Indigenous cultures are more likely to be revered as accounts that reflect higher truths.

[2] For clarity and flow, this edition avoids substituting "coming to know" for "knowledge" throughout the document, as well as many other possible ways of trying to reflect Indigenous perspectives in English. Ultimately, the best way to understand Indigenous perspectives is through fluency in an Indigenous language, rather than twisting English into knots.

The idea of coming to know is reflected in some of the characteristics and practices of inquiry-based learning:

- The end point or final product is not known at the outset, but rather attained along the journey of learning.
- Prior knowledge and experience are elicited during this journey.
- There is a greater emphasis on interactivity with children.
- There is respect for learner agency and understanding one another, with an emphasis on seeing the same thing from multiple sides, over multiple times (revisiting questions), and through diverse methods.
- There is more time provided for reflection and guarding against cursory observations.
- There is emphasis on
  - process-oriented (vs. goal-oriented) learning
  - lifelong, seamless, holistic learning
  - many entry points to learning
  - listening to and carefully watching students over time, rather than talking to (or at) them
  - emotional security, supported through informal and non-judgemental (versus highly scrutinizing) approaches

All of these ways of supporting inquiry-based learning respect that the journey to knowledge is unique to each individual, best achieved when each of us is respected for the gifts we carry inside of us, and touched in ways that support the *natural emergence* of these inner gifts. This is why many Indigenous cultures have ceremonial ways of naming children in relation to the spiritually endowed gifts they bring. Such gifts are our sacred responsibility. Our names reflect our mission, and we must *find the meaning of our names, and live them out in the process of living our lives.*

Spiritual Relationship

Children intuitively connect everything in ways that inform their outer world from a spiritual place, seeing how all things are unified from within. In the teachers' stories in Part 2, Carol Stephenson shares her struggle to help Senior Kindergarten children consider their external world while also "looking in":

> One student's question, "What is your life about?" seemed a little challenging ... I was astonished and impressed by their responses, and the generosity of their vision. It was yet another reminder to not let any of my own hesitations stand in the way of what children, even as young as 5, can engage with. Here were some of their answers:
>
> *It means the moonlight and the Sun.*
> *It means being with your family.*
> *It's about being with friends.*
> *And your brothers and sisters.*
> *And your cousins.*
> *It's about people being nice to us.*
> *And us being nice to other people.*
> *It's about having food and living in a house.*
> *It's being nice to older people.*
> *And to younger people.*
> *Do not try to trick people or hurt them.*
> *Do not lie.*

From an Indigenous perspective, these answers are an excellent basis for relating to and learning about our world. The Moon and Sun cannot be divorced from love for family or from the responsibility for human kindness. They are, in a very real sense, our Spiritual Grandparents in the unending, sacred, unified circle of life.

Quality and Character

It is perfectly natural that a 5-year-old should arrive quickly at kindness as an essential quality of the universe. Given the chance, children are receptive to what is good.[3] Reaching a child's inner fire requires focussing on their *qualities*, which always precede and assign value to any quantity.[4] An emphasis on inner qualities connects with an emphasis on values and character in the learning process. *Mino Bimaadiziwin* ("living in a good way" in Anishinaabemowin) is a phrase reflecting how we must strive from an early age to follow our life path from a spiritually centred place of kindness, respect, and love.

Healthy parenting instincts tell us that the goal of nurturing children is the same as protecting what is sacred. We help our children come into their better nature by making them feel respected, safe, and loved. This is why an emphasis on emotional security – the foundation for developing empathy and compassion – is so essential in an inquiry-based environment. Compassion supports learning that is more fully felt in relation to what is within and around us. A sense of separation, of being apart from what we learn, has little place in such a learning process.

Knowledge approached from a foundation of good character and values takes on a different quality. It is imbued with meaning based on deeper understanding rather than being a collection of mere information. This requires a radical step away from creating citizens who are satisfied with surface knowledge about things, towards the nurturing of people who have the capacity, inner motivation and habit of delving deeply into what they would really *love* to know and *need* to know. It is a shift from merely living *under* what is legal (the letter of the law) to living *up to* what is good (the spirit of the law). It is the difference between knowledge as advantage over others and knowledge that is shared in the service of others. Emotional security, and the development of inner qualities like compassion, supports the sharing and *building of knowledge with others*.

Heart-based Knowledge Building

Learning from a heartfelt personal level does not mean an individual can ever own knowledge. The goal is *not* a society of specialists and technocrats who work in isolation from one another and from the people in general. Closely connected to the importance of learning from the heart is the Indigenous value placed on *putting our best knowledge together*, which is related to the principles of knowledge building and "idea diversity" emphasized in both editions of *Natural Curiosity*.

---

[3] Only a society preoccupied with war and conquest, where much of religion has degenerated to serve material interests, and where children are torn from their mothers and communities and thrown into boarding schools, could produce the savage children in Lord of the Flies, a novel widely read in Canadian schools. Indigenous people know too well the sad results of radical experiments that wrench children from family and institutionalize them. The residential school experiment was designed to crush the values and character of whole nations of people, and led inevitably to community breakdown, violence, and despair.

[4] A focus on quality should have the effect of improving quantitative aspects of learning, since larger quantities of knowledge can be assimilated with proper internal motivation. The emphasis on qualitative standards of learning is reflected in how we assess students in an inquiry-based learning environment.

The Anishinaabe value of *Debwewin* lends insight into knowledge building, and the importance of respecting diverse ideas in a context of inquiry-based learning. Debwewin can be translated as "heart-based knowledge." When we truly approach knowledge from our heart and spirit, such knowledge *cannot belong to a mere individual*. Another way to translate Debwewin is "to *speak* from the heart" (Goulais & Curry, 2005). If a person can find Debwewin within, it is her responsibility to share that truth as well as she is able. This is not the same as sharing any old thing; if knowledge is not connected through the heart, then it is hardly worth sharing, and the *quality* of what we know is in question. We may have facts, but without deeper understanding and connection with a wider holistic context, facts can too easily be turned to destructive ends.

The principle of Debwewin is *integral to community life*, since anyone who has a heartfelt truth contributes to the whole community when they step forward to share that truth. But even the most highly valued truth arising from an individual is only part of the full truth; there are in fact many of these truths, so great value is also placed on hearing and understanding the perspectives of others. Human knowledge is enriched by the diversity that comes from our highest individual truths being put together. Spirit manifests differently through different beings, so the fullest approach to the truth appreciates and attempts to unify these manifestations. *And so we need to assemble, hear and consider our highest and most deeply considered personal truths* (Borrows, Johnston, as cited in Simpson, 2011, p. 59).

The ideas embedded in the value of Debwewin indicate why Indigenous worldviews are less likely than Eurocentric views to see diversity as a source of conflict. Some practices emphasized in the inquiry-based approach to learning reflect the relatively high Indigenous value placed on diverse truths; most notably, the practice of "Knowledge Building Circles" resonates with Indigenous cultural and social tendencies.

The Circle of Learning

Indigenous societies have distinct ways of assembling knowledge, ways that encourage people to speak their own truth from the heart, to better reach the ears and hearts of others. Meaning and knowledge are made on an ongoing basis through the sharing of diverse personal truths across the community. The shared generation of knowledge and meaning across a community is often grounded in ceremony, and involves detailed systems to ensure accountability to a range of concerns. Indigenous political and ceremonial traditions are detailed and diverse, but generally have ways to increase how knowledge comes alive, and ensure that the widest consideration is given to an issue. This means taking the time to hear many possible angles.

The "talking circle" is one simple way in which diverse truths can be assembled and respected. It serves to bring us to a shared understanding of our common truth or purpose. A talking circle is by no means a full expression of any particular Indigenous nation's governance structure (these are quite complex), but it does distill some key principles common to many of those structures. Knowledge Building Circles, encouraged as part of inquiry-based learning environments, owe much to the talking circle.

Talking circles differ according to the Indigenous cultural context, but they share some common underlying principles:

Table 11: Principles of Talking Circles

- All are heard who wish to be heard
- Non-interference
- Deep consideration and respect
- Common purpose
- Speak from the heart

The ideas embedded in these principles owe much to oral teachings shared by Harold Ashkewe with the author (1989-93), and to Simpson (2011) as cited in Wemigwans (2014).

All are heard who wish to be heard

The opportunity to speak is offered to each person in the circle, even though every person's opinion or desire may not be acted on. Speaking is never mandatory.

Non-interference

People should not be interrupted. This principle reflects the value of non-interference: all must be free to follow their own spirit. This principle extends far beyond our human family to the wider world around us.

Deep consideration and respect

We need to listen and speak out of respect for others. As we love one another, we truly see one another, and deeply respect what we see in others. It is vital to be slow to judge each other, and take care in how we speak of others' ideas, even if we disagree. Patience and kindness are critical.

Common purpose

Movement in any direction, such as making a decision or rejecting an idea, or considering all possible consequences of a decision, is focused on the idea or decision, rather than on the people who speak.

Speak from the heart

People are encouraged to speak from the heart, with honesty, so that we may hear and consider their truth as well as possible. Building knowledge in this way is centred in how we serve and live in balance with our relatives, continually defined by our inner qualities and truth, which ultimately emanate from our spirit.

In a classroom environment, the consideration and understanding of each child's reality is the ideal, along with a way to help children understand one another's realities, to the greatest extent possible. We need to support children to move as deeply as possible within themselves to the seat of their being, where their individual truth lies, and then to move together and assemble those truths. Then, even in the dire world circumstances in which we now leave them, the path to the healing and recovery of their world can be made clear – not by us, but by them.

Our failure to ignite and share our spirits is barbarism. Set apart from one another, it becomes easier to succumb to self-interest, indiscriminately accelerated material progress, and the acquisition of *things*. In such a world, our shared purpose, our deeper selves, and love itself, are dimmed. But together we survive. Given a chance, our inner fire can be shared sincerely, which brings light to others. Our combined light is the real meaning of civilization. The great Nehiyaw (Plains Cree) Chief Payepot exhorted his people to remember this truth on his deathbed in 1908.

> My people, love one another. I want you to keep together. You don't know what the future holds. There will come a day when carts will no longer need horses. The white man may even be foolish enough to try to fly. Mark my words. Stay together. Love one another.
>
> – Abel Watetch, *Payepot and His People* (2007)

Branch II: Experiential Learning
Building a Sense of Place

Theoretical Underpinnings

> Basic understanding begins with exploring how things happen. Observing how things happen in the natural world is the basis of some of the most ancient and spiritually profound teachings of Indigenous cultures. Nature is the first teacher and model of process. Learning how to see nature enhances our capacity to see other things.
>
> – Gregory Cajete, *Look to the Mountain: An Ecology of Indigenous Education* (1994)

What Is Experiential Learning?

At its core, inquiry is about lived experience. It places our learning deeply within our living, breathing interaction with our surroundings.

In *Experience and Education* (1938), John Dewey writes, "There is an intimate and necessary relation between the processes of actual experience and education" (p. 7). His theory stresses that experience does not just supplement, enhance, or make learning more palatable; rather, it is the very condition of learning. This view speaks to some of the fundamental premises of environmental inquiry.

Of course, there is an important sense in which everything is experience: books and direct teaching, a walk to school, weeding a garden, conversing or overhearing a conversation, attending a lecture or a documentary, engaging in imaginary play, climbing a tree, solving a math problem. Some of these experiences are more immediate while others are more vicarious or mediated through institutions, technologies (including print), or knowledgeable others. Experiential pedagogy tends to focus on the more direct, relatively unmediated experiences available to children. It values the practical and hands-on, involving the body as much as the mind in encounters with the world. As Dewey suggests, such immediate experience lies at the core of real learning, and it makes little sense to conceive of environmental inquiry without direct and active participation in the world around us.

In its essence, experiential learning

- engages students in direct encounters (sensory, cognitive, and affective) with the immediate environment, including close observation
- moves beyond authoritative sources of information (teachers, books, etc.) as the sole providers of knowledge
- involves an ongoing dynamic interchange between immediate experience and reflection on this experience
- transforms experience into meaningful knowledge (Dewey, 1938; Kolb, 1984)

Inquiry and Experiential Learning: Experience and Reflection

While concepts that are ungrounded in experience may lack substance or meaning, experience in itself does not build concepts. Rather, to derive knowledge or meaning from experience requires conscious reflection upon its connection with current understandings, past experiences, and the experiences and understandings of others, both past and current. This offers a clear point of convergence with principles of inquiry, in which encounters with the world trigger questions and theories which inform subsequent encounters with the world (and so on). In this way, experience and reflection are intimately bound; unreflected experience fails to move thinking forward, while reflection needs something to reflect upon.

A recent Ontario Ministry of Education document, *Community-Connected Experiential Learning: A Policy Framework for Ontario Schools, Kindergarten to Grade 12* (Winter 2016 – Draft for Consultation, pp. 9-10), envisages a continuous experiential learning cycle in which students participate, reflect, and apply new understandings to new experiences.

- *Participate: What?* Students are immersed in an experience, acknowledging what they are doing, what they are thinking, and what they are feeling during the experience.
- *Reflect: So what?* Students think about their experience, guided by reflective questions and prompts, and identify what they learned as a result of the experience – about themselves, other people, the world, their opportunities, or the subject of study.
- *Apply: Now what?* Students describe how their learning stimulates further inquiry; how it has influenced – or may influence – their decisions, opinions, goals, and plans; and what they might do differently if they have a similar experience in future.

There is seldom a natural or definitive endpoint to this kind of learning process. The dynamic interplay of experience, reflection, and new observations or questions is potentially limitless. In this model, learners continually formulate and reformulate their ideas and theories within each added layer of lived experience, as Dewey compellingly described almost 100 years ago.

Why Is Outdoor Experiential Learning Essential for Children?

> People discover properties of the environment and their own competencies through action in the world, as they directly perceive the environment through movement and all five senses.
>
> – Louise Chawla, "Growing up Green" in *Journal of Developmental Processes* (2009)

It has been repeatedly demonstrated that direct, active involvement in learning increases engagement and deepens knowledge. Even beyond this, there are compelling reasons for taking children into the natural world, both for their own benefit and for the benefit of the Earth.

In his 2007 work, *Last Child in the Woods: Saving Our Children from Nature-Deficit Disorder*, Richard Louv has famously proposed that a dearth of experience in healthy natural ecosystems – for reasons ranging from helicopter parenting to the erosion of habitats to the proliferation of personal technologies – has resulted in a kind of "nature deficit disorder" in today's children. Numerous studies such as those compiled by Charles, Louv, Bodner, Guns, and Stahl (2009) have stressed the urgent need to reverse this trend, and have provided evidence of the benefits of outdoor experiential education, demonstrating that:

- Daily exposure to natural settings improves children's capacity to focus and enhances their cognitive abilities.
- Children who play outside every day, regardless of weather, display better motor coordination and concentration compared to those who do not.
- Academic achievement improves when school curricula are centred in the outdoor environment.
- Nature-based experiential learning at school significantly improves student outcomes in many subject areas.
- "Greening" of the everyday environment improves the ability of children with symptoms of Attention-Deficit Disorder (ADD) to manage their learning challenges.

Additionally, in one study, 90 percent of respondents reported increased student enthusiasm and engagement when learning occurred outdoors. Seventy percent of teachers in this study also reported increased motivation for teaching in outdoor settings.

Why Is Outdoor Experiential Learning Essential for the Planet?

> Authentic environmental and social commitment emerges out of first-hand experiences with real places on a small, manageable scale over time.
>
> – David Sobel, *Childhood and Nature: Design Principles for Educators* (2008)

To raise a generation with both the knowledge and the commitment to halt and reverse the rapid degradation of the Earth, we need children who have first come to care about it. This emotional investment is far less likely to arise from a life spent indoors or in totally managed outdoor environments. Without a significant and continuing accumulation of direct experiences in nature, research suggests that didactic environmental education consistently fails to translate into environmentally responsible behaviour (Sobel, 2008; 2013).

There is widespread agreement that to love nature you need to spend lots of time in it, and studies have shown powerful connections between childhood experiences in nature and the subsequent development of environmental consciousness and concern. Two factors stand out as particularly influential. The first is having frequent opportunities for free, unstructured exploration in natural settings. The second involves experiencing nature in the company of an environmentally aware adult within a close relationship (Chawla, 2009). In a retrospective study, Wells and Lekies (2006) showed that participation in "wild nature" (e.g., hiking, camping, playing, hunting, and fishing), in places relatively unchanged by humans, strongly predicted later environmental attitudes and behaviours, while engagement in "domesticated nature" in more humanly controlled settings (such as gardening) correlated with later attitudes but only very marginally, if at all, with behaviour. To their surprise, participation in various forms of environmental education, both in and out of school, utterly failed to predict environmental attitudes or behaviour in adulthood. While all forms of involvement in nature are important, it is therefore incumbent on educators to find ways for their students to get to know nature's wilder side.

Nature as a Complex Environment

> In natural habitats, children discover infinitely new iterations. No two crickets and no two birds sing exactly the same song. No two rotting logs hold exactly the same constellation of insects. No stream floods and pools exactly the same way when children dam it, nor does the water flow with the same music and force, or reflect the same gleam of light, on different days in different weathers ... Thus even down in the same stream and the same mud bank for the 237th time, children can discover a world that is inexhaustibly new.
>
> – Louise Chawla, "Childhood Experiences Associated with Care for the Natural World" in *Children, Youth and Environments* (2007)

In Branch I, we remarked on the close relationship between children's curiosity and their attraction to complexity. Yet even the richest indoor learning environment cannot begin to replicate the limitless sources of information and opportunities for discovery in a simple encounter outdoors. This complexity encompasses both sufficient predictability for sense-making – asking causal questions and building theories – and the ongoing deviations and surprises that keep things eternally interesting (and the questions inexhaustible).

Complexity extends to children's sense of themselves as bodies in a physical world. Walking on irregular surfaces (such as rocks, root-heavy ground, soft mud, and so on) has been shown to play a critical role in developing balance and coordination in children. Even the most cleverly engineered playground will eventually become predictable in ways that a natural environment never will. It is difficult to overestimate the sense of efficacy gained by children as they master the challenges of a natural setting and see the clear effects of their actions in the world around them. If our education system hopes to graduate people with a commitment to environmental and social justice, it needs to make it a priority to foster students' belief in their ability to have an impact in the world.

Nature's complexity also encompasses moral and aesthetic dimensions. Not all of nature is beautiful or easily pleasing to the senses – along with the blue lakes and leafy forests, we encounter rot and stench and poison ivy. There are stinging creatures and slimy ones. There are life-threatening situations. There are predators and bloody prey, and scavengers feeding by the side of the road. In one Grade 2 classroom, children's excitement as the class pet gave birth turned to fascinated horror as the mother proceeded to eat her babies. Being in nature gives children access to a world beyond the sanitized and carefully managed environments of many schools and homes. Inevitable confrontations with such cyclical and elemental forces as birth, death, and sex enable children to explore and raise questions about more difficult or emotionally laden concepts in manageable contexts at their own level of understanding.

Ghafouri (2014) describes a class of kindergarteners' encounter with a dead squirrel in the park behind their school. This experience triggered a week of intense observation, examination, and questioning that touched upon children's deep interest in (and associated fears about) the nature of death. Begging to return to the site, they spent long periods each day examining, sketching, and pondering the mysteries of the dead squirrel. They expressed concern for its current well-being (despite its being dead) and showed a growing reluctance to leave the animal when they returned to school. The evident decomposition did nothing to deter their caretaking impulses. After a week, concerned about the children's burgeoning preoccupation, the teacher secretly removed the squirrel, triggering a flurry of questions and speculations about where it had gone. Many months later, when two of the children's fathers unexpectedly died, the teacher wrote to Ghafouri, "It was very sad, but relating to the squirrel I believe assisted them in understanding about death more deeply. Using the squirrel as a reference helped them to relate" (2014, p. 66). Later that spring, one of the chicks they had hatched in their classroom also died, and in connecting all these deaths over the year, the children were able to more fully explore and put into context their thoughts, fears, and wonderings about life and death. This became an example of a year-long inquiry driven purely by the concerns and interests of the students, who took control of what they needed to know and how they chose to know it.

Carol Stephenson, Senior Kindergarten teacher at the Lab School, describes a similar experience in her classroom one year:

The Death of Downey

The summer a red-tailed hawk moved into my urban downtown neighbourhood, I decided that my Senior Kindergarten class would begin the school year thinking about birds. I bought lots of books, both non-fiction and story-based, and looked into local programs and venues that might give us the opportunity to see birds up close. In a stroke of luck, the teaching student who would be working in the class happened to own a pet bird, and offered to "lend" it to the class for the duration of our study.

Downey, the zebra finch, was a lovely addition to the classroom community, though she did have a tendency to hide in one of her little boxes whenever we wanted to study her. Still, her song trilled out regularly during play, lessons and storytime, and the children delighted in opportunities to replenish her food and water. The study of "Birds" itself, however, seemed a little dry. The children had lots of questions – about eggs, flight, migration – but that spark of deep engagement that makes an inquiry really take off just hadn't happened.

Two things turned our study around. The first was a decision, sparked by the children, to let each student choose a particular bird to study. The second came as a complete surprise. One morning, I came in to find Downey lying still on the floor of her cage. I brought Downey's cage down to the floor where we gathered each morning, and waited for the children to arrive.

The regular morning routines were put aside that day. We had a long, and for some, teary, discussion about Downey. "Why had she died?" "How old was she?" "Did she die for a reason or was she just at the end of her life when she arrived?" It was a quiet and profoundly moving talk, as many children shared their favourite thing about having Downey in the class. A number of the kids talked about how she always hopped away whenever they tried to draw her.

"Well," I offered, somewhat hesitantly, "if anyone is interested, we could carefully try sketching Downey now…"

The children leaped on the opportunity. Not only did they draw her in their sketchbooks, they made wreaths and coloured paper ribbons for her – "to decorate her for the funeral." Before Downey was buried in a solemn ceremony next to a butterfly garden, we drew Downey, we weighed Downey – "But maybe she will weigh less now than when she was alive." "Yeah, because her blood is all dried up." "Or maybe because her soul isn't there anymore." – and we wrote stories about Downey.

The opportunity to connect deeply with this little creature, in life and in death, was remarkable, and brought us together as a learning community in a way I can't imagine many other things could.

Students Say Goodbye to Dead Chick Hatched in JK Classroom

Putting It into Practice

Take Your Students Outside

The outdoors offer students a range of opportunities to use all of their senses as they explore their surroundings. The Ontario Ministry of Education policy framework, *Acting Today, Shaping Tomorrow* (2009), articulates its vision for Environmental Education: "Students will come to understand our fundamental connections to each other and to the world around them through their relationship to food, water, energy, air and land, and our interaction with all living things" (p. 6).

For students to grasp their fundamental connections with all living things, they need opportunities to connect directly with the environment and to reflect on that experience. We cannot expect children to develop a relationship with the natural world if we confine them, and our teaching approaches, within the prescribed boundaries of classroom walls, worksheets, and textbooks.

Lost opportunities for direct experience invariably lead to 'default' teaching options, as David Sobel (2008) describes: "When direct experience in nature falls to the wayside, the opportunity to explore the ditch gets replaced by memorizing lists of the plants you might find if you actually ever went to the ditch" (p. 11). He speaks about the importance of learning to "read nature's book" by spending time in it, reminding us that environmental knowledge is another form of literacy, involving deep mastery of a complex interpretive code.

Bringing Children into Nature

Many types of experience can stimulate a productive cycle of reflection and idea development within a learning community. Educators practicing environmental inquiry will find various ways to provide experiences in nature for their students. Table 12 summarizes some of the possibilities with a few examples of each.

Table 12: Some Direct Experiences Fostering an Ongoing Experiential Learning Cycle

Type of Experience	Rationale	Examples in Practice
Close observation of natural phenomena	Close observation stimulates student curiosity, enhances attention to detail, and compels students to confront their existing understandings in the light of observable evidence.	• studying the sky over time • sketching natural phenomena • analyzing soil • following and identifying animal tracks • studying animal behaviour in the wild or in captivity • using a field guide to compare and classify
Designing experiments	To build and test their theories, students are supported in the process of designing and refining experiments.	• constructing and reconstructing gliders for efficient flight • seeing how seeds grow best • designing experiments to determine patterns of animal behaviour
Open-ended exploration of an outdoor environment	Following their own interests, students gather materials and information using their senses, which provides a basis for subsequent questioning and knowledge building.	• collecting • foraging • sketching • hiking and climbing • listening to forest sounds • observing closely • smelling, touching, and tasting
Artistic design	Students develop and express their understanding in visual and tangible ways.	• drawing or painting outdoors • sculpting or collage-making with found materials • photographing • collecting and sculpting with riverbed clay
Play	Students engage with the environment on their own terms, including imaginary play, physical play, and constructive play.	• building forts and dams • digging • treasure hunting • climbing trees • developing imaginative scenarios • counting, classifying, and patterning
Active engagement in field research	Students are encouraged to actively participate in research, engaging with the topic and environment from many angles (e.g., conducting interviews, collecting physical data, and analyzing information).	• collecting, classifying, and graphing specimens • observing, experimenting, hypothesizing, theorizing • analyzing causal relationships • interviewing experts • using tools to analyze materials (e.g., magnifying lenses, prisms, microscopes, pH strips, filters, measuring devices)
Field trips to off-site locations	Field trips both activate and further develop students' curiosity, either at the beginning of an environmental inquiry or as an opportunity to investigate questions throughout an inquiry.	• exploring the local community through neighbourhood walks • visiting local ravines and parks • visiting Nature Centres with guided exploration • visiting museums or zoos • visiting conservation areas • visiting local farms

The importance of play

There is a great deal of evidence that children who take a role in constructing their own learning engage more deeply on both a cognitive and an emotional level. When given time to freely explore natural settings, following their own inclinations as they discover the intricate wonders of nature, they not only learn more but also develop the sense of connectedness and belonging that grounds them as humans within their world. They show a "total involvement" in which "there is little distinction between self and environment" (Csikszentmihalyi, 1975, as cited in Ghafouri, 2014, p. 57).

Taking seriously the call for unstructured learning time in nature, we need to give children of all ages time to play outdoors, to build a relationship with nature on their own terms, to follow their own interests as they muck about with materials, get wet, scratched, and muddy. They should be allowed to test the limits of their physical prowess, and use elements of the setting for their own purposes, whether it be collecting, balancing, constructing, pretending, or simply taking time to watch what is going on. When children choose what they want to do, their investment is usually guaranteed. Children who have plenty of time to play with materials and ideas gain skill in higher-order and counterfactual ("what if?") reasoning. They show increased persistence, focus, and keen habits of observation that will support all their learning, especially their engagement in inquiry. Given more responsibility for their own actions, they learn to regulate themselves within safe limits.

In free exploration in nature, cultural and learning differences tend to find a comfortable place. The child who is challenged by the confinement of a classroom takes leadership in building a dam. Verbal skills no longer assume priority. And there is nothing more powerful than free individual exploration within a group of equally engaged peers for strengthening a child's sense of community. Students return to school energized and with a new sense of their classmates. Meanwhile, teachers are able to observe their students in a new light and come to learn more about how they think and what they truly treasure.

As a class moves from this kind of open-ended outdoor experience into the first reflective phase of an environmental inquiry, the biggest challenge is the overabundance of possibilities; this leaves the educator free to ponder which are most likely to bear rich fruit for the majority of students. While this need for pedagogic decision-making can provoke some anxiety, it helps to realize that there is nothing momentous at stake; if a first approach falls flat, there are many alternative avenues to try.

Risk-taking

Genuine play involves both imagination and risk. It has even been suggested that children's safety ultimately suffers when too many controls are put into place, as their perceived need for self-regulation declines. A New Zealand principal notes the marked decline in his school's playground injuries when safety rules were relaxed, allowing children to climb trees, engage in wrestling matches, and use sharp sticks; another study cites an increase in physical injuries after British playgrounds installed soft surfaces (Tierney, 2011). There is a great deal of evidence that contending with reasonable risk – both physical and psychological – is essential for building the security, resilience, and resourcefulness children will need to fully and satisfyingly engage in their own lives (Alliance for Childhood, 2012). Learning to manage graduated amounts of risk at their own

pace gives children resources for managing anxiety and developing a sense of mastery.

If we want students to take risks in their learning, we need to also allow them to take manageable risks in the real world. A skinned knee or wet clothing is a small price to pay for the sheer joy of throwing one's whole being into attempting and mastering something new.

Of course, this doesn't mean that a teacher forgoes responsibility for ensuring the basic sense of physical and psychological safety that allows children to take risks within its boundaries. No one benefits from chaos or neglect, and students depend on their teacher to use professional judgement in setting the kinds of limits that both the group and the setting demand. Teachers generally find that when the risks are perceived as real rather than adult-generated, even quite impulsive children can show a remarkable degree of care and responsibility.

Active interaction with nature

When bringing children into natural settings, we need to find a way to promote respectful behaviour toward plants and animals without losing sight of children's driving need for active interaction with their world. While there is a range of opinion among environmentalists, thinkers such as David Sobel (2008) and Robert Pyle (2002) stress the need for children to touch as well as look, to pick things up and use them in many ways, to climb trees, wander off the trail, build forts, catch frogs or insects, collect specimens. Citing a strong link between childhood foraging (collecting objects for some use, whether aesthetic, magical, or practical) and children's knowledge of biodiversity, Sobel makes an argument for encouraging "hunting and gathering" rather than discouraging it in the interests of environmental sanctity. When children are allowed to build experience in places where nature is robust enough to withstand their incursions, they can be extraordinarily careful and restrained in more environmentally sensitive areas. In the end, a "look don't touch" attitude to the natural world simply reinforces the idea that we are separate from nature rather than a living part of it.

More structured opportunities

Not all outdoor experiences need to take the form of unstructured play and exploration. In the educators' stories in Part 2 of this resource, we see a range of valuable ways to engage with the world outside the classroom walls, each offering its own possibilities and purposes within a broader environmental inquiry. Structured gardening programs, local walks, and guided visits in conservation areas all offer enriching experiences that expand understanding.

Even within a more structured excursion, however, students need to encounter choices and some possibility of exploring in their own way and at their own pace. Many teachers note the marked decline in engagement (and consequent increase in management challenges) when children are "herded" through a setting. It is therefore worth thinking about which constraints are minimally needed to achieve the purposes of the trip. For example, young children hiking along a trail can be free to travel anywhere between the leading adult in front and the one who takes up the rear (rather than walking neatly with partners in a line), leaving them free to observe their surroundings and explore their interests more or less at their own pace. Older children might be trusted to venture farther afield on their own without losing their connection to the group.

Field trips: Sending the right message?

Outdoor environments for experiential learning can range from a forest trail or ravine to a city park or school garden carved out of asphalt (Louv, 2007). Both rural and urban schools have access to a host of opportunities for outdoor experiential learning.

Field trips to natural settings in more distant locations are worthwhile experiences for students for a number of reasons:

- Field trips broaden horizons. They give students an opportunity to explore new environments beyond the everyday and to make comparisons between local and distant environments. Outside experiences offer new perspectives on the local.
- Field trips give students a chance to gain direct contact with environments, objects, or processes that are not readily accessible within the school community.

- Guides or expert speakers allow students to learn from someone with a level of specialized knowledge that triggers new questions, enriches knowledge, and puts existing beliefs into a different perspective. Working with an outside expert gives children the chance to genuinely view their teacher as a co-learner. A knowledgeable outdoor guide helps both children and adults attend to details of the environment that might otherwise pass them by.
- Field trips provide memorable opportunities for students who are unlikely to encounter such experiences outside of school.

However, field trips are not the ultimate solution for engaging in outdoor experiential learning. Relying too heavily on one-time events in locations that are not readily accessible to all learners can signal the wrong message – that the environment is something far away, detached from, and irrelevant to their everyday lives. Teachers need to be wary about perpetuating this misconception.

Explore the Local Community and You'll Find the Curriculum

If deep familiarity with a natural setting is the key to building a meaningful relationship with it, then children need repeated experiences in nearby places that can be part of their everyday life. As both Dewey (1938) and Sobel (2008) emphasize, a child's learning begins with coming to know their own environment in the familiar world of neighbourhoods and communities. In their mix of the built and the natural, urban neighbourhoods are complex settings that offer children a wide range of possible actions, roles, and opportunities for exploration. Cities provide unique learning environments that encompass a dense diversity of people and ways of living along with irrepressible natural forces.

Going on community walks heightens children's awareness of their surroundings. It also opens up numerous curriculum connections, including number sense and numeration, geometry,

structures, simple machines, flight, energy, matter, growth and change, daily and seasonal changes, habitat, air, water, soil, history, sociology, art, and more!

Exploring the local community can sometimes trigger investigations into broader issues of social justice. While teaching a Structures and Mechanisms unit, Rhiannon Kenny brought her Grade 2/3 students on a community walk to identify different structures in the neighbourhood (see Photo 6). The class then engaged in a Knowledge Building Circle to discuss the question: **"Of the structures that you spotted, what kind of structure is the most important in your life?"** Not surprisingly, the Grade 2/3s identified houses as the most essential structures in their lives. Through writing and drawing, they conveyed their personal reflections on the importance of 'home.'

The combined experiences of community walks, Knowledge Building Circles, and individual reflections shifted the focus of the initial inquiry. The children became interested in social justice issues such as the lack of affordable housing, homelessness, and substandard housing in Toronto and Canada.

Photo 6: Structures in the Neighbourhood*

*Text enhanced to ensure legibility. Original grammar has been maintained.

The Indigenous lens provided in this resource speaks eloquently about the value accorded to a "sense of place"; this deepens as children visit and revisit places and experiences that have meaning in their everyday lives. These include both the special places (often hidden) that children choose to make their own and the places that adults help them make sense of. When teachers afford students regular opportunities to get to know the surroundings of their school, they help to foster children's sense of place and their understanding of where they fit in their community.

Through repeated experiences in the same location, children become acutely aware of what changes and what persists through time (including their own perspectives), and thereby come to experience and better understand natural processes and cycles. In the educators' stories in Part 2, we see many examples of repeated visits to a place, whether a manicured urban park ("Carol's Story," p. 168), a nearby city ravine ("Zoe's Story," p. 187), the "camp" beside a country school ("Marge's Story," p. 150) or a single tree that students get to know intimately through the year ("Stephanie's Story," p. 142).

Dewey has noted that when children perceive school as something detached from their community, their experience of school tends to be less meaningful. Children's important sense of themselves as operating within intersecting or reciprocal communities – a class, a school, a family, a neighbourhood – is deepened and enriched through conscious efforts to bring families into the learning, especially in less formal contexts (not just as audience or expert) where they learn and experience alongside their child.

'Unnatural' Outdoor Spaces: Why They Count

Especially in urban school settings, it can be easy to assume that the school's outdoor surroundings offer few meaningful opportunities for students to engage with the natural environment. Yet, all teachers need to do is look outside their doors to find inspiration. Pyle (2002) stresses the potential of the weed-ridden vacant lot, reminding us that, "Just as real life does not consist primarily of car crashes and exploding buildings, quotidian nature is more about grasshoppers in the pigweed than it is rhinos mating on a pixelated screen" (p. 319).

Zenobia Barlow, executive director and co-founder of the Center for Ecoliteracy, describes an experience of this kind:

> We explored a three-block radius of neighbourhood around the school for half an hour. I asked the students to write three lines of poetry or narrative based on what they observed, and bring back a found object. We then used the writing they brought back to create a poem, and we placed the found objects on an oversized map of the school and its surroundings. The results were incredible. You don't need to be in the wild to use the environment for learning. Life is erupting everywhere. Weeds grow out of cracks in cement ... Many urban campuses are covered with asphalt, but even there, one can still find a special place. Children have this tremendous ability to focus on minute things. If you're small yourself, you're more likely to see all these other tiny life forms – ants and such – that the rest of us pass by.
>
> – Zenobia Barlow, Interview with Derrick Jensen (March 2002)

Rose Avenue Junior Public School Garden

Kindergarten Students at Rose Avenue Document Observations of Their Class Tree

There are many varied and wonderful examples of environmental learning in urban environments. Rose Avenue Junior Public School is located in a densely populated community in downtown Toronto, in the midst of 22 high-rise apartment buildings. Its playing field is made of artificial turf rather than grass. Such a setting offers an interesting perspective for investigating the coexistence of natural and built environments, raising such questions as "Why isn't there real grass here?" "Is it possible to grow grass here?" "How could we find out?" "How and where can we create more natural spaces around our school?" Within this intensely urban setting, Kathleen Quan and her Grade 4/5 students developed an innovative and meaningful outdoor learning experience that benefitted the entire school community – transforming a portion of the schoolyard into an edible garden.

Observing the dramatic difference between built and natural environments can spark deeper questions about the impact of urban development on ecosystems. For instance, some Grade 5/6 students in Ben Peebles' class noticed that there were far fewer forms of wildlife in their schoolyard compared to what they had encountered on a fall camping trip in Sandbanks Provincial Park. This observation led one group of Grade 5s to choose urban sprawl as the topic of their environmental awareness documentary, which they created in the final term of the year.

The Laboratory School at the Dr. Eric Jackman Institute of Child Study is situated in the heart of downtown Toronto. The playground is a mix of asphalt and wood chips, with a scattering of smallish, recently planted trees. The Lab School teachers regularly use this playground as well as nearby outdoor spaces to foster environmental inquiry.

Informal learning

For children in city schoolyards, the drive to find nature in the unnatural is quite compelling. Opening our eyes to informal as well as formal learning opportunities, it is inspiring to see how persistently children work – wherever they are – to probe their surroundings for meaning. In an examination of a large inner-city primary school in South Wales, Waters and Maynard (2010) found that students spent significant amounts of time engaging with and remarking upon the most ordinary, common elements of the outdoor environment, such as bugs or plants. During unstructured recess periods in the Lab School's small playground, with students largely left to their own devices, these are only a sample of children's observed activities:

- collecting bugs and worms
- making homes for ants and snails
- collecting berries from vines
- picking dandelions
- planting fallen maple keys
- dropping maple keys from the climber and watching them spin
- checking out the sky
- digging in the ground
- playing with shadows
- exploring the limits of their physical capabilities
- exploring with magnifying lenses
- collecting and transporting piles of snow
- covertly eating snow (liberally laced with salt, against adult warnings)
- moving water from puddle to puddle
- jumping over puddles, wading in puddles
- sliding on ice, breaking up ice, transporting ice, building with ice and snow
- playing in mud
- collecting sticks, stones, and leaves
- sorting and combining found materials
- disposing of trash
- climbing and swinging on young trees (despite adult strictures against doing so)
- building pulleys with skipping ropes slung over a tree limb
- watching birds, chasing birds, and chastising each other for chasing birds

Just because an experience is informal or child-initiated doesn't mean it can't become the basis of sustained and focused learning. Recess is not only an important part of the school day for children, but also a valuable time for a teacher to see what their students truly know, care, and wonder about.

The following conversation was transcribed by a teacher as two kindergarten children came together in outdoor play to debate a rusty shovel. Resisting the temptation to simply remove the object as unsafe, she moved closer to keep an eye (and ear) on what happened. The child without the shovel began:

You should throw that out. It's old and ugly.

No, it's part of nature and I won't throw it out. Nature is good.

It's not part of nature. It's made of metal and it's sharp. And rusty and broken.

Well, metal is part of nature, anyway. People don't make it. You find it in the ground.

So? Someone made the shovel. So it's not nature.

Yeah, but now the shovel part is broken, so only the nature part is left. If we put it on the ground it will go back into the ground where it came from.

Can nature be broken? Or just things people make?

What do you mean? You can break sticks off trees.

So – I actually think metal is nature cuz you find it in your body, and your body's nature.

I don't get it ...

Well, things that rust are iron. And there's iron in your blood. It makes your muscles strong, that's what my mom said.

OK, I'll eat this! (laughs and mimics eating the shovel)

(laughter) I know. Let's hide it where no one can find it.

Yeah, come on ...

Tellingly, although their teacher was standing close by, neither child appealed to her to adjudicate their discussion. Their brief dialogue considers some interesting and fairly profound ideas: What is nature? Can human artifacts be considered nature? Can the natural and manufactured coexist in a single object? Can nature be broken? Are people nature? In this exchange between five-year-olds, we see knowledge building in its earliest stages, in spontaneous peer-on-peer conversation around an issue of common focus. This suggests that the introduction of knowledge building discourse in school easily builds on to children's natural inclinations to figure things out by testing their ideas on one another.

A Place for Solitude

> On our first field visit with Trevor, a hush fell over the group, to the point where all that could be heard was the sound of the river rolling in front of us, the rush of the wind in the trees above and the calls of jays in the distance. This lasted nearly a minute and was only ended by one gregarious student saying, "This is the sound of calm".
>
> – Joanne Nazir & Erminia Pedretti, "Educators' perceptions of bringing students to environmental consciousness through engaging outdoor experiences" in *Environmental Education Research* (2016)

The intensely social nature of school can lead us to disregard the value for children of spending time alone, thinking their own thoughts without immediately relaying them to others. When compared to more socially dependent peers, children who value solitude have been shown to experience reduced anxiety and aggression along with an increased sense of autonomy (Galanaki, 2005). When questioned, they cite many benefits of solitude, including a sense of peace; opportunities for reflection and problem-solving; a sense of self-reliance, self-control and mastery; the opportunity for privacy; time to daydream; reduced boredom and increased engagement; better concentration (Galanaki, 2004). Adults have identified similar benefits that include creativity, inner peace, intimacy, self-discovery, and spirituality (Long, Seburn, Averill, & More, 2003).

It is therefore important to consider how to encourage *all* children – not only those introverts who are so inclined anyway – to find ways of achieving solitude in the social bustle of school life. As children build their own relationship with the natural environment, they need time and space to do this on their own as well as with their friends. For this reason, an educator may at times set parameters that support more private reflection and exploration.

Successful efforts to observe wildlife often require immense control and stillness. E. O. Wilson (1984) has written of "the naturalist's trance, the hunter's trance – by which biologists locate more elusive organisms" (p. 6). Learning to be still in nature further deepens the relationship that emerges through more interactive involvement. It may even open the possibility for spiritual connections that link to some of the ways described in the Indigenous lens on Branch I. Asking students to each choose a "sit spot" ("Ellie's Story," p. 194) in which to quietly attune themselves to their surroundings is one way to encourage a more contemplative way of being in nature. Making time for children to pursue individual investigations such as drawing, recording, or collecting is another. Quietly listening to ambient sounds helps to build both the deep absorption and the acute awareness that go along with truly getting to know a place. Collective learning will be immeasurably enhanced by the rich private worlds that participants bring to the group.

Summary of Chapter

Connecting children with their surroundings, both constructed and wild, helps them to securely situate themselves as curious, caring individuals in their world. It expands meaningful inquiry beyond academic learning. Nature can provide the questions, content, and investigative drive that propel an inquiry. Deep engagement – through hands-on, hearts-on, and minds-on immersion in the real world – is the starting point, leading to a learning spiral of experience, reflection, informed actions, and new experiences. This involvement of the mind, emotions, and senses has rich potential to build awareness and understanding, and opens up possibilities for both action and insight. The following branch (Branch III: Integrated Learning) considers how we can best capture that richness and complexity in ways that connect and interweave all the threads of curriculum and learning.

Sending out Roots: Grounding Learning in Place
Indigenous Lens on Branch II

Sending out Roots

Once our inner fire is lit, powerful roots can emerge from our core, anchoring us in our place in ways that serve our higher and inner purpose. We know why we are here, and our affinity with the world is personally felt and embodied. Our Spirit permeates our place, and our place permeates our Spirit.

Being in and of the World

Broadly considered, Indigenous perspectives tend to be holistic and cyclical rather than analytical or linear. Compared with Eurocentric perspectives, there is less emphasis on time and abstract knowledge as concepts taken apart from their realities. Reason is not considered the highest form of intellect (intellect, in its original Latin roots, implies much more than reason). This does not mean time, abstract ideas, or reason are neglected, only that they are considered through a different lens that frames space as multi-dimensional reality. Beings in our world are not separate from the spiritual "idea" that transcends their corporeality. Indigenous perspectives highlight a multi-layered relationship to space and place, over many generations, that cuts across time, both in our physical world and in the subtle and metaphysical realms. These differences in perspective are comparable to the difference between thinking in one dimension and thinking in many dimensions, or to seeing things in black and white versus technicolour.

This deep relationship to place conceives of the Earth as more than an objectified noun, and ecology as more than an abstracted field of study. An Indigenous sense of place has little in common with modern notions of nature. Indigenous worldviews and ways of life radically challenge, and have the potential to significantly deepen, our usual conceptions of the environment and experiential learning.

A Eurocentric scientific lens tends to view the environment as our physical surroundings, unless we explicitly refer to the social, economic, or learning environment. A spiritual environment is almost never considered. Mainstream culture analytically subdivides environment into categories. The mainstream scientific meaning of environment attends only to the intellectual and physical dimensions of human experience, emphasizing the accumulation of knowledge about our physical surroundings.

An Indigenous sense of place grounds Spirit in a physical space, making it impossible to consider our surroundings as separate from ourselves. And so, rootedness in place is not about mere territory, as in the European sense of possession. When Indigenous peoples refer to "our territory," it would be more apt to say, we are this land, and this land is us. For example, to introduce oneself as from Oneida Nation – *Onyota'a:ká: niwakuhutsyó:t^* – is to say more precisely something like, "I am Oneida kind of land." This phrase has undergone lexicalization and more commonly translates to the English meaning, "Oneida is my nation."

We have roots in the soil and are embedded in and completely reliant on Mother Earth. We are a part of Her rather than apart from Her. Our identification with the world around us ultimately extends far beyond our usual, narrow range of human concern. For example, water is respected metaphorically as the blood of Mother Earth, which means water is our own mother's blood, related closely to our own blood. Polluting water is as murderous as injecting poison into our own mother's veins – worse, in fact, given the scale of life affected.

Rooted in Everything

But even saying we are part of the land or the water does not convey the full meaning of place as seen through Indigenous worldviews. Our affiliation with water, for example, extends much further into the universe, including spiritual aspects of the universe that are unknown to modern science. In other words, our blood and water, at every level, has spirit, an inner or higher water that is reflected in Creation stories from various world traditions. The same can be said of our flesh and the soil, or of our nerves and the force of fire, and so on. All things we know in our small conceptions of the immediate world are connected at every level to everything.

The Anishinaabe word *Aki* is often translated as "the land" or "earth," but this is just a translation of the word into English thinking. Some Anishinaabemowin speakers say *Aki* can translate as "everything." An Indigenous sense of place extends to anything conceivably related to a place: the waters around us and the blood in our bodies, which are, of course, both connected with Grandmother Moon; all the stories of place that sing in local ways to the mysteries around us; all the dead and unborn who have walked or will walk where we do, and who once breathed or will breathe the same sacred molecules of air; the dew at our feet, which speaks with the star beings above us, and so on, in every direction and in relation to everything.[1]

> **Aki includes all aspects of Creation: land forms, elements, plants, animals, spirits, sounds, thoughts, feelings, energies and all of the emergent systems, ecologies and networks that connect these elements. Knowledge in akinoomaage flows through the layered spirit world above the earth, the place where spiritual beings reside and the place where our ancestors sit.**
>
> – Wendy Makoons Geniusz, Anishinaabe Scholar, *Our Knowledge is Not Primitive: Decolonizing Botanical Anishinaabe Teachings* (2009)

Indigenous ways of seeing go much further than even the more expansive experiential learning models of modern North American theorists, which emphasize the cyclical, open-ended nature of learning. Through Indigenous eyes, not only is there no definitive endpoint to the learning process; Eurocentrically conceived boundaries of space and time are completely erased.

The world around us is so much more than an object of study or a range of things to be used, managed, or helped. We cannot really approach the truth about our world without feeling how our identities are intimately woven into place, without truly *being* our place, in every way. And when we do feel this way, the patterns of waves or the appearance of certain birds at certain times assume profound meaning, inspiring an expansive love for where we live.

Indigenous art offers us powerful representations of how we are rooted in all things around us, including Spirit: consider Woodland art, with Spirit lines radiating out in every direction from every being, connecting, communing, and moving through one another; or the elaborate, transformative West Coast dance masks, with Thunderbirds opening great beaks into wide wings holding up the face of a great ancestor, or of the living spirit of the Sun as Being.

Learning from place becomes rooted in everything that is around us through experience, extending in every direction – and ultimately beyond what we know as "direction." For example, Indigenous rootedness in place also considers, "Who has been here, and who will come? What is the essence, or spirit, of our place?" If we begin to see ourselves as not just rooted in the ground, but also deeply connected to everything around us, everything changes, including how we feel, think, and behave.

---

[1] "Dew forms under clear, windless skies when the temperature falls below the dew point, forcing the air to release its moisture in the form of droplets. Thus many little drops of dew tend to form when many little stars are out" (Garnett, 2005, p. 114). Indigenous peoples the world over have always known and observed such phenomena, along with innumerable other details of how our world speaks to us through many thousands of voices and forms.

Christi Belcourt, Michif artist, and Isaac Murdoch, Ojibway storyteller and traditional knowledge holder, collaborate with the Laboratory School community to paint murals based on Naneboozhoo stories.

Place as Culture

Indigenous identification with place extends into and informs deep cultural knowledge and practices that have endured over time, and which can be used in social, economic, and political realms to address contemporary problems. One reason Indigenous knowledge remains valuable is because it has evolved as very specific knowledge about particular places. Indigenous processes of coming to know place are spiritual (gained through vision, ritual, and ceremony); traditional (passed along through stories and intergenerational experiences); empirical (gained through careful observation over time); and contemporary and scientific (developed through experience, education, and problem solving) (Cajete, 2015).

Indigenous people hold expert knowledge acquired through deep experiential and land-based inquiry that includes traditional activities such as ceremony, hunting, farming, decision making, art, medicinal practice, and other aspects of living in the land. Key to this notion of inquiry is *relationship*. Indigenous people know through doing, and through embodying a relationship to place. Because place is alive, it is inhabited by spirits who confer ceremonial, medicinal and other information related to everyday living. Indigenous people might ask place itself for answers to some of life's most important questions. For example, in traditional fasting, a knowledge seeker abstains from food and water for days, offering prayers to receive guidance from spirits of the place around them.

These interactions with place are the basis for Indigenous worldviews, including knowledge systems, identities, and philosophies, which are all internalized to form the deepest parts of consciousness. Because Indigenous sense of place is cultural, and not inherently racial, non-Indigenous people may also act and see themselves as an intricately interwoven part of place. As a consequence, they can develop intimate relationships with place and rely on methods of inquiry that are deeply personal. Through these relationships, place for any people can become imbued with cultural meanings, collective historical memory, and spiritual significance. But such a process is also inseparable from the longstanding cultures that have developed in specific places over many millennia. Because place is inseparable from Indigenous cultures, fully recovering essential information about our place means Indigenous cultural recovery – the uncovering of what has been deliberately buried.

> In the process of settler colonialism, land is remade into property and human relationships to land are restricted to the relationship of the owner to his property. Epistemological, ontological, and cosmological relationships to land are interred, indeed made pre-modern and backward. Made savage....
> Indigenous peoples are those who have creation stories, not colonization stories, about how we ... came to be in a particular place – indeed how we ... came to be a place.
>
> – Eve Tuck and K. Wang Yang, "Decolonization is Not a Metaphor" in *Decolonization: Indigeneity, Education and Society* (2012)

Place Is How We Live

An Indigenous perspective conceives of place as a process, because it refers to what is happening in a place rather than the mere contents and location of a place. Place is a web of dependent interrelationships with everything in Creation, and it includes human responsibilities to care for those relationships, to maintain balance within the universe so we can survive, and to participate in the sacred processes of Creation.

And so Indigenous economic, social, and political systems outlining how to live are an intricate reflection of place, inextricable from place. Indigenous ways of living take direction through observing and interacting with place, and are deeply connected to and informed by the behaviour of the Sun, Moon, stars, winds, waters, trees, birds, animals, and other, greater-than-human entities. Anishinaabe scholar John Borrows (as cited in Simpson, 2014) explains that:

The Anishinaabe word akinoomaage is formed from aki, our place in the world, and noomaage, which means to point towards and take direction from. As we draw analogies and metaphors from our surroundings and appropriately apply them or distinguish what we see, we learn about how to love, and how we should live in our place (p. 14).

It can be said that plains nations, for example, hold a powerful tradition of "buffalo politics," derived from a deep observation of the roles of male and female buffalo, and how the large herds live and move safely. Other nations have place-specific political systems reflecting diversity in age, sex, and being – including non-human beings ordinarily relegated to the department of the "environment" in Eurocentric cultural frameworks (Armstrong, 2013). Indigenous place-based political frameworks are effective and detailed, affecting every aspect of governance – who leads, how they lead and when, how they are chosen, how conflict is resolved, how war and peace are made, and much more.

Implications for Experiential Learning

Indigenous multi-dimensional rootedness in place can inform and deepen experiential learning. Identification with all of life, with everything around us, whether spiritual or physical, is not easily developed in modern classrooms. An Indigenous perspective might see experiential learning as a temporary measure, a way station on the road to understanding the reality of our relationship to place as human beings. Eurocentric perspectives have created the necessity for what is called "environmental education" and "experiential learning" through the objectification and separation of nature. Environmental education as conceived today is a good thing in many ways, but it is still only an artificially constructed way to begin shaking us out of blinkered and institutionalized ways of thinking.

If environmental education is a point in a movement away from certain rigid characteristics of Eurocentric education, where could we be moving if we approach Indigenous perspectives in experiential learning? Because we are talking about the Indigenous meaning of the word "everything," the many possibilities obviously cannot be covered in this resource, but a few modest examples are included here. Meaningful movement in this direction is a long-term process that is just beginning, and involves detailed relationship and discussion with Indigenous people over time.

We are taking steps toward Indigenous understanding when we take students outside and provide opportunities for them to use all their senses, to make fundamental connections with as many aspects of the world around them as possible, as recommended in both editions of *Natural Curiosity*.

But how might these practices be deepened through Indigenous perspectives, and what other realms might be linked and explored in relation to developing a more powerful sense of place?

Engage Locally and Much More Deeply

An Indigenous approach challenges us to ask, "How do we deepen our relationship with the place we are in? How do we send out roots?" Ideally, we can help children come to know through a direct, *personal* understanding of their world and their place within it. All of this can be done in ways that engage emotional learning and memory, and which respect children's intuitive sense of what they need individually.

Bringing children out into their humanly built and natural environments can help them develop a better sense of how these spaces *affect them personally*. Specifically, we can

- Make increasingly significant links between the places around us and science education. Science education should support immediate community research rather than abstract curriculum checklists.
- Consider what makes the children come alive, laugh, and connect with one another and their particular context. Teachers may need to spontaneously change the direction of their own preconceived learning activities when they find that something unanticipated moves the children.
- Think about the particular challenges children are faced with. For example, what conflicts exist among a given group of students, and how can addressing these conflicts form the basis of learning that reaches them where they are most invested in their hearts?
- Learn about the range of place-based realities faced by children and their families. A big question: Where is the land where I belong, and how do I belong? What are the local foods?
- Try to get the kids out in the land with their families (and not merely on it). Crucially, this is going to be land they can return to on a regular basis, across the grades, with grandparents or other trusted caregivers. Connect the parent-child relationship with the development of place-based knowledge.
- Get outside with parents and children at night; light a fire; watch the stars, planets, and the moon; tell remarkable stories, and sing; observe everything together.
- Introduce stories about the place where the children live. What are the stories of the stars above us that correspond with our place? What are the Indigenous constellations, and the cosmologies from this place? What is the significance of the river or land formations where the children live? What life lived here 65 million years or 12,000 years ago?
- Discover the plants and animals that are in our place, or that belong here. What are their uses? Do we use them? Can we use them? Why or why not?
- Support meaningful exploration of birth, death, and connection with our ancestors and future generations. Whose bones lie under our feet? What nations have lived here? Who is still here?
- Consider how we are connected to our grandparents. How do our great-great-great-grandparents come alive to us? How do we love them? And our great-great-great-grandchildren? How are they immediate, and in the room with us now?

The possibilities are endless, and will often require the introduction of resources we have not typically accessed in contemporary learning contexts. What are the stories from this place? The life of the land is embedded in stories from where we live. Indigenous stories have always included detailed information about life in our place that has only recently been uncovered by modern science, giving detailed information about giant beasts long after their extinction, or lake formations that have disappeared for millennia. Stories of spirit beings embedded in diverse Indigenous cultures explain important forces and phenomena that are reduced to the level of superstition or overlooked entirely by modern science and culture. Stories and knowledge of our place ultimately live in people, not books.

If we are severed from such stories, we are severed from our place. Greek myths are fine, but the real stories of the place where we belong should not be neglected, or we do not fully belong. The Indigenous knowledge specific to the northern shores of Lake Ontario, embedded in Creation stories and political histories, are essential knowledge for people living there. For example, it is not enough to know that the white pine was used extensively for British warships. This is not significant historical knowledge, but more like trivia. The White Pine is the central symbol of a confederacy that stretched across eastern Turtle Island (North America) and which has lasted for a thousand years up to the present day, in spite of British, American, and Canadian genocidal practices. It is the law of the land, and holds clues to things like the reinvigoration of democracy. It connects us with where we live. Every part of the Americas has these important stories.

Children Are Ready

Children can move into a deep sense of place faster than we might think. An Indigenous sense of place is the normal state of human relationship to the world around us. It is the adult world that sets up barriers to such a state; we need to catch up to the learning needs and natural intuition of children.

One story from the first edition provides an excellent example of how children are intrinsically inclined to develop a deeply embodied relationship with place. In this story, kindergarten children had forged a strong relationship with the courtyard at their school through a variety of detailed, emotional, and place-embodying inquiry projects. Without warning, the school board sent groundskeeping staff in the spring to remove invasive plants and the whole area was "cleaned out" in the process. The children were disappointed and saddened at what they had lost. Their newly emerged Painted Lady butterflies had nowhere to eat. It seemed like their emotional connections to nature had been wiped out. The destruction of the children's special place, their "Classroom in the Courtyard," is a remarkable microcosm of how Indigenous peoples must cope with the broad desecration of their whole territories.

This particular case epitomizes the challenge we face in setting down roots; we are hamstrung in every direction by technocratic responses where a shared common purpose is needed to bring learning to life. In this case, the administrative response to invasive species in the courtyard was to bring in "experts." Their reaction was to eliminate everything, without any connection to the children or any understanding of their relationship with the place. The opportunity was lost for children to learn what plants belong and don't belong, and why, how we remove the harmful plants while retaining the rest of our little part of the world, and how to be even more grounded. Instead, the children and their place became victims of mechanical expediency.

If given the chance, children will show us how our spirits can both nurture and be nurtured by our place. Our sense of safety, stability, and beauty can grow through our relationships with and participation in everything around us, seen and unseen. And our survival can be ensured by these relationships with both everyday things and the ever-unfolding mysteries behind them.

Branch III: Integrated Learning
Making Connections and Broadening Perspectives

Theoretical Underpinnings

> All education is environmental education. By what is included or excluded, students are taught that they are part of or apart from the natural world. We must be wary not to imprint a disciplinary template onto impressionable minds and with it the belief that the world really is as disconnected as the divisions, disciplines, and subdisciplines of the typical curriculum. Students come to believe that there is such a thing as politics separate from ecology or that economics has nothing to do with physics. It just happens to be dead wrong. The same is true throughout the curriculum.
>
> – David Orr, *Earth in Mind: On Education, Environment, and the Human Prospect* (2004)

What Is Integrated Learning?

Environmental education offers an especially generative context for integrative interconnected learning. More than 100 years ago, John Dewey's (1915) call for localized experiential learning stressed the many-faceted nature of his approach, forecasting contemporary ideas such as those of Orr (above). Dewey wrote, "Experience has its geographical aspect, its artistic and literary, its scientific and historical sides. All studies arise from aspects of the one earth and the one life lived upon it" (1915, p. 91). Integrated, interdisciplinary learning is inherent in environmental education and naturally follows from an emphasis on place and local experience. Based on a holistic view of education, it "recognizes the necessity for learners to see the 'big picture' rather than to divide learning into small pieces" (Brazee & Capelluti, 1993, as cited in Brazee & Capelluti, 1995, p. 10).

Integrated learning transcends subject areas as educators encourage students to see connections among disciplines and draw upon content and skills from multiple areas. Outside the artificial boundaries of some classroom settings, children's questions and thoughts about the real world are seldom contained within a single academic discipline. If we place these ideas and questions at the core of their learning, then our approach has no choice but to incorporate different perspectives, skills, and ways of understanding.

From a developmental perspective, the play of young children perhaps shows integration in its most authentic, natural form. As children freely and purposefully engage with materials and peers, an observant educator sees a multitude of emerging concepts in math, science, literacy, the arts, physical and social development, and so on – the list is pretty much endless (Ontario Ministry of Education, 2016). For kindergarten-age children, separating this seamless whole into some of its component concepts (often through adult instruction) begins to make these concepts more explicit and available to reflection, building a common language for communicating and refining ideas. In school settings, this often entails disciplinary language (e.g., mathematical vocabulary), which sets in motion a lifelong process of exchanging ideas, reflecting upon them, and using them in the real world. These newly explicit concepts in turn begin to infuse and shape children's experiences, including their play, in an ongoing cycle of teaching and learning, of analysis and synthesis, of reflection and application. In this way, the integrated whole of early childhood gains depth and richness through being broken apart and reintegrated, in a kind of spiral development that repeatedly circles back to concepts at levels of growing complexity.

Some Benefits of Integrated Learning

Benefits to students of an interconnected curriculum include

- deeper understanding of a topic by exploring it through multiple perspectives
- stronger grasp of each subject's purpose and varied applications in different contexts
- greater appreciation for the way in which subject areas, skills, ideas, and perspectives

are enmeshed and come together in the real world
- deeper understanding of complex systems, such as scientific, environmental, or political theories and structures
- increased relevance of reading, writing, and mathematics to real-world understanding and expression
- deeper levels of student engagement (identified by teachers as the most positive aspect of integration, Drake & Reid, 2010)
- opportunities to cover a wide range of curriculum expectations in a single broad unit of study

Children spend nearly half of their waking hours at school, a setting that ultimately shapes a large portion of their experience and understanding of the world. Learning to look for the interconnections among all aspects of life will serve them well throughout their lives.

Western schooling has traditionally tended to reinforce the separation of knowledge into discrete disciplinary areas. There are times when this partitioning has clear uses, enabling educators to focus on the specialized skills or concepts needed to solve particular problems. Disciplinary learning also allows students to develop a knowledge base in an unfamiliar area before they start building connections with other areas. Moreover, disciplinary knowledge crucially connects learning to the rich history of ideas and thinking in a given area.

To reassemble the various disciplinary pieces requires awareness of what those pieces are. However, when students only encounter curriculum in a fragmented way, their perceptions of the world in its interrelated complexity tend to be limited and skewed. They need opportunities to integrate their knowledge and skills from different disciplines and to think critically about how all these separate pieces of school learning fit together. Rather than being cast aside, disciplinary knowledge is itself deepened and enriched through being understood in relation to other disciplines and applied in different contexts.

Integrated, interdisciplinary learning encourages students to approach problems from multiple perspectives. This approach supports the values of a democratic classroom, ensuring a genuine role for different skills and strengths within communities of learners. As discussed in Branch I, this appreciation for diversity has significant implications for assessment. "By its very nature, community-connected experiential learning provides rich opportunities for students to acquire knowledge and skills in a variety of ways, and this richness should be reflected in the assessment and evaluation of student learning ... Gathering evidence of student learning from multiple and varied sources ensures that evaluation will ... most accurately reflect the learning that has occurred" (Ontario Ministry of Education, Winter 2016, p. 20).

As this chapter's opening quotes from Orr and Dewey suggest, environmental inquiry powerfully encompasses many facets of what it means to be human in the world. Because environmental issues are fundamental to all global systems – economic, political, historical, cultural – it makes pedagogic sense to incorporate environmental education throughout a student's learning, rather than add it as a separate area of study. As they develop understanding of the environment's interconnections and interdependencies, students become increasingly equipped to make informed, sustainable life choices.

Viewing curriculum through the lens of environmental inquiry enables a student to create linkages both within and among disciplines. For educators who are considering how to foster engagement in focused, purposeful learning through the integration of different curricular areas, environmental topics provide a natural starting place.

Building an Integrated Learning Program

Some approaches to environmental inquiry, as described in the educators' stories in Part 2, include the integration of subject areas, curricular strands, skills, and perspectives over the year. While there is often considerable overlap among these approaches, the following section clarifies each in turn.

Integration of subject areas: Interdisciplinary learning

Cross-curricular or subject integration provides opportunities to link content from more than one subject area within a single unit of study.

The integration of subject areas is never arbitrary, but intended to exploit the particular possibilities that each area can offer. For example, one key learning goal in environmental inquiry is to build observation skills; learning to view and produce art equips students with valuable tools for this. As a result, representing their observations and ideas through visual art not only provides a window into their understanding, but also uniquely helps them to build this understanding. Similarly, specialized mathematical tools (such as measurement or graphing) may offer the best approach for coming to grips with a hypothesized pattern in the world. Experimenting with building and construction materials in the classroom builds understanding of real-world physical forces. Hearing, enacting, and producing narratives enhances the social perspective-taking required for knowledge building and develops the empathy required for environmental activism. Recent innovations in medical education, in which doctors exposed to art and literature show improved skills in observing, diagnosing, and treating patients, provide some confirmation of these ideas (Shapiro, Rucker, & Beck, 2006; Katz & Khoshbin, 2014).

Subject integration allows students to absorb and express ideas in different ways, whether through language, art, technology, drama, or other modes of expression. This gives them new ways to consider an issue and helps to ensure that every student has a voice in the classroom community. "Mike's Story" (Part 2, p. 251) offers a number of examples in which students build their understanding of climate change through different curricular perspectives, including poetry, journalism, photography, and math.

Integration of curriculum strands

Strand integration provides opportunities to explore relationships within a subject area by linking content from two or more designated curriculum strands. For instance, the Ontario Ministry of Education's *Science and Technology Curriculum* (2007) is organized into four separate strands: Understanding Life Systems, Understanding Structures and Mechanisms, Understanding Matter and Energy, and Understanding Earth and Space Systems. Each strand represents a major area of knowledge and skills within the curriculum area of Science and Technology.

Robin Fogarty argues that "both integration within a discipline and integration across disciplines are necessary to fully integrate the curricula" (1991, xiv). Strand integration is a logical starting place for integrating learning since the strands within a subject are already related within the discipline (see Table 13 for an example). If students are to appreciate the complexity with which global subsystems interact, it is helpful for them to see how smaller systems function within the larger area of study.

Grade 5 Students Visit The Edge of the Earth, a Climate Change Photography Exhibition at the Ryerson Image Centre

*Image students are discussing is *Quaternary IV (Anthropocene)* by Isabelle Hayeur

Integration of skills

Skills integration aims to develop essential learning skills that apply across all subjects and strands of the curriculum, including

- **Critical Thinking and Problem Solving**: predicting, hypothesizing, categorizing, inferring, analyzing, synthesizing, comparing, generalizing, evaluating sources of information, assessing conflicting priorities, thinking hypothetically, making informed decisions
- **Social/Communication Skills**: listening attentively, agreeing or disagreeing respectfully, developing arguments and counterarguments, effectively paraphrasing, communicating ideas coherently and concisely, recognizing the perspectives of others, collaborating with others
- **Organization**: sequencing ideas logically, planning, managing time and space, balancing priorities, giving and following instructions
- **Self-regulation and Engagement**: persisting, concentrating, showing curiosity, demonstrating patience, self-monitoring, reflecting, paying attention, controlling impulses
- **Conceptual Flexibility and Application**: applying information or skills to new situations

These lifelong learning skills strongly affect how successfully students access and interact with every aspect of the curriculum. Even more to the point, perhaps, they play a key role in most aspects of daily life.

In addition, there are a number of broadly applicable academic skills (such as reading, writing, mathematics, or technological expertise) that are critically important across almost all areas of learning. Finding ways to integrate such skills into different curricular contexts has the dual advantage of strengthening the skills while enhancing understanding of the topic under study.

Integration of perspectives

Perspective integration involves the exploration of a topic from different points of view. While an interdisciplinary focus in itself offers different lenses through which to consider an issue, subject- or strand-based integration are not the only strategies for widening the scope of students' thinking. The fundamental premise of a knowledge building classroom is that the exchange of individual perspectives expands group understanding. Differences among learners are valued for what they add to the learning community. As well, the social perspective-taking abilities that develop in and through such negotiations have far-reaching applications that go well beyond the classroom. When students examine global topics from different viewpoints, they show a growing capacity to take the perspective of the animals, plants, landscapes, and people affected by global events and decisions.

In the rapid growth of industry and technology over the past two centuries, environmental perspectives have been overlooked and undervalued. Deforestation, habitat loss, species extinction, and global climate change are among the catastrophic consequences. More than ever before, the current generation of children is being asked to consider the impact of human decisions and actions on the sustainability of the planet. Affirming the crucial importance of the environmental perspective, the Ontario Ministry of Education's policy document, *Acting Today, Shaping Tomorrow* (2009), strongly urges educators to integrate environmental and sustainability education into all areas of the curriculum, considering the relationship between humans and their environment through science, social studies, arts, humanities, and other appropriate areas. Looking at topics through an environmental lens, students can begin to consider the reciprocal and interrelated perspectives that are essential to the survival of animal and plant species.

Indigenous perspectives have also been systematically ignored, undervalued, or actively suppressed in Canadian education for a long time, yet are crucial for coming to grips with the challenges of restoring a faltering planet as well as for engaging in a reconciliation process with descendants of the first inhabitants of our now-shared land. This resource's Indigenous lens shows us how intimately enmeshed the Indigenous and environmental perspectives can be, and it is our hope that this edition of *Natural Curiosity* represents one tiny step toward such reconciliation. Indigenous views of learners and their relation to the natural world offer transformative possibilities for refining and rethinking our practice.

As children mature, they begin to recognize that their own perspective is only one view among many, shaped by their personal experiences, culture, family history, and other factors. They begin to appreciate that studying a topic from a single viewpoint provides an incomplete picture that can result in misinformed opinions and unbalanced decisions. It is therefore important for educators – within the reality of developmental constraints – to encourage their students to incorporate different perspectives into their thinking about topics and to recognize the value in beliefs that conflict with their own. Coming to see that even experts disagree on major environmental issues is an important step toward the realization that facts alone may be insufficient to fully resolve an issue.

As students move up the grades, integrating social and environmental concerns becomes essential to building a more complete picture of the world and how it works. Students must learn to think systemically and see the interconnections among ecological, economic, and social systems, drawing explicit links between environmental perspectives and other critical global issues. The vision of sustainable development put forth by the United Nations Educational, Scientific, and Cultural Organization (UNESCO) underscores the importance of such an integrated perspective. Sustainable development requires simultaneous and balanced progress across interdependent social, economic, ecological, and political dimensions (UNESCO, 2010).

Putting the Pieces Together

Integrated learning is always implemented for particular purposes, never arbitrarily or for its own sake. It would be impractical, and not necessarily useful, to indiscriminately bring together all possible integrative teaching strategies at the same time. A more pragmatic way to begin is to gradually incorporate a variety of strategies over the course of a school year in a way that makes sense for the educator's strengths, the topic, and the individuals in the class. Many of the teachers' stories in Part 2 show this gradual widening of the learning lens.

Putting It into Practice

Getting Started

When considering which approaches to integration make the most sense for a topic, it can be helpful for educators to reflect on a few key questions as they plan:

- Which subject areas provide meaningful contexts for understanding the topic?
- Which forms of integration are likely to engage the students in this class?
- What skills might students need to pursue their questions on this topic?
- How can integrated learning help to make the learning accessible to all students?

Student Questions and Big Ideas

Integrated learning and an inquiry-oriented approach are natural allies. Children's broad questions and ideas – rarely organized into discrete disciplinary categories – often provide the catalysts for authentic integration that capitalizes directly on students' sense of wonder and enthusiasm for learning.

Educators may opt to create an integrated learning program by mapping their students' questions onto different subjects or strands in the curriculum. This responsive process, as shown in Tables 13 and 14, reveals some of the possibilities for integrated learning that arise when students' questions are placed at the centre of their learning.

Howard Gardner (1991) suggests that "a unit on water … provides opportunities for exploration in virtually every area of the curriculum. Students can write about their own beliefs … and enjoy classic or humorous texts … all kinds of counting, measuring, and comparing activities. Historical and geographical issues arise naturally … [there are] a host of questions that one can investigate in a scientific manner" (p. 214).

Tables 13 and 14 illustrate how some actual questions about water in a Grade 2 classroom led to opportunities for strand integration and subject integration respectively. The students' questions were linked to the curriculum's broader overall expectations, for three main reasons:

- Focusing on broader ideas, issues, or concepts (rather than on narrowly defined expectations) creates more room for students to pose and pursue relevant, generative, and multi-leveled questions.
- A broader focus makes it more likely that each learner will find a way to genuinely engage with the material.
- This approach accords with Ontario Ministry of Education strategies that ask teachers to focus student evaluations on their achievement of the overall expectations (2010).

Given the number of curriculum connections revealed in Tables 13 and 14, there are clearly many possibilities for addressing the overall curriculum expectations. Solid knowledge of the mandated curriculum area will enable an educator to connect students' questions and ideas to different aspects of the curriculum.

Table 13: Integrating Students' Questions into the Curriculum: STRAND Integration in Grade 2

STUDENTS' QUESTIONS	LINKS TO THE ONTARIO CURRICULUM – SCIENCE AND TECHNOLOGY: GRADE 2 (2007)	
	Strand & Topic	**Big Idea (BI) and Overall Expectation (OE)**
Why is a lot of water polluted?	**Strand:** Understanding Earth and Space Systems **Topic:** Air and Water in the Environment	**BI:** "Our actions affect the quality of air and water, and its ability to sustain life." **OE:** "Assess ways in which the actions of humans have an impact on the quality of air and water, and ways in which the quality of air and water has an impact on living things."
	Strand: Understanding Life Systems **Topic:** Growth and Change in Animals	**BI:** "Humans need to protect animals and the places where they live." **OE:** "Assess ways in which animals have an impact on society and the environment, and ways in which humans have an impact upon animals and the places where they live."
Why do so many species live in water?	**Strand:** Understanding Earth and Space Systems **Topic:** Air and Water in the Environment	**BI:** "Air and water are a major part of the environment." **BI:** "Living things need air and water to survive." **BI:** "Changes to air and water affect living things and the environment." **OE:** "Demonstrate an understanding of the ways in which air and water are used by living things to help them meet their basic needs."
	Strand: Understanding Life Systems **Topic:** Growth and Change in Animals	**BI:** "Humans need to protect animals and the places where they live." **OE:** "Assess ways in which animals have an impact on society and the environment, and ways in which humans have an impact upon animals and the places where they live."
What part of our bodies is water?	**Strand:** Understanding Earth and Space Systems **Topic:** Air and Water in the Environment	**BI:** "Air and water are a major part of the environment." **BI:** "Living things need air and water to survive." **OE:** "Demonstrate an understanding of the ways in which air and water are used by living things to help them meet their basic needs."
	Strand: Understanding Life Systems **Topic:** Growth and Change in Animals	**BI:** "Animals have distinct characteristics." **BI:** "Humans are animals." **OE:** "Investigate similarities and differences in the characteristics of various animals."
Why does everything need water?	**Strand:** Understanding Earth and Space Systems **Topic:** Air and Water in the Environment	**BI:** "Air and water are a major part of the environment." **BI:** "Living things need air and water to survive." **OE:** "Demonstrate an understanding of the ways in which air and water are used by living things to help them meet their basic needs."
	Strand: Understanding Life Systems **Topic:** Growth and Change in Animals	**BI:** "There are similarities and differences among different kinds of animals." **OE:** "Investigate similarities and differences in the characteristics of various animals."
Why do some fish live in salt water while others live in fresh water?	**Strand:** Understanding Earth and Space Systems **Topic:** Air and Water in the Environment	**BI:** "Living things need air and water to survive." **OE:** "Demonstrate an understanding of the ways in which air and water are used by living things to help them meet their basic needs."
	Strand: Understanding Life Systems **Topic:** Growth and Change in Animals	**BI:** "Animals have distinct characteristics." **OE:** "Investigate similarities and differences in the characteristics of various animals."

Table 14: Integrating Students' Questions into the Curriculum: SUBJECT Integration in Grade 2

LINKS TO THE ONTARIO CURRICULUM – SOCIAL STUDIES: GRADE 2
(Ontario Ministry of Education, 2013)

STUDENTS' QUESTIONS	Strand & Related Concepts	Overall Expectation (OE), Big Ideas (BI), and Framing Questions (FQ)
Why does everything need water?	**Strand:** People and Environments: Global Communities **Related Concepts:** Cause and Consequence	**OE:** "Describe some similarities and differences in the ways in which people in two or more communities in different parts of the world meet their needs and have adapted to the location, climate, and physical features of their regions." **BI:** "The climate and physical features of a region affect how people in that region live." **FQ:** "How do physical features and climate contribute to differences in the ways people around the globe live? How does the natural environment affect the ways in which people meet their needs? Why do people live where they live?"

LINKS TO THE ONTARIO CURRICULUM – MATHEMATICS: GRADE 2
(Ontario Ministry of Education, 2005b)

STUDENTS' QUESTIONS	Strand	Key Mathematical Skills (KS) and related Overall Expectations (OE)
Why do so many species live in water?	**Strand:** Data Management and Probability **Topic:** Data Relationships	**KS:** "Read and display data using line plots and simple bar graphs." **OE:** "Read and describe primary data presented in tally charts, concrete graphs, pictographs, line plots, simple bar graphs, and other graphic organizers."
How do snowflakes form themselves?	**Strand:** Geometry and Spatial Sense **Topic:** Geometric Properties	**KS:** "Compose and Decompose Shapes." **KS:** "Locate a line of symmetry." **OE:** "Compose and decompose two-dimensional shapes and three-dimensional figures."
What part of our bodies is water?	**Strand:** Number Sense and Numeration **Topic:** Quantity Relationships	**KS:** "Investigate fractions of a whole" **OE:** "Read, represent, compare, and order whole numbers to 100, and use concrete materials to represent fractions…"
	Strand: Number Sense and Numeration **Topic:** Quantity Relationships	**KS:** "Investigate fractions of a whole" **OE:** "Read, represent, compare, and order whole numbers to 100, and use concrete materials to represent fractions…"
Why do some fish live in salt water while others live in fresh water?	**Strand:** Data Management and Probability **Topic:** Data Relationships	**KS:** "Organize objects into categories using two attributes." **KS:** "Read and display data using line plots and simple bar graphs." **OE:** "Collect and organize categorical or discrete primary data and display the data, using tally charts, concrete graphs, pictographs, line plots, simple bar graphs, and other graphic organizers, with labels ordered appropriately along horizontal axes, as needed." **OE:** "Read and describe primary data presented in tally charts, concrete graphs, pictographs, line plots, simple bar graphs, and other graphic organizers."

The topic of water is also a galvanizing force for confronting pressing issues of race, poverty, and Indigenous rights. In his September 2017 address to the United Nations General Assembly, Prime Minister Justin Trudeau "highlighted the lack of safe drinking and bathing water in Indigenous communities across Canada and then pointed to the government's elimination of more than two-dozen boil-water advisories and its plans to end those that remain" (Zilio & Stueck, 2017).

Bev Caswell, a former Grade 4 teacher who is now the director of the Robertson Program for Inquiry-based Teaching in Mathematics and Science, designed a water-focused lesson that integrates mathematics, environmental science, geography, Indigenous culture, language arts, and social justice issues. Grounded in rigorous mathematics, this introductory lesson has sparked rich, socially committed inquiry in groups of teachers as well as in junior and intermediate level classrooms (Caswell, 2017).

Bev developed the lesson in response to the shocking realization that undrinkable water was a feature of many First Nation schools in which she worked. As she says, "Can you imagine what the response would be if people in major cities in Canada had to put up with this issue for weeks, let alone years on end? We have to ask ourselves: Why is there no public outrage on this pressing issue?"

Water Inquiry

Developed by Dr. Bev Caswell, Program Director
The Robertson Program: Inquiry-Based Teaching in Mathematics and Science
www.therobertsonprogram.com

Water Connections: Initial Activity

Materials
- PowerPoint presentation*
- Sticky notes and pens or pencils
- Blackline Master (BLM): Anishinaabemowin Water Words handout* – compiled by Jason Jones, Nigigoonsiminikaaning First Nation
- Computer with internet access
- Projector

Could I ask you to shut your eyes. Now, open your minds. With eyes closed, look down, down through the surface veneer beneath your feet, past the floor joists and structural shadows, look down until you see the earth. The building disappears, and you are a witness, but time has collapsed and you are not here. Look around you. At first you see forest, great pines and rich flora, then you see water, a riverbank and you hear the sound of fish swimming and butterfly wings – that's how attuned you are to your surroundings, how inseparable you are from the natural world.
– An excerpt from "The Opposite of Prayer: An Introduction to Tomson Highway" by John Moss, found in *Comparing Mythologies* (Highway, 2003)

1. Begin lesson by reading the excerpt above.
2. Give everyone time to write words on sticky notes that come to mind when they think of water. One word per sticky note. Provide time for each student to read word aloud.
3. Ask students to think about an experience they've had that has connected them to water in some way. For example, it could have to do with oceans, lakes, storms, rain, drinking water, tides, floods, canoeing, camping, swimming, etc. Talk in table groups or in pairs about experiences. Ask 3–4 students to share their experiences with the entire class.
4. Introduce Anishinaabemowin words that relate to water.*
5. Share Anishinaabe cultural practices relating to water:

- Liz Osawamick's Water Song (The Robertson Program, 2016)*
- Water walks

Math Exploration I: Central Tendency & Capacity

Materials
- Whiteboard & marker
- 1-litre water bottle (one per group)
- Dimensions of bathtub: L x W x H, 48" (122 cm) x 32" (81 cm) x 25" (64 cm)

1. Ask table groups to brainstorm ways in which they use water in their lives. Hear from each group. Create a list of all the ideas.
2. When students mention bath/shower, hold up a 1 litre water bottle and ask groups to estimate how many bottles of water they think it would take to fill a bathtub. Document the estimates on board at the front of the room. Have the students put the numbers in order. Give a mini lesson on mean, median, and mode using these numbers. Invite students to think about what the average estimate is. Highlight various strategies students mention.
3. Give each group a 1 litre bottle. Ask them to think about how they might calculate the capacity of a bathtub, for example ask, "What information do we need to calculate the capacity?" Give time for students to revise their estimates now that they have tub measurements. After groups have shared their ideas, you may decide to introduce the formula for calculating volume.

Math Exploration II

Materials
- Blackline Master (BLM): How much water do you use in a week?*
- 1 litre water bottle (one per group)
- Whiteboard & marker
- Computers with internet access

1. Ask students to think about approximately how much water they consume weekly?
2. Distribute BLM: How much water do you use in a week?
3. Ask everyone to use the worksheet to calculate approximate number of litres of water used per week.
4. Invite groups to write these numbers on the board at the front of the room and/or find the average for each table group then write the numbers on the board.
5. Discuss water consumption. Any surprises?
6. For further exploration, visit the CBC Water calculator (CBC News, 2012).

Introduction to Water Problem

Materials
- Sticky notes
- Chart paper and markers

1. Introduce a statement on current boil water advisories in your province. For example: "Nearly half of the 133 First Nations in Ontario currently have boil water advisories, and it has been more than ten years since ten First Nations in Northwestern Ontario had clean drinking water" (Porter, 2014).
2. Invite students to think about the statement above and to use the sticky notes

provided to write one word that comes to mind. Ask students to read their words to the class. These can be collected for later use in a language arts activity (e.g., performance piece or poetry to raise awareness of issues).
3. Now ask students to use the stickies to write any questions, thoughts that come to mind, or emotions that arise as they think about this fact. Give time for students to write questions and remind them to use a separate sticky note for each question or response.
4. Distribute chart paper and markers and invite table groups to sort the sticky notes into categories.
5. Each table will share the way they categorized their questions such as sources of water pollution, legislation, engineering systems to clean water, etc.
6. Students can choose a specific area of interest to study. Discuss ways in which we might go about answering our questions.

Water Problem II

Materials

- BLM: First Nations Drinking Water Advisory*
- Roadmap of Ontario (one per group)
- Circle stickers: red, orange, green, blue
- Large First Nation Map(s) of Ontario
- Same map but smaller versions in plastic sleeves

1. Give each group a list of the names of First Nation communities in Ontario that are under boil water advisories (BLM: First Nations Drinking Water Advisory).
2. Divide up the list and assign an equal number of First Nation communities on the list to each table group.
3. Distribute a roadmap of Ontario to each table group.
4. Highlight that First Nation communities are not usually listed on Ontario roadmaps and ask the students to consider why?
5. Ask groups to act as cartographers and investigative journalists to locate each of the First Nation communities and write the names of these communities on their roadmaps. Then place a colour-coded sticker on the map and write a number to identify the particular community:
    a. Red = do not drink the water under any circumstances
    b. Orange = boil water advisory
    c. Blue = water shortage

   Note: You can have a couple of large First Nation Maps of Ontario to help students locate the First Nation communities or the smaller versions at each table. Alternatively, students can use computers or digital devices to locate the communities on the list.
6. At the front of the room, hang the large version of the First Nation Map of Ontario. Ask groups to place colour-coded stickers on the large map to represent various types and numbers of drinking water advisories in First Nation communities in Ontario.
7. Provide additional information about drinking water advisories for First Nation Communities in Ontario. For example, show YouTube videos such as those by HumanRightsWatch (2016) for firsthand accounts of people's experiences with boil water advisories.

*Available at www.therobertsonprogram.com

Next Steps in an Inquiry

Invite participants to view the colour-coded map. *Any further questions to add to our lists?*

New Questions:

- Which questions can be answered quite quickly?
- Which questions are going to take more time?
- Which are the burning questions?

Have students write these questions on construction paper and place them on an "inquiry board" in the classroom.

Inquiry Ideas

Put students into working groups according to their areas of interest (as demonstrated in their questions). Students begin researching their area of interest. Gather as a class for discussions or knowledge building circles to share findings. Groups can display their findings prominently in the classroom.

Teaching children how to "take action" on issues of social justice is an important aspect of informed citizenship. Brainstorm ways in which research groups can make their "findings" public (e.g., creating posters or public service announcements, writing blogs, creating podcasts, documentaries, letters to the editor of local newspapers, etc.)

Math refreshers for teachers:

What is volume?

Volume relates to the amount of 3-D space an object or liquid occupies. For example, if I have a tank, how much space does it take up? For more information on volume, visit the UK Metric Association (n.d.).

How to find the volume of a rectangular prism:

To find the volume of a rectangular prism, you have to find the product of the area of the base and the height. For example, if you have a tank with the following dimensions: 50 cm (L) x 40 cm (W) x 30 cm (H), the area of the base is 50 cm x 40 cm = 2000 cm^2. Then you would multiply the base area by the height: 2000 cm^2 x 30 cm = 60 000 cm^3. Since 1 cm^3 = 1 mL, 60 000 cm^3 = 60 000 mL. And since 1000 mL = 1 L, 60 000 mL = 60 L.

Converting units of volume:

Volume is measured using liters (L), milliliters (mL), cubic meters (m^3), and cubic centimeters (cm^3).

1 cm^3 = 1 mL
1 000 000 cm^3 = 1 m^3
1000 mL = 1 L
1000 L = 1 m^3

Why is 1 000 000 cm^3 = 1 m^3?

1 m^3 = 1 m x 1 m x 1 m
1 m^3 = 100 cm x 100 cm x 100 cm
1 m^3 = 1 000 000 cm^3

Building Connections, Planning for Possibilities

> To be effective, teachers must simultaneously overplan – making sure they have a variety of resources and activities to accommodate students' interests – and underplan – remaining flexible instead of spelling out each week's activities.
>
> – Keith Barton and Lynne Smith, as cited in *Ontario Secretariat Capacity Building Series: Integrated Learning in the Classroom* (2010)

When planning, it is useful to keep in mind opportunities that are likely to arise for connecting topics of study. This may occur either through a concurrent integration of topics or through intentionally building connections among topics over the course of the year. Anticipating possibilities for connection helps to create a coherent and meaningful year of learning. Topics can be explored in an order that makes it easier to create bridges between topics rather than bringing each to an abrupt halt. For example, Cindy Halewood, a Grade 2 teacher at the Lab School, deliberately followed an environmental inquiry into trees and forests with a study of North American salmon. Cindy asked a question that encouraged students to think about the relationship between these two topics: "How do you think trees might be connected to salmon?"

Along similar lines, a kindergarten class started the school year with a hands-on look at the metamorphosis of a butterfly. In the following spring, the class incubated and hatched chicken and salamander eggs. Those studies were enhanced when one child serendipitously brought in tadpoles collected from a local creek and another contributed baby snails from their garden. Close observations and comparisons of these diverse life processes expanded into a deeper and more general look at life cycles (including the children's own life patterns) and cycles of all kinds (e.g., biological, astronomical, social), which naturally led back to reflections on the original butterfly experience. The school year came around full circle for the children, and the growth in their understanding of key concepts as well as in their ability to ask and pursue focused questions was apparent to both the children and their teacher.

Teachers find many ways to build connections:

- A Grade 3 teacher might plan to follow a study of Strong and Stable Structures (Ontario Ministry of Education, 2007) with an investigation into Communities in Canada: 1780-1850 (Ontario Ministry of Education, 2013). A possible way to create a link between these disciplines (Science & Technology and Social Studies) might be to compare present-day structures to those in the past, both Indigenous and settler, and to explore how different building approaches have responded to and affected the environment.
- This same Grade 3 teacher might decide to follow a study of Strong and Stable Structures with a Social Studies unit on Living and Working in Ontario. Among other possibilities, this sequence would allow students to compare and contrast urban and rural structures, while also investigating the environmental impact of these different structural approaches on urban and rural communities.

As Fogarty has observed: "Just by rearranging the order of topics, teachers can help kids make those critical connections" (1991, p. 35).

Though the order in which topics are introduced will affect the way students perceive them, these connections among units of study are most relevant for students when they themselves identify them. There is an ongoing interplay between a teacher's planning and the way students understand and work with the plans. Educators encourage children to draw connections by asking questions such as, "Does this remind you

of anything?" or "What does this make you think of?" A flexible, responsive approach to planning ultimately helps educators and students to delve more deeply and creatively into the curriculum.

Example: Grade 5s link government to energy

During their initial study of Government, students in Cathy Bertucci's Grade 5 class began to pose questions connected to another topic: Energy. Even though Cathy had not planned to begin the topic of Energy for another two months, she rearranged her long-term plans to support the interests and curiosity of her students and provide an authentic opportunity for making connections. This story is reminiscent of the example given in Branch I, in which a Grade 4 student's observation and expression of puzzlement in a literacy study led to a class-wide inquiry on the subject of light, a mandated science topic originally slated for later in the year (see p. 32).

> Subject matter is not discarded: It is re-positioned in a new form.
>
> – Edward Brazee and Jody Capelluti, *Dissolving Boundaries: Toward an Integrative Curriculum* (1995).

Place as a connecting thread

Several of the teachers' stories in Part 2 show a similar interweaving of thematic threads, such as seasonal change, throughout the school year. At other times, the connecting thread is less a topic than a *place*, such as the ravine in "Zoe's Story" (p. 187), a camp in the woods ("Marge's Story," p. 150) or an urban square ("Carol's Story," p. 168). As each of these classes moves through a series of investigations, each topic under study gains resonance from its connection to a single place the children come to know well. Reciprocally, the children's knowledge of the place gains depth through its developing connection with different areas of study.

Broadening Perspectives

Perspective integration occurs at many levels, starting with the rich possibilities of interdisciplinary study. For example, a Grade 4/5 class in a Toronto public school combined the Social Studies strands of Political and Physical Regions of Canada with First Nations and Europeans in New France and Early Canada (Ontario Ministry of Education, 2013) from a number of disciplinary vantage points, including Physical Geography, Indigenous Studies, Environmental Studies, History, Science, Math, Visual Arts, and Literature. The unit culminated in a persuasive writing project in which each child sent to an appropriate government agency a carefully composed and edited letter advocating on behalf of an environmental issue (Grade 4 students) or Indigenous rights issue (Grade 5 students) they felt strongly about. The result was a cohesive and meaningful trajectory of learning that explored and connected several subject areas. Looked at in this way, teaching a combined grade presents unique opportunities for, rather than obstacles to, rich learning.

Other kinds of perspective shifting are evident in the teachers' stories in Part 2. "Robin's story" (p. 234) is fundamentally a story of transforming both student and teacher perspectives on the Indigenous people of Ontario and their relationship to the students' own worlds. In Marlo's Grade 3/4 class (p. 226), a simple look at rocks and minerals broadens into a nuanced consideration of the moral, economic, and environmental complexities posed by mining in the North. Along the way, the students come to view their own community of Aroland in a new light. In a third example, through juxtaposing investigations into distant Space with a close look into their own lives, Carol's kindergarteners expand their five-year-old perspectives on the universe and their place within it (p. 168).

While most would agree that environmental sustainability is a global priority, the best means for achieving this are not always readily apparent or straightforward. It becomes essential for students to reflect upon conflicting perspectives in order to "appreciate the challenges faced by the human community in defining and implementing the process needed for environmental sustainability" (Ontario Ministry of Education, 2009, p. 27). Various interests must be weighed and balanced in the equation. Economic, social, and environmental goals sometimes appear difficult to reconcile, as highlighted in current controversies around pipeline construction. Electric cars reduce harmful emissions, but building and maintaining roads to sustain an automobile culture consumes land and energy (while creating jobs). Asking "benefit for whom?" becomes a critical question in many environmental and social justice issues. How are conflicting priorities to be reconciled?

Working to achieve a balanced solution often requires investment in tackling conflicting perspectives. Many older elementary-aged children, starting to question the values and assumptions they have grown up with, are passionately interested in engaging with such complex issues. "Mike's Story" (p. 251), for example, tells of ten-year-olds' efforts to make sense of climate change denial. During an inquiry into Government, the Grade 5/6 students in Ben Peebles' class conducted research and simulated through role play the process of drafting legislation to restrict car idling. As they learned more, they came to understand that diverse constituents in a metropolis such as Toronto are likely to have opposing interests and perspectives on key issues.

Summary of Chapter

Integrated learning that considers a topic through multiple lenses has pedagogic advantages that mesh easily with an inquiry-based approach:

- Learning easily builds upon ideas and questions that cross disciplinary borders.
- Knowledge and skills develop in meaningful contexts that make information more interesting, accessible, and easily retained.
- Learning is less fragmented and more relevant to learners.
- Through the application of skills and concepts across different contexts, the understanding of discipline-specific skills and concepts is deepened and solidified.
- By contextualizing learning, children are enabled to apply their school learning in other aspects of their lives.
- Children develop a habit of drawing connections and viewing scenarios from multiple perspectives.

Environmental inquiry is integrated in its very nature, most effectively centred in the interconnected environment and community in which students live. Significant implications for schooling lie in the possibilities for integrating aspects of students' lives into their learning and bringing their learning back into their lives, both within and beyond the school walls. Experiential learning is a fundamentally integrated endeavour, as place-based education gives a profoundly meaningful context to all that students learn about, think about, and act upon. Taken together, the experiences of inquiry, experiential learning, and integrated learning provide a solid ground for the development of environmental consciousness and socially responsible action.

The Flow of Knowledge: Everything Is Related
Indigenous Lens on Branch III

The Flow of Knowledge

If we take time to approach knowledge by grounding ourselves deeply in place, then knowledge can be built around who we really are, right where we stand. Such knowledge then flows together from every direction, to serve our shared life and purpose. Such knowledge is unified in its diversity, because it *is* our life.

The Sacred Web of Life and Knowledge

Eurocentric thought tends to study how disparate things may or may not be connected by looking at their tangible manifestations. Indigenous perspectives are more oriented to how all things are related from within, on the basis of their spiritual reality. When we see everything in creation as coming from and containing Spirit, we are more inclined to try to understand the sacred aspects and inner essence of things. At this higher level, everything is related. If we respect these relationships, they become vital to how we see, feel, think, learn, and live (Hampton, 1993). The connections binding the universe flow through everything like water, so knowledge of anything requires a moving knowledge of, and relationship with, many things. Knowledge itself must flow like water.

Because everything is alive with Spirit, we are related to everything, and our relatives include animals, plants, the elements, past and future beings, subtle levels of being, and the spiritual world beyond time and space. This living, connected quality of all reality is not an abstract theory to be used for framing how we think about the world. An Indigenous reality supports how we experience and embody what is around us – how we live – rather than a dispassionate observation of our surroundings as objects. The names of people, or of anything, are more likely to be lived spiritual and physical reality in an Indigenous universe, rather than mere labels. Arts and economics, for example, are intimately intertwined, equally filled with inner meaning and informed by ceremony.

Holy people who actually experience the totality and connection of everything in the universe are extremely rare. However, we can all seek to heighten our sense of this connection in relation to our personal responsibilities, and to what is around us. In other words, we can all connect more deeply with our place. A sense of inner personal kinship with our place helps ensure integrated learning, bringing biology and history or literature and geometry together to sustain us in spiritual and material ways. Since knowledge is a living, fluid process (and not a cold, segmented abstraction) no single strand of knowledge, nor any specialty held by any individual, can ever be taken as things unto themselves. Rather, these strands and bodies of knowledge must be seen in light of how they both inform and are informed by other strands of Spirit and reality. Such a view challenges the modern mind educated in Eurocentric thinking.[1]

Implications for Integrated Learning

Some concepts outlined in *Natural Curiosity* as essential to integrated learning correspond with the recognition that everything is related, such as the notions of holism and the interconnectedness of all systems. However, Indigenous perspectives invite us to approach knowledge integration through a lens that extends far beyond typical notions of our environment. Indigenous views broaden the basis for knowledge integration to include *everything around us*, ultimately erasing the environment as a concept, immersing and connecting us in a blooming sense of place, until everything we are, every aspect of our existence, is one whole, inseparable, living system, united from within.

Coming to know is not just aimless, random curiosity about everything (this would be overwhelming); Indigenous emergent learning processes are centred and embodied in *how, where, who, and what we really are* (or should be) – unique beings with intuitive gifts, purpose, and instructions integrating us into *an immediate, living and unified system of life*. This system is what should define and unify various functions and strands of knowledge held by diverse individuals: ceremony, songs, food, relationships, governance, economics, sciences, mathematics, history and so on.

Integrating our realities helps us restore balance both within and among ourselves and in the

---

[1] Of course, this is not the same as saying people of European extraction only think in certain ways; great European minds often hold views similar to Indigenous views on the integrated nature of knowledge and reality at high levels, expressed so well through Keats' line, "beauty is truth," or in Einstein's views on the convergence of art and science, for example.

world around us, since every aspect of our reality is ultimately unified from within, rather than competing. "The environment versus the economy" becomes a false dichotomy, since they are one. We may not be able to reach this kind of unity and balance as adults in the early 21st century, but we *must help our children get there*. We can begin if we proceed with humility and respect, in partnership with Indigenous people in our region.

We must also emerge quickly from the only era most people in the modern West have ever known, epitomized by the Cartesian duality of mind and matter. Separating the natural world from our cultural intellect is no longer a viable mental habit. Our economies, social structures, every aspect of human life, are all holistically one, and inseparable from the environment. The idea that "holistic views of education" unify diverse subjects and themes on the basis of their separate, external manifestation (from below, as it were) is still a Eurocentric view of holistic education. The idea that we need to "balance conflicting priorities" is an example of binary thinking.[2] Such conflicts are aggravated by reductionist Cartesian concepts, so foreign to Indigenous holistic thought, which considers diversity in light of "total continuity without interruption" (Solomon, 1990, p. 79).

Indigenous worldviews challenge us to consider holism and interconnectedness in spiritual ways that are not part of Eurocentric conceptions of nature. While the environment can be a basis for shared knowing, a unifying Spirit lies within the environment. To ignore the higher unity of this inner level makes any consideration of the environment hollow.

The Challenge: Integrating Knowledge from Within

> Meaning then is derived not through content or data, or even theory in a Western context, which by nature is decontextualized knowledge, but through a compassionate web of interdependent relationships that are different and valuable because of that difference. Individuals carry the responsibility for generating meaning within their own lives – they carry the responsibility for engaging their minds, bodies and spirits in a practice of generating meaning.
>
> – Leanne Betasamosake Simpson, "Land as Pedagogy" in *Decolonization: Indigeneity, Education and Society* (2014)

If we search for meaning through disparate subjects or areas of learning that remain intellectually detached from each other – and even worse, from which we ourselves are detached in our own spirit and life – many problems arise, and meaning itself is incomplete. We are then detached from the world around us, and this is dangerous.

Indigenous worldviews challenge us to engage with the web of life in a much more inwardly connected, personal way – to deepen our relationship with all that surrounds us, using mind, body, and spirit to the greatest extent possible. Through an Indigenous lens, knowledge is seen as having less value if we are unable to develop it through holistic perspective and practice, where we see and live with our surroundings from as many different angles (or subjects) as possible – and above all, from our heart.

To take a simple example, if one were a hunter, it would be hoped that one would not just need to know where to find a deer and how to shoot it. This would merely be a kind of mechanical deer murder. In some Indigenous cultural frameworks, one might ideally also be gifted with the responsibility of hunting as part of one's personal vision, attained through ceremonial interaction with the Spirit World as a youth. On this basis, one would be empowered with the need to know what plants deer like, how to attract or charm the deer, how to speak to the Deer Spirit, how to use every part of the animal responsibly (and who in

---

[2] Binary thinking has its legitimate place – in making decisions at the grocery store, designing useful machines, or programming a computer, for example; but when applied to the higher or inner nature of reality, it leads to false dichotomies.

your community has the skills to use them), how to give thanks for the deer, and so on. The learning process could also include accessing knowledge of certain songs for hunting, or of certain medicines to heighten one's own senses and the songs for those medicines, or of certain kinds of training to heighten one's own senses.[3] All of this would be attained not through any rigid educational course, but through a personal, inner *relationship* with the widest possible range of factors supporting the success and sacred aspects of the hunt.

What applies to the hunt applies to anything. Being Indigenous is not synonymous with hunting, but is about how deeply and respectfully we can enter into relationship with everything around us, in ways that integrate many aspects of knowledge related to what we urgently need to know. As long as we can connect with what children need, we can help them approach this level of care in their relationship with the small piece of Mother Earth in which they stand. We can help them explore heartfelt and closely linked questions regarding the place where they belong (not *their* place, the *place where they belong*), in ways that transcend and unify all subjects.

We do not need to be explicitly spiritual; bringing spirituality into learning can be challenging even for those educators who wish to be (especially in secular public school systems). We just need to feel something strongly together, from our hearts. If we are able to *identify* with our locale together, our knowledge of our place will emerge in ways that are unified. Simply asking what birds sing outside our door opens innumerable learning pathways. Do the same birds who sing at sunrise also sing at dusk, and if so, do they sing differently at those times? If we can get children out with their parents for a dawn chorus near the school, the shock of being all together in the early morning as the sun rises can help us form a powerful, emotionally connected and commonly held memory. Such an experience takes us beyond our modern scientific tendency to reduce birds to their physical manifestation. Rather than throwing some seeds at the birds and walking away, we may well ask, "If a bird feeds my spirit, how do I feed the spirit of birds?" Let us not be too discouraged at our own helpless feeling in the face of such "impossible" questions; small children are much better at addressing these things than adults. In considering birdsong, the smallest child may quite easily wonder *what songs we can sing back to them*, and then happily sing or hum something for the bird, especially if encouraged by an adult.

Depending on the child's vocalizations and the bird's nature, conversations may even ensue. From a place of *caring about the birds personally*, it is much more likely that we will come to know what our bird relatives want and need, which even in the confines of our small piece of Mother Earth, is everything. We will need to know the insects and plants, and how the sun travels at different times and seasons. We may well arrive quickly at seemingly unrelated questions: where is our watershed, what is thirst, and why do we need to be grateful for water? Above all, what is our relationship with the birds, the water, this piece of Earth, and this tree? What are the emotional qualities of that relationship? What happens when we gather under that tree or on that little piece of Earth or by that water? (A mere birdbath or puddle is fine.) What happens if we can have a relationship with each other and the tree, or even just a pinecone? How does the place feel to us, and how does the *place itself feel about us?* (Another "impossible" question!)

---

[3] Some Indigenous games have such training as their explicit aim. Of course, most anthropologists tend to completely miss such aims, reducing these games to their simplest external manifestations.

We can leap from here into the stories and histories of the place we share with the birds. Who are the regional Indigenous people who can bring this information to light in ethical ways? Learning the words for dawn in the local Indigenous language can lead us to the stages and purposes and meanings of the sunrise, depending on the language, and even to some surprising details not usually considered in modern scientific inquiry, such as when the birds start to sing, and pause, and why. We may also find ourselves asking about what else has happened in this place we love. For example, there may be a person in the area who knows the birds very well. What other people in the community hold knowledge of our place, and can connect us more deeply with it? Who is the oldest person in the neighbourhood? Who has lived there longest? What can they tell us about what the place was like 70 years ago?

The questions and exploration that may arise through a deeper relationship with our own place can unify language, geometry, geography, science, art, media literacy, social studies, and much more. But all subjects are unified through a focus on what is most immediate to our inner lives, through heartfelt connection – *through love*.

Integrating Knowledge Around Our Shared Purpose

Integrating themes and subjects is a natural outcome of common purpose. When we feel something urgently together, our human family – all the people in our place – is most motivated to address the integrated nature of reality. This is when all the various "experts" work hardest to connect their separate knowledge. Deep inside, everybody intuitively knows the interconnectedness of all things. If we can focus on the big idea, and bring students together around our common connection (rather than the separate pieces of the curriculum by using disconnected examples), then we can bring together the strands of knowledge that different individuals are drawn to personally, and learn about different subjects together in the most memorable ways. If the big idea is about our place, then what songs or stories exist in the cultural traditions held by children's families that tell us about the land, or water, or the sacredness of life?

Integrating knowledge as a group in a shared learning environment need not be limited to a Eurocentric idea of nature. Many questions arise from any unifying invitation to consider who we are, where and how we belong, and more importantly, how we belong together through shared priorities. Hopefully our questions have an immediacy that unifies the diverse strengths and tendencies of the children into a common purpose.

The common cause can be whatever sparks the class. The spark could be the powerful emotions children experience in something as mundane as food. Ask any group of children, "Who fights with their parents over food?" We can then connect with many topics by discussing the children's lunches. Why do parents want them to eat certain foods (health)? How much did the lunch food cost (mathematics)? Where does it come from and what does it look like on the land (research skills)? How do the food plants or animals grow, what do they need, and what is in the food, the water, and the soil (science)? Where did this food originate (geography)? What plants grew here before the Europeans arrived (history)? What has happened to these plant relatives (ecology)? A more ambitious activity could be the establishment of a school garden, managed through family engagement. If our children are part of a community in school, so too are the parents and other relatives.

Going deeply into and relating deeply with our immediate world can be the hub around which all subjects revolve. Seeing our local park as a source of food is combined with an analysis of what goes into our food. How do history, math, or science support our reconnection with local food? Rather than being mere areas of study, how do these subjects become applied in integrated ways to our lives, in ways that help us build communities? What does this mean for every child, of every age? How do we help children think integrally so that the capacity is developed for transcendent rather than technocratic knowledge? There is no end to integrating school subjects, once we allow the integrity of all knowledge to flow like water through any aspect of our immediate place.

Branch IV: Moving Toward Sustainability
Living and Acting in the World

> If we can harness our knowledge, the deep reservoirs of human wisdom accumulated over millennia, and our unique gift of foresight, then we can achieve sustainability within one or two generations. Saving ourselves and countless other species from the brink of ecological disaster would be the greatest comeback of all time.
>
> – David Suzuki, *David Suzuki's Green Guide* (2008)

> [W]e find ourselves in this moment where there are no non-radical options left before us. Change or be changed, right? And what we mean by that is that climate change, if we don't change course, if we don't change our political and economic system, is going to change everything about our physical world.
>
> – Naomi Klein, Interview with Michael Winship (February 3, 2016)

Theoretical Underpinnings

Situating Ourselves in Nature

> The more people understand that Native Americans have their own religious rituals and objects of veneration – which to many non-Native people are simply features of the landscape – as well as cathedrals and churches, the better. Understanding the natural world as more than just a resource for energy, or a recreational opportunity, or even a food resource, gives moral weight to the effort to contain catastrophic climate change.
>
> – Louise Erdrich, "Holy Rage: Lessons from Standing Rock" in *The New Yorker* (December 22, 2016)

Since the first edition of *Natural Curiosity* appeared in 2011, thinking has started to shift about how to characterize an optimal relationship between humans and the land in which they live. In keeping with its times, the first edition put forth a view of environmental stewardship as consisting of "human actions that contribute to a sustainable future for humans, animals, and plant species alike" (Chiarotto, p. 54). It described how "acts of stewardship grow from a deep respect for, and desire to protect, the balance of nature within Earth's biosphere" (Chiarotto, 2011, p. 54).

Recently, however, the term "stewardship" has come under scrutiny for its implicit protectionist stance ("save the Earth"), which places humans strictly outside the natural world of which they are a part, and may thereby inadvertently perpetuate the very alienation it seeks to overcome. Indeed, some scholars (e.g., Malone, 2016) go further to caution against the over-romanticization of children in nature as ultimately serving to maintain an undesirable "nature-culture binary" (Malone, 2016, p. 42). The idea of reciprocity provided in the Indigenous lens on this chapter (Branch IV) offers a very different vision of what it means to be a person in the world. As Glen Aikenhead, Professor Emeritus at the University of Saskatchewan, has commented, it emphasizes the "web of interrelationships and responsibilities" in which we are all enmeshed, "that naturally requires sustainable living day in and day out for a community's survival" (personal communication, July 30, 2015).

While continuing to encompass aspects of stewardship, the broader notion of "sustainability" comes somewhat closer to this idea of reciprocity, stressing a long-term intergenerational locus of responsibility. As defined very simply by the World Commission on Environment and Development (Brundtland Commission) report to the United Nations (1987), sustainable development is "development that meets the needs of the present without compromising the ability of future generations to meet their own needs" (p. 41). The report expands upon the interrelated ecological, economic, and social dimensions of sustainability, proposing that "even the narrow notion of physical sustainability implies a concern for social equity between generations, a concern that must logically be extended to equity within each generation" (Brundtland Commission, 1987, p. 41).

Facing today's environmental crises, sustainable

> But even to think that we are separated from Nature is somehow a thinking disorder. You cannot be separated from Nature. Why we think that way is the interesting thing.
>
> – James Hillman, *The 11th Hour* (2007)

living may be as much at issue as sustainable *development*. As we expand our earlier ideas of stewardship to incorporate broader concepts of sustainability, the Indigenous lens gives us something deeper to aspire to – a new framework for our understanding of how it is possible to act as a moral agent in our world. However, such a radical transformation in thinking is not likely to happen all at once. In the meantime, there is reason to embrace all efforts to limit or reverse the damages that continue to be perpetrated on the Earth. As we reflect upon what it means to approach a condition of reciprocity, there may still be a place for the narrower notions of stewardship or caretaking, especially for children who have grown up witnessing the human/environment relationship as primarily one of separateness and control. For these children, thinking about a shift to a more benign and protective form of control is an important first step. For this reason, we do not, in this second edition, entirely eschew the idea of environmental stewardship, while acknowledging that it may not be the desired endpoint but rather a significant step along the path to something more complete.

Natural Curiosity's four-branched approach does not intend to imply that every environmental inquiry needs to directly culminate in immediate acts of environmental sustainability. It is more realistic and useful to see this learning as supporting the lifelong growth of understanding, within an extended accrual of learning experiences that help children situate themselves as moral agents within their many intersecting worlds, natural and human. Accordingly, the stories told by educators in Part 2 show a range of action levels contained within the umbrella of environmental inquiry. Some inquiries are more focused on building insight, while others lend themselves to concrete and simple acts. In still others, emerging insights catapult students into impassioned calls for justice. Each has its place.

The ways in which children are willing and able to commit to meaningful sustainable or restorative action will depend upon many factors, including their age. In her story (p. 160), Beverly describes the process of scaling down her ambitions for awakening stewardship impulses in her kindergartners until she identifies a situation they can genuinely relate to – keeping a few birds fed in the winter months.

Environmental responsibility is two-pronged, entailing both awareness and emotional investment. Decades of research, along with more anecdotal observations, provide evidence that knowledge alone is unlikely to spur environmental action. The approach to learning we espouse, which involves the whole child – cognition, emotions, and all – results not only in more engaged and joyful learners but also hopes to provide the conditions for building new ways of living and acting in the world.

In the previous three chapters, we have laid out a pedagogic framework within which children develop a sense of agency through *inquiry*, a sense of place through *experiential learning*, and a sense of interconnectedness through *integrated learning*. Although we consider each branch separately, they are, in reality, quite intertwined. In the end, though, all this wonderful learning is in vain if children fail to incorporate it as feeling, thinking, physical beings with the power to act upon their knowledge to make a difference where they can.

Even at the most local level, the development of environmental awareness has global implications:

- It recognizes that we all share the responsibility to maintain a healthy planet (of which we are a part).
- It empowers learners "to take informed decisions and responsible actions for environmental integrity, economic viability and a just society for present and future generations" (UNESCO, 2017, p. 7).
- It develops in students "the knowledge, attitudes and capacity to respond to the challenge of sustainability throughout their professional and personal lives" (UNESCO, 2017, p. 50).
- It challenges the notion that nature is an unlimited body of resources available for human consumption without consequence.
- It rebalances the values of traditional ways of living, learning, and knowing, stressing the importance of listening to Indigenous voices from around the world.
- It honours the idea that nature has rights (Global Alliance for the Rights of Nature, 2017).

Fostering Environmental Responsibility

> Indigenous protocols may approach the human condition not as a struggle to know the universe; the condition, rather, is to know ourselves well enough so we can act morally in the universe. Forms of scientific inquiry – sustainability or Indigenous – have important roles to play in this process.
>
> – Kyle Whyte, Joseph Brewer II, and Jay Johnson, "Weaving Indigenous Science, Protocols, and Sustainability Science" in *Sustainability Science* (2016)

For educators, incorporating the branches of environmental inquiry into their practice provides a foundation for building environmental responsibility in students. A number of research studies (e.g., Bamberg & Moser, 2007; Chawla, 2009; Hungerford & Volk, 1990; Thomson & Hoffman, 2004) suggest that environmentally committed behaviour is most closely associated with three things: a **sense of efficacy** in the world, a caring **relationship with nature**, and solid **knowledge** about environmental issues and action strategies. In school settings, these tend to emerge under the following conditions:

- Children develop a sense of efficacy through assuming agency over their own learning.
- Children build "ecological identity" and sensitivity to nature through spending meaningful time in natural settings.
- Children's environmental actions are linked to classroom learning in which they build knowledge about environmental issues and effective strategies for action.

In the sections that follow, each condition is described in more detail.

Student agency: Sustainability and inquiry-based learning

Children are empowered when they are genuinely able to act upon their own decisions. Placing their questions and ideas at the forefront of their learning conveys that what they think and how they act makes a difference. Over time, this belief can spur them to initiate and participate in thoughtful, relevant action in the world.

> I wanted students to leave my classes not just better informed, but more prepared to relinquish the safety of silence, more prepared to speak up, to act against injustice whenever they saw it.
>
> – Howard Zinn, *You Can't be Neutral on a Moving Train: A Personal History of Our Times* (2002)

Effective environmental education produces citizens who make sustainable life choices as they assess the impact of their actions on the balance of global ecological systems. To support this goal, learning environments must encourage students to critically consider what is happening in the world around them. Learning to probe beneath the surface and question assumptions helps students to

- identify problems of understanding in different contexts
- develop critical thinking and problem-solving skills and strategies
- work toward achieving balanced solutions

When questioning is solely the prerogative of the teacher, students tend to receive curriculum content passively and accept that life within the classroom, the school, and the world at large has already been decided for them. This kind of learning can be alienating and disempowering. When young learners come to believe that school is not a place to pursue the ideas that matter to them, they are likely to assume that they are unable to make meaningful contributions within that setting, let alone have an impact in the larger context of real environmental or social issues.

David Orr (2004) warns of the larger implications of such a scenario. "We were not taught to question the physical, biological, and psychological reordering of the world taking place all around us. Nor were we enabled to see it for what it was ... The orchard beside our house was drenched with pesticides every spring and summer, and we never objected" (p. 158).

If we want to nurture students' belief in their own efficacy, we need to provide opportunities for them to make small differences from the start. It is not enough to listen to children's ideas if we take control of every other aspect of their lives. Children thrive when they see themselves as working contributors in their community, and there is much to learn from Indigenous models in which children are expected – and helped – to participate and pitch in to the best of their abilities. Many educators have commented on the unusual persistence, industry, and sense of achievement shown by students who engage in what they perceive as genuine work, no matter how repetitive – clearing a trail, boxing up cans at a food bank, planting and maintaining a garden, clearing the schoolyard of ice and snow – work that goes well beyond the somewhat artificial jobs often assigned in classrooms.

Students' confidence in their ability to take effective action grows along with their developing knowledge of topics, issues, and action strategies. The opportunity to make informed choices about important aspects of their lives, including their school learning, motivates students to seek new knowledge. They also gain the confidence to act upon this knowledge by challenging established norms and effecting change within their community.

> Knowledge plus motivation equals action.
>
> – David Suzuki, *David Suzuki's Green Guide* (2008)

Time spent in nature: Sustainability and experiential learning

> People around a child foster a bond with nature not only by giving the child freedom to move about and engage autonomously with natural areas, but also by their own example. What they need to do, it appears, is to set an example of noticing nature in an appreciative way. By the direction and quality of their attention, they communicate nature's value and promote the child's interest in this world too.
>
> – Louise Chawla, "Childhood Experiences Associated with Care for the Natural World" in *Children, Youth and Environments* (2007)

The agency offered to students through inquiry-based learning is supported and furthered through opportunities to build joyful, productive, and autonomous relationships with nature. Branch II (Experiential Learning) summarized some of the cognitive, physical, and emotional benefits associated with immersion in the natural outdoors. There is also evidence to suggest that frequent childhood experiences in nature play a key role in building an "ecological identity" that is strongly associated with environmentally conscious behaviour.

One retrospective study found that daily positive childhood experiences in natural habitats were the most frequently reported influences leading to activist behaviour in adulthood (Tanner, 1980). Moreover, positive memories of outdoor experiences more strongly predicted subsequent stewardship actions than did the acquisition of content knowledge about environmental issues (Finger, 1993).

These findings have been supplemented by research (e.g., Chawla, 2007; 2009) revealing that time spent outdoors with a caring adult in childhood uniquely predicts later inclinations toward environmental activism. Significant elements of such mutual experiences in nature include adult modelling that

- expresses care for the land as a limited resource
- criticizes destructive practices
- shares pleasure at being in nature
- attends closely to details of the "earth, sky, and living things" (Chawla, 2007, p. 158)

When Janice Matthews interviewed amateur entomologists to discover the origins of their passion for insects, they, like the activists, commonly described formative childhood experiences in nature characterized by "a contagious attitude of attentiveness on the part of those adults who have meaningful relationships with the child" (Matthews, 1992, as cited in Chawla, 2007, p.157).

It is plausible that the joint attention to nature fostered by caring adults builds the reflectiveness that transforms experience into learning. This suggests that educators' attitudes toward, pleasure in, and attentiveness to details of the natural world have the potential to strongly influence their students. For educators who are uncomfortable or unfamiliar with wilder natural settings, finding manageable ways to gain personal experience in this realm is likely to have marked benefits for their students.

> Children need to develop a relationship with nature before they can be expected to heal its wounds … Without that deep, abiding sense of comfort in and love for the natural world, no amount of chastising about turning off the lights or biking to school is going to make a bit of difference.
>
> – David Sobel, *Childhood and Nature: Design Principles for Educators* (2008)

Along with the attentional scaffolding provided by caring adults, children develop a meaningful relationship with nature through opportunities to wander about and explore the natural environment, unhampered by rigid expectations of what they must learn or do. In order to forge deep bonds with their environment, their initial experiences need to be open-ended and rewarding.

Ideally, the foundation for developing environmental responsibility is laid during the early childhood years, where the main aim is to provide interesting and pleasurable experiences in nature – exploring, gathering treasures, identifying wildlife, noticing patterns of change over time (Sobel, 2008). Children need to start small, tending to things they truly care about, such as individual plants or animals. On a larger scale, it takes time for them to build awareness of what is usual (such as seasonal patterns) before they can begin to grasp the significance of deviations (such as global warming trends). As they get older, students acquire more context and perspective for tackling the complexities of global issues and applying this understanding to their own practice. Even at these later ages, however, they still benefit from continuing opportunities to cement their emotional connection to the natural world.

There is, of course, genuine risk in coming to love something that is endangered. While it is often possible to find developmentally appropriate entry points into difficult topics, an educator sometimes walks a fine line between building urgent awareness and overwhelming children with counterproductive anxiety or hopelessness. This kind of delicate balancing act is inevitable in education when something real is at stake.

Linking environmental action to classroom learning: Sustainability and integrated learning

Informed and productive action requires deep knowledge, yet knowledge alone is insufficient to motivate environmentally responsible behaviour. When learning is integrated and coherent, the emphasis on students as whole learners in an interrelated world supports the growth of motivation, skills, and knowledge that together drive effective action for sustainability. Children's experiences in nature are crucially tied to their developing understanding in a cyclical interaction of experience and reflection. The emotional as well as cognitive sides of their development and learning are recognized and supported through adult modelling and thoughtful curricular planning. Their sense of themselves as contributing members of intersecting communities is strengthened as they bring aspects of their lives into classroom learning and classroom learning back into their lives. An integrated approach encourages students to incorporate other ideas and perspectives into their thinking as they move beyond the limitations of a single point of view.

Integrating environmental perspectives into classroom learning contexts is vitally important for a number of reasons:

- Developing environmental responsibility is fundamental to becoming an informed moral agent in the world.
- Belonging to a community inherently entails environmental responsibility.
- Environmental action contributes to sustainable development in real world contexts.

When educators integrate an environmental perspective into classroom learning, they acknowledge that the desire and capacity to exercise responsible environmental and social practice is at least as important as the ability to memorize math facts or use decoding strategies.

Putting It into Practice

Fostering Environmental Agency

The mutually supporting roles played by inquiry and experiential learning in fostering environmental agency in students are reinforced when educators challenge students with probing questions, such as

- "Now that we have all this information, what do you think we should do with it?"
- "What is really going on here?"
- "Who is this good for? Who is this not good for?"
- "Does this decision respect everyone's rights?"
- "Who might think differently about this issue?"
- "Does this seem fair to you?"
- "Do you think anyone else should know about this? Who?"
- "How can we help?"
- "How might we be part of the problem?"

An effective response to children's heartfelt expressions of concern helps them to develop realistic and concrete strategies for implementable action. In his story of investigating climate change in Grade 5, Mike recounts his early attempts to curb students' immediate impulses to spring into action. He felt that they needed to better understand the issues before jumping in to fix what they perceived as terrible wrongs. After a while, though, the class reached a point at which the need to *do* something became galvanizing. At that point, by encouraging his students to take on action projects of their own choice – from technology design to advocacy, fundraising, or consciousness raising – Mike helped them to identify the wide range of possibilities available for taking responsibility. When children realize that there are many different ways (big and small) to make worthwhile contributions, their awareness of far-reaching global and environmental injustices becomes more manageable and less overwhelming.

Example: The Grade 4s tackle waste management

Focusing on an issue within the school community supports meaningful action on a workable scale. Vessna Romero, Grade 4 teacher at Victoria Village Public School, followed up on a question that emerged from a knowledge building discussion: How much garbage does our whole school send to the landfill? The Grade 4 class wanted to know whether the students and educators at their school were making environmentally responsible decisions about the waste they produced each day. They carried out a school-wide waste audit that revealed an alarming amount of waste. In response, the Grade 4s challenged each class at their school to devise strategies for reducing the amount of waste in their classrooms and launched a Garbage Reduction Contest in the weeks leading up to Earth Day.

Structuring Outdoor Time

As described in Branch II, valuable outdoor learning experiences can range from highly structured programs to open-ended play and exploration, depending on the context and intent of the outing. Building a school garden, for instance, requires a series of well-defined and carefully ordered tasks. In freer exploration, an educator's skill in drawing children's attention to interesting or important features of the landscape – perhaps in conjunction with such observation tools as cameras, binoculars, magnifying lenses, or field guides – will have a strong impact on how their students learn to relate to the outside world. Though such explorations in nature are often less overtly structured, they may still be organized around a few broad questions that provide a common focus for students to explore in individual ways.

Example: The Grade 1s explore seasonal changes

To investigate the topic of "cycles" with her Grade 1 students, Zoe Donoahue reserved a full morning, every six weeks or so throughout the school year, for her students to observe and experience seasonal changes in a nearby Toronto ravine. She guided the children's explorations with a few open-ended questions, including

- "What signs of the season do you see, hear, feel, or smell?"
- "How can you tell that it is fall, winter, spring, or summer?"
- "What has changed since the last time we came to the ravine?"
- "What effect might this (these) change(s) have on other ravine life?"

Students ran to her with evidence – a large pinecone, a crimson leaf, an icicle. Meanwhile, she rushed about with her camera, snapping shots of whatever interested them, such as the frozen stream, which, as the students pointed out, had flowed freely only a few months earlier. The children trudged through mud in their rubber boots, made snow angels, and used sticks to crack through the frozen stream to test how frozen it was. They ran through tall grasses and cattails whose height exceeded their own. They paused for a while, sketching observations in their lab books, all in an urban ravine a short subway ride from their school.

Linking Sustainable Action to Classroom Learning

In many schools, student engagement in actions for sustainability typically occurs in an extracurricular context. Environmental clubs provide motivated students with opportunities to assume leadership and model conservation behaviour, as interested representatives across the grades meet periodically to discuss greening initiatives around the school or in the community.

However, there are two primary reasons to deepen and extend these approaches:

1. to ensure that all environmental action is tied to deep learning
2. to ensure that every student has the awareness and power to make a difference

The following examples illustrate a few ways in which educators have integrated action for sustainability into classroom learning.

Example: The Grade 4s and 5s build a school garden

Kathleen Quan, Grade 4/5 teacher at Rose Avenue Public School, wanted her students' experience and practice of sustainability to build upon knowledge gathered from previous inquiries into human health and nutrition, as well as energy conservation. With the assistance of the non-profit organization Green Thumbs (2017), the Grade 4s and 5s took leadership in building an edible garden for the entire school community, located in one of the most densely populated neighbourhoods in Canada.

By participating in the design, building, and planting of the garden, the students took on the roles of producers as well as consumers, creating a hub for community engagement, interaction, and ownership. Through a combination of knowledge building discourse and expert sources, they examined the larger purpose behind their efforts, gaining insight into the social, health, and environmental benefits of local gardening.

Example: Restoring salmon to the rivers

Over a number of years, Grade 2 classes at the Laboratory School have participated in the Lake Ontario Atlantic Salmon Restoration Program. This is an initiative of the Ontario Federation of Anglers and Hunters (2017), which provides equipment and guidance for classes to incubate salmon eggs and release the young fish into local habitats. The classes supplemented their work with tree planting to provide cooling shade along the creek into which the salmon were released. Each class concluded its study with a student-produced newsletter packed with environmental advice, poetry and fiction, drawings and information about salmon, and children's reports about their learning and experiences. In the excerpt below, one child's memory of the culminating outing beautifully captures the mix of interests, knowledge from a previous inquiry (on birds), and emotional significance brought to the experience (punctuation and grammar preserved):

> We saw very cool things at Duffin's Creek not just salmon but a lot of birds too. Something like 20 or 25 birds there including a Blackburnian warbler, a lot of eastern kingbirds (I would say about 20). We also got a lot of tree swallows and one about a foot away from my face.
>
> Now to the salmon … The first thing we did was release the salmon after we split up into groups and went on hikes or some people just looked around and explored. On the second hike some people got some pretty good birds. Cindy's group got a least flycatcher…. Also we had a really nice look at all our salmon too and just the bank of Duffin's creek. All the song sparrows chirping around in there warmed your heart. It was very nice right there.
>
> Some things that you should not do and that kills almost a quarter of the Atlantic salmon:
>
> 1. Don't litter.
> 2. Help Atlantic salmon.
> 3. Remember that Atlantic salmon need help from you.

This seven-year-old's vivid construal of a shared environmental project brings to light the potent blend of emotion, fact, and values (both ethical and aesthetic) that informs meaningful experience and action in the world.

Example: Exploring actions to counter climate change ("Murray's Story," Part 2)

> While the students focused on their knowledge about climate change, a big question emerged: "Shouldn't we be trying to do something about climate change? It seems like a big deal." This prompted the creation of a new category called "Actions," and a type of momentum began to build in the class. I have to admit it was a bit of a struggle to not force my students to begin to look at actions right away. I now doubt it would have had the same impact. By giving them time to understand the mission, letting them pursue their own areas of inquiry, the "action" part came naturally from them and it was much more impactful.
>
> – Murray Dee, Grade 6 Teacher, Rideau Heights Public School

In his story (p. 262), Murray describes a process of building knowledge within a class-generated category titled "Actions." Rather than immediately moving students into action projects in response to their emerging understanding, he first gives them time to probe the scope of what "action" might mean in the problematic context of global climate change. As the students mull over a wide range of reparative actions, from individual "micro-changes" (such as turning off lights) to larger-scale interventions (such as eliminating fossil fuels), they come to realize the complexity of actions and decisions within both personal and global contexts. One student remarks that even the categories of "micro" and "macro" changes are context dependent, not absolute – that what counts as a small act from one person becomes widespread when taken on by many. They become aware that, while many micro-changes are readily implementable on a personal basis, more systemic changes require more indirect tactics, such as writing persuasive letters to global decision-makers. The inquiry culminates in a Climate Expo, in which the class shares its learning with other classes and invites them to join in a school-wide venture dedicated to exploring and acting upon issues of climate change. Many months later, into a new school year, the students return to their old classroom to remind Murray of a tree-planting project still pending from the previous year. Finally, five trees are planted, that "represent the difference a single class can make, and provide shade, capture carbon, produce oxygen, and offer enjoyment for future students … for years to come" (p. 270).

Murray's story provides a compelling demonstration of "the transformative power of inquiry," as his students move from "compliance to engagement to empowerment" (p. 269). Their growing ownership over their learning slowly begins to translate into genuine agency in the real world. This story highlights how deeply enmeshed action and knowledge can be. A better grasp of the ramifications of possible actions deepens students' understanding of the problem they are trying to address. Conversely, as they learn more about climate change, their awareness of strategic and realistic action possibilities is expanded and made concrete.

Which comes first – environmental knowledge or environmental action?

One element common to each of the classroom examples is the importance of community, which develops through classroom learning but is deepened, strengthened, and expanded as groups of students jointly participate in actions to build a sustainable world. These examples also show how knowledge and action support each other; either can serve as the starting point (main goal) for an inquiry. Neither Mike's nor Murray's inquiries into climate change begin as action-oriented investigations; their students are motivated to take on action projects only after delving into the issues from many different viewpoints. In contrast, the Grade 4s and 5s at Rose Avenue Public School start with a clearly defined action project – to design and create an edible garden for their school. However, to succeed in this requires a great deal of thinking and learning about gardening and nutrition. In the case of the salmon restoration program, the explicit goal from the start is to repopulate the local streams. With this as the driving focus of the learning, students engage deeply in inquiry that explores their questions and builds their knowledge about salmon, life cycles, and ecological health.

Regardless of the starting point, environmental knowledge and environmental action propel each other forward in an ongoing cycle of experience, reflection, informed action, and relevant new learning.

Environmental Consciousness and Social Justice: Building Connections

> A country and its values are measured not by the number of extremely wealthy people but by the state of its poorest and most vulnerable. Many environmental problems are tied to societal inequities – hunger and poverty, chronic unemployment, absence of social services, inadequate public transit and often conflicting priorities of corporations and the public interest – as people at the lower end of the socioeconomic scale are disproportionately affected by environmental hazards and toxic pollution.
>
> – David Suzuki, "Environmental Rights are Human Rights" in *Science Matters* (January 21, 2016)

Many environmental issues are closely related to imbalances of wealth and power in human societies; a disproportionate number of those most severely affected by environmental devastation are poor, Indigenous, of colour, or otherwise disenfranchised. No integrated study of water, for example, can easily ignore the human side of such environmental catastrophes as the aftermath of Hurricane Katrina, the pervasive problem of contaminated water in Ontario's First Nations communities, or the global dispersions of climate change refugees. In deciding how to most effectively draw attention to the connections between environmental and social/political issues, it is useful to first probe students' own understandings of these matters. The following discussion with Grade 5 students provided their teacher with a glimpse into how they thought about the issue.

Educator: Looking at the UN sustainable development goals (there are 17 in total), #1 is "no poverty" and #2 is "zero hunger." But why, if we are worried about the environment, are poverty and hunger sustainable development goals? What do poverty and hunger have to do with the environment?

Student 1: If no one has any money or food, how can they help with the environment? Then you can't do anything about it, so that's why climate change is number 13.

Student 2: Imagine where you and your family barely have any food. I mean, it's hard to imagine, but imagine that you are living in poverty … and you're, like, what can I do to help the environment? It takes down confidence. Sometimes people have to use cheating ways and they can't really go buy things that are more environmental….A lot of people can't afford that … you are kind of stuck where it's hard to do both at the same time, where you really want to focus on having food three times a day, maybe even once a day, so you have to take shortcuts that don't necessarily involve thinking about the environment.

Student 3: Quality education might be fourth because you need people to be educated about the problems we're having, like pollution and stuff and all the climate change. We need to be educated to teach other people about the problems in the world so they can change them.

Student 4: I think clean water should be #1 or #2, with food. I think quality education should be fifth. To make your argument better, you need education, but to get education you need clean water, food, good health so your brain can develop and you can take in information.

Student 5: In my opinion, I think climate change should be number 1 because these problems that we have aren't anyone else's fault, but all these problems [poverty, hunger, etc.] or most of them only affect our species. But, like, now we've created a huge problem that aren't just affecting people who have made the problem but also other species, so I think we need to fix that. 'Cause, like, if you made a mistake that affected other people, and then you also make a mistake that affected you as well, which one would you fix first? I would fix the one that affects other people as well as me.

In their responses, we see clearly the scope and limitations of their thinking. Four students are making an effort to imaginatively project themselves into the situations of individuals with different life experiences from their own, considering the impact of poverty, health, and education on environmental choices. In different ways, they all suggest that poverty and malnutrition will limit the capacity for sustainable living. Their thinking is still largely on an individual human level rather than on a more systemic scale. The fifth student makes a moral argument for moving beyond species-centred thinking, but perhaps downplays the human dimension. In this introductory conversation, students have not yet begun to identify a direct link between environmental problems and social justice issues. This information will help their teacher to figure out the most accessible and relevant level of analysis to begin to nudge their thinking in new directions.

Inquiring into wants and needs

As any parent or educator knows, fairness is a topic of passionate importance for children. At all levels of development, therefore, issues of fairness provide a natural starting place for thinking more broadly about social and environmental justice. Educators often find that issues of justice touch deep chords in students.

Viewing human consumption through the lens of wants and needs can provoke fruitful conversation at all ages, though the complexity of children's understanding is often tied to development. Asked for their ideas, a class of Grade 5 students listed "needs" that included food, water, clothing, medicine, education, and shelter; "wants" included computer games, TVs, and the internet. Grade 6 students showed a far more sophisticated understanding, expanding the binary distinction into four categories: **wants** (jewellery, toys, fancy phones), **needs for survival** (food, water, shelter, clean air), **needs to function in society** (jobs, a sense of belonging, democracy, education) and things considered **helpful but not essential** (money, computer access, expressing your opinion, play). Beginning to think about consumption in these terms offers a productive starting point for working out realistic and balanced ways to tread more lightly on the Earth.

Building empathy: A foundation for activism

The ability and impulse to take a stance on environmental and social issues begins with the developing capacity for imaginative identification with other lives and other ways. Empathy demands an attentiveness to others that includes both awareness and feeling, and educators can make it a priority to foster cognitive perspective-taking and the feelings of care that ideally accompany it. By elementary school, most children are able to identify with people who are not present or whom they may not personally know. In later childhood, this empathy can be extended to include more distant individuals, groups, or even societies as a whole. But without a classroom culture of care and kindness, it is much less likely that many children will show the inclination – at school, anyway – to assume their share of responsibility for the well-being of other lives beyond their own.

Empathy and resilience

With empathy come strong emotions. As children become acutely aware of the inequities and violations perpetrated among people as well as on our planet, they need time to process this difficult knowledge and come to terms with their own distress. It is reasonable and appropriate to respond to tragic events with fear, sadness, or rage; acknowledging and talking about these feelings respects their legitimacy. Naturally, we don't want to leave children mired in depression or anger, but when we move them too quickly from mourning into action and positivity ("We don't have to feel sad – let's just do something to make it [ourselves feel] better"), we risk sending a message that strong negative emotions are too threatening to safely experience or contemplate. The resulting expense of energy required to suppress such feelings can lead to detachment, anxiety, and a reluctance to engage with difficult emotional realities, as Joanna Macy (1995) has persuasively argued.

To actively participate in caring for the world beyond themselves, children need resilience as well as empathy. This resilience is built in part through facing and dealing with challenging but manageable emotional experiences. As educators or parents in today's world, we will sometimes be faced with critical decisions about how much and what kinds of information our children are ready to safely and productively engage with. Our well-intentioned efforts to shield them from all sources of potential pain do them no favours, yet we also need to be careful that an overload of frightening information does not end up alienating them from the very world we hope to connect them with.

As with many aspects of teaching, finding a balance is the challenge, and reading our students' emotional responses to their learning may be the most important form of assessment we practice. In the end, it has been convincingly shown that a focus on the human benefits of sustainable living which stresses "positive, informative strategies" has a stronger effect on behaviour than fear- or guilt-provoking "apocalyptic doomsday narratives" (Strife, 2010, p.181).

Literature as a route to empathy

Among the many strategies for building empathy, stories provide a powerful entry point into other worlds and lives, and children's literature has been shown to offer an especially effective entry into difficult issues of equity and justice (Yokota & Kolar, 2008). Fictional stories in particular tend to more strongly promote empathic imaginative absorption than argumentative or informational texts (e.g., Oatley, 2011). In narratives that possess this power to draw an audience into their frame, the implicit or unspoken is often as important as what is said; stories do not always need to explicitly address a concern to elicit empathic involvement. At all ages, children expand the boundaries of their world from hearing a diversity of stories that foster their understanding of lives under different circumstances, both near and far, and help them develop a fine-grained awareness of the commonalities and differences among us.

Opportunities to write or tell stories of their own – both personal and fictional – also help to develop children's critical perspective-taking abilities. Identification with animals is one of the very earliest manifestations of environmental empathy in children, and one that is closely connected to their developing imaginative and narrative capabilities. As Brenda Peterson puts it, "By telling their own animal stories, children are practicing ecology at its most profound and healing level. Story as ecology – it's so simple, something we've forgotten. In our environmental wars, the emphasis has been on saving species, not becoming them." (as cited in Sobel, 1998, para. 27).

Based in real events, biographical narratives that imaginatively pull a reader into the world of their subject also play a compelling role in building perspective and awakening the drive to make a mark in the world (Morgan, 2009). There is a rapidly growing body of wonderful picture book biographies of figures from all cultures and walks of life (among them naturalists and environmental crusaders), which provide realistic and inspiring models with whom children can identify. In Robin Shaw's explorations of Indigenous history and culture in Grade 4 ("Robin's Story," p. 234), biographies play a central role. As she puts it, "I tended to choose stories that represented life journeys characterized by adversity and challenge closely followed by empowerment and personal triumph. My experience was that when children heard stories of real people's lives, those journeys inspired in them compassion and open-mindedness …"

Branch IV: Moving Toward Sustainability

Thinking Developmentally

> What happens when we lay the weight of the world's environmental problems on eight and nine year-olds already haunted with too many concerns and not enough real contact with nature? ... My fear is that our environmentally correct curriculum will end up distancing children from, rather than connecting them with, the natural world.
>
> – David Sobel, "Beyond Echophobia" in *Yes! Magazine* (1998)

David Sobel has laid out some simple, developmentally informed guidelines for environmental educators. In early childhood (ages 4-7), children's worlds are still quite small, centred in their home, school, and immediate community. The main aim of environmental teaching at that age is to foster empathic bonds with nature. This may include the use of stories, songs, movement, and play to help children identify with and care for animals, such as imagining what it feels like to be a bird or looking after a snail. Bringing animals into the classroom – even for limited periods of time – is a sure way to evoke both deep fascination and caring ways. "And so we must begin in empathy, by becoming the animals so we can save them" (Sobel, 1998, para. 27).

By middle childhood (ages 8-11), rich curriculum responds to children's drive to explore beyond the known, to find independent ways of being in the world, especially the wilder world, beyond familiar experiences contained within adult-defined boundaries: building forts, following streams, hunting and gathering, planting, caring for animals, map-making, treasure seeking. These kinds of independent explorations build the necessary confidence and resourcefulness for children to develop and act upon their ideas. This emphasis does not suggest that children of this age (or even younger) do not also care about perceived injustices, but rather reminds us that their concern typically remains on quite a small scale, largely through empathic identification with individuals (even those far away), rather than through engagement with the abstractions of global systems.

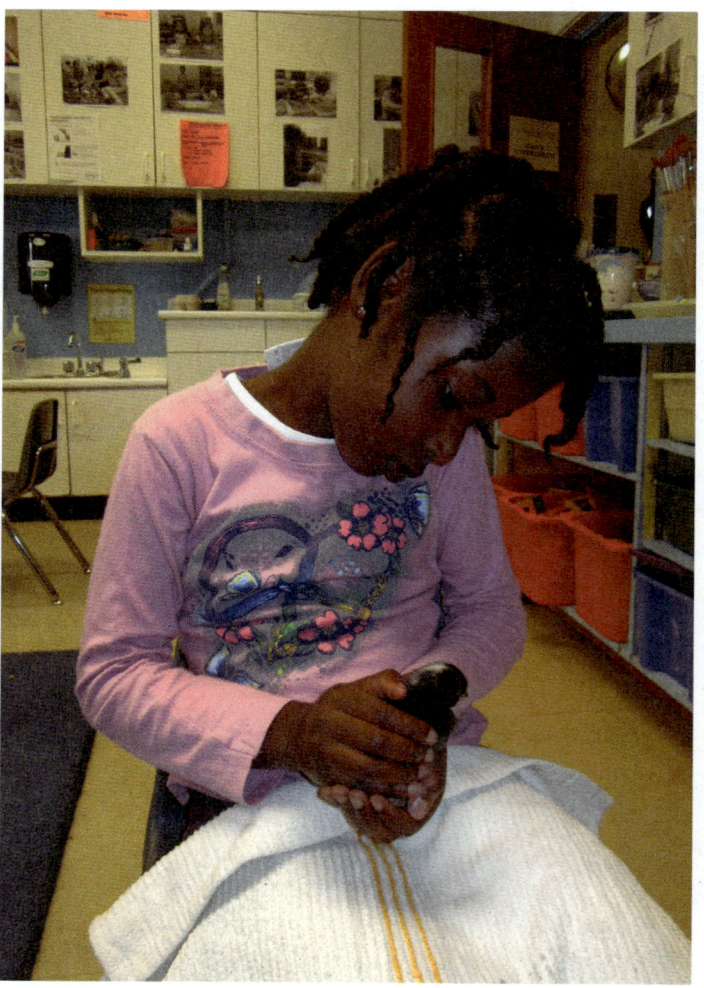

By the ages of 11 or 12 and beyond, idealistic social action becomes a driving force. This is the age of emergent activism, in which children respond both passionately and analytically to both local and systemic inequities, building on the independence and resourcefulness developed in middle childhood. By sixth grade, they are strongly aware of themselves as independent agents within an interconnected web of relationships, with opinions that may be starting to diverge from those of the adults in their lives. At this age, students' hunger to make a difference in the world provides fertile ground for their learning.

The beauty of inquiry is that an attentive educator is unlikely to stray too far from the developmentally informed concerns and interests of the students. In that sense, responsive curriculum is inherently developmental. By equipping themselves with knowledge of basic developmental trajectories, such as those proposed by Sobel, educators can better prepare themselves for some of the possibilities that are likely to emerge in their class.

How Do Children Understand Environmental Sustainability?

> Because children's experience of nature remains a vital and irreplaceable source of healthy development, nothing less than the future of our species is at stake in maintaining and, when compromised, restoring this relationship ... The crisis of deeply diminished connections between children and the biological basis of our humanity is too great for us to remain passive. The scale and scope of the problem calls for bold steps and a deeper understanding of what is at stake.
>
> – Stephen Kellert, "Reflections on Children's Experience of Nature" in *Children and Nature Network Leadership Writing Series* (2009)

Working within a sustainable model or taking action on environmental issues takes many forms. These include conscious acts of restraint, such as reducing consumption, and direct actions to sustain the land, such as planting native species or releasing salmon fry. Raising awareness in the community, raising funds to support sustainable projects, attending protest rallies, and engaging in concrete acts of advocacy are among some other possibilities for taking action.

While developments in science and technology bear their share of responsibility for today's environmental problems, they also remain a potent vehicle for solutions, and a child may aspire to gain the expertise to design ecologically sound technologies. Over their years of schooling, it is our hope that children will encounter possibilities for engaging in all of these actions and more. Environmental inquiry aims to develop in students a habit of seeking new perspectives on established practices, awakening them to the possibilities of innovation and creative problem-solving in response to the enormous environmental and social challenges we all face.

As they learn and develop, children's understanding of environmental agency and sustainability continues to broaden and deepen. Recognizing how their students perceive issues of sustainability will help educators determine which learning approaches are most appropriate. Simply asking them what they think may be a perfect starting place.

One Grade 2 boy wrote:
Conservation is about helping animals. Keeping stuff like plants, animals, and soil is important. Animals might die if we don't. Animals use trees for oxygen and to live in. Polluting water is bad for salmon. Putting garbage in the water is bad because fishies might die. They cannot breathe in dirty water. Please don't kill fishies by eating them or by throwing garbage in the water. Salmon are endangered so let's do something about it.

A child in Grade 5 offered:
Sustainability is, well, pretty much you're giving everybody what they need without future generations not getting what they need. So kind of making sure everybody gets what they need, but not taking away from what people in the future need.

Children's ecological identity – how they perceive their connection with nature – grows through all their experiences and learning, and strongly influences their commitment to sustainable practice throughout their lives (Chawla, 2009). The drawings and writings on the following pages offer some snapshots of how urban elementary school children situate themselves in the natural world. Additionally, across the great diversity of ages, topics, settings, and learning strategies, every educator's story in Part 2 illustrates ways in which children come to better understand the natural world and their place in it.

It is always worth remembering that the language we offer children will shape their perceptions. Norah L'Espérance, who works with the very youngest children at the Laboratory School, offers a few poignant words on how her thinking and teaching have evolved: "The more I've learned about ecology and the story science tells us of the unfolding universe, the more my language has changed in my teaching. When I talk about the planet earth, I no longer say, 'we are on the earth.' Now I talk about 'the planet that we're part of.' It's a small change in words, but a big shift in consciousness: we're not separate from everything else on the planet – we are actually, literally, completely a part of it."

Children Reflect on Their Connections with Nature

Grade 1

It's about when we went into this ravine kind of forest-y place and we got our pictures taken and we saw a snake and I held it and it was really cool. Nature is nice.

This is at my farm at my playground. I just like it because of the forest beside it. We love to play hide and seek there. We go to the bridge, we get our bathing suits and we go play in it. Since I love animals nature sort of means it's a home for animals. My relationship with nature is how quiet it is. It's another place where I go if I'm a bit mad at the farm. And then I get a bit of quiet time to play with my stuffies.

It's in my backyard and there's a swing set, a slide, monkey bars, a pool, and a sprinkler. Nature is where everyone can be free and play with nature. My relationship with nature is that you can play with it however you want.

My favourite place in nature is the swings in the park close to my house. The tree in the very middle of the two swings is my favourite tree because I can climb on it. Nature means where you can play and where you can be free. I like it because it's beautiful and I take care of it.

It's at school and there's a kid shooting a basketball. Nature means that animals shouldn't get killed. The forest shouldn't get killed.

Grade 3

I drew my family looking at things in nature. There's sun and a waterfall, making a rainbow. One thing I really want to know is, where do rainbows come from? I know it's when sun and water come together, but how? It feels good to be with nature, in the forest, by the water. It's relaxing.

I think nature is beautiful - the forest, the bright sun, all different kinds of animals. I feel very safe in nature. I know sometimes when animals are in the forest, people get scared. But I don't feel that, I don't know why, I just feel safe and happy and interested to see the animals.

I drew my favourite tree. It has the trunk of a birch tree and the blossoms of a magnolia, I combined my favourite parts of trees. Me and my friends are having a perfect time. The sunlight is coming out, just spreading, the clouds are purplish because I wanted to show there's just the perfect among of sunniness - not too bright, not too dark. There's stepping stones to cross the river. When you go in the river, the fish all come to you. I'm holding a bird's nest and the bird is flying toward it with found in its mouth. The flowers grow back immediately when you pick them, so you can pick as many as you want without feeling bad. It's a place where you can't throw away garbage because it gets composted right away, becomes beautiful soil.

This is how you get there. When you look up at the sun, all the butterflies come and lead you along the river. But only if you're going to be a good part of nature. Only people who are good in nature can find it. The garden is open in all seasons, and each season is perfect for the season. In winter, you can skate on the river without wearing a jacket, it's the perfect amount of cold.

I drew a secret garden behind a waterfall, full of plants and animals. If you touch a plant with the colour you want, the plants grow that colour. That's why it's a magical place. People can go there, but it's very hard to find. When it's night-time, the plants still glow. The garden only appears in spring and summer and there's never snow or cold. There's no fall, because the leaves never fall. When the garden's disappeared - in fall and winter - all the animals go to sleep for two seasons. When hikers go behind the waterfall, they don't see the garden, only rocks. Because when the animals sleep, the garden turns black, it stops glowing. It's the animals that control the garden. Nature means that you can be free - it gives you peace, air, and joy. And beauty and love.

I like everything about being in nature. Spotting animals, birdwatching, identifying species. Especially when you get to see really rare birds, it's cool. Nature is pretty much everything, it's everywhere. As a whole, we're not respecting nature. Because we're cutting down trees, killing animals, farming. You have to cut down trees to farm and you have to feed animals, and that destroys nature too. Eventually if you keep destroying nature, you won't be able to live. Terrible decisions benefit some people in the short term but nobody in the long term. All the Aboriginal people, they fit in with the environment, nature is important to them. It's another way to live.

Nature is a big part of the world and we have to respect it. And if we don't, it will be really hard for animals to live on the planet. If you made a list of the most dangerous animals, who kills the most, humans would be first. And mosquitos would be second because of the diseases.

What I like best about nature is just looking at all the things around you. You walk into the forest and you just pay attention and see all the interesting things in the forest. Like everything surrounding you. It's fun to see all the different birds and things. And then if you take pictures and show people, then they come to see them too. And then they take pictures and more people come to see what is so interesting. Some birds are really rare, really hard to see. But sometimes birds and animals are not so shy. Like in the Galapagos, where they haven't learned that people can be dangerous.

Branch IV: Moving Toward Sustainability

Grade 4

To me nature means peace, harmony, and a safe place to be and a place to relax.

To me nature means love as in shelter, home, food and this is provided for all kinds of animals. Nature means beauty as in leaves, vines, trees, bushes, and berries to decorate our future in a world of wonders. Nature means adventure as in climbing mountains, swinging on vines, finding animals you've never seen, eating berries, climbing trees, finding leaves, and jumping in puddles to make a future for your children. Nature means exercise, as in swimming, walking, running, dancing, skiing and jumping, which keeps us alive. Nature means live as in the trees give us clean air. The water grows our crops. The animals give us milk, eggs, and cheese. Habitats give us animals to eat. Trees give us logs to make cabins. Stone to make castles. Leather to make clothes and shoes. Feathers to make pillows. Trees give us paper and pencils. Water to drink. Nature is everything to me!

Grade 5

This is a picture of me fishing. I usually like fishing because my parents fish. I have a cottage and fish there and I find it relaxing and fun. When I was a little kid my Dad would fish, and then I would try to fish so I ended up like it. Every summer I go and fish. I think that my relationship in nature is that it makes me feel at home, because I've been in nature a lot. My grandparents have a farm and we used to have a cottage so I have a lot of memories in nature. When I'm out in nature fishing, I feel happy and I kind of feel like safe. It makes me calm and relaxed just to be in nature, sometimes fishing or doing something else. If you're feeling stress, it makes me feel calm and happy and forget about what's stressing me out. We have a responsibility to give back to nature. If you cut down a tree, then plant another tree. And try to be as eco-friendly as you can. Eco-friendly fishing is not wasting plastic, like no plastic worms. Like trying to use only biodegradable bait.

I have a park across from my house and I like to just go down there in the summer. I usually sit under the tree and look around. I can see little birds flying. Sometimes I go with my friends to the park, but sometimes I go alone. This drawing is just me sitting, looking out at all the people, having a picnic. Sometimes I sit against a tree just to think. I think about different stuff going on in the world and different stuff going on in my life. I think about life. It helps me concentrate and think about stuff because I'm not in my house, which can be really crazy with my siblings around. If you have a little bit of stress, like before a race or something, like when I have a race soon and that's kind of nerve wracking, and if I just sit down outside and think about it, it helps relieves the stress. Nature means that people can be free and have a way of looking at different colours. It makes me feel really grateful to have so much greenery around you. Being in nature makes you feel like you.

Nature is too amazing for all of our forms of communication. One aspect of Nature that inspired this drawing is colours. In the background you see dulled down colours because nature is a key to a door, your eye. When you open the door you see gorgeous colours and feel an undescribable feeling.

Looking Forward: Building Communities of Sustainable Practice

> Place-based educators do not dismiss the importance of content and skills, but argue that the study of places can help increase student engagement and understanding through multidisciplinary, experiential, and intergenerational learning that is not only relevant but potentially contributes to the well-being of community life.
>
> – David Gruenewald, "The Best of Both Worlds" in *Educational Researcher* (2003)

> Environmental education, with an expansive definition of environment, incorporates diverse perspectives of what it means to live well in a place…. Instead of conceptualizing the environment as a place where humans interact with ecological systems, the environment becomes a place rich with dynamic cultural, social, economic, political, historical contexts and perspectives that frame and construct the ecological processes within them.
>
> – Anna Cole, "Expanding the Field" in *The Journal of Environmental Education* (2007)

Coming around full circle, it is worthwhile to once more reflect upon the threads of agency, experience, connectedness and participation that run through all four branches (though to differing degrees). Inquiry begins in curiosity – the sense of wonder and the drive to find out more. Honouring curiosity as the dominant driving force of learning prioritizes student agency – in all its forms – and consequent student engagement (Branch I). This emphasis on agency and engagement resurfaces and is deepened in experiential learning, which provides essential opportunities for autonomous, playful, and meaningful engagement in the natural world (Branch II). In integrated environmental inquiry, the environment beyond the classroom provides the integrative context for learning. As students come to better understand their world through distinct though related disciplinary and perspectival lenses, it is the world itself that gives meaning to their learning and spurs the desire to understand more (Branch III).

Finally, this chapter (Branch IV) explores the combined potential of the three pedagogic approaches for bringing environmental learning back into the world as students gain the motivation and understanding to work toward sustainability as members of a wider community. Throughout the branches, the significance of community is an underlying theme – from sharing a common interest in the earliest years to building knowledge as a community of learners to envisaging the more global sociocultural, historical, and ecological contexts in which our children will eventually need to find their place. Especially at the elementary school level, finding ways to bring families into the school community extends learning beyond the classroom walls in ways that can have dynamic implications for our children and our planet. This final chapter concludes with a parent's memory of a Lab School outing. It suggests the depth and power, still relatively untapped in our schools, of Indigenous approaches to ecology, as well as to children and their learning. She evocatively conveys how people of different ages, interests, and histories briefly come together, united in their mission to better know a piece of land.

Tracy's Story – A Parent's Perspective

At the beginning of the school year, I joined my daughter's Grade 1 class on a field trip to a stretch of land alongside the Humber River in Toronto's west end. Led by urban Indigenous people who had been working with the land and members of the surrounding community, we were invited to learn about methods – based on Indigenous principles, knowledge, and practices – being used to heal the land we were about to explore. The children were invited to participate in a smudging ceremony and encouraged to give thanks to their natural environment by making an offering of tobacco on a rock, a tree branch, or a plant of their choosing. They were remarkably uninhibited by what must have been a new experience for most of them, dutifully accepting the smoke of burning sage to wash over them as a classmate walked from child to child holding it in his hands.

One of our guides laid down a fish he had just caught from the river, revealing to us the life existing just beneath the surface of the nearby water, taking care to acknowledge it as a gift from nature to give sustenance to the people. We then began to walk along a path beside the riverbed, interwoven with brush and bramble amidst the graffiti-covered concrete posts of the bridge that towered above us. As our guides described the plants growing along the path and their traditional uses for food and medicine, such as the wild sumac known for its antiseptic properties, I wondered if the children fully grasped that this project of healing nature extended beyond the earth, rock, and brush into the people of the surrounding communities. They were happily engaged, playing freely amid the grass and brush, occasionally stopping to listen attentively to descriptions of plants and even taste the odd one, and I realized that they were taking in what was important and relevant to them. We were immersed in an experiential lesson based on Indigenous ways of knowing and being that revealed to us the inherent connections we all have with our environment. It was a dynamic that we could feel just by touching the earth, tasting the fruit of the plants, and breathing the fresh air into our lungs. I do not think this was new or unfamiliar to the children. It was natural and totally accessible.

I also realized that the principles our guides were sharing were not given to the children and attending adults to be consumed or adapted. We were simply recognizing the land with each other, and then walking out into that land to reflect upon our relationship with it, and the plants, in the new ways we were seeing them. The full impact of this experience occurred to me just over a year later, when I returned to the same stretch of land with my daughter and witnessed the incredible change that had occurred since we had last been there. Dog strangling vines and other invasive plants removed, the river bed no longer littered with trash, the space was alive with the spirit of people coming together, united by the desire to learn, grow, and simply live in harmony with each other and the land.

Breathing with the World:
Applied Learning Through Reciprocity
Indigenous Lens on Branch IV

Breathing with the World

If we have been able to find some spark that lights the learning process, if we can find a way to stand more firmly in our place, and if we can gather in that place and begin to assemble our knowledge, then we have a powerful basis for acting in the world. The application of our learning now becomes a living, breathing way of life.

All of Life Is Breathing Together

Indigenous cultures place great value on reciprocity. This value is expressed through cultural practices of giving when we need to receive something. In many Indigenous cultures, people offer tobacco or some other "gift" for what they seek, whether that gift be food or medicine from the land, or help with a ceremony. These offerings are not just about harvesting things from our environment, or celebrating a marriage, or asking for healing or knowledge from an Elder. They are a way to give thanks for everything that is given to us, including our own lives and the Spirit that flows through everything around us. Ultimately, these offerings are a way to recognize our affiliation with all the gifts of Creation.

Reciprocity is not just a cultural tendency. Nor is it a mere recognition of the importance of symbiosis and ecosystems.[1] It is a sacred law. We live in a reciprocal world, with reciprocal acts flowing around and through us at all times. Our reciprocal nature is expressed in every second of our lives, in each breath of every creature and plant in Mother Earth, in the dance of water with rock, and in the movement of subtle forces through all things, including how our own thoughts and feelings interact with and affect the world around us. The interdependence symbolized in the ongoing exchange of air and other elements is absolutely unavoidable. We are responsible to all things around us, not out of superiority to them, but because we are part of them, and cannot be safely disconnected from them. Our lives need to be an expression of this truth: whenever we take something – and we are always taking something – something should be given back. If we can live this truth, every facet of human cultural expression, from the economic to the artistic, reflects the vital question: How do we live in thanksgiving and reciprocal action, in ways that extend in every direction?

Cultivating a sense of gratitude and reciprocal practice in our lives is not merely a matter of mimicking Indigenous cultural practices, such as offering tobacco, as appealing as these practices may be to some. It is problematic for various reasons to appropriate Indigenous ceremonies without any holistic cultural context. Participation in such rituals is not restricted by ethnicity; however, these practices can be rendered meaningless if a deeper sense of them is not developed through ongoing exchange, understanding and relationship with the world around us, and with Indigenous people and principles.

Even if we are unable to connect with an Indigenous cultural context, we can all ask: How do we grow from a rootedness in our own place and context into a life of gratitude, a collaborative life with everything around us? Living out the answers to such questions can and should be the work of educators, children, and all of us.

It Is Not About Stewardship of the Environment

Because the terms "nature" and "environment" as commonly used do not reflect an Indigenous sense of place, they also lack the ability to support Indigenous ways of thinking, doing, living, and being. Such terms tend to objectify material aspects of the world, ignoring our spiritual connection to everything around us, and robbing us of a deeper relationship with our place.

Modern science tends to be about controlling nature through a kind of vaunted expertise available to only a few. Human control of nature tends to bring a sense of superiority over, and separation from, nature-as-object. This human control over the natural world is also closely tied to Eurocentric notions of stewardship, where humans take care of particular parts of nature by protecting them from human activities narrowly dedicated to material "progress" (reflecting the artificial dichotomy between nature and economic survival). Certain human "stewardship" activities (often belonging to a compartmentalized "environmental" focus) are promoted to contribute to a sustainable future, but the whole of society

---

[1] Modern science writers may be tempted to reduce Indigenous ceremonies to a kind of superstitious affirmation of obvious, mundane scientific realities, when in fact ceremonial functions are higher rather than lower reflections of truth. Symbiosis is no mechanical "accident" arising from below, but is rather a reflection or outer symbol of higher principles.

is not really engaged much beyond this level of particular causes that only reach part of our lives. Although well-intentioned, attempts at sustainable lifestyle practices in this context are far from being a way of life, or the basis of living.

Practicing reciprocity means more than just "stewardship of the environment" – as if nature were something apart from humans. If we do not help our children grow into an awareness that expands beyond our usual modern notions of nature, we leave them with superficial survival tools for the future. "Saving nature" as an outsider to nature, a thing from which we are alienated, becomes a daunting and hopeless burden. We are more likely to entrust the work to experts and reduce our own participation to the humdrum level of consumers, sorting our recycling every week or investing in a low-flow toilet. As alienated from the land as most of us are, our best efforts may not go further than planting trees through a "stewardship" program.

Indigenous awareness of our complete dependence on nature leads to a sense of unity with what is around us in ways that necessitate reciprocity and cooperation with the environment as a way of life. Every aspect of living – physical, emotional, intellectual, and spiritual – reflects the sense that we are helpless without our expansive family, which includes all our relatives in Mother Earth – water, minerals, soil, air, fire, plants, animals, our fellow humans, and many beings and levels of existence we cannot see – and ultimately leads beyond what we consider existence, beyond all forms or ideas.

> First Nations people view themselves not as custodians, stewards or having dominion over the Earth, but as an integrated part in the family of the Earth. The Earth is my mother and the animals, plants and minerals are my brothers and sisters.
>
> – Henry Lickers, Environmental Biologist of the Seneca Nation, as cited in *Lessons in Learning: The Cultural Divide in Science Education for Aboriginal Learners* (2007)

It Is About Family and Intimacy

Eurocentric notions of stewardship disappear through an Indigenous lens. Even the term "sustainability" fails to really capture what would be implied, since this term is often limited to looking at natural resources, that is, how we might more responsibly consume some *thing* that is apart from us, extracted from elsewhere. We need to ask rather: what would be different if we lived with a strong sense that *water, land, all of the world around us, are relatives*? What if we *love the world* around us deeply, as our family? Our actions would then begin to reflect reciprocity in how we live and move in any direction, including seven generations into the future. Rather than *contributing* to a stewardship *cause*, we would *ensure balance in all our interactions with the world around us*, through space and time.

Where modern conceptions of ecosystems suggest that nature consists of *things* that must be *protected from us*, Indigenous reciprocity is an *intimate relationship with* a living universe – familial respect, a *daily exchange* with a river or a forest or field (or even a room full of people or a high-rise apartment building) and the many layers of beings there. It is about *engaging in and using* the world around us *more, not less*, but in a reciprocal manner, in ways that can actually regenerate balance in our environment.

Our reciprocal relationships with the world should inform all human activity. To take the example of governance, a Eurocentric stewardship lens tends to focus us on how we manage the environment more effectively – as if "the environment" could be a government department. But through an

Indigenous lens we ask instead, "How do we live with respect and humility for all our relations?" This has profound implications for decision-making structures. Who speaks for the water? Who speaks for the birds or soil, and so on, not out of bureaucratically assigned roles, but out of a deep *identification with that water, or with those birds?* (Perhaps one who was gifted with a song for the birds as a child.) And how do such people speak for all aspects of Creation, not merely as resources, but as sacred, as having being and life and value in themselves?[2]

Erasing the false dichotomy between humans and the rest of nature resolves many issues that seem most challenging to Eurocentric thought. And so we have to ask: how can we help children develop a culture where they have an ongoing, intimate, and deeply informed relationship with their environment, rather than a sense that their environment must somehow be *protected from them, and managed by experts?* How can we help future generations shift from suffering with the burden of "stewardship for the environment" to a life of active participation in, coupled with deep love and respect for, Mother Earth?

The Challenge: Learning Reciprocity

Everything changes if we shift from asking how we foster stewardship in children to asking how we help children relate to their world, love their world, and value reciprocity with all our relations. This includes approaching a life of mutual collaboration as a higher guiding value, in every direction and every sense. This expansive reciprocity seems daunting but it is absolutely approachable. It brings the classroom to life in ways that may surprise us. Branch IV of Natural Curiosity suggests principles and practices that can help students to move in this direction. The observation is made that children's love for the natural world is comparable to the bonds that characterize close kinship. This observation is linked with other ideas found in this resource. For example

- The idea that building a positive relationship with nature (through experiential learning) is an important foundation for stewardship and sustainability.

- The idea that learner agency (through an inquiry-based approach) lies at the centre of meaningful engagement with the world.

Placing an Indigenous lens over these ideas in relation to helping children develop a wider, lasting sense of reciprocity is challenging – but this challenge is necessary today, and greatly enriches learning. And so, we are faced with the exciting possibility of working with Indigenous people as allies in bringing a paradigm shift to life through our children.

One of the greatest challenges of learning reciprocity – and potentially the most richly rewarding for educators, students, and their families – is to build the practices of experiential, inquiry-based learning into a community-building approach. The idea of contributing to community knowledge is magnified, it even explodes, if we tie it into an expanded resurgence and empowerment of community, and to a sense of the whole world as our family. What can we learn from the idea of community seen through an Indigenous lens?

Weaving Communities

> Service to the community is paramount for Indigenous value systems. The individual does not form an identity in opposition to the group but recognizes the group as relatives (included in his or her own identity). Education is to serve the people, not individual advancement or status.
>
> – Eber Hampton, Chickasaw Nation, Oklahoma, *Toward a Redefinition of American Indian/Alaska Native Education* (1993)

The principle of reciprocity is reflected through an Indigenous sense of service to community that includes human and non-human community members. Our children need to become partners in maintaining balance across diverse systems – to enter into a loving and mutually beneficial relationship with all that surrounds them. Their health and survival depend on their ability to be in healthy communion with their world. This is not the way most modern humans (including many Indigenous people) generally feel about the world, or act, today; but from any traditional Indigenous

---

[2] This is not as utopian or far off as it might seem; for example, leaders from spiritual traditions around the world have signed a document titled the "Rights of Nature." While this document is not a complete reflection of Indigenous value systems and departs from them in some ways, it at least is significantly informed by those values.

(and some would argue any human) viewpoint, it is the normal way we are inclined to feel and act – at least, normal in the sense of how we would act if we were living in a healthy and balanced way.

And so in fairness to ourselves, we must begin by acknowledging that we too often live in abnormal, unbalanced ways, and that our relationships with the world in general are fractured. It can even be said that not only our sense of kinship with "nature," but also our sense of community with other humans is weak. Widespread human displacement, mobility, and the pace of living are certainly not contributing to any kind of stronger "village" life (with the sad exception of electronic ones). For many, we are not only detached from our relatives in the wider natural world; our extended human and even nuclear families are shrinking, and we have come to live in an increasingly atomistic reality. Indigenous wisdom traditions have always seen a direct correspondence between the breakdown of social and natural systems.

Learning for the future needs to be linked wherever possible with place-based community building. The way to re-weave community with the human and wider natural world is simple, if not always immediately practical given our current context: spend more time with them. Work and play together more – a lot more. For educators, this can be a relatively simple step, if support can be gained from school administrators and parents: rather than visiting a nearby park or landscape every once in awhile, visit every day, or at least several times a week. When there, get to understand it better. What makes it happy? How can we help? Does that make us feel better too? How does this relate to the way we get along with other people in our human family? (It is hard to develop a healthy, reciprocal sense of community with the world around us if we are not equipped to see our own human family in this way.)

> …[T]eachers need to provide their students learning experiences that are genuine and lead to real and measurable improvements not only for their immediate community but hopefully for the larger community as well.
>
> – Veronica Ignas, "Opening Doors to the Future" in *Canadian Journal of Native Education* (2004)

This assumes that there is at least some basis or possibility for community building; where this basis or possibility is extremely limited, educators may need to work on a much more rudimentary community-building process. "Stephanie's Story" at the Fraser Mustard Early Learning Academy, included in this resource, is a wonderful example of an inquiry-based, experiential approach to building the basics of community for a class of students.

Community Knowledge Building

Children exploring their place are likely to find that there is much that is needed, and much they can do to be a more integrated part of that place. Students can become researchers who explore their local environment-as-relative, connecting academic information with their own lived experience. Cindy's account in the educators' stories section of this edition about how her class came to explore local bird life provides a wonderful example of how deep seven-year-olds can go, even in a mostly concrete schoolyard. Cindy's example raises many exciting questions that can be explored immediately:[3]

- How can we explore the world around the school so that classroom activities support what happens outside, reversing the way we are usually conditioned to look at school (where we venture out mainly to find something to help meet curriculum expectations in the classroom)? For example, how can we build our own books, cataloguing the history, life, and being, right around our school, and our experiments in recovering them (including mathematical applications and scientific or artistic explorations of the process)?

- How can we extend an outdoor focus to demonstrate real reverence for the local area? For example, can school gardens go beyond planting random plants with no relationship to our area, or which often die over the summer? How can we explore our site in much greater detail – finding unique indigenous seeds, for example, and protecting diverse, endangered life forms through the re-creation of lost worlds that enrich us?

- How can we help children explore their community in ways that are shared across wider circles, with parents, grandparents, and other children in different grades or other schools (after all, nearby schools share the same place)?

- How does such exploration evolve into reciprocal relationships, through research that serves the community, including all our non-human relatives? How can various departments of universities support localized research on the ground, through ethical research frameworks that focus on local knowledge-building and capacity that stays in the emergent community?

With the help of educators and other adults, children can feel empowered to research, understand, and find solutions to restoring the world around them, to re-weaving their wider family of birds, plants, rocks, soils, insects, water, air – if they are given the opportunity to do it in ways that contribute to the healing and resurgence of all our relations, right where we live.

Relating to Everything, Using Everything

The greatest questions for our current age have to do with learning through relationship and mutual care. How do we help a community of children and families grow relationships with their local world in their own culturally specific ways, informed through ethical consultation and meaningful partnerships with regional Indigenous peoples, wherever possible? How do we help children reclaim the local world as their own family?

How, from a place of joy and *mino-bimaadiziwin* – living in a good way – do we relate to our local world and its gifts? How do we understand the ecological connections and the significance of various life forms, and how they relate to our past and future? We can begin by using that local world. We need to define sustainable harvest in ways that support more life and which give back to and enrich the participation of our local family of insects, birds, plants, waterways, and Spirit.

We need to ask, how do we not merely restore an ecosystem as something we must not touch, but rather, begin *using it every day*, through reciprocal relationships? It is a common modern misconception that the Americas were an "untamed wilderness" before the arrival of Europeans; in fact, Turtle Island has long been highly managed by Indigenous people. Indigenous management of nature has long been in place in northerly, forested regions as well as in densely populated agricultural areas. For example, oak trees were deliberately planted, and sugar maples purposely culled as saplings and used, for very specific reasons that serve both human and tree

---

[3] Not all at once, of course – and in many cases, only with support, flexibility, and participation from administrators, families, policy makers, and other local stakeholders around us, such as religious leaders, community agencies, and businesses.

nations. Indigenous people have long known that for every animal, there is a plant. Indigenous Elders with traditional knowledge know that using plants and animals in certain ways that are beneficial to humans also improves rather than harms the overall survival rate of those plant and animal relatives, and maintains balance in the world around us. We are – *we must be* – an integral part of the places where we live, or, through a lack of belonging there, we *will* destroy ourselves, along with much of the life around us. We are already well along that road.

Children need support to develop their own inwardly connected, active relationships with their place, and the skills to fruitfully and ethically engage with an expanding circle of life. This relieves well-meaning and devoted "environmental educators" of the grim tendency to focus learning, too early, on ecological collapse. It is not age-appropriate to give elementary schoolchildren messages, however subtle, that they are somehow faced with the need to "save the world." If we, as adults, struggle to face such a horrible burden, how hard must it be for an eight-year-old? This may be why so many of us have too long avoided facing – or preparing children for – the escalating devastation that is currently underway.

The burden of responsibility for the wider world comes later in life. We need to help children find an emotionally secure sense of unity and relationship and free movement within their immediate world. They need to know what parts of their place can be used, in ways that help their own small corner of the universe. They need to know all about the good things, the gifts they carry, and the gifts their world can give them, and begin to use those gifts, year after year, in cycles that quietly and incrementally *begin to clean the water or invite back a certain kind of bird*. Dying forests and rivers can be revived, but people need to walk into them and have a good time, and eat berries, and catch fish – or the world around us will continue to deteriorate. If we fail to engage and use our local worlds and regard them as sacred, they are more likely to suffer, to become garbage dumps overrun with invasive species.

If we can support children to engage in and use their world-as-relative, we set them on a path to radically rethink the spiritually vacuous, preposterous lifestyles that still drive us. If we can do this, we set them on a path to synchronize their lives and cultures and nations with the stars, in a dance which reflects and radiates a harmony that transcends human understanding. If we can do this in small ways, in many places, Mother Earth will be able to *breathe* well once more, and will cry with joy. Then, in ways we have long, long forgotten and can now barely imagine, *she will begin to sing to us again.*

Part 2
Environmental Inquiry in Action: The Educators' Stories

Teachers constantly adjust their models to fit their students and the changing realities of education. Through such constant and creative adjustment, teachers and students engage in a symbiotic relationship and form feedback loops around what is being learned. In this way, teachers are always creating their stories even as they are telling them.

– Gregory Cajete, *Look to The Mountain: An Ecology of Indigenous Education* (1994)

As with the first edition of *Natural Curiosity*, we invited educators to share their experiences with environmental inquiry. The new stories in this section have been generously shared by educators from the following schools:

Belfountain Public School is a public elementary school located in Caledon within the Peel District School Board. The focus of the school is environmental education and community citizenship. It supports a learning community of 160 students from Kindergarten to Grade 6.

Dr. Eric Jackman Institute of Child Study Laboratory School is an elementary school located in downtown Toronto, supporting a learning community of 200 students from Nursery to Grade 6.

Elmdale Public School is a public elementary school within the Ottawa-Carleton District School Board. Elmdale Public School is home to 500 students enrolled in French Immersion from Kindergarten to Grade 6.

Fraser Mustard Early Learning Academy is a Kindergarten public school within the Toronto District School Board. The school supports a learning community of 24 kindergarten classrooms with 675 students, 95% of whom speak a home language other than English.

The Grove Community School is a public alternative elementary school within the Toronto District School Board. This school, which focuses on environmental education, community activism, and social justice, is home to 130 students from Kindergarten to Grade 6.

Johnny Therriault School is a federally funded First Nation school located in Aroland First Nation, Treaty 9 area. This school offers an Ojibwe language program and supports the education of 90 students from Kindergarten to Grade 8.

McMurrich Junior Public School is a public elementary school located within the Toronto District School Board. This school supports a learning community of approximately 450 students from Kindergarten to Grade 6.

Mine Centre School is a public elementary school located near Fort Frances, Ontario. Students attend from three communities in Treaty 3 area: Mine Centre, Seine River First Nation, and Nigigoonsiminikaaning First Nation. This school is within the Rainy River District School Board, which partners with the Seven Generations Education Institute to offer Indigenous curriculum and language programs that support a community of 70 students from Kindergarten to Grade 8.

Rideau Heights Public School is a public elementary school located in Kingston within the Limestone District School Board. This urban school is home to 220 students from Kindergarten to Grade 8.

Stephanie's Story
Junior and Senior Kindergarten

Fraser Mustard Early Learning Academy, Toronto District School Board (TDSB)

Starting the Environmental Inquiry Process

In my Kindergarten classroom, the first inquiry of the year always begins with one question, "How will we become a community of learners?" With that comes a consideration of what my Junior Kindergarten and Senior Kindergarten students bring with them when they walk through the door. Some of my students begin the first day of school with little to no English, while for others, English is their first language. Some students have never been away from their parents while others have attended daycare since they were small. I have students on Individual Education Plans (IEPs), students with identified exceptionalities, and students who require support with self-regulation.

My role is to meet each student where they are and help them move forward in their learning. In the first few weeks it is hard to imagine how these 28 individuals, with their nine different languages and a broad range of learning needs, will come to care, respect, and respond to each other in the classroom. Yet, the value I put on establishing relationships – with each other, with the teachers, with the classroom and learning materials, and with the outside environment – helps make it happen. I believe that students must learn to live and play in their world together before they can share what they understand and know. They need to trust one another and feel safe in order to ask questions and share theories.

Setting the Stage

As I set up my room I use the furniture to create learning spaces for small groups of students and larger areas for collaboration, making sure there is room for 28 students to sit together comfortably. Next, I select and arrange materials in the learning areas that might be reorganized once I have a chance to see what the students are most drawn to in the classroom. I closely observe the students engaged in play, alone or with others, in this first week, planning how to modify the classroom to become a more comfortable space for the children. I consider questions about space (too much? too little?), traffic flow, noise, materials (too many? too few? too unclear?), and whether the overall space is inviting. I view the classroom as a living, changing thing, and respond to cues from the students that tell me what they need to feel safe, happy, and engaged at school.

This year I observed early on that my students were an active group that needed lots of movement. To establish trust, I always spend a lot of time getting to know them through play and classroom songs and games. I live on the floor for the first week, helping to build a train track or painting at the art studio. I model how to play and share. I engage the children in Sharing Circles at the end of the day, encouraging them to both listen to one another and express their own voice. Since holding something soft often seems to calm shy or nervous students, I offer a small stuffed animal for them to hold as they speak to the class at the start of the year. The child holding the stuffed animal is the speaker while the rest of us focus on them. I encourage students to directly address the child who is speaking, rather than look at me as they are talking.

For the first few Sharing Circles I don't record on my computer or notepad. I allow my focus to be fully on the students, again modeling the behaviour I want them to copy. Then I introduce the recording of their words. I explain how I will write down what they say because what they share is important. By then, the Sharing Circle routines are already established and though the computer might initially be a small distraction, it eventually fades into the background. After some time, I might provide a framework for our Sharing Circle by asking a question: "Who was nice to you today and why?" or "Who did you play with today and what did you play?" The Sharing Circle sets the stage for Knowledge Building Circles (KBCs), which will come later.

The Spark

The "Crocodile Game"

There comes a time in those first few weeks when there is a "spark." This year it happened during a game with large building blocks. I looked over and the entire class was talking and laughing on the big carpet, encouraging each other to play something they called the "Crocodile Game." It involved walking on the large blocks to avoid the pretend crocodiles swimming below. Rich in student voice through words and actions, the moment started with the students and ended with the students. This "spark" is what I value most about inquiry-based learning, when the joy in a shared experience and the process as a group is valued more than the work of the individual. I remember taking photographs of the process and going home at the end of the day thinking to myself, "We're going to get there. They're starting to care about each other. We're starting to get to a good place."

The next day I posted photos of the game on the wall at student height. They immediately noticed and began to talk about the photos with each other – "Remember the Crocodile Game? It was so much fun." This reflection on their learning together is important, as they begin to understand how much I value what they do together.

Flexibility and a space for large class collaboration is key to making this happen. This game happened at the end of the day, at a time when the students were supposed to be cleaning up and preparing to listen to a story. But I knew that the learning happening before my eyes was more important than any book I might read, and saved the book for the following day.

Witnessing more of these collaborative games during the week told me that the children were on the path to seeing themselves as a community of learners. Building onto each other's ideas, helping, encouraging, and talking – lots and lots of talking! The next step was taking everything that was happening inside, outside.

The Collaborative Indoor Games

Stephanie's Story: Junior and Senior Kindergarten

Getting Outside

Experiential Learning

As in the classroom, the students need to develop a trusting relationship with the outside spaces around our school; they need to feel safe. At first, they need to simply explore and play outside, taking time to experience their local environment before they ask questions and talk about it. Eventually, the children begin to explore these outdoor spaces more purposefully. I help to make this happen by giving children a lot of time outside – every day if possible.

Our school has a fenced-in space we call the "Learning Yard," shared among 635 kindergartners (at different times). Venturing out from this known space, we begin with small walks around our community, visits to the local public parks, and eventually hikes to the Don Valley ravine when we've worked up our walking endurance. You don't need a huge space to explore outside; a small patch of grass, a single tree, or a mud puddle can be all students need to explore. I always make sure to revisit the same locations.

Outside – A Short Walk Around Our Community

When we go outside, I model relevant language. Naming common animals and plants helps students who simply don't know the names for local wildlife. Walking in pairs encourages discussion while shortening the line. English-language learners may point and gesture with their hands, using facial expressions to communicate. Often another student will try to be their voice, for example, "She's saying the tree is so big!" Other times, students will pull me by the hand and excitedly point to an interesting object they've found. I label the item for them in English and they echo it back to me, for example, "Leaf."

As we take walks together, the students begin to tell me what they see and what they are thinking about. We start to bring back nature treasures for the classroom. A leaf, a feather, and a piece of bark are placed in our Discovery Area, honouring what the students find interesting. We also start to talk about ways of respecting the outside space, avoiding picking flowers or tearing branches off trees. Back in the classroom, during read-alouds or shared reading, I incorporate both non-fiction and fiction books related to what they have seen outside. The students start to tell me what they saw on their morning walk to school with their family. When trust, relationships, and experiences are all in place, inquiry will happen.

Discovery Area: November, December, and January

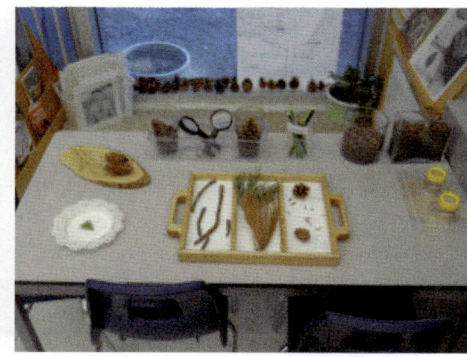

Outside - A Walk to the Don Valley

The Pine Cone Inquiry

Our first real student-driven inquiry emerged from one of our community walks. We came back with a brown maple leaf, a seagull feather, a cedar twig, a closed pine cone, and an open pine cone – five nature treasures to be displayed in the Discovery Area. The students observed the items, smelling and touching them, and talking about what they noticed and understood. Some students decided to sketch their favourite treasure. I recorded their observations and questions, noticing that the pine cones seemed especially interesting to many children.

The very next day something extraordinary happened that I wasn't at all prepared for (making the inquiry even better). At entry time a student noticed that the closed pine cone had opened up overnight. "Hey! Pine cones are both open!" The students called out to each other, wanting to share the exciting news with their friends. I knew that the next step was to have a Knowledge Building Circle (KBC) with the pine cones placed in the middle of the circle as the students shared their ideas, questions, and theories.

Discovering, Observing, and Sketching Pine Cones

Stephanie's Story: Junior and Senior Kindergarten

> **"What are the brown objects inside the tray?"**
>
> **Student 1:** Pine cones.
> **Student 2:** We had open and closed ones.
> **Student 3:** But we have two open now.
> **Student 1:** The one that was closed opened.
> **Student 4:** It growed.
> **Student 5:** Yeah, when everybody was sleeping it growed.
> **Student 6:** It opened up very quietly in night time.
> **Student 1:** It quietly wake up.
> **Student 7:** When people were sleeping they grow.
> **Stephanie:** Will the closed pine cone keep growing?
> **Student 5:** The night will come again and it will grow bigger and bigger.
> **Student 8:** No, because it's already big.
> **Student 6:** Because all of this cannot grow anymore.
> **Stephanie:** Can you tell me how you know that?
> **Student 6:** Because it don't move.
> **Student 9:** Because it's just like the pumpkin seeds, but it can't grow.
> **Student 6:** The pumpkins seeds are not growing anymore because the sun is gone.
> **Stephanie:** What did we need for the pumpkin seeds to grow?
> **Student 10:** Life.
> **Student 4:** Water.
> **Student 11:** Soil.
> **Stephanie:** If you think that the pine cone is growing, what might happen if we plant the pine cone?
> **Student 2:** I don't think it will grow.
> **Student 1:** I think it won't grow.
> **Student 12:** It won't grow.
> **Student 13:** It will grow bigger.

Integrated Learning

Examining Pine Cones Across Disciplines

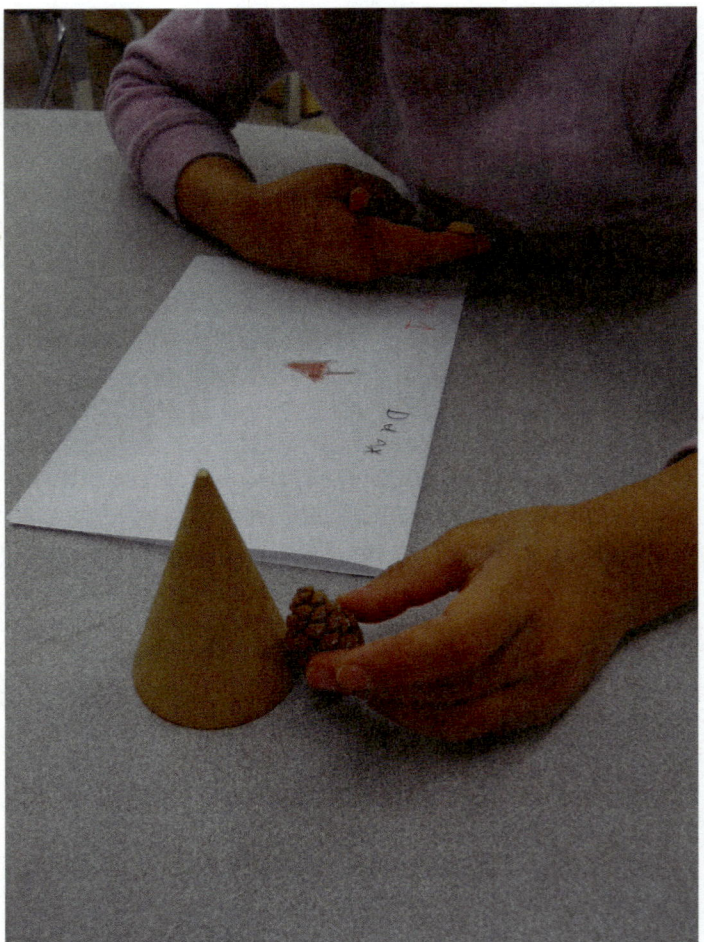

The students and I made a survey that asked what students thought about planting a pine cone in soil. I recorded their initial ideas about why the pine cone had opened and why they thought the pine cone would or would not grow in soil. At the end of the morning we read the survey. I reminded students that several different ideas in a single classroom is okay, and they understood that there was no right or wrong answer. The next day we got out soil and a cup and planted the pine cone that had opened up. I then encouraged students to record on a blank piece of paper the planting of the pine cone along with their ideas, predictions, or theories.

Our student-generated inquiry about the pine cones sustained itself over a long period because the learning that happened through the process was much bigger than just learning about pine cones. Students were learning about growth and change, trees and seeds, outdoor plants and indoor plants, and weather and seasonal changes. They were learning about experiments, research, sketching, and how to collect and read and survey data. Their learning process covered many expectations of the Kindergarten program, including literacy, visual arts, science, and math, as well as personal and social growth. As a community of learners, they were building on one another's theories and questions, and encouraging each other to share what they were thinking. One student, who had started the school year with little English, revisited the pine cone documentation in February, asking questions and sharing what she knew with her friends. With her new English fluency, she could better explain her thinking in complex sentences instead of using gestures, single words and drawings. She returned to a part of the inquiry process that was important to her and felt that she still had something to contribute as her friends encouraged and listened to her.

Documenting Our Learning About Pine Cones

A lot happens during an inquiry. Some days, other planned activities have to be put on hold. Knowing that all program expectations can be achieved through inquiry justifies these delays; inquiry is the foundation from which so much learning flourishes.

Continuing the Inquiry: November – January

A second nature walk to the same location unearthed six more closed pine cones, which we brought back to class. When three were observed to open up in the classroom, students sketched and recorded their ideas about what was happening. In a KBC, there was further discussion as to why some had opened while others remained closed. Students again sketched their observations as they compared the two types of pine cones.

One student decided to immerse an open pine cone in water overnight. When, in the morning, they saw that it had closed up, the children began to generate theories about what had happened. They conducted further experiments, leaving more pine cones in water, still wondering why they closed up each time.

As these investigations were continuing, some students noticed that our pumpkin plant had died. Why had it died? In a KBC focused on this question, the topics of weather and seasonal change came up, expanding the scope of our inquiry.

One day, students returned to school to discover that the three closed pine cones had opened up and "exploded," leaving the tray filled with tiny "things." Prompted by the question – "What came out of the pine cones?" – the consensus in our next KBC was that the small particles were seeds. Students concluded that the pine cones had failed to grow when planted because pine cones are containers for seeds rather than seeds themselves.

Changes and Differences Among Pine Cones

To help students organize their understanding of the sequence of observed events, I provided a template in which they recorded their ideas in columns labeled "First," "Then," "And," and "I wonder," with a blank space at the end for further theories or questions. This gave me new insight into their thinking.

One day, a student brought a small "mystery stick" to a KBC. After looking at, touching, and smelling the stick, students suggested that it might be connected to the pine tree because it smelled like a pine cone. This hypothesis was confirmed when we walked with this boy to where it had been found and, under a pine tree, discovered many similar sticks. As they continued to sketch their findings, they were developing a vocabulary to distinguish among pine trees, pine cones, pine needles, and pine cone seeds, and we read non-fiction books about trees in small groups. This culminated in a collaborative drawing of a pine tree, showing all they knew as they shared new wonderings (such as why some pine needles were brown and some green, or the differences and similarities between pine and cedar trees.)

Our questions were moving beyond pine cones. Another KBC focused on two questions: "What happens when something grows?" (to which some responded "it turns into something different") and "How do you know something is growing?" ("It has to be real.") Building on to the idea of change as turning into something different, students created a list of things that change, including weather, leaves, trees, pine cones, plants, people, and colours.

Growth of Student Ideas

This is where assessment fits into inquiry. I can compare KBC transcripts to see how student ideas change over the course of an inquiry. When it comes to individual student work, I keep notes on student theories and ideas on their work, having them periodically explain to me what they were thinking compared to what they know now. This self-reflective exercise, which often incorporates photographs of past work and a First/Then/And graphic exercise, allows students to show their understanding of their learning while leaving space for new possibilities with further questions, "I wonders…", or conclusions. While managing so much information and documentation for each child can be a challenge, I'm never worried about assessment when it comes to inquiry.

Reflecting on One's Growing Knowledge

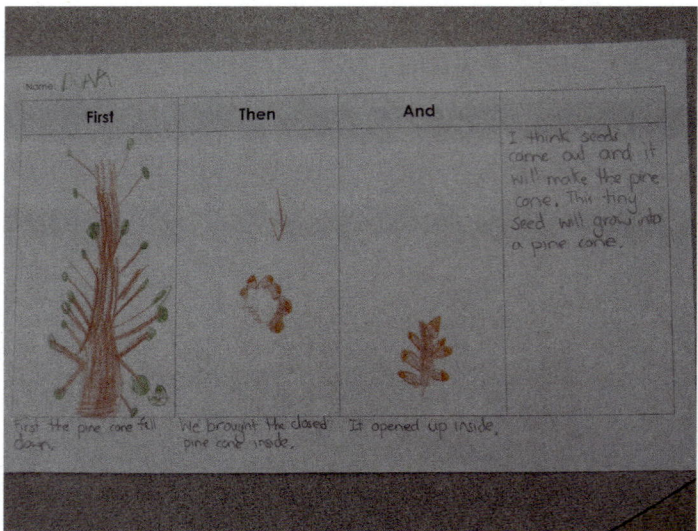

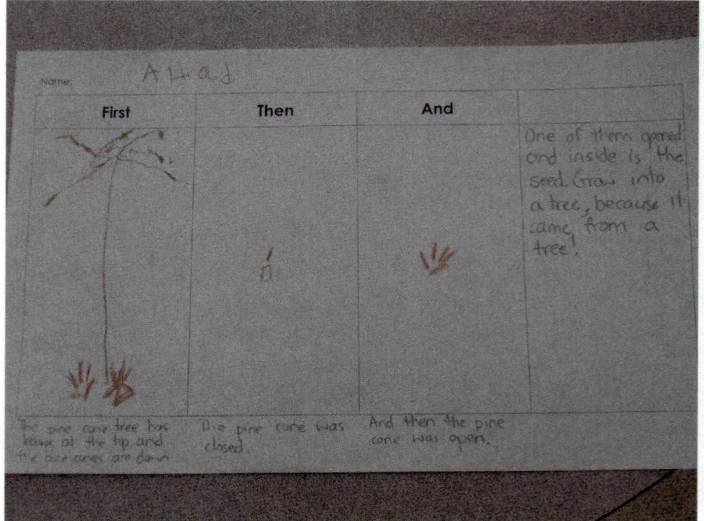

Our pine cone inquiry allowed students to dig deeper into their understanding of what makes something grow. For a long time, many students believed that the pine cone itself was a seed. They were shocked when they found the smaller seeds that popped out of the pine cones we brought inside. Now they had to think why the tree needed a pine cone for the seeds. Would the seeds grow into a tree or another pine cone? More questions, more theories, more research required. Once that was undertaken by researching more about seeds, the students began to articulate the cyclical nature of the pine tree. One student shared her observation in a KBC: "It came from a tree and the seed comes out and plants and a tree grows and then it, the pine cone grows and drops again and the seed comes out again and it just keeps going!" Students began to make connections to other living things we had observed in the classroom, such as our pumpkin seeds that we planted in November and the apple seeds we planted just before March break. The students in my class don't just learn something and move on. We revisit, reflect, and learn all at the same time.

Growth of Classroom Community

This snapshot of our pine cone inquiry demonstrates how student voice is honoured and always brought back to the classroom community. Someone can have a great theory or idea for an experiment, but it can't be in isolation. With three months left in the school year, we are at a great place with each other, while still working on maintaining the relationships and the trust. It's never-ending, just like inquiry-based learning.

Our Community

Marge's Story, with Sara, Glenda, and Gail

Junior and Senior Kindergarten

Mine Centre School, Rainy River District School Board (RRDSB)

The Outdoor Camp at Mine Centre Public School

The Lean-to in the Outdoor Camp

Starting the Environmental Inquiry Process

While our school is surrounded by forest, lakes, swamps, and ponds, we often fail to take full advantage of nature's closeness and the many wonderful opportunities there are for students to explore it. Wanting my students to engage with nature more deeply and become more active in inquiry-based learning, I had them embark on an environmental inquiry that would explore growth and change in animals through the seasons.

A short distance away from the school, we created a camp in the forest. Within our camp there are two lean-tos, a child-sized picnic table, an area for roasting wild rice, and a firepit with play cooking toys. Scattered throughout are student-created structures such as teepees and wigwams, and next to the camp are two flagged hiking trails. This camp has become a wonderful way to immerse students in nature, providing a space in which they can investigate how things work, why things happen, and what might be hidden beneath and within the forest. At the beginning of the school year, our school's cultural educator, Gail Jones, placed tobacco down at our camp as an offering, thanking the Creator for this place, and praying for the safety of students as we embarked on our learning in this environment. We collectively thanked the Creator for providing the trees, plants, and animals that we would be learning about, and the things we would be touching, digging up, or moving.

Looking in the Teepee

Observing a Frog

Our focus during visits to the camp has been on the effects of seasonal change on plants, animals, and people. Students are encouraged to both explore and respect the land and water, placing tobacco as a gift in place of things that are removed. To help students notice seasonal change, each student picked a tree to observe throughout the year. They described and labelled their tree by name, visiting it many times. As the year progressed, they chose a second tree to learn about.

In addition to weekly visits to the site itself, we expanded our explorations to other outdoor spaces, visiting a beaver pond and exploring a nearby lake. Early in the school year, a student found a frog outside the school entrance, providing an opportune learning moment. After observing the frog hop around, we took it inside the classroom. Some students wanted to keep the frog, while others seemed indifferent. After discussing its needs (Where would it sleep? What would we feed it?), the class decided to keep it in our classroom for the day, adding grass, dandelions, and water to a fishbowl. While some students seemed fascinated and watched intently as it breathed and moved, I found it disquieting that others showed no interest. I had assumed that these rural kids would be more aware of and curious about nature. It was then that I decided to make it a priority for my class to become more engaged with the world around them.

During our discussion I tried to connect the students to the frog's world, posing questions that were both open and focused, to get them thinking. Becoming a skilled questioner and taking the time to listen to responses are key strategies to encourage thinking and questioning and avoid controlling the conversation. Valuing and acknowledging the different ways in which each child contributes to the discussion is also very important.

A key part of these strategies is teaching students to listen to one another, often a challenge for young children. We have worked with the MindUp curriculum to help students be more mindful and practice some calming strategies, such as deep breathing and MeMoves. As the year has moved along, students' listening and inquiring skills have improved. They have been learning to stick to tasks and keep working when things became hard. Along with behavioural routines and expectations, these were all important processes to get in place at the beginning of the year.

As summer turned to fall, we noticed changes – leaves changing colour, flocks of birds preparing to migrate, and temperatures beginning to cool. On our treks to camp, we often stopped to say "Hi" to a cow in a neighbouring field. By the end of the fall, this cow was no longer there. One student's suggestion that the cow was dead led to a discussion about raising cows for food. We talked about how people and animals get ready for winter, and considered the traditional fall harvest activities our cultural educator had planned. During these festivities, parents and volunteers roasted wild rice, made fry bread, organized a nature scavenger hunt, and built structures. Our school secretary, a master gardener, showed us photographs of the food she harvested from her amazing gardens.

We focused on the bear, duck, and beaver getting ready for winter, learning about what it looks like inside a beaver lodge, a beaver pond, and a bear den. Full of questions, students expressed a wish to see inside the beaver lodge next to our playground. We walked to a nearby lake and watched the ice forming along the shore, observing natural ice sculptures that had formed on rocks and low tree branches as the waves splashed up. This year, the snow failed to arrive until the end of November, which was unusually late in the season.

Hiking down to the camp one day, a group of students saw a white rabbit. Because there was no snow on the ground, the rabbit stood out against its background, yet it behaved as if it were camouflaged and allowed us to come close. This got us thinking: "Why was the rabbit white already? Shouldn't there be snow on the ground before it turned white?" With that, our next inquiry began. We set out to learn about rabbits, or "wabooze," as they are called in Ojibway.

A White Rabbit

I always begin an inquiry by eliciting what students already know and identifying any misinformation they may have. From there I determine our next steps, often using backwards planning. Sometimes it is a challenge to give up control of a plan and go where the students are leading, or to admit that you don't always have answers to their questions. While small-group discussions often seem more productive for students of this age, large-group conversations can sometimes be richer as ideas springboard off each other.

Following this methodology, we began our inquiry by talking about what children knew about rabbits, recording a series of large-group discussions. Then, working in small groups, students drew a picture of a rabbit while sharing their ideas. It was intriguing to see what emerged from these discussions, including the beliefs that rabbits hibernate or climb trees, but the children were able to delve more deeply into the inquiry as a result.

> **"What do you know about rabbits?" – Seasonal Change**
>
> **Student 1:** Rabbits hibernate.
> **Student 2:** Rabbits turn brown and white.
> **Marge:** When do they turn brown and white?
> **Student 2:** In the summer they turn white and brown. In the winter they turn all white. I have seen a rabbit.
> **Marge:** Have you seen a brown and a white rabbit?
> **Student 2:** Yeah.
> **Student 3:** Rabbits can jump high. Jump as high as me.
> **Student 2:** Jump as big as a giant.
> **Student 4:** Rabbits can jump up to here.
> **Marge:** What else do we know?
> **Student 4:** They are good hiders. They hide in a hole.
> **Student 5:** They hide behind people.
> **Marge:** We already said they can turn brown or white. How can they hide in the winter?
> **Student 4:** They hide in a hole.
> **Marge:** How does being white help them hide in the winter?
> **Student 5:** They can hide in the winter.
> **Marge:** How do you think rabbits turn white?
> **Student 5:** The snow makes them white.
> **Student 1:** They hide and the snow makes them white.
> **Marge:** Remember when we saw the rabbit, was there snow on the ground?
> **Student 3:** There was no snow on the ground.
> **Marge:** [Student 5] is saying they are turning white because of the snow. What do you think?
> **Student 2:** Maybe 'cause they just turn white on their own.
> **Student 6:** Probably turn brown in the summer and they turn white in the winter.
> **Marge:** So why do you think they turn brown in the summer?
> **Student 6:** The white wears off in the summer.
> **Student 2:** It's because of the snow they turn white.
> **Student 6:** Yeah, it's because of the snow too.

"What do you know about rabbits?" – Eating Habits

Marge: What else do we know about rabbits?
Student 7: They can jump.
Student 2: They are little bit fast runners. They hop too. They went in the bushes.
Marge: Have we seen where they hopped?
Student 6: Yeah.
Student 4: They hopped in their bunny hole.
Marge: How did we know they were in the bushes?
Student 4: We saw the tracks in the road.
Student 3: We sawn a bunny at the camp.
Student 2: I saw the tracks.
Marge: How did the rabbit behave that you saw?
Student 3: He just sat there. The bunny turned white all by itself. It was sitting still.
Marge: At first you told me you thought it was a white garbage bag.
Student 4: Yeah, we thought it might be a white bag.
Marge: When you went closer, what made you decide it was a rabbit?
Student 4: Because it had fur.
Student 3: It hopped.
Student 2: And we saw the ears.
Student 3: And we saw the fluffy tail.
Student 4: And when we got really closer, he started hopping away.
Marge: A while ago we tied some carrots to a stick. Did the rabbits eat the carrots?
Student 4: But he still didn't eat the rotten one [hung there for a long time].
Student 2: No.
Marge: I'm wondering why. What do you think?
Student 6: Because you peeled the skin off the carrots. They like the skin. Rabbits don't peel the skin off, they just eat it off.
Marge: Oh, just like we noticed the branches with the bark nibbled off. Is that how they eat carrots, just nibble off the skin?
Student 6: Yeah, they eat off the skin.
Student 3: Yeah, they eat the skin.
Student 5: They eat the carrot with the skin on.
Marge: What do other kids think?
Student 8: We have been taking pictures of rabbit tracks at camp and pictures of rabbits.

"What should we try to do to see a rabbit with our trail camera?"

Marge: We tried to get pictures [of rabbits] on our trail camera. But we haven't yet.
Student 5: Sneak up on it and take a picture.
Student 4: We could hide on it and when he's jumping, take a picture of it.
Student 6: But we can't see the trail.
Marge: We know what bunny tracks look like. Should we put our camera where we see tracks?
Student 3: Yeah.
Marge: That sounds like a good plan. If we hide like [student 4] is suggesting, we might have to sit there for a while. How can we not let the rabbit see us?
Student 4: We should wear bunny ears like him.
Student 3: What!
Student 4: And make a bunny costume.
Marge: When we go to camp tomorrow, we will set the camera up where we see tracks and maybe we should give it some food. We know they don't like carrots. We tried it. What should we feed him?
Student 4: Carrots.
Marge: But he doesn't like carrots.
Student 4: Marshmallows, the colour like him.
Student 6: Hot dogs.
Marge: Rabbits are going to eat what they see out in the bush. Would they see marshmallows?
Student 4: No.
Marge: Hot dogs?
Student 3: No.
Marge: What would they see out there?
Student 2: A moose.
Student 6: Lettuce.
Student 5: A rabbit can't eat a whole moose.
Student 6: He could eat a little moose.
Marge: What food are you going to bring to camp tomorrow?
Student 4: Carrots, baby carrots. I know – birch bark.
Marge: That's interesting, [student] says they nibble the skin off things. Remember the stick we saw that was nibbled and I hung the carrot right there, thinking maybe he would eat it and he didn't eat it.
Student 4: Maybe the rabbit couldn't find the carrot.
Marge: I hung it right where he was chewing before. Does anyone else have something to tell us about rabbits?
Student 9: Rabbits are white in the winter time.
Student 10: They change colour.

As the conversation evolved, the children's comments began to reveal clear connections to what was previously said, resulting in a rich discussion that reflected their expanding ideas. I then asked students what other things they wondered about rabbits. They were full of curiosity.

> **"What more do we want to know about rabbits?"**
>
> **Student 1:** Do bunnies like water?
> **Sara:** Why do bunnies have such long ears?
> **Student 1:** Do bunnies hibernate?
> **Student 8:** How come there are Easter bunnies and other bunnies?
> **Glenda:** Where does the Easter bunny get the eggs?
> **Student 9:** Why do bunnies change colour?
> **Sara:** I wonder where bunnies find water in the bush.
> **Student 4:** How do they hold baby bunnies?
> **Student 1:** Do bunnies climb trees?
> **Student 4:** Why do they live in a bunny hole?
> **Student 3:** How high can bunnies hop?
> **Student 4:** How fast can a rabbit hop?
> **Student 5:** How do they hop?
> **Student 7:** Do they eat more than carrots?
> **Student 1:** Do bunnies eat sticks?
> **Student 3:** Why do bunnies eat sticks and get bigger and how big?
> **Marge:** I wonder if rabbits make noises.

Establishing a Personal Connection with Nature and One Another

Throughout the month of October, we made weekly visits to our camp in the forest. The students had become quite comfortable in nature, showing respect for the land while locating their trees and confidently hiking the trails we had made. Using Ojibway words, we identified medicinal plants and trees such as spearmint, willow, balsam, and cedar. We learned that tea made from spearmint, willow bark, and a species of red berries, which the students called "little apples," helps to soothe a sore throat. Balsam sap heals wounds, and was used as a glue long ago to seal up birch bark canoes. We also found out that we were not the only visitors to our camp. The disappearance of food we had left out made us wonder what animals might be around. We saw other evidence of animals such as nibbled branches, scat, tracks, fresh small holes in trees, and feathers. To learn more, over the weeks we set up a trail camera in various areas of the camp.

It is difficult to describe the deep connection that our students had developed with this place. Our treks to the camp were tiring for both students and adults, yet we always came back inspired, focused, and calm. Our experiences of the camp also continued to have an impact on our thinking and our discussions once we returned to the classroom. An older student shared photographs of her pet rabbits, including six babies. She brought one into the class for everyone to touch; the students' contact with the pet rabbit enabled them to connect to those they had observed in the wild. Later, the sighting of a white rabbit outside our classroom window prompted the children to wonder where it lived and what it was nibbling on near the edge of the forest. With their parents' help, the students were asked to write about their experiences with rabbits. This assignment helped the parents and the children connect with the inquiry.

Experiential Learning

Though the pet rabbit had helped to expand our learning, how could we help our students to have direct experience with rabbits that were so difficult to see in the wild? We really wished rabbits would appear every time we visited our camp, but that didn't happen, of course. Instead, we drew students' attention to the signs rabbits had left behind. We followed their tracks in the snow. We noticed their scat and where they had nibbled on willows. The students soon were able to recognize rabbit tracks whenever they hiked the trails or walked down the road.

Student's Rabbit

Several possible directions for our rabbit inquiry were emerging. The most nagging question was "Why did we see a white rabbit when there was not yet snow?" Some students still insisted it was the snow that made them white, rubbing its colour off on the rabbit. Though the tame rabbits were brown and black, it didn't seem to trouble students; they were not concerned that they had not turned white like the wild ones. Another area that continued to be of interest concerned what food rabbits ate. Students were sure that rabbits ate carrots even though no carrots grew in the forest and the carrots we had set out did not get eaten. We asked the students how we could find out what rabbits living in the wild eat.

> **"What do wild rabbits eat?"**
>
> **Student 1:** Rabbits eat seeds.
> **Student 2:** No, rabbits eat carrots.
> **Marge:** Do carrots grow out at our camp?
> **Student 2:** No, but we did put carrots there.
> **Student 3:** They might eat them from a garden.
> **Marge:** We did put out carrots, but they were not eaten. Remember they hung there for a long time, all dried up. What else lives at our camp that rabbits might eat?
> **Student 1:** Rabbits eat bark.
> **Marge:** Yes, we saw the branches chewed when we were at camp. What else might rabbits eat?
> **Student 4:** Maybe grass.
> **Student 1:** Not now, there's snow on the ground.
> **Marge:** So rabbits might eat different food at different times of the year.

Having previously set out different foods to determine what the rabbits might eat, such as bagels with peanut butter and sunflower seeds, a container with only sunflower seeds, dry grass, and carrots, we had observed that bagels with peanut butter and sunflower seeds had been eaten.

Preparing for Our Food Experiment

"I think the rabbits will eat seeds."

"I think the rabbits will eat carrots."

"We think the rabbits will eat dry grass."

Photo of Rabbit from Trail Camera

Each student posed for a photo beside the food they expected rabbits to eat. This exercise provided them with opportunities to wonder about many things, such as why we chose particular spots to place the food, how to hang carrots in a way the rabbits could reach them, and what would happen if other animals ate the food. I also posed questions for them to think about, such as, **"Why would this be a good spot to put the food?"** and **"How do we know rabbits have been in this area?"** While not all students could fully verbalize their thinking, we noticed that the less verbal students talked a lot more at camp than elsewhere.

After setting out the food, we set up the trail camera facing down a trail that was covered with rabbit tracks. When we returned at the end of the day, the bagel had been eaten and nothing else was disturbed. To our disappointment, the trail camera had failed to record any rabbit pictures. We were not able to prove much with that experiment, as we were not sure what had eaten the bagel; we suspected a squirrel or birds. When we checked again two weeks later, everything had been eaten and the area had many rabbit tracks. We moved the trail camera to a different part of the trail and were excited to get a picture of a large white rabbit in the new location.

We continued to leave out the bagels with peanut butter, sunflower seeds, and carrots in the middle of our camp. Each time we returned, the bagels were eaten, but not the carrots. On an early morning visit to the camp, we saw chickadees flitting around in the trees. They appeared to be fighting over the bagels.

Our observations eventually confirmed that rabbits liked to eat seeds and nibble on willow bark. On closer examination, we noticed the outer layers of the willow branches were chewed away, leaving the indent of teeth marks. Several willows had more extensive chewing.

Willow Tree with Bark Eaten Off

156   Part 2 – Environmental Inquiry in Action: The Educators' Stories

Back in the classroom, we learned from an information book that rabbits' teeth keep growing. We compared this with what we knew about beaver teeth, which also keep growing. We set out more seeds and added some pellets – tame rabbit food – to see if our rabbits would eat them. Several days later we noticed the seeds and food pellets had been eaten.

Why Does the Rabbit's Fur Change Colour?

Closely examining the photo on the trail camera, we noticed the rabbit was white. It was now spring; why had the rabbit stayed white even though the snow had melted? To understand more, we consulted the internet and books. We found that while primary-level books failed to explain why animal fur colour changes, the internet provided the necessary information, yet we needed to find a way to simplify it for these young students.

On one trip during the winter, we saw no fresh animal tracks at the camp. No sign of birds, rabbits, deer, or mice. This didn't make sense to us. We wondered where the animals had been. Our cultural educator informed us that there had been a "stingy moon" that night. During this time, animals stay in their burrows because it is too dark to hunt for food or avoid predators. Trappers even take home their traps.

Over the course of the year, our frequent and lengthy visits to camp led to the development of a strong emotional connection to this place. Hiking to camp in a snowstorm with driving wind and snow pellets did not faze the children; it allowed them to experience what the animals and plants would experience, which was very exciting for them. Taking time to play at camp, walking the flagged trails, displaying collections of found items in the classroom, noticing the plants and animals, and looking at photos had helped students form a bond with the camp. The impact of this kind of immersive experience was very powerful.

"Why is the rabbit white?"

Marge: (Recall the sighting of the white rabbit before we saw the snow and from the picture on the trail camera.) Why were we able to see the rabbit so clearly?

Student 1: Because it was just sitting there alone and everybody was quiet.

Marge: It was white and the land around it was not white.

Student 2: The bunny moved when we got close to it.

Marge: Why would he move, I wonder?

Student 3: We scared him.

Marge: He probably didn't feel safe.

Student 4: I thought he moved 100 steps.

Marge: Because the rabbit was white we noticed him very easily, right? Because the land around him was like the forest. It was grass, moss, and trees. I'm wondering why was the rabbit white?

Student 5: I think the bunny was just white.

Marge: Why was the rabbit white?

Student 5: Not sure.

Sara: Is it white because we are going to get lots more snow?

Student 3: Yeah.

Marge: When we saw the rabbit there was no snow yet?

Student 1: I think the rabbits, he's too a little bit small to go in the deep snow. Maybe that's why they are white.

Marge: You think they are white because they can't go in the deep snow.

Student 1: Yeah.

Student 6: When it was spring, and no snow at all, the bunny returned brown.

Marge: It's spring right now, so you're expecting it to turn brown.

Student 3: He's not brown yet, he's still white.

Marge: When we saw our bunny it was fall, no snow, but here he was. He was white. I wonder why.

Student 4: Because in winter it's white, except some people can see it and some people cannot.

Student 3: Some people can see it now.

Marge: Now that there is snow on the ground, and the bunny we saw on our trail camera was white – so, white bunny, white snow. How does that help the bunny?

Student 4: It just hops and hops.

Student 1: Easy to hop over the snow. Helps it hop away from people, something that is dangerous.

Marge: What could be dangerous for a rabbit in the winter?

Student 6: Us.

Student 7: He could be scared of any animal, like a wolf.

Student 6: A fox.

Marge: If he is white and the snow is white how does that help him?

Student 3: Yeah.

Marge: How could that help him?

Student 7: He can blend in with the snow.

Marge: Remember the game where we had the white sheet? We were hiding on the trail, someone was covered in the white sheet, someone was the wolf. The wolf had to find us. The one who was wrapped up in the sheet was hard for the wolf to see. And that's what it is like for the rabbit out in the snow. It is hard for us to see him. When do you think the rabbit will turn back to brown? How long will he stay white, do you think?

Student 1: Little bit.

Student 8: I don't know.

Student 9: Don't know.

Student 3: In summer, in a little while.

Marge: I wonder how it's going to get brown. What will make it brown? How will it do that – get brown?

Student 3: It will get brown in 10 min.*

Marge: What will make it brown?

Student 3: The sun, it's melting.*

Marge: What do you think? What might make it go brown?

Student 10: I don't know.

Marge: That is a hard question to answer.

Student 9: The warmness.*

Marge: The warmness and sun will make it brown. That is a hard question to answer. I don't know why rabbits can change their colour. We will have to look for answers, maybe on the internet or in books.

*These comments may foreshadow the concept of photoperiodism, described below.

Having discussed the fur colour in depth, a simple PowerPoint presentation that touched on the concept of photoperiodism later allowed the children's observations and theorizing to be measured against science. The children learned that a rabbit's fur changes depending on the length of the day. As the seasons and the light cycle change, rabbits produce melanin in their fur depending on how much light they sense in their retinas. When the brain receives less stimulation, melanin production slows down and the new fur that grows is colourless; it looks white. This process takes ten weeks. In the discussion about the rabbit's white fur, the students seemed to be grasping in a simple way the reasons the colour changes – "the sun, it's melting, the warmness, the warmness and the sun will make it brown."

A Transitioning Rabbit

In the spring, several students noticed rabbits near their homes. One student had seen a rabbit that was transitioning – part white and part brown.

Integrated Learning

Integration allows students to deepen their understanding, improve their skills, and share their knowledge. Experiencing habitats, seeing and coming into contact with nature and wildlife first-hand, writing, drawing, counting, measuring, colouring, and reading about rabbits provided continuity for our inquiry.

A great deal of the learning took place in the follow-up activities we engaged in after visits to our camp. Learning songs, games, and poems about rabbits and other animals, and having in-depth discussions both at the camp and back in the classroom, allowed students to not only develop and solidify their knowledge, but also to expand their vocabulary by using words and terms related to their inquiries. Writing and drawing about their experiences, creating and labelling diagrams, drawing maps that showed the route from school to the camp, and hearing and discussing stories about rabbits allowed the children to go deep. Keeping information in special "rabbit books," the students wrote about something they had experienced and felt connected to. Through their writing and drawing, I saw what information they were acquiring and tracked their growth in writing skills, letter and sound recognition, print conventions, sight word acquisition, drawing, and colouring skills.

Writing and Drawing About Rabbits

Gavin saw 7 rabbits on the hiking trail.
Carl saw 3 rabbits on the other hiking trail.
Kealin saw 1 rabbit by the camp.
How many rabbits did they see altogether?
Use numbers, words or a picture to show your thinking.

Beverly's Story
French Immersion – Senior Kindergarten
Elmdale Public School, Ottawa-Carleton District School Board (OCDSB)

Starting the Environmental Inquiry Process

When I taught Grade 3, environmental inquiry was a fundamental part of the program. My students and I were able to access the "outdoor classroom" almost every day. I could open the doors of the portable classroom I was teaching in and the school yard and beyond became a setting for our lessons. When I was given a Senior Kindergarten class to teach, it was an entirely new experience for me.

Not realizing at first how different inquiry-based learning would be with this younger group of students, I brought my enthusiasm and experience with environmental inquiry into the Kindergarten classroom. I set about navigating an entirely new learning environment with my five-year-old students.

Trying Snow Goggles Made from Caribou Bone

In late fall we visited a bird sanctuary in a forested area along the Ottawa River called Mud Lake. The children observed and thought about how both the weather and aspects of animal life were starting to change. Guided through the forest and along the watershed by Grade 6 students who have become unofficial guides of the area, we learned about the creatures who live there and how they prepare for winter: turtles, snakes, and fish under the ice and in the mud; beavers in their lodges; and birds, who hang around fattening themselves up. The students' first-hand experience of seasonal change provided a good foundation for our winter inquiry.

Our winter inquiry started with the first snowfall of the year. Glorious, white, sticky snow, enough to shovel and slide a toboggan over. Since October, we had been learning French vocabulary to describe the weather and to identify winter clothing. The students were really excited about putting this learning into practice. Our days began with a 50-minute outdoor learning period, and on this particular morning we hauled out a collection of toboggans and shovels that our school had purchased.

Multiple curriculum areas, including language, science, and physical education, were accessed that morning as the students pulled, piled, rolled, and slid on the snow. Later, they wrote about their day. Some children met the winter experience with less enthusiasm than others, expressing their dissatisfaction with statements such as "I don't like snow because it's cold and winter is long." Still, I felt hopeful that such valid opinions could be transformed by more positive engagement with our long Canadian winter.

While preparing for the winter inquiry, I sought ways to link our learning to the Kindergarten science curriculum. Guided by the expectation to "demonstrate an understanding of the natural world and the need to care for and respect the environment" (Ontario Ministry of Education, 2016, p. 125), students gathered information through observations and discussions about what happens outside in winter. They observed that there is more darkness, cold air, snow, and ice, plants lose leaves or die off, and earthworms tunnel deeper down into the earth. The children commented on the various changes that creatures experience: growing thicker coats, hibernating, flying south, or digging deep in the mud at the bottom of a lake.

The "I Know, I Wonder, I Have Learned" (KWL) model (Je Sais, Je me Demande, J'ai Appris) provided a framework for our investigations. The inquiry progressed through these stages, culminating with a sustainability activity of the children's choice.

- **Know** – A winter web of ideas was gathered in a Knowledge Building Circle that identified what the students already knew about "What happens in winter?"
- **Wonder** – A winter wonder wall consisting of questions the students would like to explore further was created.
- **Learned** – Students were guided to demonstrate, in a variety of ways, what they had learned. This allowed for evaluation of the knowledge they had acquired.
- **Sustainability** – I considered how children's acquired knowledge helped them to demonstrate a need to care for and respect the environment.

Classroom Setup

In my classroom I dedicated space to our winter inquiry, highlighting students' thinking on a whiteboard Wonder Wall which delineated the three components of the KWL model.

I Know/Je Sais

In pairs, the students brainstormed what they knew about winter. Many mentioned plants dying and animals, particularly bears, hibernating. Many students wrote using inventive spelling, enabling their ideas to be captured efficiently following the momentum of our class discussion.

Ideas about Winter

I Wonder/Je me Demande

Our team found books such as *What happens in Winter?* (Latta, 2006), *Who lives in the Arctic?* (Canizares & Chanko, 1997), and *Grandmother Winter* (Root, 2004), which highlighted the cooling and darkening of the Earth and the variety of ways creatures adapt to the change in season. We read a beautiful book called *Ben and Nuki Discover Polar Bears* (Valberg, 2012). This is a wonderful story of two boys – one from a big city in "the south," the other from a village in the Far North – who learn about polar bears as well as each other's cultures. As a provocation[1] about polar bears and life in the arctic, it was a fantastic launch.

As a result of these readings, the Wonder Wall quickly filled up with questions about animals who don't hibernate in winter (when we had previously assumed that they ALL do), as well as questions about the people who live in wintery climates for much longer periods of time than we do. Students' questions included

"What do seals do in the winter?"
"How do people get their food?"
"What do they make their clothes out of?"
"What is fur made of?"
"How do they build an igloo?"

They wrote their questions during our Writer's Workshop period, using inventive (phonetic) spelling when unsure of a word. The result was a fine collection of inquiry questions that demonstrated both the direction of the children's learning and how deeply they were connecting with the topic.

In this section of the inquiry, we assessed evidence of student engagement in the subject and the learning process. Were questions relevant to the topic? Did students demonstrate through play, visual art, writing, or oral expression a connection with the topic of winter and the life of the Inuit that showed development in their knowledge? More specifically, did they venture beyond knowing that animals hibernate and plants die in the winter?

---

[1] "The term 'provocation' describes a stimulus or trigger for creative thought or action. This may be in the form of an object, an experience, an idea, a question or a challenge which provokes a reaction of some nature." (Thornton & Brunton, 2015, p. 100)

What I have Learned/J'ai Appris

True to form, the trajectory of inquiry can never be predicted. After a couple of short weeks of exploring winter, our students had pushed well beyond their initial, limited knowledge. During a visit from Dion Metcalfe, a teacher from the Ottawa Inuit Children's Centre, the students learned how a wintery landscape has influenced the lives and culture of the Inuit, and how everything the Inuit need to survive can be found in nature, including food, clothing, shelter, tools, and toys.

Dion Metcalfe from the Ottawa Inuit Children's Centre Displaying a Sealskin

An SK Student Who Was Born in Pangnirtung, Nunavut is Wearing Her Own Amauti, Sealskin Slippers and Mittens

The students were able to share some of what they had begun to explore about people and animals in the arctic with our guest teacher. He was impressed with their background knowledge and responses to his questions, and his saying so encouraged the students to engage further in the discussion.

During Dion's presentation the students had opportunities to touch seal, fox, and rabbit pelts, try on an amauti (anorak), kamik (boots), and caribou bone snow goggles. They played a caribou skin drum, used seal knucklebones to create pictures during storytelling, and, for a full hour, learned and played Inuit wrestling games involving strength and stability. They discovered that these games are also easily played outside in the snowy schoolyard.

Exploring an Arctic Fox's Summer Coat

Playing the Caribou Hide Drum

Igloo Made from Seal Knucklebones

Our KWL bulletin board filled up with sentence strips on which the students wrote about and drew what they learned and liked about the visit:

"I learned that sealskin is best for clothes and boots because it's warm and waterproof."
"I learned that Inuit live in houses not igloos. I liked playing Inuit games."
"I learned that sealskin is waterproof."
"I learned that foxes don't hibernate in the arctic – they change colour."
"I learned how warm Inuit clothing is."
"I learned how the Inuit tell stories using seal bones."

At the art table, some students chose to paint what they had learned.

KWL Bulletin Board: Dion Metcalfe's Visit

"Dion taught me how to play a drum. How men play it and how women play it."

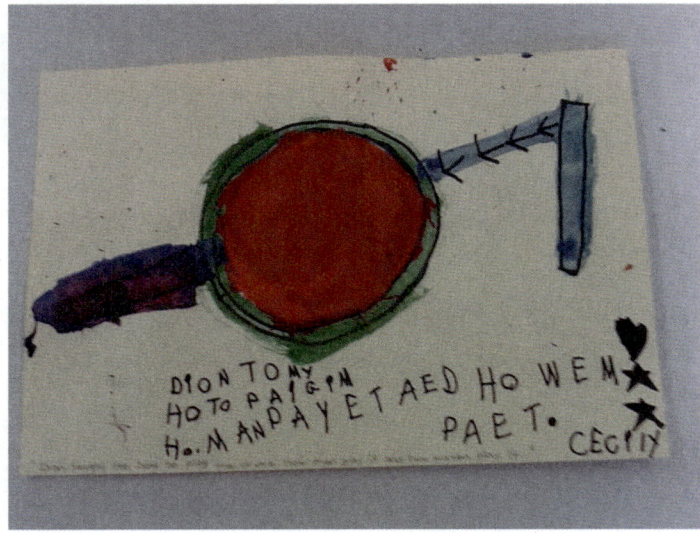

Beverly's Story: French Immersion, Senior Kindergarten

The variety of ways the students demonstrated their understanding of Inuit traditions and ways of life, as well as of arctic animals, made it clear to us that they each acquired learning in ways that made most sense to them. Some students used a paint brush and paper to illustrate what they learned and liked, while others chose to build something related to their inquiry either indoors or out. Those who enjoyed writing wrote meaningful sentences to express their understanding. Students demonstrated a sense of connection to their learning by identifying images in books of an inuksuk (a human-made stone landmark used for communication and survival) or the northern lights. They also showed their familiarity with Inuktitut words by easily using amauti, inuksuk, and kamik in the proper context. One student was surprised when she noticed that her winter boots had the brand name "Kamik" written on them.

How the Classroom Was Transformed

Following Dion's visit, we set up activities and centres in the classroom and outdoors, offering the children more opportunities to draw on their learning. In math, after discussing the best shape of rock to build an inuksuk, students were challenged to draw an inuksuk with more than five rectangles, tallying the total number they used. In the block centre, several students took the challenge further and built freestanding, student-sized inuksuk.

Student-sized Inuksuk

"Hunting" Seal and Polar Bear

A few days after the presentation, students "hunting" seal and polar bear spontaneously got into character and began tipping over chairs to be used as blinds. Later, they were redirected to the art table to make seals, polar bears, hunters, and dog sleds for a puppet theatre version of their dramatic play.

Another provocation involved posting Inuktitut syllabics on chart paper. Next to each symbol I wrote out the sound it represented. While some students recognized that there were several triangles in the alphabet, others attempted to find the syllables they needed to write their names or simply to experience the act of writing in Inuktitut.

Inuktitut Syllabics (Alphabet)

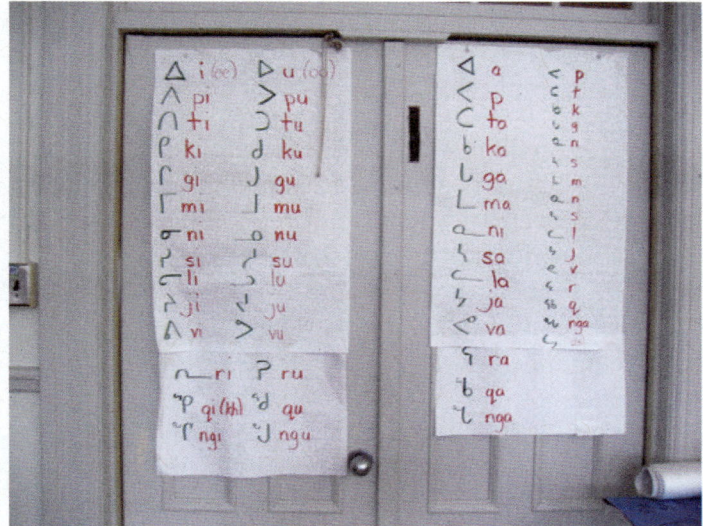

Student Writing Using Inuktitut Syllabics

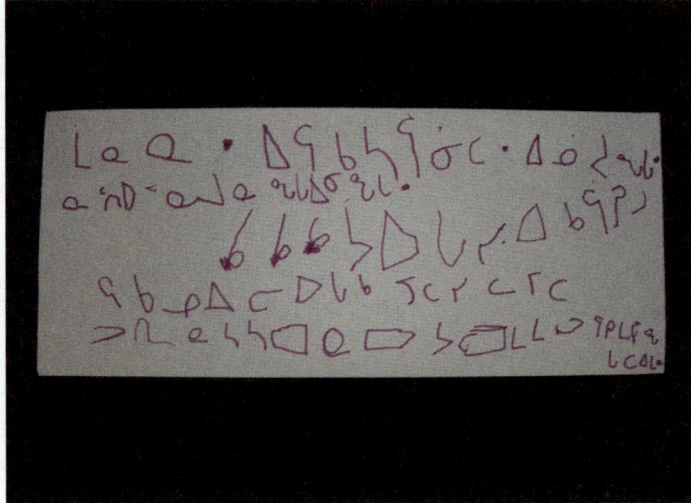

At this point in the inquiry, I began to ask questions about the snow, the sky and clouds, and animals during our daily outdoor learning period. This inquiry led the students to become very aware of the living things that inhabited their schoolyard, and they eagerly shared their observations of the environment around them.

> **Beverly:** If we had to build a shelter, would this be good snow to use? Why or why not? Let's find out.
> **Student 1:** This snow is too fluffy to build with. You need sticky snow.
> **Student 2:** Or really hard snow like bricks.
> **Beverly:** Can you hear any animal sounds?
> **Student 3:** I heard a cardinal on my way to school this morning.
> **Beverly:** Have you noticed any signs of animals such as scat, tracks, or birdsong?
> **Student 4:** We found bunny poo over by the fence!

I also asked the children to consider: "What do you notice about the weather today? Is it different from yesterday?" "What are the clouds telling us?" "What do you think the animals are eating in the winter?

Building a Snow Shelter

Playing Inuit Wrestling Games – Demonstrating Pushing Strength

A Winter Walk Looking for Signs of Life in the Woods

Stewardship and Sustainability

With our winter inquiry coming to an end, my biggest challenge was to find a way to awaken the children's empathy and concern for the environment we had been studying, fostering in them an awareness of stewardship and sustainability.

Hoping to galvanize the students into action, I wrote a note from the creatures the students had observed around our schoolyard. In the note, the creatures complain that the snow is unhealthily dirty.

> "Chers Amis, Our homes are not healthy any more! When the snow melts, the water we need to live is making us sick. Many of our friends have already left to find a cleaner place to live. We don't want to leave! Can you help us? Signed, your friends – Earthworm, Chickadee, Rabbit, Crow, and Cardinal."

I folded the note and tucked it into a space between the bark and trunk of one of our maple trees growing along the fence in the schoolyard.

The next morning, I challenged the students to hunt for evidence of living things in the schoolyard. I was beginning to wonder if anyone would find the note, when finally a group of students came running back, all talking loudly about what they had found in a tree. I gathered everyone together and read the note aloud, then asked what they thought. They turned and talked with their neighbours excitedly. "Rabbits can't write!" "Yes they can." Speaking about the unclean snow, they had many thoughts. "It's true! There is sand in the snow. I can see it." "Snow looks clean but it's actually really dirty." Others mentioned the dirt from cars as well as the dogs that dirty the ground. When I asked if we ourselves could drink the water if we melted this snow, the answer was clear. "Ewww! No way!"

I was hoping the students would acknowledge that since humans had created the problem we were all responsible for addressing it. However, I quickly realized that figuring out how to clean up the planet is a controversial question even for those with professional expertise, let alone a group of five-year-olds. At this age, they are more focused on helping one animal at a time through actions such as putting out a bowl of clean water to drink, as they would for their pets at home. It became clear to me that rather than ask how we might help the creatures, a better question was what if … ? So I started over again, asking what they thought would happen if there was no more winter. I explained the effect of climate change on the Earth, noting that scientists think this is happening because of pollution caused by people using cars and airplanes and building factories to make things.

At first, the group was rather quiet, but then one of the students commented that a warmer Earth meant that the snow would melt. Right away, more students began to add their thoughts:

> **Student 1:** If the snow melts, then the polar bears would have no home.
> **Student 2:** And the seals and foxes too.
> **Student 3:** There would be no habitat for the animals.
> **Student 4:** All the animals would lose their habitat and then they won't have anything to eat.
> **Student 5:** Their habitat is broken and the animals would get dead.

Losing habitat is something the students could visualize and understand, so I asked them, "How do you think we can be habitat helpers, then?" They were happy to articulate how they have bird feeders in their backyards, how they compost and recycle garbage, how they plant gardens with their families, and how sad they are when they see trees cut down or dried-out worms on the pavement. Rather than engaging in large-scale activism, these five-year-olds came to realize from this inquiry that they already had a positive impact on the environment. My own learning came when I had to acknowledge that the understanding of sustainability in an SK classroom is, of course, closely tied to the developmental worldview of five-year-olds, with themselves firmly at the centre of it all. I was reminded that everything does, after all, start with the individual.

Through their explorations of Inuit life, our connection to nature, and our impact on our environment, the children gained a much greater understanding of our relationship with the natural habitat in winter. At the same time, our inquiry remains unfinished. Winter's transition into spring brings with it unlimited opportunities to build upon the knowledge we have all gained. I am inspired by the perspectives and curiosity of the Kindergarten students that are waiting to emerge as we move forward.

Signs of Life in the Winter Woods

Carol's Story
Senior Kindergarten
Dr. Eric Jackman Institute of Child Study Laboratory School

Starting the Environmental Inquiry Process

I began this year wanting to challenge myself. I had heard, again and again, that the surest way to connect ourselves and our children to a deeper sense of our natural world was to get outside. I had done this over the years, in fits and starts, but this year I wanted to embed this value right into the structure of our days. With the support of my principal, I scheduled a weekly, hour and a half visit to our neighbourhood park on Monday afternoons. Rain or shine, snow or sleet, we were going!

I wasn't sure how parents would respond to the news, but the uptake was overwhelmingly enthusiastic, with many offering to join us. Surprisingly, some of the children were less positive. "But we won't go if it's raining," one suggested. I assured him we would. "But not if it's raining hard." "Yup!" I said. "But not if there's lightning." I assured him that we would not go if it was actually unsafe. "But we won't go if it's snowing," he countered.

Since that initial conversation we have only missed one park visit, late in the term, due to extreme cold, and even that very child, the one who had initially been so worried, tried to convince me that it wouldn't be that bad. The shift in imagining what's possible had happened to us all.

Hardly a grand forested space, our neighbourhood park occupies a smallish city block in downtown Toronto. It has a few clusters of trees, some formal plantings, a dirt playing field, and a playground. It is only two blocks from school, but is a place much greener than our concrete- and woodchip-covered schoolyard.

On our first visit, the children ran straight past the trees and flowers and shrubs, and threw themselves onto the climbers at the far end of the park. "Why are we here?" I asked myself. It was fun, but was it school? On subsequent visits, I decided to begin with a question, story, or other gathering activity. We each chose one special tree in the park to observe and track through the year. The children photographed their trees and drew them. We measured the circumference of our trees, and tried to judge their age: were they "baby" trees, "mommy" trees, or maybe "grandfather" trees"? We discovered birds' nests, squirrels' nests, and wasps' nests in their boughs, and creature-made holes at their base. We sat beneath our trees reading stories.

My favourite visit occurred on a rainy day that followed weeks of sunshine. The sky looked heavy and grey as we walked in our raincoats and rubber boots to this place we now all considered "our" park. The lightest rain began to fall. We gathered underneath Luke's pine tree, and seated ourselves on the hard earth where the pine needles had kept grass from growing. I started to read a book called *The Memory Tree* (Teckentrup, 2014). As I read, the rain fell harder and harder, but it barely touched us. The boughs of the trees provided the perfect cover. When the story ended we all sat in the quiet for a moment, watching the rain fall in a circle around us. Then we jumped up and the children ran to play.

The Memory Tree

The park visits became the backbone of our year, something that we looked forward to and also back at through the week. From a study, in the fall, of growth and change in living things, our focus shifted in the winter to tackle our place in the universe.

Looking In, Looking Out: Grounding Inquiry in a Sense of Place

My SKs often start the winter term thinking about how our Earth might look from space. But this year, I wanted to broaden our thinking about the environment, to consider it as something we are part of – physically, emotionally, intellectually, and even spiritually – rather than as something external that we act upon or that acts upon us. I was hoping to shift the focus of our inquiry to tackle Earth's place in the universe, and our place in Earth. Of course, I wasn't sure how I was going to manage that.

The first day back from the winter break, I retold a version of Raven Steals the Sun, a Haida origins tale that was one of the children's favourite stories. I challenged them to imagine flying as high as Raven, so high that they could see our world as a whole. I told them to keep that image in their minds because after lunch they would draw it with chalk pastels.

Highlighting the Colours of Earth's Water, Land, and Clouds

Thinking About What Makes up Earth, Inside and Out

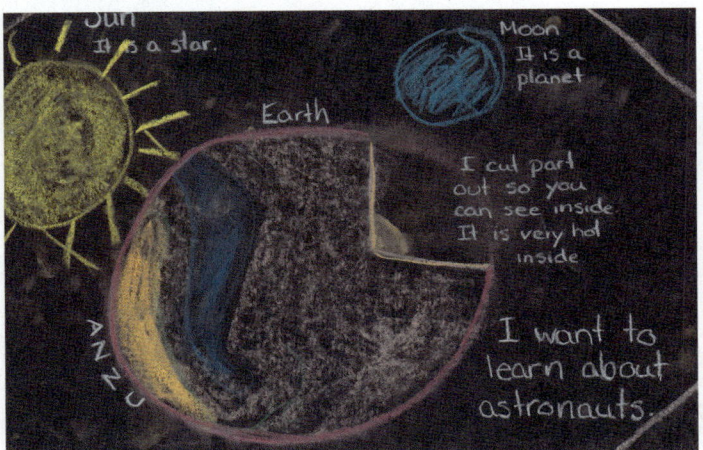

Layers of the Atmosphere Rising Above Earth

Our Solar System

Carol's Story: Senior Kindergarten

"What does our world look like?"

After labeling each child's drawing to their specifications, I scribed any further questions or thoughts they wanted to share.

Looking In: What Makes You Be You?

While gathering these initial understandings about space, I was wondering how we could look out and in, simultaneously. The next morning I read the children a book called *Earthdance* (Ryder & Gorbaty, 1996). The cover shows a colourful multitude of figures dancing all over the Earth. "So many people," I said. "Do we know anything about any of them? If we wanted to know, what kind of questions do you think we should ask? What kinds of questions would you ask to get at 'What makes you be you'?" I asked them to think about this until we resumed our discussion. As we sat on the sand beneath Tom's maple tree, I repeated my question, asking what kinds of questions might get at the core of who a person was. Their suggestions were amazing:

What is your favourite thing to do?
Where do you most like to be?
Who do you like to be with?
What makes you feel bored or mad or frustrated?
What do you want to be when you are an adult?
What is your life about?
Who gave you your name?
Where does your name come from?
What does your name mean?
What does your name mean to you?
Do you have a secret name, or a nickname?

Most of the children's ideas were immediately actionable, building on their delight in sharing aspects of themselves through writing and encouraging family discussions at home. The questions about names offered an impetus for the children to become active researchers – about themselves. From there, many more questions emerged!

"What Makes You Be You?"

> **"What Makes You Be You?"**
>
> Dear SKs, last week we began talking about our Earth and its place in the Universe. At the park on Monday, we started to think about our own place, and who we are. You came up with some great questions to help us find out, many about your own name. For your homework, please ask your parents to help you answer these questions.
>
> 1. Who gave you your name?
> *me mommy*
>
> 2. Where does you name come from?
> *Japan and Israel*
>
> 3. What does your name mean?
> *my love and motion*
>
> 4. Do you have a secret name, or a nickname?
> *Noo Boo and Boo and Short Pants*
>
> Please feel free to write anything you would like to add on the back or another piece of paper. We want to know!
>
> By: NOA

One question, however, seemed more challenging to me: "What's your life about?" I couldn't imagine how the children would respond to such a question – I didn't know how I would respond to it! – but I was worried that if we didn't tackle it in some way, Frances, the child who offered it, would feel left out. I decided to bring my own uncertainty back to the group.

Seated on the carpet, I repeated Frances' question and asked how they thought people might begin to answer it. Once again, I was astonished and impressed by the generosity of their vision. It was another reminder to not let my initial hesitation stand in the way of what young children can engage with.

That evening, I sent a letter home:

Dear SK families,

As you may have heard, the SKs have begun looking at the Earth and its place in the universe. In tandem with that path of inquiry, we have also begun to look into ourselves, or as Ella helped us articulate "What makes you be you?" Sitting in a circle on the cold sand at Sibelius Park Monday afternoon, the children continued a conversation from the morning, thinking about the kinds of questions we might ask to get at the heart of what makes each person who they are. (You can see the list posted in the classroom). Tomorrow we are sending homework based on some of those questions. We hope you enjoy them as a family.

Please feel free to support your child's writing of the answers as works best for you. That may mean helping them sound through each word. You may help them with some standard spellings. If the response is long, you may even scribe for them. We would appreciate having the homework returned by Monday. Thank you in advance for your help!

We tackled one question today as a group – a question that, frankly, I thought would be a challenge for these very young children to connect with. How wrong I was:

"What is your life about?" (a question suggested by Frances)

It means the moonlight and the sun.
It means being with your family.
It's about being with friends.
And your brothers and sisters.
And your cousins.
It's about people being nice to us.
And us being nice to other people.
It's about having food and living in a house.
It's being nice to older people.
And to younger people.
Do not try to trick people or hurt them.
Do not lie.
Have a great family!

Looking Out: Tackling Big Ideas About Space Together

During this time, we continued to look out towards space. Our first knowledge building discussions focused on the interrelationships among the sun, the moon, and the Earth. One question I brought to the SKs came straight from a child's drawing:

> **"What Is the Sun?"**
>
> **Student 1:** It is something made out of fire and lava.
>
> **Student 2:** No one made it. It was made in the Big Bang. That's when the solar system was created. No men or volcano made it.
>
> **Student 3:** It has ash.
>
> **Student 4:** And Earth-like lava.
>
> **Student 5:** The sun is just a whole chunk of fire.
>
> **Student 6:** When it's in space you can see it from Earth.
>
> **Student 7:** In the night-time you can't see it.
>
> **Student 8:** Or behind clouds.
>
> **Student 9:** It's actually made out of gases. If it was lava it would have hardened into rock.
>
> **Student 10:** It's gases that look like fire.
>
> **Student 11:** It's really hot, though, right?
>
> **Student 12:** The sun makes the Earth light.
>
> **Student 13:** When it's winter the sun moves far away, but in the summer it moves closer.
>
> **Student 14:** Actually, the sun stays put.
>
> **Student 15:** The Earth moves around.
>
> **Student 16:** It looks like the sun turns around, but it is just the Earth.
>
> **Student 17:** It takes a whole year for the Earth to go around the sun.
>
> **Student 18:** Actually more.
>
> **Student 19:** Yeah, like a month or a season.
>
> **Student 20:** The sun is 8 thousand, million miles away!

This wide range of understandings turned my attention to two concepts about which five-year-olds tend to hold deep misconceptions: "What causes day and night?" and "How can we explain the apparent changes in the moon?" We gathered the children's initial thinking before setting out to shape steps that would give the opportunity for them to learn from experiences, books, experts, and one another.

"What causes day and night?"

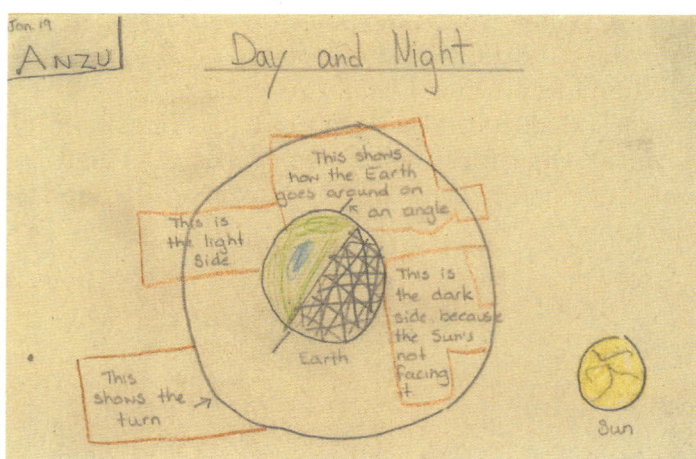

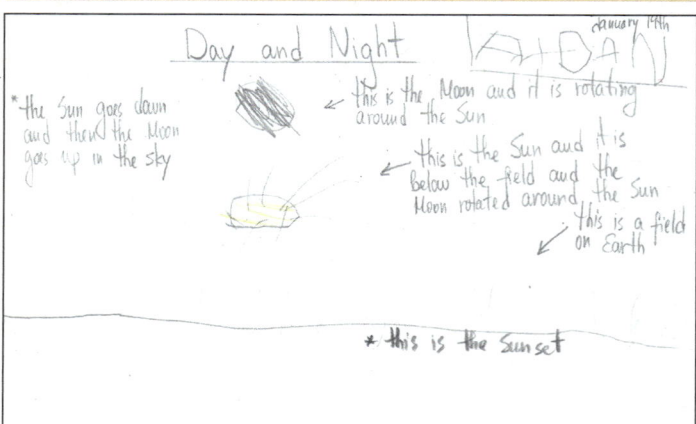

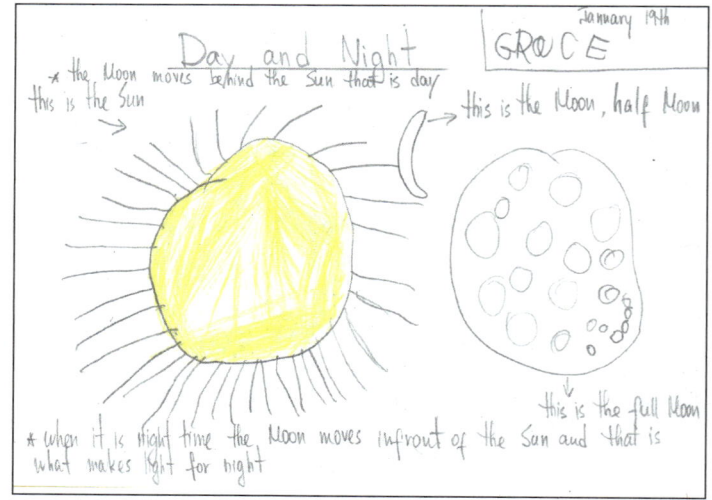

"How can we explain the apparent changes in the moon?"

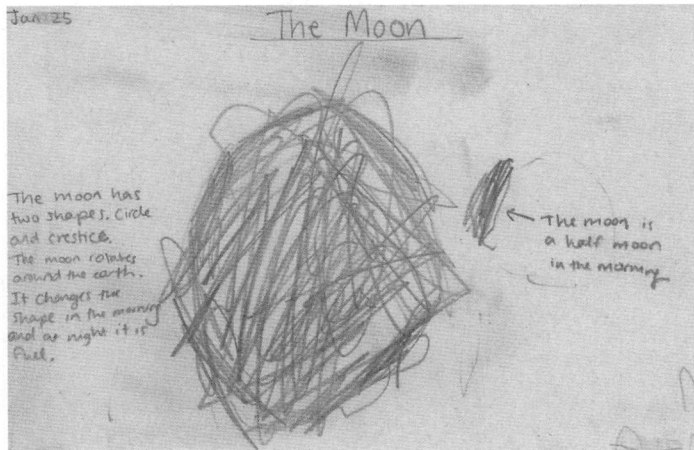

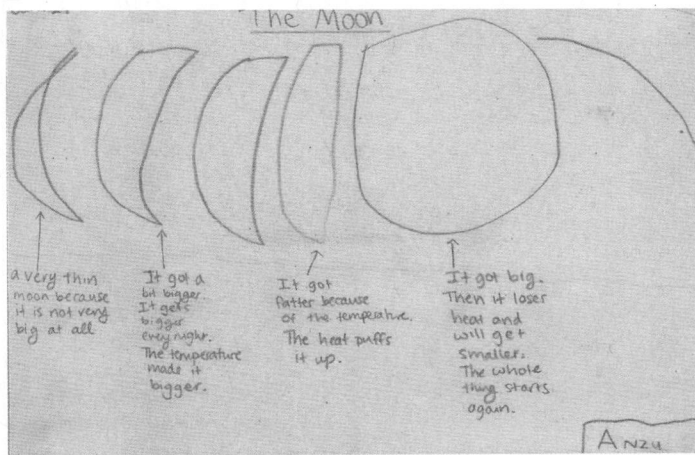

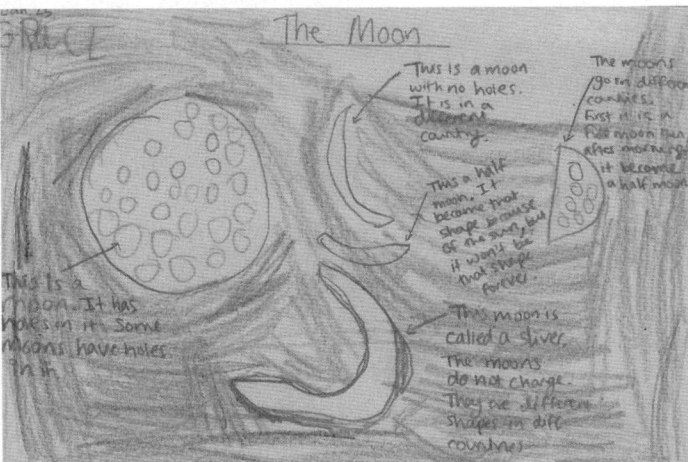

We scanned the internet, looking for useful video clips. We gathered books from libraries and our homes. And we drew, painted, played, and talked about everything under the sun!

The transcript of our next whole-class discussion on the topic demonstrates how the children's understanding really began to shift.

"The Sun and the Earth"

Carol: Looking back at our previous discussion, people had some ideas about how the sun and the Earth move. Could someone begin to explain that relationship for us?

Student 1: It's like this, the sun is staying still just like this [hand flat on lap] and the Earth is moving around it like this [other hand moving in a circular motion above]. It's called rotation. The Earth rotates around the sun.

Carol: [We all try replicating the motion.] So we are always going around the sun. Is there ever a time when we don't see the sun, as some people suggested in our last conversation?

Student 2: Yes, when the moon goes in front of it.

Student 3: That's when it's night.

Student 4: The moon comes out and that means it's nighttime.

Carol: Is the moon ever out when it isn't night?

Student 4: No, only at night.

Student 5: Or when it's a solar eclipse.

Carol: Now, this is strange. Didn't we see the moon in the sky during recess, not so long ago?

Student 5: Yeah. But it was behind the sun.

Carol: Hmmm. Let's think about the sun and Earth again. Could someone be our sun? [One child sits in the middle.] Should she move or should she stay still in one spot?

Many voices: Stay still!

Carol: Now we need someone to act as our Earth. [Another child stands.] Should the Earth move or should it stay still in one spot?

Many more voices: Move!

Carol: [Our Earth begins moving on the spot, spinning around and around.] Wait a minute. Our Earth is moving. Is that what you were expecting?

Student 6: The Earth moves like that, too.

Student 7: The Earth moves in two ways – around the sun and around itself like that.

Carol: What does that look like?

Student 8: [This child stands and begins moving in two ways – spinning and circling the sun.]

Carol: Now our Earth is spinning and circling our sun. The spinning can be called rotating, like you heard earlier. Look, our Earth has pictures on his sweater. If we were living on that Earth, where would we be?

Student 9: On the cactus.

Carol: Where is the cactus facing?

Carol's Story: Senior Kindergarten

Student 10: The sun!

Carol: And when it starts moving around and spinning?

Student 10: First the sun and then away from the sun.

Student 11: And then at the sun again!

Carol: So what do we see when we aren't facing the sun?

Student 12: It's dark!

Student 13: That's night.

Student 14: And when it's facing the sun, it's day, 'cause we can see the sun.

Student 15: So it's day and night on Earth at the same time. Half the Earth has day and half has night.

Student 16: But if it's a quarter turn you still see the light some, because you're not turned all the way away.

Carol: Okay, you guys have brought up some really interesting ideas for us to follow. Thank you so much for your time.

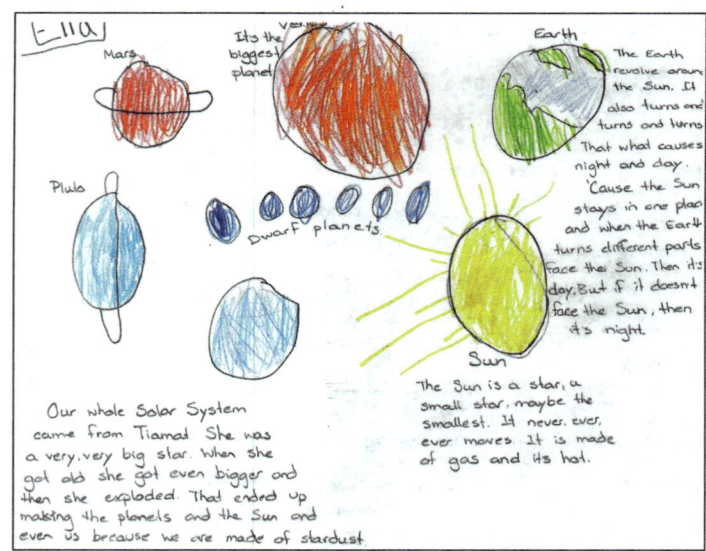

"What does it look like when a star gets born?"

As new questions began to fill the walls, I looked for ways to connect them to the broader concepts we were tackling:

How was our solar system made?
What made our moon?
Is our sun a big star or a little star?
Why doesn't Earth have colours, like the moon?
What does it look like when a star gets born?
What does it look like when a star dies?

Leaping from the children's ideas about the moon's surface, my student teacher had small groups of kids drop, toss, and hurl marbles into wet plaster as they talked about meteors and impact. The idea of gravity was frequently mentioned and became another natural jumping off point.

We introduced a series of simple experiments to help illustrate how gravity works on Earth. In small groups, the children dropped marbles into sand from different heights. Next, two tennis balls were dropped from the same height, though one had been weighted with sand.

Each time, we encouraged predictions – "What do you think is going to happen?" – close observation, and reflection upon what they noticed.

Each child was then asked to draw something they noticed about one of the experiments.

"What did you notice?"

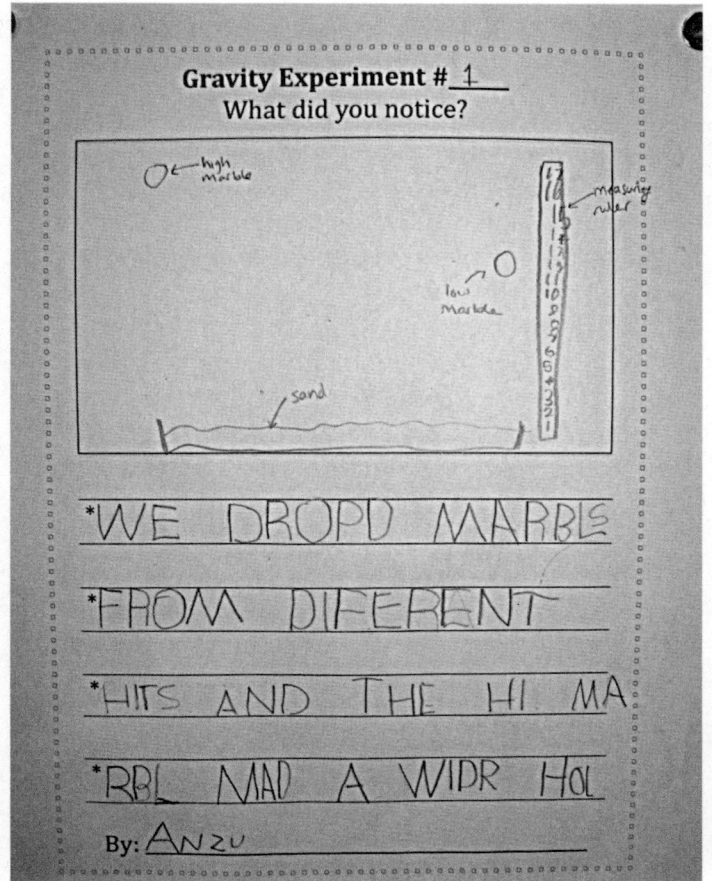

Gravity Experiment # 1
What did you notice?

*WE DROPD MARBLS
*FROM DIFERENT
*HITS AND THE HI MA
*RBL MAD A WIDR HOL

By: ANZU

Gravity Experiment # 1
What did you notice?

*THE HIYER THE
*MARBL WAS
*DROPD FROM THE
*WIDR THE HOL

By: MAE

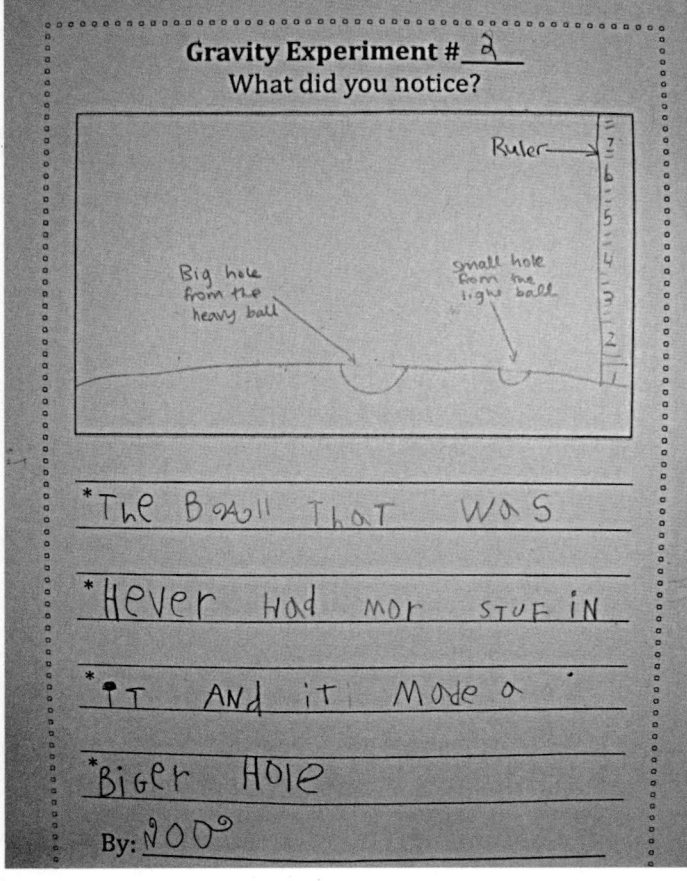

Gravity Experiment # 2
What did you notice?

*The Boll That was
*Hever had mor stuf in
*it And it Made a
*Biger Hole

By: NOO

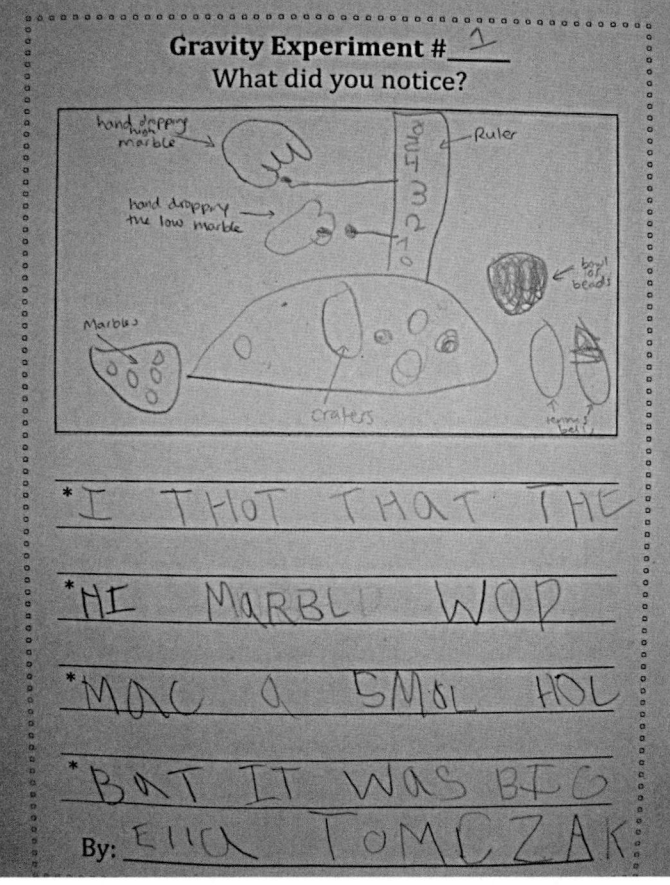

Gravity Experiment # 1
What did you notice?

*I THOT THAT THE
*HI MARBL WOD
*MAC A SMOL HOL
*BAT IT WAS BIG

By: Ella TOMCZAK

We were looking to see whether children were making reasoned predictions or more fanciful guesses, and whether their reflections remained strictly observational ("The high marble made a bigger hole.") or incorporated causal thinking ("The higher the marble was dropped from, the wider the hole."). Some even reflected on how their ideas changed ("I thought that the high marble would make a small hole but it was big.").

We then brought their ideas back to a whole-group discussion that aimed to pull together their individual discoveries about gravity.

> **Carol:** I didn't get to see you doing your experiments. Can someone describe to me what happened?
> **Student 1:** We dropped marbles from different heights.
> **Student 2:** The marble that was bigger made a bigger hole.
> **Student 1:** No, what's heavier made a bigger hole.
> **Student 3:** Yeah, like the heavy tennis ball.
> **Carol:** Can you explain that a little more?
> **Student 1:** We had two tennis balls, and they were just the same size.
> **Student 2:** But one of them was heavier. It had sand inside. And it made a bigger hole.
> **Student 3:** Not just heavier makes it bigger. When you drop a marble from high up it made a big hole. When you drop it from lower down it made a smaller hole.
> **Carol:** Why do they fall down?
> **Student 4:** Thin air.
> **Student 5:** Gravity is pulling them down.
> **Student 6:** It pulls everything down.
> **Student 7:** If there was no gravity, we wouldn't be able to touch the ground. We would just float up in the air.

From this discussion we pulled out two basic rules of gravity on Earth, which we posted in the class.

1. The higher an object is dropped from, the greater the impact.
2. The heavier the object, the greater the impact.

That's when we tried dropping two plastic animals, one large and heavy – a bear – and one small and light – a fox. This time we all worked together. I asked, "What do you think will happen if we let the fox and the bear go from the same height at exactly the same time?"

Three theories were offered. Many children offered a version of "The bear will fall to the table first, because it is heavy and it will cut through the air faster and gravity will pull it down harder." Some predicted the fox would hit the table first, "because it is small and light and it will fall fast." One child suggested that maybe they would fall at the same time, though she couldn't articulate why that might be. "Just because it might happen that way."

With everyone watching intently, the suspense building, we counted down and I let go. THUMP. I said, "Did you hear that? Sometimes our ears can tell us something our eyes cannot. How many thumps did you hear?" A child replied, "One! They fell at the same time!"

The children suggested testing other objects. An even smaller animal – same result. A plastic owl, with wings! – same result. A feather – a different result, and they knew it before we even started, their hands demonstrating the wafting motion the feather would take as it fell. But why? The children offered their theories: "Maybe because it is so light." "Maybe the shape." "Maybe because feathers kind of have holes that let some of the air go through it."

A piece of paper was also suggested. This gave us the opportunity to test the weight theory. When we dropped the paper it fell more slowly than the bear, though not as slowly as the feather. Then we tried a piece of paper crumpled up: same weight, different shape. As almost all the children now predicted, it fell at the same speed as the bear. Tom wanted to try and add some paper to the plastic owl to see if we could make it fall more slowly.

Though I had engineered the beginning of the experiment, the children had taken over the process, and in doing so had come to some fundamental understanding which allowed them to extrapolate in interesting ways.

> **"Does gravity work the same way on the moon?"**
>
> **Carol:** What would happen if we dropped a marble, like the ones we used in our experiments, on the moon?
>
> **Student 1:** It would make a tiny dot, cause the marble is so small compared to the whole moon.
>
> **Student 2:** It would make a tiny crater compared to on Earth because craters on the moon were made by bigger things than marbles, so the real craters are bigger.
>
> **Student 3:** It's not because they are bigger. They're meteorites. They're faster. The faster they go, the bigger the crater.
>
> **Student 4:** Inside the moon there are rocks. The marbles are going to go into the moon. They are going to sink in.
>
> **Student 5:** When you dropped the marble, it wouldn't make any hole because you are so much higher than the Earth.
>
> **Student 6:** Do you know the moon is the Earth's satellite? The moon doesn't have any gravity so when you let go of the marble it wouldn't drop down. It would just go out, into space.
>
> **Student 7:** It would float.
>
> **Carol:** In the pictures we have seen, does it look like people or things are floating?
>
> **Student 8:** Astronauts don't kind of touch the moon. They just touch a toe and bounce off. There is so little gravity. So maybe the marble would kind of just float down. Kind of go down to the moon slowly or something.
>
> **Student 9:** It would go down slowly to the moon but bounce back up.
>
> **Student 10:** Maybe the craters were made by just a few meteorites that bounced.
>
> **Student 11:** Astronauts have super heavy boots so they can stay on the moon.

The next day I brought out a book on space, and sure enough, many of the children's observations were echoed in its pages.

Had all the children moved from their original misconceptions? Definitely not, but over the coming weeks, as we continued to engage in experiences that they helped shape, I kept track of the growth of their understanding, recorded their discussions, observed how they engaged in various aspects of our inquiry, and asked them to illustrate what they knew while scribing their ideas.

We planned to take this experiment, and many more, to our park. Could the children find natural objects in the park that would either fall at the same rate as the bear or more slowly? Was there some way they could modify the objects to change how they fall?

Of course, spring was soon to be with us, and new paths of inquiry were sure to arise as the park awakened. Who knew what we would discover next?

Understanding Ourselves and Our Place

In connecting ourselves to the wider universe, we ended up following some rich paths of exploration and discovery. On one hand, the children drew pictures of nebulae, giant gas clouds where stars are born; on the other, they collected funny or interesting stories from their parents about when they were babies. They brought in baby photos of themselves, and their classmates tried to guess who was who. We plotted where our names came from on a map, which led to thoughtful discussions about what "up" and "down" mean when gravity pulls us into place wherever we stand. We watched videos from space which captured our beautiful planet in all its round, spinning glory. "There's the atmosphere, wrapping up our Earth!" the kids shouted.

I didn't notice the switch from the Earth to our Earth right away. Once I did, I realized it reflected how we now thought of our park – as a place where we belonged, that welcomed us in all conditions, a place that protected us and to which we owed our protection.

Hopi's Story
Junior and Senior Kindergarten
McMurrich Junior Public School, Toronto District School Board (TDSB)

Starting the Environmental Inquiry Process

After being told that children learn by "constructing their knowledge" during my teacher training at the Jackman Institute of Child Study in the late 1990s, I set out into Toronto's public school system to "construct" for myself whether that was true in practice. Like many Toronto public school teachers in the last two decades, I encountered an amazing diversity of students and an education system intent on standardized assessment and improvement measures. In that environment, constructivist theory and knowledge building did not seem to fit.

When the first edition of *Natural Curiosity* (2011) was given to me as part of the Ontario Ministry of Education's Early Primary Collaborative Inquiry (EPCI), I was still sceptical as to whether the diverse students I taught had a natural sense of wonder and curiosity. In my experience, teachers would ask questions about a subject they already knew about and students would then either guess or be told the answer. *Natural Curiosity* and the professional learning community of EPCI challenged me to ask real questions, both of my students and myself, that would require genuine inquiry and research. This profoundly changed the dynamics of the classroom. Rather than listening for answers that confirmed what I already knew, I started listening to how students explained their learning, listening for clues that would help me understand what they wondered about.

Because English was a second language for many of my Kindergarten students, I started using pictures and video to document their thinking. Using this method of pedagogical documentation, I found I could "listen" to my students as they expressed themselves through painting, sculpture, building, drama, and outdoor exploration. When children saw their thinking shared visually through photographs, videos, and written words, they would light up. It was like watching a flower bloom.

Through the process of visual documentation, I began to notice that asking real questions (where I did not already know the answer) and actively listening to children's responses changed my relationship with the students. Through the daily practice of Knowledge Building and sharing circles both with the whole class and in small groups, the students began to trust me and each other on a deeper level. While learning to sit in a circle, listen, and ask questions respectfully took a lot of effort with Early Years students, the daily practice made our learning community flourish. Even though creating enough space for a circle of 30 students in a crowded Toronto school was difficult, it was worth sacrificing furniture for the community it created. Gradually, as our reciprocal relationships strengthened, students began to take greater risks in sharing their wonder, their curiosity and their learning. For me, respecting and valuing this relationship became the heart of inquiry.

The practice of documenting inquiry learning through pictures, video, and text permanently changed me as a teacher. Through the process of reflecting on the evidence of learning in collaboration with students, educators, and families, I noticed a pattern that kept repeating. And I found that the pattern aligned with the Kindergarten Inquiry Process (Ontario Ministry of Education, 2016, p. 23) outlined in the Ontario Curriculum. I would often describe the Kindergarten Inquiry Process to parents in the following way:

1. "Get me interested." (Initial Engagement)
2. "Let me muck around and play with the ideas." (Exploration)
3. "Let me do something with what I learned." (Investigation)
4. "Let me talk about it." (Communication)

I noticed that this pattern of learning happened naturally during recess time and after school during unstructured play. When I took my three young daughters to our local ravine or park, their play would naturally follow this pattern. If they were given enough time, particularly in the "mucking about" stage, their investigations would go off in directions my adult mind would never have anticipated. For instance, in the grasslands of the local oak savannah, they created a game that mimics the behaviour of wild horses. While I saw my children learning through natural inquiry, I also found that my role as an active listener was critical to sustaining the learning. Had I not asked them about what they were doing, or noticed the learning that was happening, I might never have brought them back to the magical place they now call "Horse Valley."

In my Kindergarten classroom, one of the students had the idea to post the story of our learning on YouTube so they could show their parents and return again and again to the places we had visited during our Andy Goldsworthy art inquiry (Martin, 2013a; Martin, 2013b). If I had not listened to her suggestion, and taken the time to communicate our learning in this way, the learning would have stopped. When the students watched their movie about their natural art, it re-engaged them and caused them to expand and deepen their learning through another cycle of inquiry. Further, the learning started to transfer beyond the time and space of the classroom. That same student came back to me years after she completed Kindergarten to tell me how many views our movie had received!

While working at Forest Valley Outdoor Education Centre on the West Don River in Toronto, I noticed a similar cycle of learning in the Anishinaabe Medicine Wheel lessons created by Jan Beaver, a now-retired Anishinaabe teacher. At Jan's suggestion, I investigated the on-line recordings of Indigenous Elders on the interactive platform, *Four Directions Teachings* (Invert Media, 2012). There I found Elder Lillian Pitawanakwat's teachings of the Medicine Wheel from an Anishinaabe perspective. Through these teachings, I realized that the cyclical story of learning I had observed in my Kindergarten class and in my own children's play had a relationship with the natural cycles and teachings of the Anishinaabe Medicine Wheel.

Medicine Wheel from *Four Directions Teachings* **(Invert Media, 2012)**

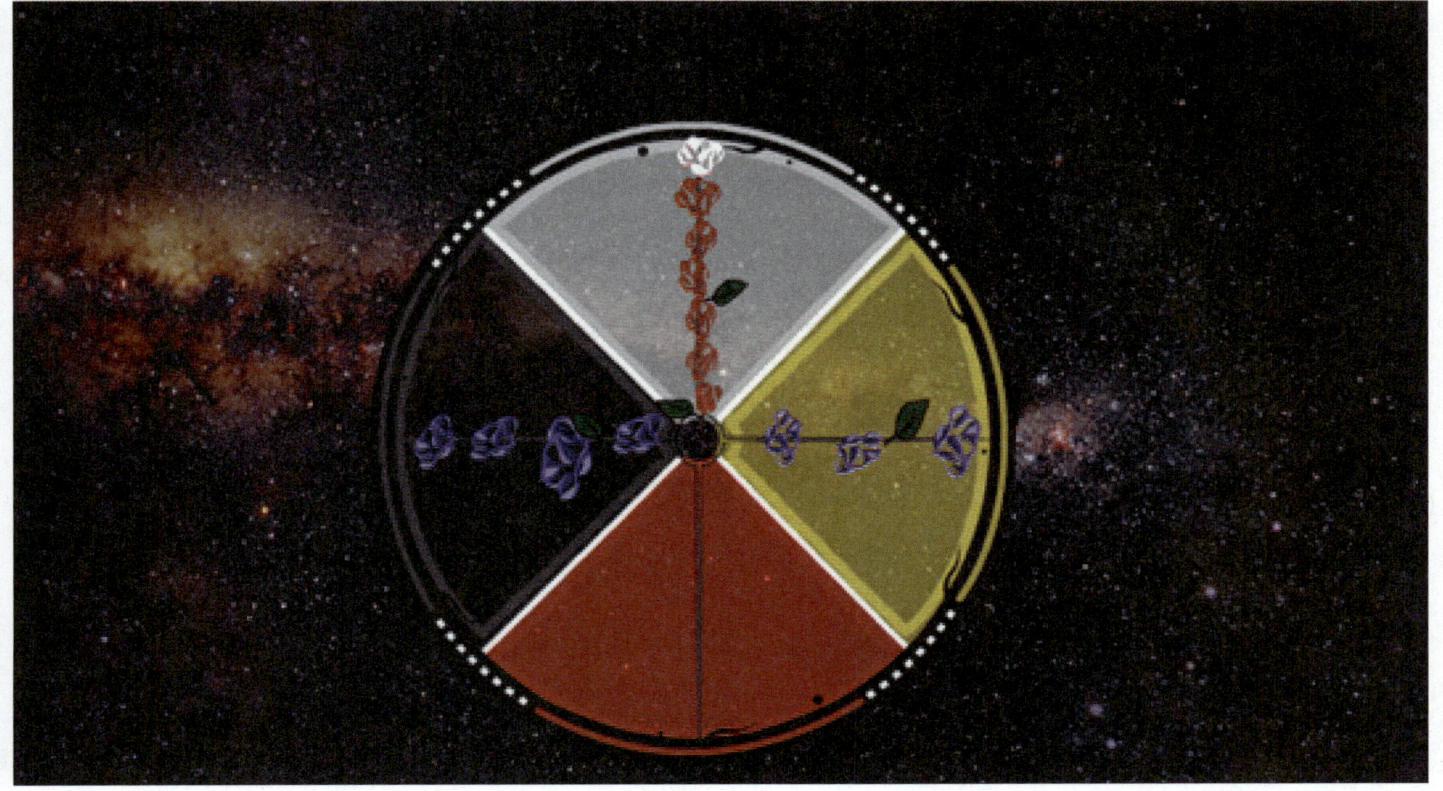

While "the teachings of the Medicine Wheel are vast" (Pitawanakwat, 2006 as cited in Invert Media, 2012), my introduction to them made me think about how learning flowed in natural circles that correspond to the day cycle (dawn, day, sunset, night) and the seasonal cycle (spring, summer, fall, winter). For me, this helped make sense of the layers of pedagogy that I encountered while teaching Kindergarten. There seemed to be a relationship between my early understanding of a Medicine Wheel, the four steps of *The Kindergarten Inquiry Process*, the four branches of *Natural Curiosity*, and the four frames of the *Ontario Kindergarten Curriculum* (2016).

However, the more I tried to learn about the Medicine Wheel, the more I realized it did not fit neatly into the same categories as the Western pedagogies I had been taught. My Western-trained mind was always looking for one "right" way to apply Medicine Wheel teachings and it took me a long time to accept that these teachings could not be abstracted from the relationship to the land and people where they came from and simply applied in a new context.

It was not until I came into relationship with Traditional Ojibwe Teacher/Kokomis, Jacqui Lavalley, an Elder-in-Residence at the University of Toronto, that I had a deeper experience of the value of context. After visiting her a number of times, I gained enough courage to ask her about how I was thinking about the Medicine Wheel. Her answer forever changed me. She told me that she knew who the Medicine Wheel teachings belonged to and it wasn't me. She said that for me, considering the cycles of the day, the seasons, and the four directions should be called "circle teachings." I remember the vivid experience of letting go of my Western approach of "trying to know the right answer" and accepting the traditional teachings she was offering with a new respect and humility. It was only through developing a relationship with Elder Jacqui that I began to understand which things can be shared for the benefit of a larger community, which things need to be kept within one's heart, and which things belong to someone else.

I hope that by sharing this story, it might help educators address the very real concern of appropriation and suggest how important it is to seek out respectful, reciprocal relationships with the community in which they are working.

Within this context, if we ask the difficult questions and actively listen to the answers, we can begin to build the trust in our communities that is essential for transforming our learning and developing the capacity for Truth and Reconciliation. This is how I tried to apply my early learning in my context of a downtown Toronto classroom.

Reflecting on "Lighting the Fire & Inquiry and Engagement"

Although I could find no mention of Spirit in the Ontario Kindergarten Curriculum (2016), both Elder Jacqui and Elder Lillian share that it is the source of all life. Elder Jacqui told me that just lighting the sacred medicine of sage represented a connection to Spirit. I was taught that this related to the sun, the source of all life and the colour yellow in Anishinaabe circle teachings. The eastern direction also relates to spring and the beginning of the day and the growth cycle. Elder Lillian described how her parents used to ask her, "My daughter, how is your fire burning?" as a way to reflect on and nurture the "fire within" (Pitawanakwat, 2006, as cited in Invert Media, 2012).

Engaging young students in this kind of self-reflective inquiry seemed like such a natural way to begin the day and the school year. Not only did it begin the pattern of reciprocal dialogue so essential to inquiry learning, it also provided a natural analogy for introducing early learners to self-regulation. The metaphor of a fire needing to be "just right" for the learning environment helped my students develop strategies that made sense to them. To "feed the fire" they could choose to eat a snack first. To "cool down" they could get a drink of water or play outside with their "big-fire" muscles. To accommodate these needs we started each day outside, regardless of any inclement weather.

How is my fire burning?

Our Circle Blanket with Some of Our "Treasures"

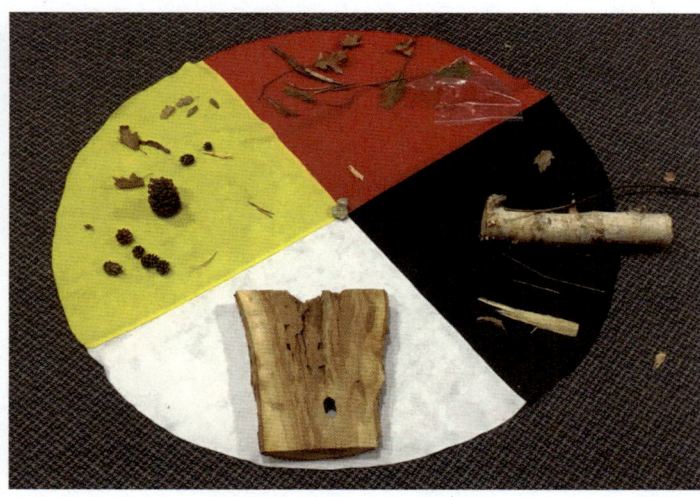

The natural world, even the outdoor yard of a school in downtown Toronto, provides the conditions for the most powerful engagement in real learning. Developing a relationship with the land is an essential aspect of environmental inquiry and a proven benefit to our mental health and well-being. To honour this Indigenous perspective, we would start each morning relating to the sun and its place in the sky and use an Anishinaabe circle to plan the cycle of the day. We would watch the sun rising in the east and relate its colour and position to the yellow part of the circle. We would talk about red being the hottest colour, and say that we would have lunch when the sun was hottest in the middle of the sky. When the sun would start to set in the west, the shadows would be black. Later at night the white moon would come up and we would be home dreaming about our great day together.

A typical school day begins with supporting children as they separate from their parents or caretakers. This can be a difficult transition time. For some children in Junior Kindergarten it is their first time away from their families. To help in a nurturing way with these morning challenges we co-wrote a song which named the people the morning sun shines on (to the tune of "The Good Morning Train Is Coming"). When it came time to acknowledge the people we couldn't see, we closed our eyes and sang to them in our hearts as a way of acknowledging that we were still connected in spirit.

Reflecting on "Sending Out Roots & Experiential Learning"

I was taught that the red direction of the circle related to the summer and to the hottest time of the day where seeds start to grow or, to use the language of this resource's Indigenous lens, to "send out roots." Young children naturally relate to the place they are in. When I worked in Outdoor Education, I loved how within five minutes of getting off the bus, young children were picking up pine cones and insects. While children will attempt to relate to any space – indoor or outdoor – by touching, tasting, smelling, looking, and listening, the outdoors magnifies this experience and immediately draws them into interaction with natural phenomena. Most teachers can attest to the fact that an insect in the classroom will totally disrupt a lesson. Conversely, outside in its natural habitat, an insect becomes a spontaneous lesson in ecology. Rather than teach students to resist their natural urge to relate to their environment, we encouraged it by making it an important first engagement to inquiry.

"Treasure!"

An Attempt to Sort Our Treasures

Natural Materials in Our Art Studio

Play-based learning is often misconstrued as a free-for-all. Educators play a critical role in active listening that draws attention to and extends the learning. To focus children's attention in their outdoor play, we constantly interacted with them, actively listening and documenting student questions. While young children will ask endless questions, notice how the ones we documented (below) have learning potential and are grounded in the immediate context of our schoolyard:

"What if we pick flowers and water them?"
"What's inside (a pine cone)?"
"Why are they (red pine trees) red?"
"Why are there little balls (ginkgo fruit) on that tree?"
"Why doesn't that ginkgo tree have any fruit?"
"Can we keep them?"
"I wonder what's inside?"
"Can you write my words to my story?"
"What's under the sand?"
"Which tree has more shade?"
"Where is the black walnut tree?"

As most Kindergarten teachers can attest, four- and five-year-olds are naturally drawn to collecting treasures. Each morning we would capitalize on this interest by collecting natural treasures in a bin so we could bring them into the classroom for further exploration. During our morning meeting, we would discuss where they best belonged in the classroom. We would then incorporate them into our math, literacy, arts, and science centres where they would support language and concept development.

It took a lot of self-discipline and patience to resist directing the exploration from an adult perspective and support students in whatever way they wanted to experience the materials. The key to negotiating success in the messy world of inquiry and experiential learning is to establish a consistent framework which helps make sense of the mess of real learning. We were inspired by the Reggio Emilia approach to develop a routine of staying with a chosen centre for the entire learning period (which only works if the materials and context are rich enough to support extended exploration). The more time children have to experience learning through all of their senses, the deeper their roots are connected to their environment.

During this exploration stage of learning, I found that the teacher's role was critical to sustaining interest and focus. We supported our students' exploration both by talking about what they were noticing and asking them what they were wondering. Documenting the exploration (through writing or photography) served a dual purpose, both as an assessment of where the children were at in their thinking and as a visual, social-emotional acknowledgement of their ideas about the learning. Assessing and paying attention to play that has inquiry potential positively encourages thinking and activity that promotes the most learning. Within a week of beginning this practice, some students were already beginning to document their own learning so that it could be recorded, shared and investigated further.

"I wonder what those little green balls are on the ginkgo tree?"

Culminating each morning with a Knowledge Building Circle served to both honour the work that had been done through the morning exploration and bring individual ideas to the larger classroom community where they might find more connections and a deeper relationship to broader, whole class inquiry. Within the circle format, focused questioning and active listening create essential links between mucking about and figuring out what to do with the learning. I found that visually documenting the circle conversation helped us co-construct a plan and demonstrate to students how we might apply and integrate their experiences through investigation.

Reflecting on "The Flow of Knowledge & Integrated Learning"

After the growth of summer, the fall is the time of the harvest, when plants bear fruit and disperse seeds. Likewise, afternoon follows morning in the daily cycle and, the farther into the west that the sun travels, the deeper the shadows become which relates to the black of the western direction in an Anishinaabe circle. If children have been inspired in real ways and have had a chance to relate to their learning by engaging their senses, then the investigations they pursue tend to naturally draw all of their learning together. When problems were grounded in the real context of the land immediately accessible to the students, they were empowered to take leadership, re-engage, and deepen their learning whenever they stepped outside.

For example, a number of students discovered black walnut shells even though we could not find a black walnut tree anywhere in our yard. The students wondered, "Where do the nuts come from? Can we eat them?" I told them a story of the old black walnut tree in my backyard, and how Elder Duke Redbird had said that they were related to the Grandfather teaching of Wisdom, as the walnuts are considered by his people to be "brain food."

Black Walnuts Found in Our Yard, but No Tree!

One student noticed that the squirrels came out in the schoolyard after the children went inside. One of the squirrels had a nut in its mouth and we wondered how he or she got it. We counted 11 squirrels, but we still could not find the black walnut tree. Since another group of students had been exploring maps, we decided to integrate mapping concepts to help us find the black walnut treasure.

"Let me show you how a map works."

Our Map to the Black Walnut Treasure

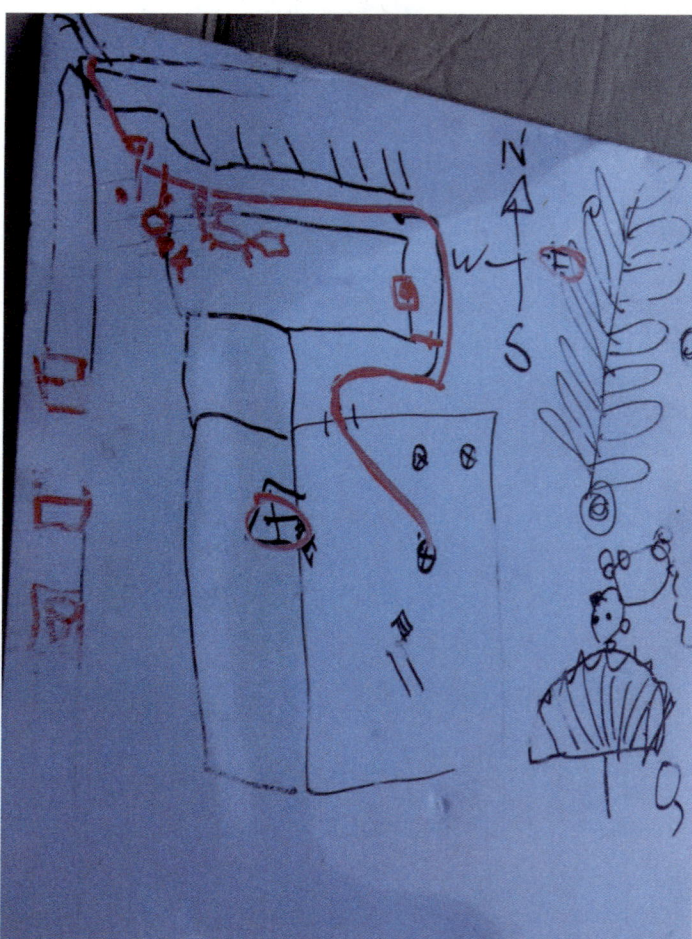

After scouting the neighbourhood for the black walnut tree, we mapped a plan for our first field trip during the second week of school. The details of our map included squirrels and leaf drawings based on our research from *Trees, Shrubs & Vines of Toronto* (City of Toronto, 2016).

The next day the investigation continued when we discovered a chewed pine cone, and noticed that squirrels were eating the seeds out of this natural treasure. Even though there were red pine trees in our schoolyard, there seemed to be more black walnut shells. We continued the investigation inside.

"There is more black walnuts because they filled 3 rows instead of 1 and this much."

When we talked about the fact that there were more black walnut shells in our yard than red pine cones, we started wondering why that might be: "Do squirrels like black walnuts better?" "Do the kids scare the squirrels?" While our environmental science was suspect, we had managed to ask, theorize, map, measure, and observe in a meaningful and integrated way.

Reflecting on "Breathing with the World & Moving Toward Sustainability"

All four branches work in a circle. I have been taught that white of an Anishinaabe circle represents the north, the night, and the winter when living things finally die and return to soil only to nurture new life in the spring.

If students are supported throughout the day in partnership and with respect for their voice in directing their learning through inquiry, they naturally want to share or give back what they have learned to their community. When educators are occupied with trying to cover the curriculum rather than bring students full circle in their learning, no time is given for students to give back to their community. Through my own learning experience, as a student and as a teacher, I noticed that it is only when I share what I have learned with others that I really consolidate the experience.

Elder Lillian Pitawanakwat called it "storytelling time" when her Elders would share stories and teachings. This reminded me of how my students naturally wanted to show me their picture and tell me about it. As a conscientious Kindergarten teacher, I would document their words and support them in writing their name and then ask them if I could hang their artwork on the wall as part of their portfolio. Early in the school year, they would invariably want to take it home to show their family. After listening to Elder Lillian this made complete sense: home was their community.

As the school year progressed and students began to trust that the story of their artwork mattered to our classroom community, the other students and educators became part of their community. Likewise, I found that if students were engaged in authentic inquiry with things that interested them and that were grounded in the land and the people in their community, this process of sharing their story and giving back was natural. My job as their teacher was to help amplify their voice and make connections in the community to support their learning.

Teacher: "Can we hang your tree in our class?"
Student: "No, I want to give it to Mom and Dad."

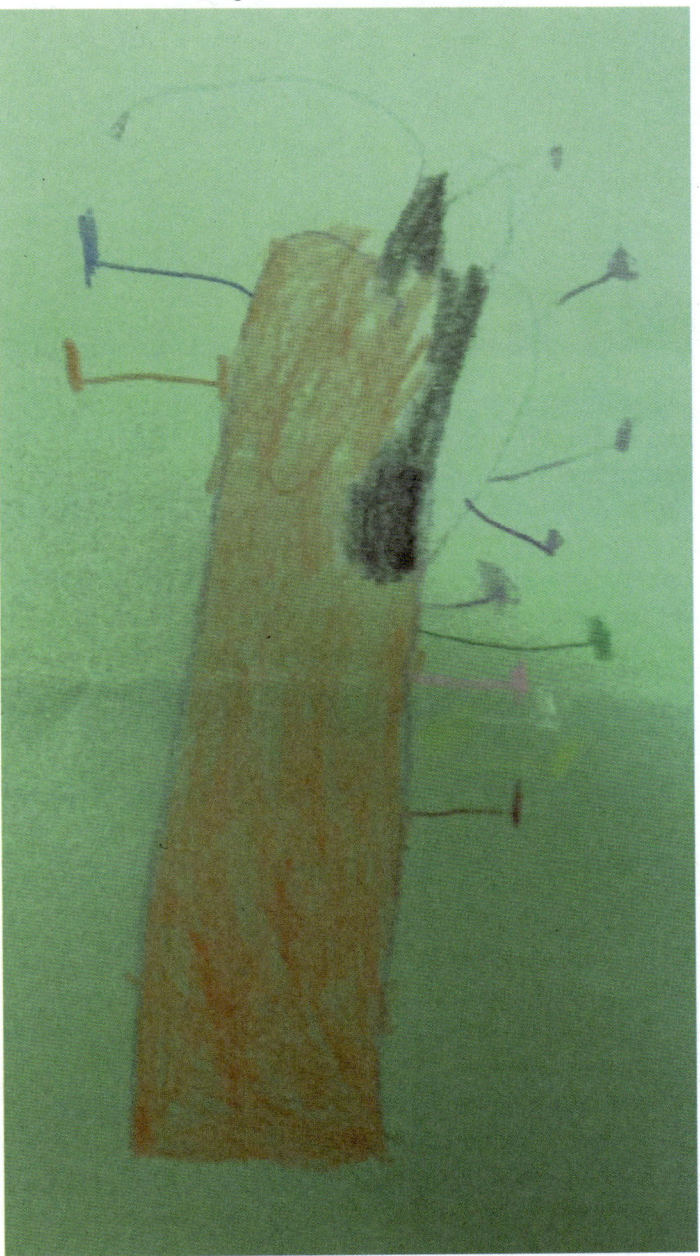

For me, the most powerful moment of teaching is when I witness people applying what they have learned to enrich their lives beyond the original learning context. For example, one student connected with our co-constructed map of our field trip to find the black walnut tree and decided that that was a good way for him to tell the story of the day to his parents. The student went a step further and thought that he might map all the black walnut trees in his community.

Hopi's Story: Junior and Senior Kindergarten

"We have to get all the way here for the black walnut tree. There is not just one. There is more than one!"

Documenting these moments along with the steps that have gone before is an excellent form of assessment, but it can also serve to link the day's story as a provocation or inspiration for the next day's learning. Thus, the circle of inquiry learning can be an expanding spiral that returns again and again through all four branches of environmental inquiry every day, every season, and every year. If we pay attention and teach in harmony with these natural cycles, learning will transfer beyond the classroom into a way of life where we are forever coming into a greater relationship with our planet and our place within it.

Transference of Learning: "Look at all the DIFFERENT leaves I found coming to school today!

Zoe's Story
Grade 1
Dr. Eric Jackman Institute of Child Study Laboratory School

Starting the Environmental Inquiry Process

I often start the year with an inquiry focusing on the local community. This focus feels especially appropriate as we begin to build a community within our own classroom; it also provides us with many opportunities to be out in nature and to connect to children's lives and experiences outside of school. This year, however, I wanted to enrich and expand our work on community by starting with a different focus – learning about seeds – hoping that this would lead nicely into an investigation of some of the Indigenous peoples of this land and how their cultures, traditions, and worldviews continue to inform us. I also wanted to tie this work into the concept of cycles, including both the seed cycle and, more generally, seasonal cycles.

Seeds and Community

To establish a connection to nature as an important theme for the coming year, I wrote to the children in the summer; I asked them to bring in some seeds and a drawing of their favourite place in nature on the first day of school. I hoped that these drawings would inspire conversation and help children to get to know something new about one another. Beginning on that first day and building throughout the fall term, we gathered an incredible variety of seeds, identifying, labelling, and examining them.

The children shared their drawings on the second day of school. We gathered in a circle to sort the seeds into categories: seeds from fruit, vegetables, trees, and flowers. We spread them out on a windowsill so that children could further examine them.

Labeled and Sorted Seeds

Gathering Questions

After an initial provocation such as this, I often ask the children for their questions, and this determines the direction of our inquiry.

On the third day of school, we gathered and I recorded their questions on chart paper. I cut the questions into strips so we could physically sort them into categories. As we sat in a circle I read each question aloud and asked if it had something in common with a previous question or belonged in a new category. There was a lively discussion and the children acknowledged that some questions could be sorted into more than one category. I glued the strips onto chart paper, hanging them in a prominent place so that the children's wonderings would be front and centre as our inquiry progressed. When I asked the children how they thought we might find answers to our questions, they suggested we might read books, go on excursions, and plant the seeds they brought in.

Our Questions About Seeds

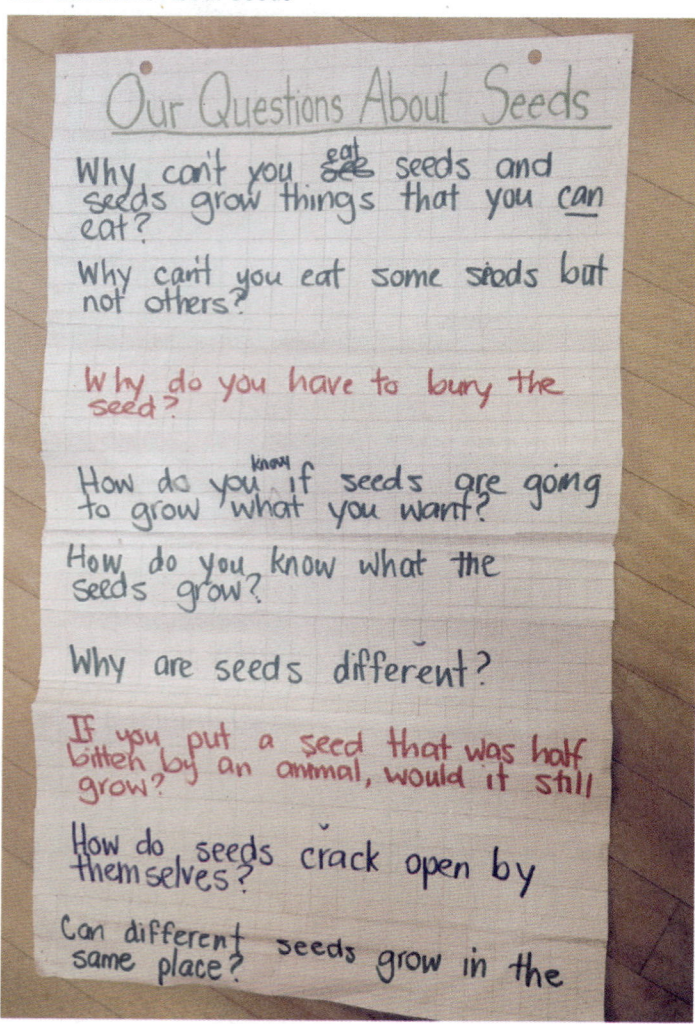

What Do Seeds Need to Grow?

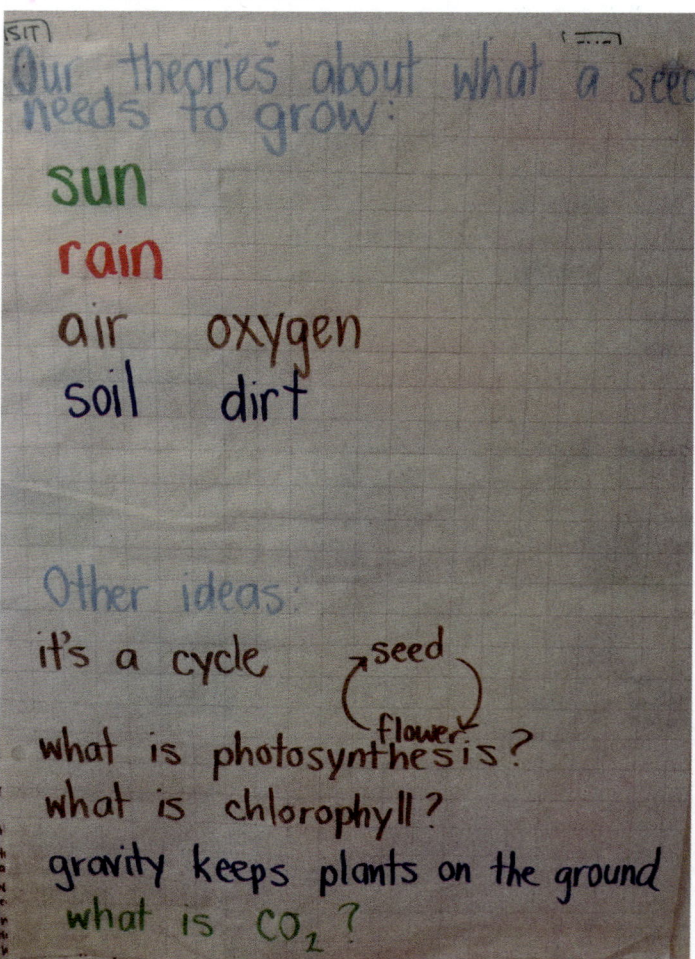

As an initial assessment, I asked the children to draw a picture in their Lab Book (a notebook used for inquiry-related work) showing what a seed needs to grow. We summarized and displayed everyone's ideas on chart paper. We then read *The Tiny Seed* (Carle, 1990), a beautiful narrative that introduced ideas about how seeds travel and grow.

Where to Begin?

At this point in an inquiry the teacher's input and decisions are critical. I chose questions I thought might capture the children's interest and lead to active hands-on work right away, asking each child to choose some seeds to plant. Over the coming weeks we observed varying degrees of success: flower, fruit, and vegetable seeds grew, while acorns, maple keys and seeds from burrs didn't. The children were eager to check on their plants each day. After a few weeks, they agreed to unearth the seeds that had not grown so we could see what was going on under the soil. We replanted some of these seeds but had no more luck the second time.

Using Non-fiction Books

Having a large collection of books about our topic, to complement our hands-on work, is an important part of an inquiry. The bulk of our collection comes from the public library. It includes books that some children are able to read on their own and others that we share together. I also select books that are beyond their reading level because children benefit from looking at the pictures and photographs.

I keep the books in bins on a low counter so that the children can independently access them. Sometimes I give them time to browse with a partner. I circulate, reading with children and listening to their comments. The first time we looked at the books, there was an excited buzz as children huddled together, finding pages that addressed their questions. They could hardly contain their excitement as they jumped up, book in hand, to show me or my student teacher something they had noticed. At times they used sticky notes to flag pages they would like me to read aloud, or to mark pages containing experiments they wanted to try.

We also use books for interactive read-alouds, as many of the texts are above the children's reading level but well within their understanding. The pace at which we read is often slow. I stop to paraphrase and the children make comments about the content, ask questions, articulate theories, share experiences, and make links to prior knowledge. It can take us several sessions to read an entire book. Alternatively, we may read bits and pieces from several books that address the same information.

After planting the seeds, we read a book called *A Fruit Is a Suitcase for Seeds* (Richards & Hariton, 2002), which described the seeds found in fruits and vegetables. Another book, *From Seed to Apple* (Ganeri, 2006), described the seed cycle – how a flower grows to produce seeds that in turn flower the following spring. This book inspired a discussion about what happens to trees during the winter.

> **Zoe:** What does it mean when trees rest?
>
> **Student 1:** They don't grow and they don't get any food because when we're sleeping we can't get any food.
>
> **Student 2:** They don't have leaves in the winter so they can't get the food. Maybe they have to store up in the summer and the spring.
>
> **Student 3:** There is sun in the winter.
>
> **Student 4:** But there is no heat. Just because it's sunny it's not hot.
>
> **Student 1:** The trees can't grow because in spring and summer they try to get lots of food in their bodies for the winter.

Addressing Misconceptions

Teachers can plan experiences and think about what they want to teach once they know what children understand about a topic and what their misconceptions are. Misconceptions about a topic often come up as we read and talk about books, but this is not a time to address them. Instead, I make note of them and consider how I might help to move the child's thinking along. I might plan a Knowledge Building Circle where children have the opportunity to discuss the misconception so that they can listen to and consider other people's ideas and knowledge. Or I might plan an experience or experiment that will challenge that child's thinking. At some point, but not right away, I might choose to read something to the children that provides "correct" information, but not until we have explored the misconception in other ways. Comments made during the interactive read-aloud, above, helped me to decide what we might do next. We read next about the seed cycle and photosynthesis because I could see that the children were wrestling with these concepts.

Knowledge Building Circles

Knowledge Building Circles are a regular part of our inquiry work. They are inspired by children's questions, both in the initial stages of the inquiry process and during interactive read-alouds or hands-on work. My goals for a KBC are that children listen to one another and either build onto one another's ideas or respectfully offer a different idea. I try to speak as little as possible and don't repeat children's comments, wanting students to listen to the child who is speaking rather than waiting for me to echo or clarify their comment. I also refrain from evaluating each child's contribution with comments such as "you're right" or "good!" I want children to know that I value a diversity of ideas and that I'm not looking for a particular answer.

After one interactive read-aloud, the children wondered where the first seed came from. The transcript below shows children engaged in and building on one another's ideas, asking questions, contributing prior knowledge, and using knowledge building phrases such as "maybe" and "I think." Another goal of these discussions is that many children participate; in this Knowledge Building Circle, seven different children made comments.

> **"Where did the first seed come from?"**
>
> **Student 1:** Maybe an apple seed [was first] because it can grow fruit and trees. I think God made it.
> **Student 2:** I have a book about God and the first seeds came from an apple.
> **Student 3:** It was a golden apple.
> **Student 4:** Maybe apple seeds came from a god's tooth.
> **Student 5:** When the world was first created by asteroids crashing together. I think that one of the asteroids had a seed in them.
> **Student 6:** There were asteroids crashing together. I think when the asteroids crashed together then a seed came and they went into space where the earth was going to be made.
> **Student 7:** Maybe the asteroids came from the other planets and then seeds came when they crashed. Or maybe when the earth came together, maybe a seed was born instead of a baby and then it came out.

Experiential Learning

Connection to the Natural World and Excursions

Another important element of an inquiry is a connection to the natural world. To introduce the concept of seasonal cycles, I invited the children to begin a year-long observation of a tree near our classroom window, hoping that close observation of a single tree would help them tune into seasonal changes. Soon after school started we went outside to sketch the tree with pastels. We planned to do a drawing each month using different media. As the year progressed, these sketches were displayed on a bulletin board along with a monthly photo of the tree. At the end of the year each child's sketches will be stapled into a booklet and they'll design a cover for it.

Our Tree Sketches

Other opportunities to focus on seasonal cycles occurred during our five trips to a local ravine – a short subway ride away – and during our three visits to a local nature centre for their "Through the Seasons" program. Visiting the same places multiple times allowed the children to develop a strong sense of place and affirmed that they could easily get out into nature in the city without much preparation.

Timing is important when planning these excursions. Sometimes an excursion can launch an inquiry, while at other times it can be an affirming culmination of all we have learned. I planned an excursion after the children had gained some knowledge about seeds so that their discoveries could be assimilated into their prior knowledge. We took our first trip to the nature centre to attend a program called "Nuts About Seeds," which included a lesson about the different ways seeds travel and a guided walk in the woods.

Our trips to the nature centre were for specific programs, but our trips to the ravine were completely unstructured. I knew the path we would walk while exploring the ravine, but how long we spent in each area and what we focused on depended on the children's interests and discoveries.

Our Ravine Outing

We visited the ravine in the fall, winter, and spring (when the buds were just starting to open), and once more when everything was in full bloom. At the beginning of each visit we talked about what we might find that was different from our last visit. I encouraged the children to be observant and to show a teacher or friend when they found something interesting. We took photographs and brought interesting objects back to the classroom for further exploration.

Classroom Environment

The classroom environment is a critical supporting element in inquiry-based learning. Starting the year with empty bulletin boards can make a statement about the inquiry work that will be central to the classroom community. The work that we choose to fill those boards has meaning for the children and reflects their thinking, wondering, and learning. My goal is that they will be able to talk knowledgeably to a visitor about everything hanging on our walls. By the third week of school we had hung up the children's questions, a chart about their understanding of what a seed needs to grow, and their drawings of our September tree.

The classroom layout is also key. A large carpet area that can accommodate everyone in a circle is essential. Children also cluster in front of the teacher's chair during interactive read-alouds so they can see the illustrations. Tables or desks pushed together into groups promotes collaborative, face-to-face work as children experiment, draw, and write about their learning.

Pervasive Knowledge Building

Six weeks into the term, children were still bringing in seeds most days. Parents told me that their children were noticing seeds when they were out in the neighbourhood, illustrating how an inquiry can become part of children's lives rather than something they only do at school, to be forgotten once they go home. I want children to live our inquiries, and hope that the topics we explore will become lifelong interests. I want them to know that all ideas are improvable, and that they can always learn more.

Shifting the Focus

In mid-October we added another layer to our inquiry as we started to think about the Indigenous people in our local community whose ancestors were the original peoples of this land. This shift seemed especially appropriate, given the inherent connection of Indigenous knowledge and perspectives with the natural world.

This shift felt like a big leap to me, as my own school learning had not included Indigenous knowledge and perspectives. I worried about not knowing enough, saying the "wrong" thing, providing incorrect or inaccurate information, and using inappropriate vocabulary. Nonetheless, in the spirit of inquiry-based learning, I knew that I just needed to jump in and learn along with the children.

I asked the children to think about what questions they had about how Indigenous people might have lived in the past, keeping in mind how this might inform our understanding of present-day Indigenous cultures, traditions, and knowledge. We ended up with an incredible diversity of questions that fell into categories relating to human needs – shelter, food, clothing, health, etc. – and also about Indigenous peoples' relationship to the land and to animals.

Our Questions About First Peoples

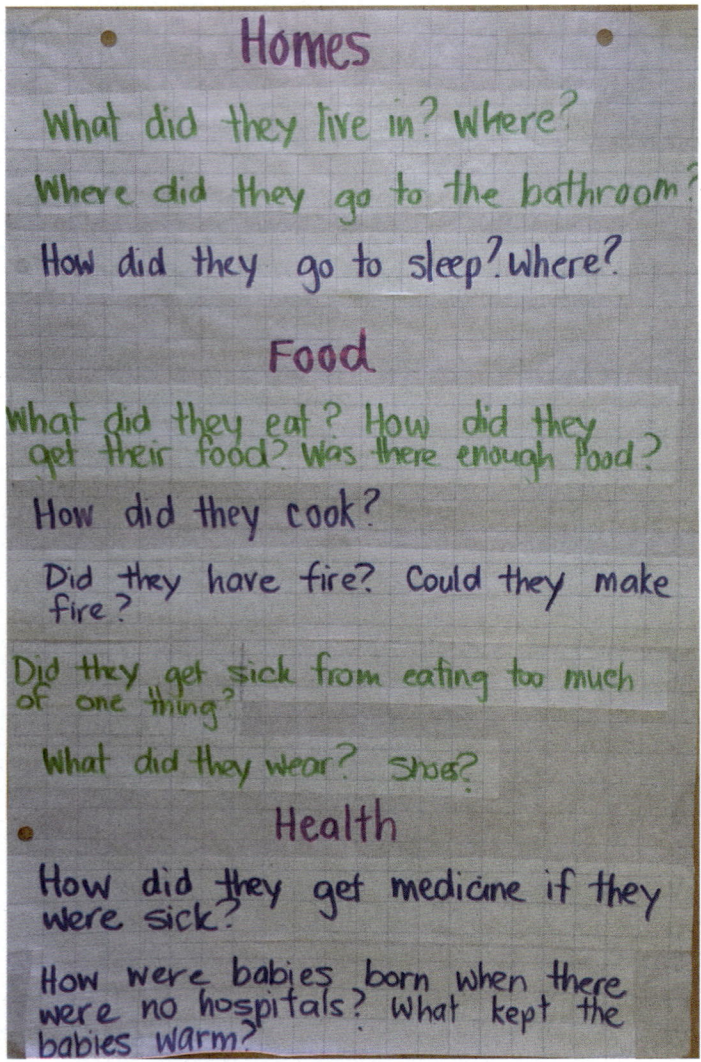

We started to build our knowledge with an excursion to an arboretum situated along the Humber River, a significant waterway and hub of human activity for thousands of years. The children learned about vegetables that were grown then (and that are still grown), explored some artifacts, and went for a guided walk in the woods. Being out in the natural world as we examined and discussed artifacts was a powerful start to our new focus.

A second excursion took us to a piece of land along the same river, where those who hosted us are working to heal the land by removing invasive species and planting indigenous plants. We started in a circle and the children were invited to smudge. One of our hosts had caught a rainbow trout, and we heard about how the salmon and trout live and reproduce in the river. The children learned about the Medicine Wheel and how it relates to the seasons. As thanks for our time in this natural place, we were each given a pinch of tobacco to leave in a place of our choosing. We then walked along the riverbank, learning about the plants and getting to know the area. The children were invited to spread milkweed seeds to help combat the invasive plant life, and we tasted sumac seeds (a medicinal plant). We stopped and listened each time our hosts had something to tell or teach us.

Learning the Wildlife and Seasons in Relation to the Medicine Wheel

When we returned to school, the children created drawings using pastels. They wrote about their favourite part of the trip, which they each recounted while gathered on the carpet.

> **"What did you like about our trip to the river?"**
>
> **Student 1:** I drew [our host] and tobacco.
>
> **Zoe:** What did you do with the tobacco?
>
> **Student 2:** Tobacco was the first plant. And we put it wherever we wanted.
>
> **Student 3:** It's going to grow.
>
> **Student 4:** We put it down to say thank you to the trees.
>
> **Student 3:** We need to replace something we took.

A Student's Pastel Drawing Depicting Our Humber River Experience

Shortly after our visit to the Humber River, one of our hosts, a parent of a student in the class, came to the school to speak to the children. We started out with a smudge[1]. Then the children had the opportunity to ask our visitor questions. In the days that followed these two rich experiences, it seemed like a good time to introduce another authoritative source. We started to read a non-fiction picture book about the longhouses of the Iroquois (Haudenosaunee). The children had so many comments, questions, and observations in response to the book that we read only a little bit each session. After I read aloud "they thanked the animals they hunted for sacrificing their lives to feed people," I asked the children if they recalled what they had learned people do to thank the land.

Student 1: If you take a plant, then you have to put tobacco down.

Zoe: You did that at the Humber River.

Student 2: At the assembly [where we had an Ojibway storyteller] some people got to put berries into the little bowl.

Student 3: Smudging. It's to clean your body.

Student 4: Washing your heart and washing your face to make you feel good if you're scared.

Student 5: It makes you peaceful.

Student 1: Or they can use it to wash your face. And one of the questions we were asking about is how they wash themselves.

Zoe: So there's washing with soap and water, and a different kind of washing for peace, or to make you feel safe.

We were also fortunate to have a wonderful school-wide connection to our inquiry work when Métis artist Christi Belcourt visited as an artist-in-residence for a week. Her colleague, Isaac Murdoch, an Ojibway storyteller and traditional knowledge holder, shared Anishinaabe creation stories and legends featuring Nanabush, and Christi worked with every class to create three large paintings depicting scenes from these stories.

As I write this account we are still in the midst of our inquiry. We have all learned a great deal, but, as with all inquiry work, the more we learn, the more we realize how much more there is still to learn.

[1] "Smudging is a tradition, common to many First Nations, which involves the burning of one or more medicines gathered from the earth. The four sacred medicines used in First Nations' ceremonies are tobacco, sage, cedar and sweetgrass... The forms of smudging will vary from nation to nation but are considered by all to be a way of cleansing oneself" (Aboriginal Education Directorate of Manitoba Education and Advanced Learning, 2014, p. 4).

Ellie's Story
Grade 1
The Grove Community School, Toronto District School Board (TDSB)

Starting the Environmental Inquiry Process

Questions about the seasons arise across many areas of the Grade 1 curriculum. I wanted to start the year exploring this important theme, anticipating that we would revisit it many times throughout the year.

Beginning an inquiry is often the hardest part for me. When I consider where the learning might lead, the possibilities branch out in many directions. To avoid becoming overwhelmed, I find it is best to start small.

Drawings are a wonderful way for students to share their understandings and can provide insights for teachers as they get to know their students. During the first week of school, I asked the children to "draw me everything you know about the seasons." I then scribed exactly what they told me about their pictures. I noticed that some students depicted only one season, while others represented all four. In addition, many illustrated seasonal weather patterns, plants, and human activities. To build upon their initial knowledge and interest, I began to pursue the themes that came up in their drawings further, though remaining open to the possibility of our route changing later on.

"In winter the snow falls and the ground is white. In spring the tulips sprout. In summer there's beautiful colours. Fall. The leaves are falling off the trees and changing colours."

"That's spring and I'm waking up in my short pyjamas and looking out my window. That's summer. That's my parents and that's me. And we're running to pick the flowers. That is winter. We're playing hide-and-seek. I'm hiding under the snow with my hat on my head to stay warm. This is fall. There is leaf piles. One is red. One is a little mixed with green and orange leaves. The tree is losing its leaves."

"Summer. A flower. The flowers are sprouting. This is a tree but it's cut off. The sun. And that's me."

"It's snowing. I'm ice skating on the ice."

Inquiry and Engagement

After examining the children's drawings, I was eager to find out what they wanted to learn about the seasons. To encourage students to share theories and build upon one another's questions and ideas, while supporting early writing skills, I developed a variant of a traditional Knowledge Building Circle.

On each of our four communal tables, I laid out a large sheet of chart paper representing a single season, along with a few photographs of natural occurrences specific to that season. The students worked in four co-operative groups as they moved around the classroom, talking, writing, and drawing their questions and ideas about the changes characterizing each season. For easy tracking, each group used a different coloured marker. While the children worked, the educators in the room recorded notes on each child that were compiled into online portfolios to share with families.

Our Shared Understanding of Fall

Once we had collected and sifted through all the questions, I was faced with a common dilemma for teachers who co-inquire with their students: **Which questions should we choose to explore?**

There is never an easy answer, but since I wanted my students to engage in holistic learning, I selected questions that would require a wide range of strategies (direct observation, hands-on experiments, research) to understand. For example, some questions could be answered through research ("Why is the sky blue?"), while others additionally lent themselves to experimentation ("What type of seed do winter birds eat the most of?").

We began to create a "We think," "We wonder," "How can we find out?" and "We learned" (TWHL) chart. Posing the question "How can we find out?" to students is a powerful part of the inquiry process, and I was excited to see what they came up with. When the children suggested ideas such as "You can ask your mom" or "You can look it up on your phone," I made connections to similar strategies used by professional scientists, such as asking an expert or doing internet research. Not surprisingly, my students (who do not identify as Indigenous) did not suggest storytelling or consulting traditional knowledge as a way of pursuing answers to our inquiry questions.

I wanted to introduce to my non-Indigenous students these ways of knowing. Wanting, of course, to find a culturally relevant resource to help us in this exploration, I turned to *Keepers of Life*, which contains "a gathering of carefully selected Native North American stories and hands-on activities to promote an understanding of, appreciation for, empathy with and responsible stewardship toward all plants on Earth" (Caduto & Bruchac, 1997, p. XVII). This resource weaves together the perspectives and wisdom of Indigenous (Bruchac) and non-Indigenous (Caduto) authors, ecologists, and storytellers to craft a holistic, interdisciplinary approach to teaching about Earth. Many teachings in *Keepers of Life* addressed seasonal questions the students had asked, such as "Why do some trees stay green all year?" or "What makes the seasons change?"

I used the stories shared by Bruchac in this resource for a number of oral storytelling lessons. Taking place in our outdoor classroom, these storytelling lessons nurtured holistic learning that contributed to our class' inquiry.

Excerpt from our lesson on "Why Some Trees Are Always Green," a Cherokee teaching shared by Joseph Bruchac.

Introducing the story:

- *Ask a child to remind the class about her inquiry question that we had added to our TWHL chart.*
- *Read the title of the story to the children and ask if they think this story could help answer her question.*
- *Discuss the location of the traditional Cherokee territory, and how this story would include plants and animals that live in that region.*
- *Introduce how the story talks about plants as medicines, and ask students what that might mean (How does medicine help you? How might nature help make you feel better? Have you ever had a time when something in nature helped you feel better?).*
- *Show students the single illustration that accompanies the story, and ask them to notice what the animals in the picture were doing (closing their eyes/sleeping).*
- *Thank the tree that gave us the paper for this book.*

After telling the story:

- *Ask students comprehension questions to ensure understanding.*
- *Reflect upon how the Cherokee people knew long ago that there was something different between these trees, and how today, biologists call trees coniferous and deciduous to reflect this difference.*
- *Encourage students to notice differences in the appearance and texture of leaf samples collected from the ground around trees in our schoolyard.*
- *Play a "blindfold tree scavenger hunt" where students have to use senses of touch, sound, and smell to determine if a tree is coniferous or deciduous.*

Sometimes, our storytelling sessions sparked connections to other subjects. For example, during our math investigations, two children began exploring the coniferous and deciduous tree materials that we had collected for our lesson about "Why Some Trees Are Always Green." They sorted the materials by colour, size, texture, and type of tree.

"These ones are yellow and these ones are red."

"This bark is really big and these needles are really small."

"These are bumpy and these are pokey."

"These ones are deciduous and these ones are coniferous. They [coniferous trees] stayed awake for the whole night and now they get to stay green all winter."

Experiential Learning

For students to truly understand natural phenomena, talk is not enough. Children need to experience the changes for themselves. For this to happen, we needed to spend much of the year outdoors.

An inquiry into seasonal cycles has no natural conclusion. Like the cycles of the year, our engagement with this topic ebbed and flowed naturally as new ideas and questions were sparked by our experiences of change.

Though located in the heart of a big city, our school grounds have spaces available as outdoor classrooms. Students tend garden plots, engage in "sit spots" (Young, Haas, & McGown, 2010), create maps, observe visiting creatures, and freely explore their surroundings.

> Find one place in your natural world that you visit all the time and get to know it as your best friend. Let this be a place where you learn to sit still – alone, often, and quietly – before you playfully explore beyond. This will become your place of intimate connection with nature.
>
> – Jon Young, Ellen Haas, & Evan McGown, *Coyote's Guide To Connecting With Nature* (2010)

We are also privileged to be located in a "city within a park," with many natural spaces to explore and free public transit for children to get there (City of Toronto, 2017). In this way, our outdoor classroom extends to other natural spaces where we build upon the environmental learning we do in the classroom.

Field Trip to High Park

Before departing, students examined maps of the Toronto Transit Commission system to plan our public transit route. Parent volunteers were recruited and children formed small groups of three or four. In these small groups, students looked at maps of High Park to decide where they would spend their time.

After arriving at the park, materials (e.g., recording sheets, pencils, clipboards, digital cameras, etc.) were distributed to groups of students. A meeting spot and time for lunch were decided upon, and then groups of children and volunteers went off independently to explore their interests in the park at their own pace. This freeform exploration allowed students to engage with the environment on a different level than would be possible in a large group. For example, my small group of students saw a dead animal down a steep hill. With a group of 20 students we would have had to pass by, but in a small group, I was able to take the time to teach the children how to safely descend a steep hill, how to treat dead creatures with respect, and also provide an opportunity for the students to see the decomposition process up close.

At lunchtime, the large group reconvened to talk about our mornings. At this point, we participated as a class in a more structured activity before travelling back to school. On different field trips, we have visited a bird sanctuary, built lean-to structures with fallen branches in the forest, and played active environmental learning games.

Integrated Learning

The inquiry process of learning allows for incredible cross-curricular connections. While predominantly a science unit ("Daily and Seasonal Changes"), our investigation into the seasons connected with areas such as Social Studies ("The Local Community"), Mathematics (Patterning, Sorting), Language (Writing), and Visual Arts.

Integrating visual arts into environmental education is a hands-on way to engage all learners. During our inquiry, two long-term artistic studies added to our growing understanding of the seasons: tree journals and plant colour wheels.

We began our tree journals in mid-September. After reading stories about trees, I told the students that we would develop a relationship with a particular tree by visiting it regularly over the year. Trying to avoid language that connoted ownership (such as "our tree"), I presented this as an opportunity to learn from this tree by observing it closely over a long period of time.

Drawing What We Saw

That first day in September, I simply pointed to a birch tree in our courtyard and provided students with the open-ended prompt: "Draw what you see." I hoped for students to engage more deeply with these tree journals throughout the year than simply repeating the same drawing activity each month. I asked myself, what would be the most effective way to support this?

As part of my philosophy on assessment, I am very interested in having students engage in alternative forms of descriptive feedback. Within these tree journals, I saw an opportunity for my students to engage in peer feedback, inspired by the educational film *Austin's Butterfly: Building Excellence in Student Work* (Expeditionary Learning [EL Education], 2012). Using the same child-created illustrations as in the video, I asked my students the same types of probing questions (e.g., "What did Austin do really well in this drawing?", "What advice would you give Austin to make his drawing even better?", "Do you think Austin took his friends' advice?"). Many students were amazed by this process, and we reiterated that the reason Austin improved was because he wanted to make his work better, and because his friends gave him useful feedback.

Each month when we reconvened in the nature courtyard with our tree journals, the students paired up with a peer to examine their past work and receive feedback about what they could do to improve their skills to better capture the beautiful details of the tree. Along with dramatic improvements in their drawings, the students learned valuable lessons about descriptive feedback, goal setting, lifelong learning, and continuous improvement. The example below shows the development in skill from September to October as this student explores how to represent the texture and pattern of the birch tree's bark and small branches.

A Student's Growth in Drawing Skill

Later, in October, we were inspired by a children's book of poetry titled *Red Sings from Treetops: A Year in Colors* (Sidman & Zagarenski, 2009), which includes poems about the colours of the seasons. After reading and discussing what we know about the colour changes of fall, we went outside to our garden. I had prepared a cardstock colour wheel covered with transparent MACtac, with the sticky side facing out. In the garden, I introduced the idea of a colour wheel in which similar colours are situated beside each other and very different colours are across from each other. I showed them how the colour spectrum goes around and around, and we talked about the positioning of different shades of the same colour on the spectrum, such as greenish or orangey yellows.

We agreed to first choose plants that had already fallen to the ground and to refrain from removing plants from the ground unless there were at least ten other plants of that type nearby. In this way, we strove to be respectful and sustainable in our learning. The children then went off to find parts of plants for each section of our colour wheel. The result was beautiful, and the children made interesting observations.

Student 1: Put the yellowy-green one in between yellow and green.
Student 2: There's no blue.
Student 3: It looks beautiful!
Student 4: It looks like a Medicine Wheel.

Our Fall Colour Wheel

I then asked the children to think about this question: If we make a colour wheel every season, how will they look similar and how will they differ from one another? This became a year-long investigation as we created a new colour wheel for each season.

In February, we gathered together in a Knowledge Building Circle to compare the fall and winter colour wheels and predict what future seasonal colour wheels would look like.

"What do you notice about the colours of each season? How are they similar and different?"

Student 1: The winter colour wheel has not very much stuff and the fall colour wheel has lots of leaves and colours.
Student 2: The winter one has only maybe two leaves and the fall one has maybe twenty leaves. There were more leaves in fall.
Student 3: The leaves fall in fall, so that's why there's more leaves in that one.
Student 4: Even in winter there is lots of green because there are evergreen trees that stay green all winter and there was also grass getting ready for spring.
Ellie: Yes, I think a lot of kids were finding grass when they looked under the snow.
Student 4: It's either getting ready for spring, or maybe because there was not much snow and it was warm this year.
Ellie: So let's make predictions about what our spring colour wheel might look like.
Student 4: Well, even though spring might have a lot of green in it, I think fall is still going to be more colourful because all the leaves change colour in fall.
Student 5: I agree with [Student 4].
Student 6: I think fall and summer will be the most colourful.
Student 2: Let's make a colour wheel on the last day of school for summer.
Student 3: Summer will only be colourful if we pick the flowers.
Student 7: I think fall and winter will be the most colourful.
Student 4: Winter has lots of grey and brown colours but those aren't on the colour wheel. The plants aren't as colourful in winter.

In this way, integrating visual art into environmental inquiry helped my students better appreciate the beauty of seasonal change. It encouraged us to develop a sense of place within our school's outdoor classroom, as the children became attentive to the blooming and fading of plants with the seasons.

Assessment

Just as every inquiry will be different, inquiry-based assessments will also look different in each learning environment. While some assessments focus on a single subject area, others may choose a variety of approaches across curriculum areas. I believe that each educator should use the approach that they feel most comfortable with at various points along this pedagogical journey.

It is important to provide multiple opportunities for assessment in order to evaluate the growth of children's understanding. Take, for example, the formative assessments of this student, carried out in the first week of September, when asked to draw everything they knew about the seasons. In this initial assessment, this student elected to draw only a single season (winter), and showed only a limited understanding of the important features of that season.

"This is a big snowbank."

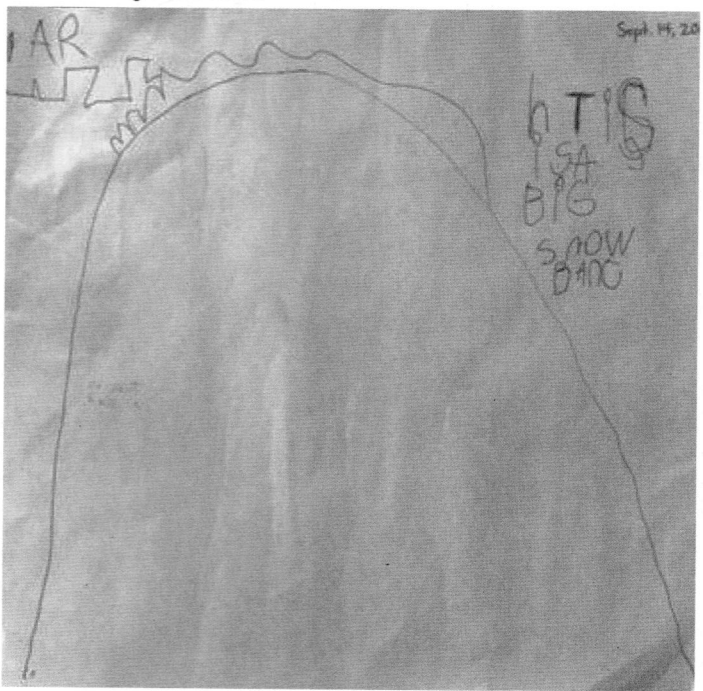

After two months, with many cross-curricular opportunities to experience, explore, and learn about the seasons, the students demonstrated a strong shift in their understanding. As a class, we read *Winter's Coming: A Story of Seasonal Change* (Thornhill & Bisaillon, 2014), the story of a snowshoe hare who sees other animals preparing for winter and wonders what to do. Having never experienced winter before, the hare worries that winter might be a big monster that will eat all her food or that she needs to hide from. Familiar with Canadian winters, the children found this story very funny. Probing further, the children reflected that as babies they too might have been surprised by their first winter. Our school community was in the process of sponsoring a refugee family from Syria and we wondered how this new family might experience a Canadian winter for the first time. I asked the children to write about how they would explain winter to someone who had never experienced it. The students showed clear growth in their understanding. The following composition illustrates one student's growth (the student who previously drew "This is a big snowbank").

"Winter is cool. In winter it is cold. In winter you can skate and sled. In winter you need a jacket and boots. In winter you can't play soccer."

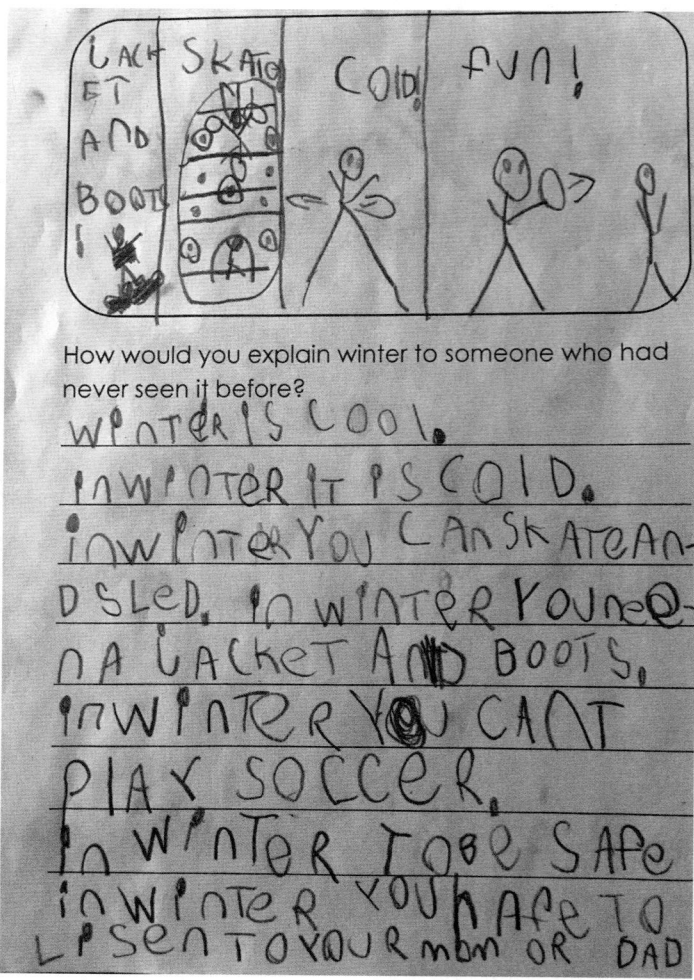

We also need to consider how to best assess individual learning in a group context. In the younger grades or in special education classes, capturing students' voices is essential. I find technology a good resource for this purpose.

Speech-to-text features are good tools for recording conversations with students, and some applications allow photographs or recorded words to be added to students' digital portfolios. Later I can easily see who participated in which discussions and retrieve meaningful anecdotes to help families understand their child's thinking.

However, it is important to remember that each individual will participate in different ways, and that just because a child does not verbally share knowledge does not mean they don't possess it. This really speaks to the importance of the branches outlined in this text, as children benefit from experiential and integrated learning, as well as from stewardship opportunities, demonstrating their knowledge through non-verbal as well as oral or written tasks.

Finally, since in an inquiry-based classroom children are actively involved in the learning process, they can also be empowered by taking some responsibility for assessment. Providing students with opportunities for both self-reflection and peer assessment builds metacognitive skills and honours the critical role of each classroom learner in collectively building understanding. Participating in peer assessment helps students understand the role they play in a democratic classroom setting, where all voices and opinions are important. It gives students autonomy as they work towards individual goals and improve their ideas by revisiting and refining prior learning.

Going Forward

Due to the very nature of the seasons, there has been no natural conclusion to this inquiry. The intensity of our seasonal learning has ebbed and flowed, reignited by natural provocations that come up as the cycles continue. I imagine that the children's questions and curiosity will continue through the spring and early summer, and I hope that their enthusiasm for learning about our planet's cycles continues beyond the end of the school year.

Using Speech-to-text Technology for Documentation

Nov 17th at 10:31 AM

Ellie Clin Today S1 and S2 were looking at maps and globes with T during Read to Self. They asked why the globe was tilted. They talked together about how the earth spinning makes day and night, but how the earth also revolves around the sun to make a year. S1 and S2 shared some theories about what makes the seasons. Maybe the moon is blocking the sun and that's what makes winter. Maybe the clouds get cold and that's why the water falls as snow. The sun is a star, but because the sun is close it looks bigger to us than other stars do.

Cindy's Story
Grade 2
Dr. Eric Jackman Institute of Child Study Laboratory School

Starting the Environmental Inquiry Process

In approaching the study of birds with Grade 2 students, I find that it's easy to "hook" their interest. This is because I am a dedicated birder myself and my passion for birding is contagious. Quite early in the year, I find that the students are excited to share their knowledge about birds. In fact, talking about birds becomes such a natural part of our group conversation that it provides us with a common language for many of our explorations. I was delighted to overhear a group of students chatting before school one day:

> **Student 1:** I saw a really nice male cardinal this weekend. It might have been a juvenile. Does anyone know how I can I tell?
>
> **Student 2:** You could look it up in your Sibley (bird guide).
>
> **Student 3:** Or you could see if it was with another bird. Could be a young bird if it's with another one.

The study of birds easily lends itself to teaching through inquiry. Local birds, with their cycle of breeding, nesting, fledging, and migrating provide opportunities for explorations and allow children to engage with nature that is part of their everyday life. As the children develop a deeper understanding of birds' growth and change, the evidence that supports their theories is in their own backyard.

This kind of learning cannot be rushed; a full year of study on one subject both expands students' understandings and demands a more rigorous examination of how they build knowledge. For instance, the mating pair of Cooper's hawks in our local park cannot be observed until late in the winter. The children can learn so much more about these birds by seeing them in their habitat, each week over the course of the second term at school.

I feel bound to honour the children's natural desires to know about what affects growth and change in the environment, especially their own. In fact, a strong connection to place allows children to deepen their understanding of their environment; a seamless way to support this connection is through traditional Indigenous teachings about honouring the land. During a field trip to a Pacific salmon spawning site along the Humber River this fall, our hosts guided us in a smudging ceremony. As the class learned about how important salmon is to the rehabilitation of local waterways, we were given tobacco to be placed on the land as an offering, so that we could thank the land for all that it gives us.

Offering Tobacco

Lofty Goals: Big Ideas

My goal is to help the students to see themselves as co-inhabitants of the Earth and to discover their duty to take care of it. The work that we do around raising Atlantic salmon is intertwined with our broader, more intense and extended study on birds, involving the children in investigations that help us tackle two big ideas: "Birds" and "Salmon." Both studies are intended to help the children establish strong emotional bonds to these living creatures.

Though I have a sense of these big ideas, I never know how each year will begin, how the inquiry will unfold, and what directions we will pursue. The provocations for our study of birds come from me, however the ideas come from the children. I start the inquiry by asking, "What do we know about birds?" and record the children's theories and questions on our "Wonder Wall."

The "Wonder Wall" serves as both a symbol of and a tool for our ongoing focus about birds. Over the year, some of these "I Wonders" will be answered, while others might be disregarded because they don't help us to learn more. I think it's important that these ideas "live" on the wall where they make us ruminate, the children circling around them, revisiting them, and coming up with new questions and theories as their understanding broadens.

A New Year: Go Outside

This year, I began by taking the learning outside, in what I refer to as "20-Minute Field Trips" (Halewood, 2014). I conduct these trips with small groups of children, so that they can be aware of their immediate environment without the distractions and pressure of a whole-group excursion. Children are provided with sketchbooks and binoculars and they are given instructions to simply sketch what is around them. These short field trips are generally quiet because I instruct the children to "notice" with all of their senses, including being able to hear what is around them. Once we are back in the classroom, we share our sketches and talk about what we observed. This is an example of a detailed drawing:

"Looking at the dray really helped me get an idea of what a bird's nest would look like. I was exaggerating but it looked like I saw a billion sparrows."

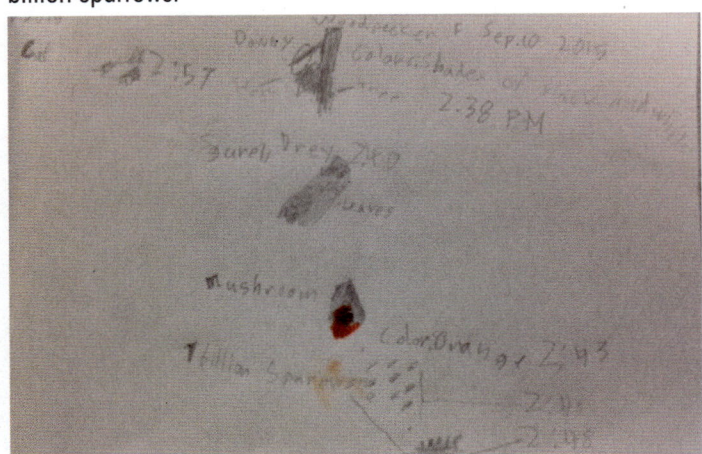

Student 1: I drew a squirrel's nest.
Student 2: That's a dray.
Student 1: Oh yeah, that's not a real nest, like a bird's nest.
Student 1: All nests are real.
Cindy: Can you tell me more about what you mean?
Student 1: It does not matter what animal, as long as it has a home. Some homes are nests.

During a subsequent Knowledge Building Circle (KBC), I asked if the children saw a connection between the kinds of birds we were seeing and their nests. They noted that many nests were built high in trees. Some children thought there was a relationship between the size of the bird and the distance of the nest from the ground, their rationale being that small birds in high nests were protected from larger predators that could not climb that high.

Deepening the Connection: The Sketching Sessions

We also had conversations about the skills required to observe and record what we saw. What made recording their observations about birds so special for the children was the opportunity to work closely with my intern, Zoë, who is a visual artist. Her expertise in the medium of sketching and watercolour played an integral role in honing the children's understanding of detail. She had them sketch using high quality artist's paper and pencils, and taught them how to add colour to their sketches by carefully mixing watercolours to create the effect they wanted. The children sketched from photographs, books, and field guides. Zoë also arranged for the class to visit the Toronto Reference Library's collection of John James Audubon engravings.

"I drew the owl to show its ears that are on the side of his head."

"This is a passerine. It is a small bird that perches on a tree or fence. It is always alert."

Sketching at the Toronto Reference Library

"Sketching with Zoë," as we came to call this time, brought the children closer to their subject matter, allowing them to get information about birds by observing the detail in pictures and paintings. As they became more confident in their drawing skills, they were able to describe the birds' anatomy, habitat, and behaviour. For some children whose reading skills are not yet developed, sketching was an entry point into some of the more complex Knowledge Building conversations we were beginning to have in class.

Migration, Adaptation, Survival: Serious Talks in KBCs

KBCs allow for candid conversations about the kinds of impact that pollution, global warming, and habitat destruction have on bird populations. I provide the children with more information by "Skyping" with experts, reading e-Bird bulletins, and participating in and exploring "Great Backyard Bird Counts" through *Bird Studies Canada* (2017). The children become aware of how the use of pesticides affects migrating bird populations and how climate change can affect the cycle of mating and nesting. They also learn about the impact of deforestation on birds' diets, migratory routes, and the overall ability to reproduce.

I don't shy away from discussing real issues that concern the environment with the children. They are aware that their world is changing and it is important for them to have a way of exploring and expressing their concerns. My role is to help them develop some perspective about the realities we all face and to support them in learning about possibilities for affecting positive change in the natural world.

An Authentic Solution for a Real-world Problem

Once winter arrived, the children noticed fewer species of local birds. In a KBC, one student offered the theory that there were more robins than other years because the weather was warmer. I asked if it would be okay if these birds stayed throughout the winter. Some children thought that there would be more competition for food with other birds if the robins stayed. Others felt that the robins would need more food, such as worms, which would put them in danger because there are no worms in the ground in winter.

> **"Is there anything we can do for the birds who stay through winter?"**
>
> **Student 1:** Well we could buy worms and put them out for the birds.
>
> **Student 2:** But the worms will get eaten by other animals. And, where would we buy worms?
>
> **Student 3:** Then we could get bird seed for them.
>
> **Student 4:** Robins prefer berries. Let's get bird seed for the birds that eat seed and we can leave the berries on the bushes for the robins.
>
> **Cindy:** How can we be sure that we are feeding the birds?

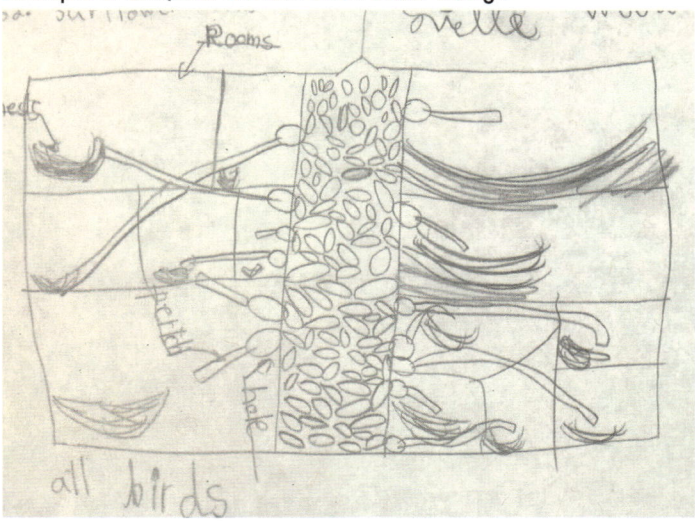

Example of an Initial Student Bird Feeder Design

This conversation continued until the group decided that they should create and install bird feeders around the school so that they could ensure that the birds had enough to eat. I was there to keep the children on topic and to ensure that everyone who wanted to contribute had an opportunity to share in the experience. The class planned to make their own, individual feeders, rather than to work in pairs or groups, so that they could have more feeders for the birds.

The Bird Feeder Project: Design, Build, Test

The discussions about bird feeder designs helped the children pull together a lot of the knowledge they had previously constructed about birds. The children had to consider trends in our local bird populations in winter, preferred habitat, bird anatomy (especially beak size), and winter-bird dietary needs. They also had to choose the size, construction materials, and placement of the feeders. These initial designs were very elaborate and imaginative. The following example depicts chambers, assorted food for "all birds," and detailed pathways that deliver seed.

The children looked at one another's designs and provided feedback. They decided that they needed to use materials that were durable. Before constructing the feeders, we took a field trip to see the hand-made bird feeders in the sanctuary in High Park, where we were lucky enough to meet the man who maintains the feeders. He told us how some designs had failed, and as a result, needed to be redesigned. As the children offered tobacco to this special place – carrying forward their experience of extending gratitude to the land during the salmon project – I noticed how thoughtful they were about placing it near special trees, bushes, and fallen logs.

Learning from Our Local Bird Feeding Expert High Park

The children saw that they needed to consider practical aspects of design such as finding ways of protecting the birds from rain and snow and keeping squirrels from eating the contents of the feeders. They went back to their original designs for further modifications once we saw these bird feeders. The following drawing is an example of a revised design with details showing perches, reinforced holes, and a "Made in Canada" recycled pop bottle.

Example of a Revised Bird Feeder Design

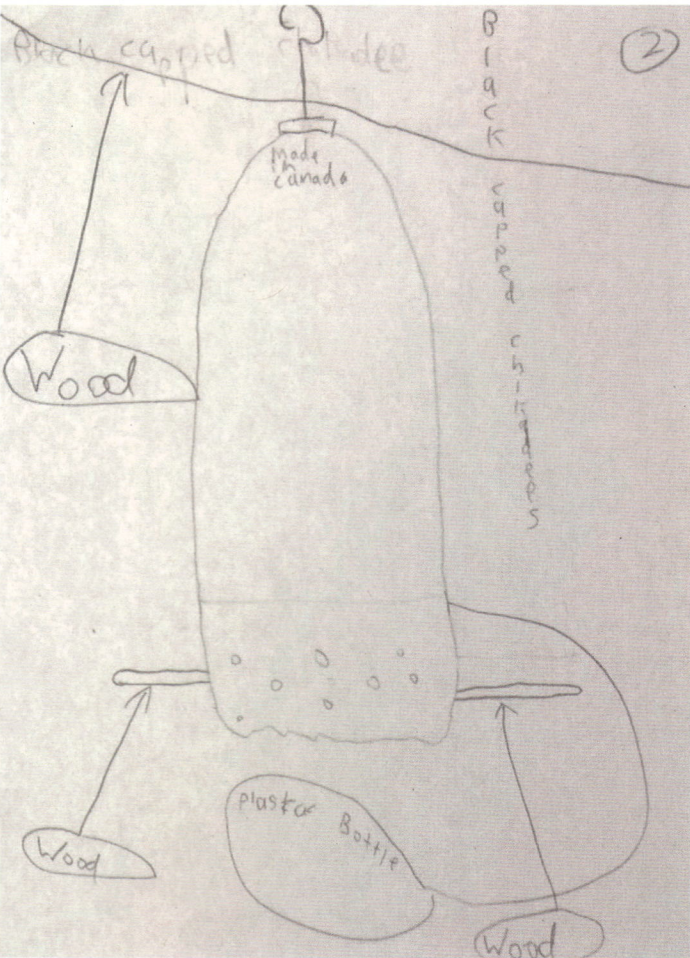

Finally, we were ready to build! The children and I put out a call for recycled materials from home and they got started. The finished bird feeders were filled with seed and installed in the schoolyard. One of the children suggested that they should give tobacco to the land before we put them up. I notice how much this ceremony means to the children and how it is such a natural way for the children to feel connected to special places in their environment.

Students Installing the Finished Bird Feeders

Moving Ahead: Coming Full Circle

Each week, the children tended to their feeders. They repaired and refilled them, and tracked the amount and kind of food the birds consumed. The conversations deepened as the students observed what birds were attracted to their feeders and how these birds were accessing the food. The children wondered about ways they could predict which birds would visit the feeders and when, suggesting ways that they might attract more or different birds.

> **Student 1:** We can add more feeders and different kinds of food.
>
> **Student 2:** We can move the feeders to areas of the yard that might attract birds.
>
> **Student 3:** We want to feed other animals that might need food too, like squirrels.
>
> **Student 4:** What happens when the weather gets warmer?

As the weather changed, so did the environment and activity of the classroom. The Atlantic salmon eggs arrived and were installed in a portable hatchery right in our classroom. The children visited the hatchery each day to look for signs of movement in the roe. They talked more about how animals are born and develop, and discussed the importance of caring for the Earth so that the birds and fish get the right message to migrate and nest.

In a KBC, I asked the children to consider what factors in the environment might cause birds to be attracted to the feeders in our yard. I asked them to consider what they already knew about birds, and how this might help them think about what birds do as the season changes. What did they observe about birds in the fall that might be helpful? Did they think we would see more or fewer birds this year? Why did they think this? The children began to consider barriers to migration, identifying weather trends, pollution, fewer trees for protection and nesting.

Growing Awareness: Stronger Voices

In another KBC, a student brought up a concern about feeding birds too much: "They might adapt to being fed and won't look for their own food."

This comment sparked a lively debate about feeding species that are not indigenous to the area. Some children wonder if this would also affect the survival of the birds that should be here.

The voices of the children had changed. I began to hear strident declarations from the class about preserving forests, making choices about how we dispose of waste in the environment, and reducing pesticides. The children were suddenly busy writing their own bird reports, and each child was becoming an expert on a bird of their choice. They would soon be presenting facts about their bird to a school-wide Earth Day assembly.

Exploring Authoritative Sources

Working on Our Bird Reports

We talked more about the connection between the Atlantic salmon we were caring for (formerly extirpated in Ontario) and the birds we had come to know. The children had proved to themselves that they can make a difference for living things, and felt strongly about helping to bring about change. They demonstrated an awareness of the reciprocal relationship between themselves and their own environment, and saw the value of what they were learning about these living things. As one child so eloquently stated, "We should take nothing from this place [the Bird Sanctuary] but knowledge."

Assessment: Embedded, Ongoing, Responsive

I left this section for last because it is the piece teachers ask the most about: How and when do you assess something that seems so student directed? In fact, my teaching is very intentional, with a specific learning outcome about environmental education.

Teaching through inquiry lends itself to the kinds of assessment that I think are important. Because the unit unfolds over the course of the year, the learning is deeper and more complex. I am looking for ways that the students come to understand the web of life and how action upon it can change the way animals grow and change. This kind of learning comes through time spent with the subject material, allowing me to tailor assessments to each step of the learning process within the inquiry and ask the right questions (How? What does it look like? What does it sound like?).

Inquiry also provides multiple entry points for knowledge acquisition along the way. Children who respond to hands-on experiences can find a way to pursue knowledge throughout the year. They can also work independently to write about their own bird. Student participation in KBCs help me to determine how far along the children are in the learning process. I use these conversations as a way of determining where the inquiry should go next, or whether we need to back up and revisit some key concepts.

In fact, I am constantly assessing throughout the year. I am able to assess individual and group understanding within the context of KBCs, through designing and constructing experiments, and before, during, and after time spent in the field collecting and interpreting data.

Teaching through inquiry provides opportunities for more comprehensive and cohesive kinds of assessment. I can see clearly where the learning has begun, where the "aha!" moments are, and where I need to go in order to help children to reflect on what they have learned. This is truly authentic assessment for authentic learning.

Velvet's Story
Grade 3
The Grove Community School, Toronto District School Board (TDSB)

Acknowledgment

Every morning at The Grove, the school community gathers in a large circle in the yard. Families, educators, and students are invited to stand together to sing, and to share our learning and important announcements.

In keeping with Indigenous protocol and building respectful relationships between Aboriginal and non-Aboriginal peoples in Canada, we start the circle by acknowledging the Traditional Territories/Ancestral Lands of Indigenous peoples. This is done before we sing the national anthem and is spoken to recognize that we are all treaty people.

"I would like to acknowledge that this school is situated upon traditional territories. The territories include the Wendat (wen-dat), Anishinabek (ah-nish-nah-bek) Nation, the Haudenosaunee (ho-den-oh-sho-nee) Confederacy, and the Mississaugas of the New Credit First Nations. As part of The Dish With One Spoon Wampum Belt Covenant, the Haudenosaunee Confederacy, and Anishinabek and Allied nations agreed to share and care for the resources on this land in the Great Lakes Region. I also recognize the enduring presence of Aboriginal peoples on this land."[1]

"As we sing, we will reflect. We honour this truth with respect. On this ground where we all stand is One Dish One Spoon Wampum Belt Land."[2]

Taking Action

Our Acknowledgement is one example of how we are trying to take action and use our power as educators to honour some of the recommendations made by the Truth and Reconciliation Commission to integrate First Nations, Métis, and Inuit learning throughout the curriculum. To me, this means recognizing the voices and the stories that are not included in the national anthem. It means creating space for storytelling, and acknowledging the complicated history of colonialism and racism in Canada. It means having the courage to acknowledge the impact that power and privilege has had in creating systems that benefit some communities over others. It means deepening our understanding of who we are and where we are, and empowering all students and educators to ask questions, to listen, and to actively challenge inequity.

My Journey as an Ally

My journey begins with my experience of family and community. I grew up in downtown Toronto in a White, working-class family that includes a younger sister, a father who is deaf and blind, and a mother who is a lesbian[3]. As a child, I learned about the importance of accessibility and inclusion, and I understood the painful impact of discrimination. I also learned about the power of advocacy, storytelling, and community. When I became an educator, I made a commitment to use my privilege to create inclusive, positive, and safe spaces where all members of the school community feel a sense of belonging and where there is room for everyone to share their story.

My name is Velvet Lacasse. I am one of the founding teachers at The Grove Community School, a public alternative school in downtown Toronto. Our school embraces a philosophy that includes teaching the Ontario Curriculum through the core values of environmental sustainability, social justice and equity, and community activism. I deeply believe in teaching our core values through inquiry and the arts.

---

[1] Instead of the Toronto District School Board land acknowledgement (2016) we used another one offered by the Aboriginal Education Centre because we wanted to acknowledge our treaty responsibilities beyond the Toronto Purchase.

[2] We worked with our Indigenous families to create our Grove acknowledgment, which is easier to say chorally.

[3] In solidarity work, it's important to be aware of one's own intersecting social identities (race, class, ability, gender, etc.) as they relate to systems of oppression, domination, or discrimination.

As an educator, I feel a responsibility to cultivate a deeper understanding of the impact of power and privilege on our students, their families, and our school communities. I have been working hard to learn what it means to be a good ally. I understand that sometimes being an ally[4] means listening; sometimes it means leading; and sometimes it means leaning in (to the fear of the unknown). It always means learning.

Everyone is in a different place on their learning journey. It's important to acknowledge where we are on this continuum and remember that we are not alone. Though it can be uncomfortable to speak about experiences that are not our own, educators have a responsibility to honour the multiple voices and the multiple ways of knowing in our school community. It's essential to make mistakes and to acknowledge that, as educators, we are also on a learning journey.

My Journey Through Inquiry

The hardest part of any journey is taking that first step.

This saying resonates for me because I believe that all learning and teaching is a journey. The hardest part about taking a risk and trying something new, such as committing to inquiry-based learning, is trusting the process. We need to trust our students, the learning process, and ourselves. We also need to trust that the journey is more important than the destination.

When I was introduced to inquiry-based learning, I couldn't figure out what it would look like or sound like in my classroom. I went to workshops, visited classrooms, and asked a lot of questions. It took me a long time to realize that inquiry-based learning was not something that I could schedule into my timetable, like "Activity Time." Now, I understand that inquiry is more about "how" I teach, and the strategies that I use to discover and "uncover" the curriculum with my students.

Like many educators, I like to feel and be in control. I like to be organized and prepared. I had a really hard time letting go of the idea that learning through inquiry meant that I couldn't plan exactly where the process would take us.

---

[4] "Being an ally means recognizing that oppressions exist and affects people that are not yourself, so as an ally you are trying to align yourself with actions, ideas, and movements that serve to undermine the systems that perpetuate that oppression and strive for liberation" (Whitecloud, 2015).

Young children are very curious, and I couldn't imagine how I could follow all the different questions my students asked every day. I was also worried about how I was going to cover the curriculum.

Educators worry about reporting and assessment. Our anxiety about "covering the curriculum" prevents us from trusting that the learning process is more about "uncovering" the curriculum. I feel more confident now that I can provide evidence for assessment. I trust that our curriculum and our report cards fundamentally support inquiry-based learning.

Getting Started

When teaching a new grade, I begin with the curriculum expectations. I look for the "big ideas." It's important for students (and for me) to integrate the curriculum. Integration makes the learning more meaningful and more manageable. Looking for connections and opportunities for integration can be more challenging with a split-grade class, but it is not impossible. Last year, I found excellent ways for my Grade 2/3 class to explore together.

This year, I was teaching a straight Grade 3 class for the first time. I decided to explore the themes of "Journey Stories." I also wanted to explore the curriculum through an Indigenous lens, which supported our learning goals as an alternative school, and my own professional and personal goals to be an ally.

Inquiry-based learning does not mean that you make no plans and "go with the flow." It means that you plan the "big ideas" or learning goals, but that you don't plan every lesson along the way. Sometimes the provocation is organic and emerges from the students, and sometimes, as educators, we have to provide the spark. As I was looking through the Grade 3 curriculum, I generated some questions that would help me to guide our inquiry. I thought about activities and projects that we could do inside and outside of the classroom, and left lots of room to explore and discover the unknown together.

I decided that we would collect our own family journey stories and investigate the impact of settlement and migration in Ontario. This project would help to make connections and strengthen the home-school connection, and also establish a sense of place by honouring the past, present, and future of Indigenous communities on this land.

We would use the Anti-bias Education learning goals (Derman-Sparks & Edwards, 2010) to explore the questions, "Who Am I?" and "Where Am I?" and integrate equity and social justice issues into our learning. We would also investigate the environmental impacts of migration and settlement as we learned about Ontario and the diverse communities that live here.

"I Wonder" Cards

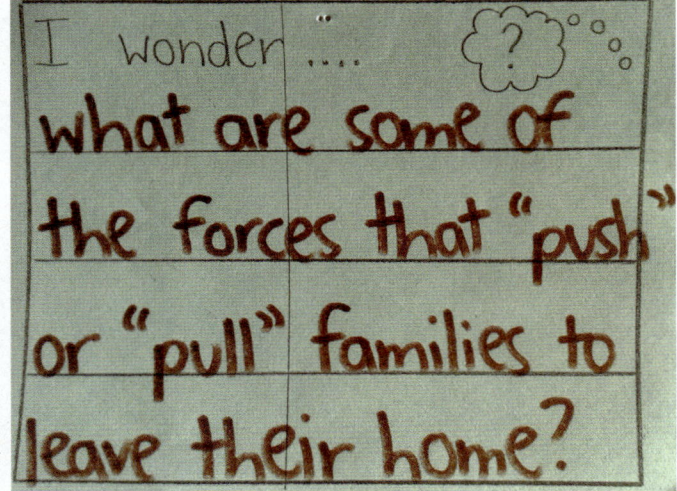

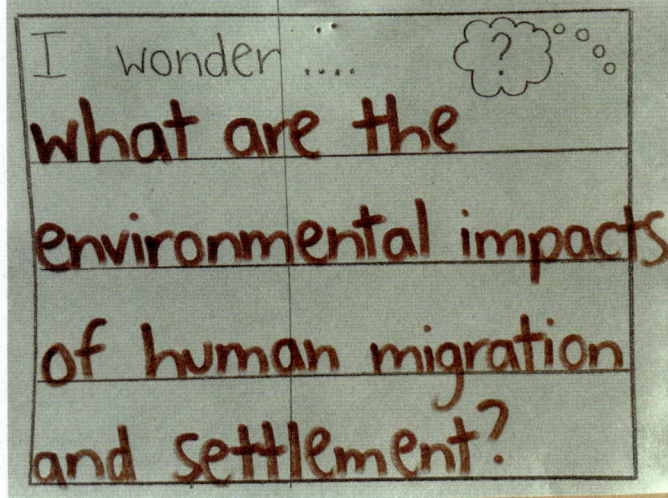

Building a Classroom Community

I have learned that building relationships and creating a classroom community that is safe, inclusive, and collaborative is vital to all learning. In September, the most important thing we can do is to work together to establish classroom agreements, routines, and expectations to support collaborative learning. If students are going to take risks, ask questions, and explore new learning, they need to feel safe, and they need to trust that the classroom is a community of learners that will support them on their journey.

Teaching collaborative learning strategies must be explicit and practiced regularly throughout the first weeks of school. For example, after using the "Think-Pair-Share" strategy, ask students to reflect on whether they feel their partner was listening attentively, and to describe why they feel that way. Use a "Thumbs-Up, Thumbs-Down" strategy to engage the whole class in self-reflection after a cooperative task. Work together as a class to generate "success criteria" about what it looks like, sounds like, and feels like to work together in the classroom. Use this information, as well as opportunities for self-assessment, as documentation for Learning Skills and Work Habits on report cards.

This year, I started building community in my classroom with activities that supported our collaborative learning strategies and Data Management and Probability expectations. We read a picture book called *Same, Same, But Different* (Kostecki-Shaw, 2011), about two boys who live in different countries and who write letters to each other about their lives. We played "Step into the Circle…" and used surveys and Venn diagrams to introduce ourselves and connect with each other in the classroom. These activities helped us to acknowledge how we are different, and reinforce the "big idea" that we all have the right to learn and feel safe in our school community.

Connecting to Place

Once there is a feeling of safety and trust in the classroom we can begin to explore new ideas together. Best practices tell us that it is important to connect new information to students' prior knowledge. Knowledge Building Circles are an excellent strategy for discovering what students already know. I also like the "Graffiti" strategy, where students are encouraged to walk around the classroom and draw or write their ideas on chart paper. Then we do a "Gallery Walk" before we share the ideas together. These strategies are active, visual, and support the idea that knowing and gaining knowledge is a collective experience.

Ontario: Yours to Discover

I decided to use the the government slogan, "Ontario: Yours to Discover" to spark interest and curiosity, and to introduce my Grade 3 students to our Social Studies inquiry about the land we live in/on. To understand my students' prior knowledge of Ontario I used the Graffiti strategy.

Postcards from Ontario

I asked students to write a postcard about a place they had visited in Ontario during the summer. I sent this work home for families to complete together. These postcards were shared as oral presentations, which helped us to create a space for storytelling and to honour the importance of listening and of sharing our personal narratives. On a map of Ontario, we marked the places that we had visited; we started to ask questions and to notice both the spaces we had marked and the empty ones.

Student Postcards

Northern Ontario

It became clear that our experiences and our prior knowledge were located in southern Ontario, and that our new learning would be about northern communities in Ontario.

It is important for educators to document the learning process and to make our students' thinking visible. It becomes a "map" of the teaching and learning journey that we are on together. I posted the slogan "Ontario: Yours to Discover" on a bulletin board. Under the slogan, we displayed our map of Ontario and our postcards. This visual documentation motivated and guided our inquiry.

I created an activity using Google Maps to introduce the students to the Computer Lab, and to generate more knowledge and questions about the North. Each student researched a community in the North and documented how long it would take to travel there from Toronto. We found these northern communities on our map of Ontario, and the students wrote "I notice…", "I wonder…", and "Now I know…" on colourful paper. This information provided ongoing formative assessment and helped to guide our inquiry.

Student Research of Northern Ontario

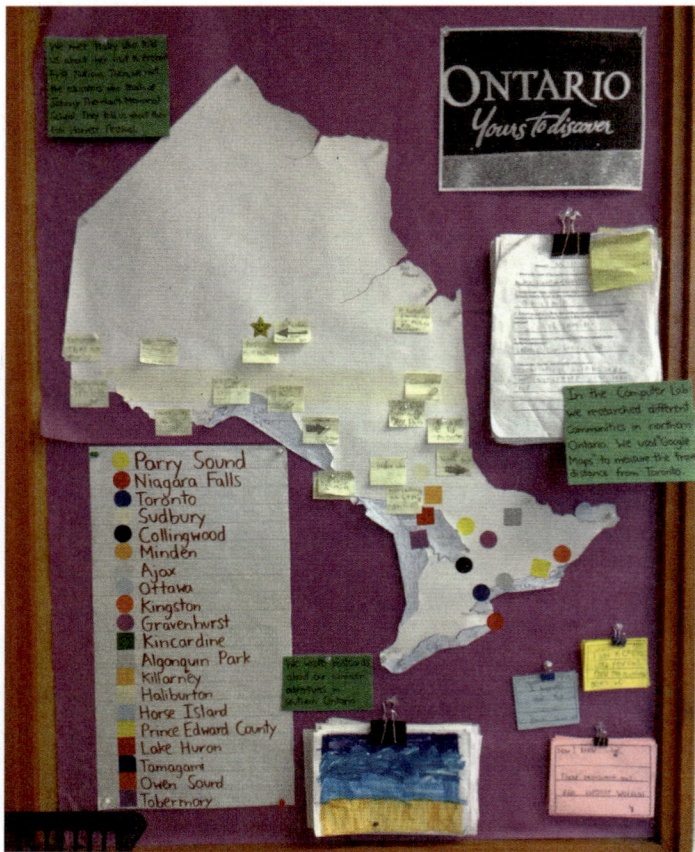

Student Questions

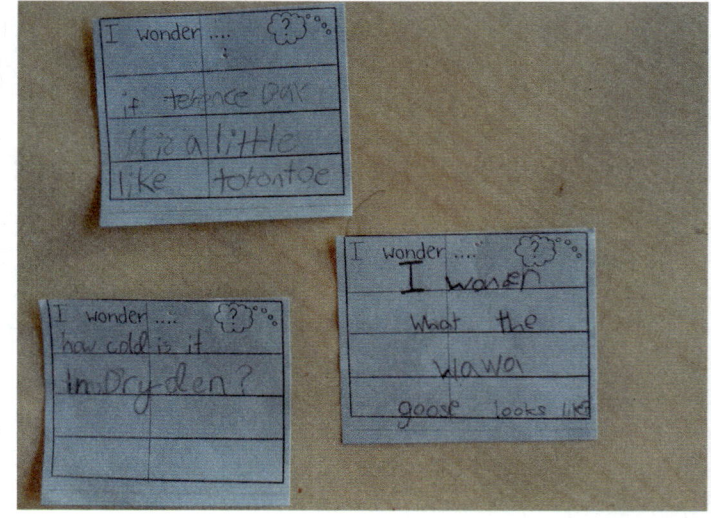

Journey Stories

In October, I introduced a family project called "Tracing our Family Roots/Routes" for students to complete at home. The learning goals of this project includes honouring our diverse family journey stories, and deepening our understanding that, with the important exception of Indigenous families, many of our families have lived in other places before settling in Canada.

Students were invited to work with their family to discuss and document the different places their family has lived and the different forces that may have "pushed" or "pulled" them to move to Toronto. Students had the option to share their family journey story, and reveal only as many details as they were comfortable with. The discussions we had were very powerful, and together we generated a list of reasons why families might be "pushed" or "pulled" to move, keeping in mind the sensitive nature of this topic. The family projects allowed us to make connections between struggles in the past and in the present, such as racial discrimination, poverty, and war.

> Excerpt from our "Tracing Our Roots/Routes: A Family Project" outline:
>
> For the next two weeks, we will work on a project at home and at school, which will recognize our diverse family journey stories. Every student will be supported to ask questions about their family, record this information, and share their story with the members of the class.
>
> Most Canadians can trace their family history to other lands. An important exception is Canada's Indigenous peoples. Indigenous people have lived in Canada from time immemorial. Please use a world map to trace your family's journey to Canada, if your family did journey to Canada. If it did not, trace your family's journey within Canada.
>
> Families are asked to gather stories, and support your child to record the answers to the following questions:
> 1. Who is in your family? List their names.
> 2. Where does your family live? How long have they lived there?
> 3. Has your family lived in different places? Can you find these places on a world map or globe?
> 4. What were the forces that "pushed" or "pulled" your family to move?
> 5. What were some of the challenges or barriers that your family faced when they moved/or were moved to a new place?

Our Journey Stories

Art Extension of a Student's Family Project

Refugee Crisis

Sometimes there are powerful, real-world events that need to be addressed. In September, the families at The Grove used their resources to organize and raise funds to sponsor a Syrian refugee family. The school staff started to collect resources and brainstorm "big ideas" that were age-appropriate to help our students understand this complex issue. We decided to explore issues related to home, belonging, and inclusion. These issues strengthened the Grade 3 inquiry about journey stories and helped make the learning relevant.

Aroland First Nation

In October, we also had the opportunity to meet with educators from Johnny Therriault Memorial School in Aroland First Nation. We were inspired to build a relationship with this school community in Northern Ontario. The educators from Aroland shared their experiences of their annual Fall Harvest Festival with us. Their stories captivated us and inspired more questions.

Letters to a New Friend

As part of our Language Arts learning, we wrote letters to the Grade 3/4 students at Johnny Therriault Memorial School. We wrote about our own school experiences and asked many questions. Our students asked about shared experiences that children might have: What games do you like to play? Do you have any pets? What costume did you wear for Halloween? Do you like Star Wars?

Being an ally means being active in the learning process and not asking racialized people to speak for an entire group or community. It means recognizing the diversity that exists within every community, and doing the work to understand the issues and the diverse experiences within them. Our letters are an attempt to build relationships and trust; this will lead us toward understanding.

Regions of Ontario

As part of the Social Studies curriculum, Grade 3 students are expected to learn about the physical regions of Ontario and the resources in each of these regions that helped to create communities and industry. We used our inquiry and research skills to learn about four regions in Ontario: the North, the Canadian Shield, the St. Lawrence Lowlands, and the Great Lakes Region. The students worked in groups and everyone was assigned a different role to support and facilitate the collaborative process. After working, we would reflect on how successful we were in our goals. Students shared their learning as oral presentations, which gave me valuable assessment data.

The Canadian Shield

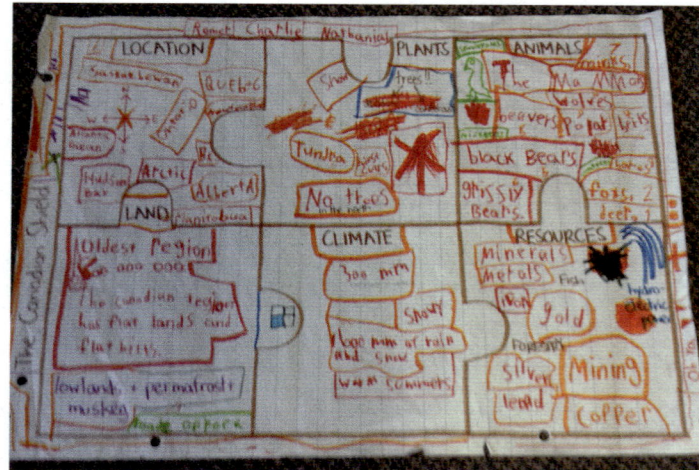

Resource Map

During Media Literacy, the students deepened their understanding of mapping skills by creating a Resource Map of Ontario, using success criteria. Each student identified the different physical regions on a map and created a legend. Then everyone created a symbol to represent the different resources found in Ontario. These symbols were glued onto the land to represent where the resources were located. Every student completed a self-evaluation and had a mini-conference with the teacher to share their understanding of the learning goals.

Some of the questions I asked were **What do you notice about the map that you created? What questions do you have? What resources are available in the North? In southern Ontario? Where do most of the people in Ontario live? Why do you think they settled there?**

Treaty Map of Ontario

There were many different directions that I could go to continue our learning journey about resources and regions in Ontario. I decided that we would learn more about reserves in Ontario and I started to look for resources to support this inquiry. The Aboriginal Education Centre in Toronto provided our school with several resources, including a Treaty Map of Ontario. This map identifies treaties, as well as different reserves and settlements.

To provoke this inquiry, I brought numerous copies of the Treaty Map of Ontario to the class. Students worked in small groups, looking at the map and then gathered to share what they noticed and what they wondered. These observations and wonderings were recorded and posted. They provided valuable formative assessment and documentation to guide our next steps.

Small Group Treaty Map Research

"We found Aroland. It's special to us."

Treaty Map: What We Wondered and Noticed

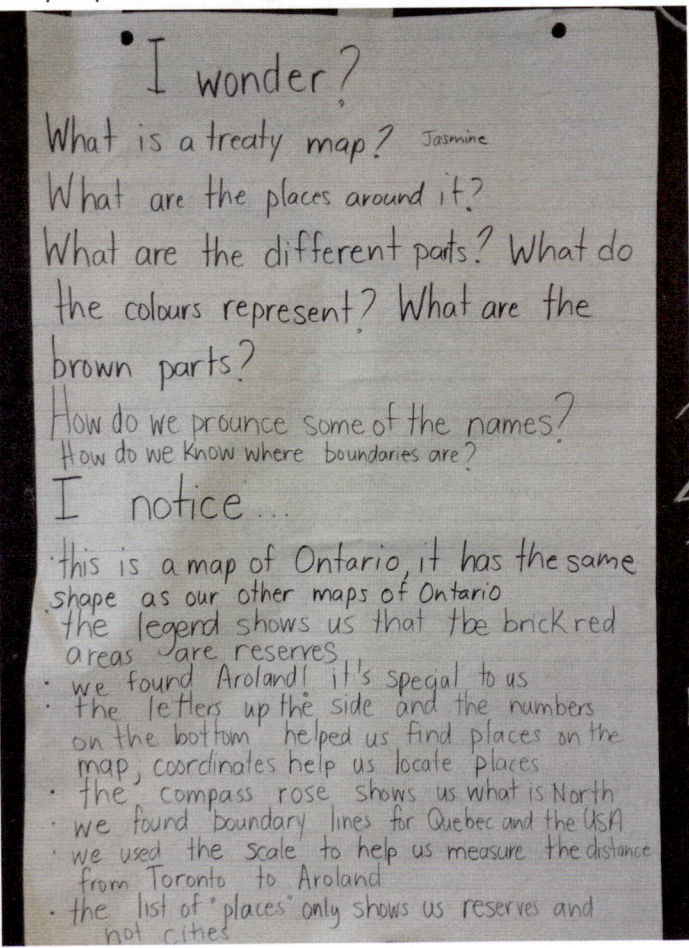

I worked with the Math and Equity Instructional Leaders to co-plan and co-teach a Math lesson about area using the Treaty Map of Ontario. As a diagnostic task, we drew the outline of four different First Nation reserves and settlements and asked students to work in pairs to measure how much land each had. During the task, we circulated and observed what strategies the students were using to measure. Later, we consolidated our learning by sharing three different examples of student work, including students who had not chosen area to measure the land. We used coordinates to locate the four different reserves and settlements on the map, and we repeated the activity the next day to strengthen our understanding of measurement.

Our Learning Goals

Measuring Land Area and Perimeter

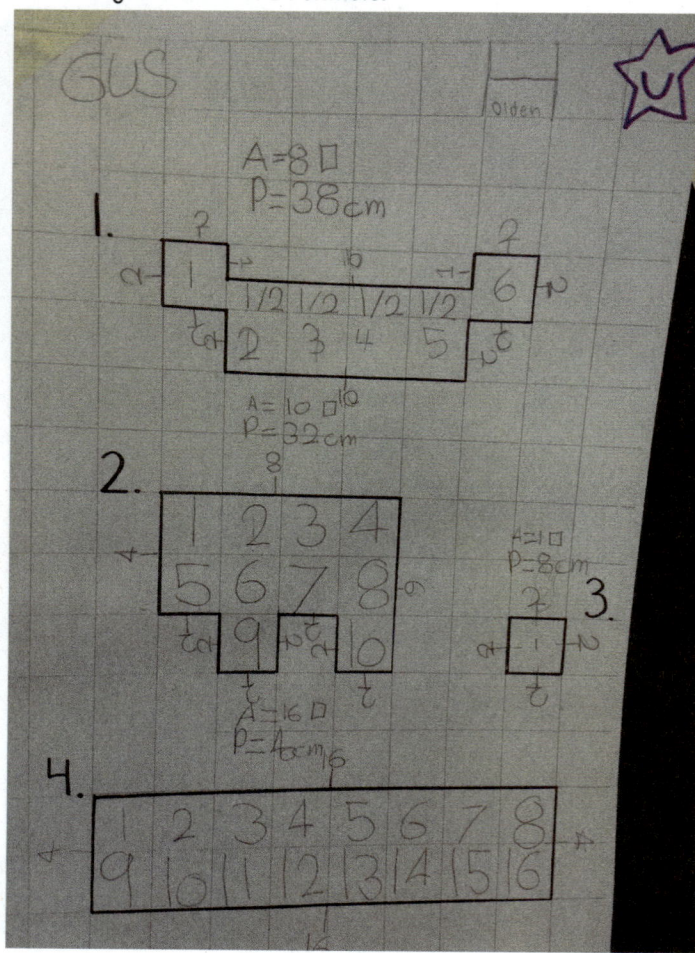

Reserves

My own guiding questions for this inquiry included What is a reserve? Where are they located? What are the resources that are available (or not available) on reserves? Why were they created? What opportunities are available to families living on reserves? What are the challenges? What can we do as allies to ensure that all children living on reserves have what they need? Students will generate even more questions to investigate.

This inquiry will take several months to investigate, and we might not answer all of our questions, but they have become "landmarks" that I can use along the way so that I won't get lost for long.

Taking Action

It is important for educators to include opportunities for students to engage in action and to share their knowledge with others. This strengthens our commitment to *Natural Curiosity's* fourth branch – Moving Toward Sustainability. Students need to understand that their voice and their story is important, and that when we join our voices we can create change.

There are many ways to empower our students and to support community engagement. Students can share their learning with families or with other classes. They can write letters or make posters or announcements. Students can organize fundraisers or whole-school events to raise awareness about issues. They can connect with community organizations, sign petitions, and join campaigns in solidarity and support.

Most importantly, students and educators need opportunities to reflect, recognize, and celebrate their own growth as learners as they deepen their understanding of what it means to be an ally and support others to take that first step.

Lisa's Story
Grade 3
Dr. Eric Jackman Institute of Child Study Laboratory School

Starting the Environmental Inquiry Process

When I was offered a job as the Grade 3 teacher at the Lab School, I was both excited and nervous. I had been teaching Special Education (five years with the TDSB and one year seconded to the Lab School) and this would be the first time in six years that I had a classroom of my own. As I prepared for this new position, as always I was looking forward to discovering how each student learned best and to finding new ways to motivate and encourage learning. Inspired by the information on an engineering website that made many connections to the Ontario curriculum (TeachEngineering, n.d.), I decided that my first big inquiry unit would involve the construction of biodomes. Now all I had to figure out was how to teach the students (and myself) everything we needed to know about ecosystems, environments, interactions between living and nonliving materials, biomes, and the roles of composers and decomposers in a meaningful, inquiry-based manner. Oh boy!

To many, the idea of teaching through inquiry can be quite frightening. The one thing that helped me stay calm and avoid becoming overwhelmed was remembering that information would be learned through inquiry. I did not need to be the expert. As a class, we would uncover information and come to new realizations as we built on our pre-existing understanding and challenged our misconceptions. I knew that I needed to have an end goal in mind, ask relevant questions, and facilitate rich discussions. I knew that I needed to expose the students to environments and experiences that proved and disproved our theories. I spent much of the summer pondering these ideas and many others.

In late September, as I was about to start my inquiry, I met with a few members of the *Natural Curiosity* team to discuss some off-site learning experiences I was planning for my students. I was blown away and excited by all the possibilities.

What? Me? Set up a saltwater aquarium from scratch? Let the children watch an ecosystem come to life in front of their eyes? I knew nothing about aquariums, or fish, or even aquatic plants for that matter, but the more I thought about this idea, the more I knew it needed to happen.

Before jumping in, I revisited the curriculum documents, reminding myself of a few key understandings that I wanted the students to walk away with. Under the overarching theme of "Systems and Interactions," we would focus on four big ideas:

- Plants have distinct characteristics and needs.
- Ecosystems are made up of living and nonliving elements.
- The composition of an ecosystem will determine its growth.
- Humans need to protect habitats.

Uncovering Student Conceptions

To begin, I wrote the word ECOSYSTEM on chart paper and asked the students to look at the word and think about what it might mean. I asked them to focus on some of the smaller words they recognized inside the bigger word. Once students had a few minutes to generate some thoughts on their own, they were assigned partners for the first step of a complex "Think-Pair-Share" structured activity.

In pairs, each student took one minute to tell their partner all that they knew, thought, or wondered about the word ecosystem. After two minutes, students were given time to write their emerging ideas independently in their notebooks, including any new information gathered from their partner. After about five minutes, students were paired with new partners to share information a second time. Using their written notes as a guide, they shared their original ideas along with any new information they had acquired. Following this second sharing, students again returned to their notebooks and added any new information they had gathered. When we came together as a group, it was evident that students were approaching this learning from very different entry points. I realized that before going any further we needed to develop some common understandings.

I discovered that for many students the word ecosystem was new, and that the "eco" part of the word failed to conjure up the ideas that I had expected. Furthermore, students didn't identify nonliving elements as components of an ecosystem; they believed that the word "environment" or "ecosystem" applied only to nature, not to human fabrications. Finally, in response to the question "Is our classroom an ecosystem?" most students were fairly certain it was not, though there was a suggestion that the presence of plants in the class might make it qualify. All students were still quite certain that without plants the classroom would not be an ecosystem.

Deepening Our Understanding

At this point, I introduced several National Geographic articles, hoping that they would help clear up some misunderstandings and add to students' knowledge. Due to the wide range of reading skills, to ease comprehension of difficult concepts and terminology and to help students extrapolate key ideas, we read these articles in adult-guided groups. Reading and discussing these articles allowed the students to return to their notebooks with new information and to make changes where necessary. To conclude our "Think-Pair-Share" learning, students got into pairs once again to share their latest understanding with each other.

Using their current level of understanding (including any misinformation yet to be uncovered), students began to make a visual image of what the word "ecosystem" meant to them. Each student also began to compile a document in which they could record both current and new "I Wonders…" during our study on ecosystems.

Example of One Student's Initial Ecosystem Visualization

The next time we met as a group to further our inquiry, we carried out a class "Graffiti" activity during which the students contributed to collaborative work on large pieces of paper. They travelled in small groups from one paper to the next, using pictures, words, and symbols to share ideas that focused on each page's big question.

"What Is an Environment?" Graffiti

"What Is an Ecosystem?" Graffiti

Following the "Graffiti" activity, we came together in a Knowledge Building Circle (KBC) to discuss and share our ideas. I was especially interested in hearing their ideas about artificial environments. Though all students had likely visited zoos or similar settings, none made the connection between zoos and artificial environments.

As a result of our numerous partner, small group, and whole-group discussions, our understanding of ecosystems was growing. We were quite certain that the definition of the term had a lot to do with the interaction of living and nonliving organisms within a specified environment. Yet many of the students were still unsure if our classroom would be considered an ecosystem. One student raised his hand and very meaningfully looked up at the plant hanging in its plastic basket from our ceiling. He said, "Hey, that plant is living and the basket it's in is not living. The plant can only grow as big as the basket will let it, so I think that is an example of how living and nonliving things interact." I was excited to see the beginning changes in student thinking. When asked what others thought about this idea, many students began to nod their heads in puzzled agreement. While some truly agreed and understood the example so eloquently described by their classmate, others were not quite in agreement.

I then asked, "Does that mean you think our classroom is an ecosystem?" Many opinions were offered, all leading us to the understanding that our classroom is an ecosystem, a complex environment in which abiotic and biotic materials are in constant interaction. Still, not everyone was convinced. My next question was "If our class did not have plants, would it still be an ecosystem?" As the discussion continued, there was growing comfort with the ideas that I was asking the students to consider.

In order to identify students who still had some misconceptions, I assigned a quick writing task. Choosing one of two sentence starters to begin their writing, they would use all the knowledge they had gathered so far to defend their position:

1. Our class is an ecosystem because . . .
2. Our class is not an ecosystem because . . .

Much to my delight, all students began their writing with the first statement.

Continuing the Inquiry

As our learning proceeded, we continued with our discussions as we gathered information from a variety of sources, including websites and videos. Three websites proved to be particularly fruitful:

- *Real World Science: Ecosystems and Biomes* (Etna Elementary School, 2014)
- *Biomes* (Kids Do Ecology, 2004)
- *World Biomes* (West Tisbury School, 2010)

We began to create a glossary to help us keep track of and remember some of the new vocabulary that was emerging, including terms such as biotic, abiotic, adapt, biome, terrestrial, aquatic, and ecologist.

We asked:

- What survives in our ecosystem?
- What do ecosystems need to survive?
- Do all ecosystems have the same needs?
- What might be some of the common needs of all ecosystems?

One Student's Questions About Ecosystems

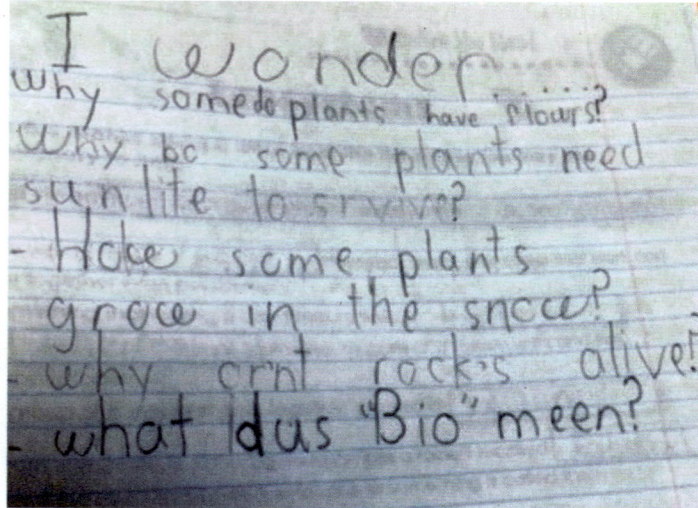

With the assistance of the school librarian, the Grade 3s used Knowledge Forum (Branch I, p. 20) in an online sharing of their thoughts and ideas in response to the above questions. Individual responses to these questions were monitored and used as a midpoint assessment before moving on.

Students Learning How to Represent Their Ideas on Knowledge Forum

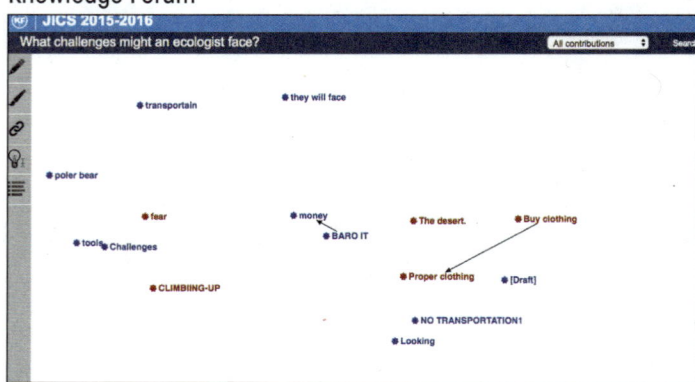

Breakthrough in Understanding

In October we gathered in our classroom for a KBC. We started off discussing the challenges that an ecologist might face, with students identifying and supporting their ideas. Still surprised by their ideas about artificial ecosystems and the reasons for their existence, I tried again to draw out their thinking about the relationship between artificial and natural environments. We eventually came to an understanding of why artificial ecosystems might be created and how they might help humans to better understand the interactions between living and nonliving organisms in particular environments.

Student Ideas for "What Challenges Might an Ecologist Face?"

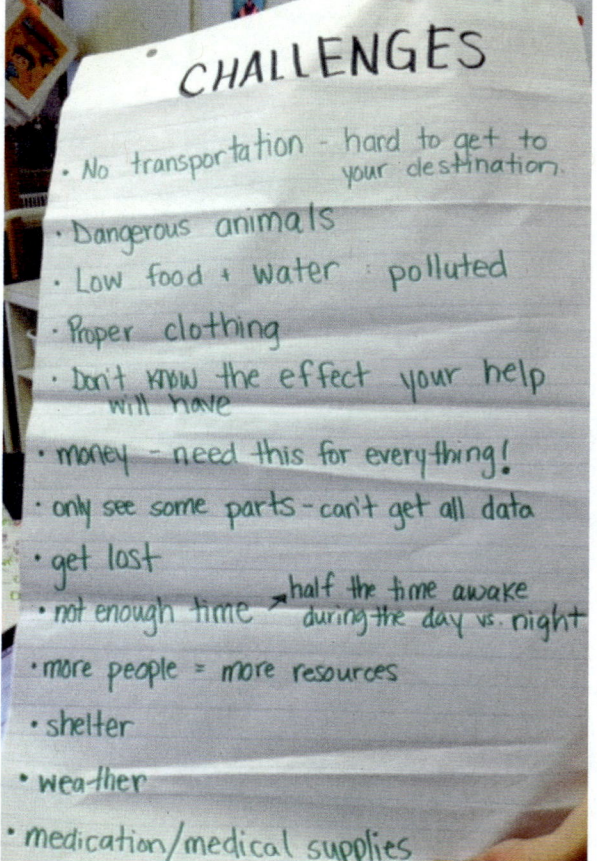

Observing an Artificial Ecosystem: Our Class Aquarium

Getting Outdoors: Exploring Real Ecosystems

In early November, we were lucky enough to explore several different ecosystems right in our own neighbourhood. On an excursion to the Humber River site, where a school parent is working with others to heal the land and provide opportunities for growth and involvement to the local community, we explored the Humber River with our hosts as our guides.

Learning About Indigenous Plants and Local Ecosystems

In the days following our outdoor explorations, we compared and contrasted our experiences in the different ecosystems that exist in our own "backyard." The students wrote personal stories about their experiences and learning.

Thinking About Biodomes: A Culminating Project

Though happy with the learning and discussions that were happening in the classroom, I realized that time was slipping away. I was still determined that our culminating task would involve the construction of biodomes and I was anxious to complete this topic before the winter break. It was nearing the end of November and we were far from having the knowledge and understanding needed for the next steps. After listening to the insights of colleagues, I realized that I needed to accept that this unit would likely need to continue after the holidays. The students were gaining understanding and experience at a rate that made sense for them. If my plans were getting derailed, it was because I was allowing the lessons to be shaped and guided by the interests and questions of the children in my class. I came to understand that this was what it meant to be the "guide" of the inquiry process. And because we had proceeded in this way, when my Grade 3 class eventually began a more in-depth study of cycles and systems, and started thinking about the energy exchange within a given system, they were ready for this new information.

To begin thinking more about the learning needed for our culminating project, the students in the class were divided into three groups. Each group was given time and resources to become an expert on one of three systems of energy exchange: the water cycle, the nitrate cycle, and the food chain. It was great to see the students learn from each other as the expert groups eloquently and creatively explained to the class how their system worked. Some used drama, some used handmade visuals with labelled diagrams, and others used video and technology to teach their classmates.

The next step was to introduce the word "biodome" and think about the connection it had to all the learning we had done to date. I wrote the word BIODOME on the board and asked the students to think about what they knew about the two parts of the word ("BIO" and "DOME") to help them figure out the meaning of the full word. The students again formed research groups with the task of gaining expertise about one of the following biodomes: the Eden Project, the University of Arizona's Biosphere 2, and the Montreal Biodôme. They gathered information and images from a variety of websites to create one page of informational text about the biodome they had studied.

During this time, we had been using materials from the Nelson Literacy 3 resource in guided reading sessions to learn more about the structure of informational text (MacKenzie, 2009). Conveniently, the topics covered in the informational texts included seeds, greenhouse growing, the functions of different plant parts, and comparisons of the basic needs of plants with those of humans.

It was the beginning of December, and we were ready to put our knowledge to the test. We were not quite ready to start our biodomes, but we were ready to get our hands dirty and record what happened when we took seeds, soil, paper towels, and a few containers, and added water and sunshine.

As we watched our seeds grow in the various environments we had set up for them, we were filled with new questions, concerns and, eventually, new understandings. The processes of photosynthesis and transpiration, as well as the role of producers, consumers, and decomposers, were just some of the new understandings that arose from our mini seed-growing experiments.

Just before the winter holidays, I introduced the students to our culminating project. We studied some sample images of biodomes and considered different ways of making them self-contained and self-sustainable. We brainstormed possible biodome models and thought about the many different types of materials we could use for each environment. Students gathered in groups to plan and pre-design, consulting their engineering design booklet, a resource created by the University of Colorado Boulder, to help them with their plans and to develop a list of materials they might need (2004).

Returning to class after the winter holiday, the students dove right into their projects. There was excitement in the room as materials began to flood in. Containers, soil, charcoal, plants, seeds, and even a few live fish were ready to become a part of their new self-sustaining biodomes. By the middle of January, the biodomes were complete. We then spent some time reflecting on the challenges each group had faced in their respective groups. Developing a self-watering system was the hardest challenge for all of the groups.

Student Biodomes Supporting Plant Life

Student Biodome Supporting Aquatic Plant Life

As we were finishing up our study of biodomes, we read a book about worms from the Nelson Literacy 3 resource (MacKenzie, 2009). Told from a worm's point of view, this text raised a lot of questions. Students' conversations and interest gave me the push I needed to ask a friend if she would help us develop our own worm compost farm. When I realized that she could only support us virtually and that I would be the one to physically prepare and handle the worms, the project seemed a little more daunting and a lot less appealing. Nevertheless, we conquered our fears and went ahead. We now have a very active squirm of worms enjoying life in their own simple biodome, which is just a small part of life in our more complex, large-scale biodome classroom.

Our Decomposers in Action

Building Our Worm Bin

Marlo's Story
Grades 3 and 4
Johnny Therriault School, Aroland First Nation

Starting the Environmental Inquiry Process

My passion for inquiry-based learning was born in the summer of 2014 when my partner and I participated in the Summer Institute at the Dr. Eric Jackman Institute of Child Study. I was very eager to begin the school year and introduce my students to this wonderful approach, yet I knew that this would involve giving up a substantial amount of control. I would be providing my students with the opportunity to offer questions and theories that would help me to navigate and closely track their learning, but maintaining such a dynamic learning environment would be a big step for me.

The "Rocks and Minerals" topic became a focus after I participated in my first sweat lodge ceremony during the spring of 2015. Though I am a First Nations person, I did not grow up surrounded by the teachings of a rural First Nations community – it is only within the past 10 years that I have been able to make a true connection to my own culture, history, and traditions. Drawn to those who have this knowledge, I am constantly asking questions. Although I have been told that I should be more cautious when asking questions of an Elder, I try to always be very respectful and approach all situations gently.

Though I had been told about the connection between rocks and the Grandfathers, the teachings of the sweat lodge healer made me more aware of the significance of rocks in First Nations cultures. I decided to select "Rocks and Minerals" as a topic of focus for my students, giving them the opportunity to learn about this amazing, important aspect of their culture while continuing to engage in regular science curriculum learning (Ontario Ministry of Education, 2007).

During the summer months, I began my own research, studying the curriculum guidelines and thinking about what my classroom might look like. Stumbling across a book entitled *Everybody Needs a Rock* (Baylor & Parnall, 1985), I immediately knew that this was where my inquiry would begin. After I read the book to my students on the first day of school, they were immediately inspired to look for rocks of their own, so we went outside. Despite having reviewed the book's guidelines for picking rocks, for some, choosing a rock was not easy. One student said that the rocks around the school "just weren't speaking to him." After picking up and replacing many rocks, he finally found just the right one. All rocks were placed into a container in the classroom, where they still sit today. Each student knows that if they move to another school, their rock will travel with them on their journey.

A Student Finding the "Right" Rock

Students with Their Rock Selections

A Student's Theory on Where Rocks Come From

After a quick writing assessment – I asked each student to write three sentences about things that connected them with their particular rock – the students brought their thoughts and questions to an "I Wonder" circle. Guided by the Ontario Science and Technology curriculum for Grade 4, I asked many questions, beginning with, "I wonder how these rocks came to be in Aroland." From this question came an enormous number of theories.

Additional questions included queries about how rocks were made, why they sparkle, what kinds of rocks are found in our village, and whether the Grandfathers had placed them on Earth before leaving for the spirit world. Students drew their ideas of where rocks might be found, in Aroland and beyond, anywhere on the planet. From this first set of questions emerged the big idea for the unit and some related learning goals. Students would investigate, test, and compare the appearance and composition of different rocks and minerals.

The establishment of our community of learners is grounded in the teachings of the Seven Grandfathers: Respect, Truth, Wisdom, Honesty, Humility, Love, and Courage. Before any classroom discussion, I remind students that these teachings were passed on to help us get along and work together. The teaching of Respect, which stresses the value of everyone's ideas, is a particular focus at the beginning of the school year and becomes the foundation for inquiry in the classroom. Students learn to bring these teachings into all of their interactions, not only within the classroom but also when working with Mother Earth and the environment.

In my classroom, the children gather in a circle to sing, pray, listen, and share ideas. At the beginning of the year, I introduce the Talking Stick and Eagle Feather, which help to facilitate this safe, sharing environment – especially important in a diverse classroom such as ours. When a conversation begins, the feather or stick moves clockwise around the circle from their starting place in the east, moving around the circle as many times as is needed to get to a deeper understanding of a topic. Only the person holding the feather or stick may speak.

Classroom discussion is often done in "clans," with self-selected names such as Wolf Clan, Hummingbird Clan, and Bear Clan. My students respond well to group collaboration, working together through problems, coming up with solutions, and developing ideas. Wait time is always crucial in our discussions. Students also go away with their thoughts and may continue to think about the topic at home. While some might ask questions of their parents or elders, others research on the computer.

The design of my classroom evolved quickly during this process. By the second day of school, students' rocks were sitting beneath a chart of the rock cycle, organized into sedimentary, metamorphic, and igneous rock categories. An early Knowledge Building Circle (KBC) resulted in many questions, which were recorded and displayed for children to see as they moved around the classroom. Eventually, the classroom began to turn into a rock quarry, as rocks were brought from home, from the schoolyard, and from hunting and fishing trips. These small offerings to our classroom often generated new and interesting conversations during our KBCs. Students would bring their latest find to the circle to see if others could guess which type of rock it was. They wondered if anyone had finally found obsidian, prominently featured in the video game Minecraft (Mojang AB, 2009).

Our Wonderings and Theories About Rocks

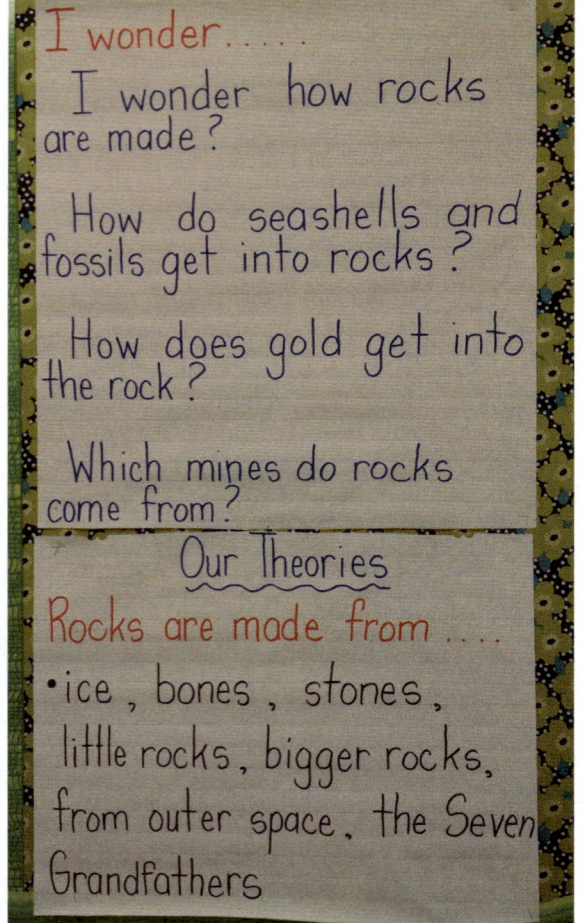

Given her deep connection to rocks, I asked our Native Language teacher, Miss Pauline, to allow us to tap into her knowledge. This provided our classroom with an opportunity to experience a traditional learning lodge. As is typical during a sweat lodge ceremony, we sat in a circle on a floor lined with evergreen boughs, a fire burning in the centre. A smudge was done at the beginning of the teaching and *aseema* (tobacco) was placed into the fire at the end as an offering to the Grandfathers and Spirits who were present during the learning.

Local Tipi Built by the Elders of Aroland for the Purpose of Teaching and Use of Johnny Therriault School Staff and Students

In this setting, the students learned from their own resident Elder about the significance of rocks for the Anishnaabe people. Miss Pauline shared her collection of rocks from around the world, brought to her from far off places (such as Jerusalem) by different people. Each student was given a sacred medicine pouch to wear around their neck each time they explored outside. In the pouch they placed tobacco as an offering of thanks to Mother Earth in return for their learning. After listening to Pauline's teachings, the children had a very different understanding of what the rocks meant and how to show respect for them. Many would say "Boozhoo Mishomis" ("Hello Grandfather") before approaching or examining a rock. Through this experience the children seem to have found a new knowledge and respect for the meaningful symbols in their culture.

Miss Pauline Leading a Lesson in the Learning Lodge

Students Examining Different Rocks from Around the World and Local Areas

Beyond the School: Exploring the Rock Quarry

Extending our inquiry beyond the school, we took a small trip to a local rock quarry where students used magnifying glasses to search for rocks that spoke to them, returning to the classroom with more to add to our collection. Many of the students had driven by the quarry numerous times, but had never stopped to look at all of the different and beautiful "Grandfathers" which lay still within it. They soon realized that within their own small community there was a whole area for exploration and learning, which many would continue to explore on their own.

Students Exploring at the Rock Quarry

The following photograph shows a collection of rocks from the quarry. The students charted their finds and assessed them in terms of lustre, transparency, hardness, and colour, attributes derived from information they had recorded about the characteristics of different rock types.

Classification of Rocks

Marlo's Story: Grades 3 and 4   229

Inspired by their visit to the quarry to make sedimentary rocks of their own, the children made a list of materials that they would need, including water, sand, and clay. Beginning with water, they slowly added silt, observing how it settled at the bottom of the glass. They then decided to place the silt in the clay.

Making Sedimentary Rocks

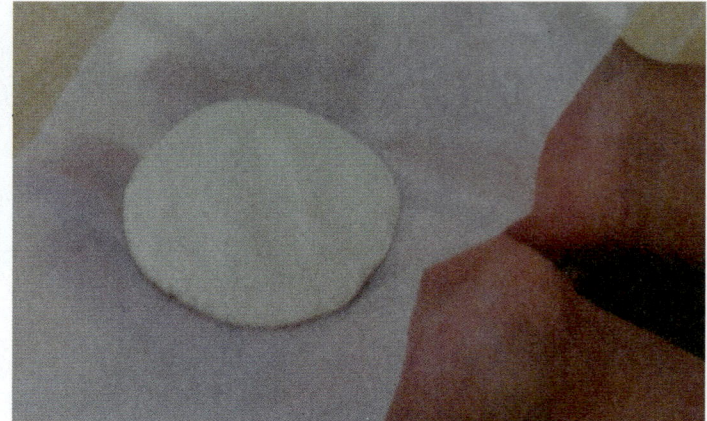

Knowing from previous discussions that sedimentary rocks need pressure to form the different layers, they attempted to create this pressure using different methods. First, they tried to roll out the clay using pencils. One student commented that this would have been like the water moving over the rocks for many years. Another wondered how silt could get into the middle of the rock to form layers. They soon discovered that they needed much more pressure and decided to press down directly on the clay, eventually cutting the clay into pieces, sprinkling silt, re-stacking the pieces, and pressing down really hard. Their end result was a triangular, layered sedimentary rock.

Medicine Bags, Which Are Worn When We Leave the Classroom. Tobacco (Aseema) Is Offered When Taking Anything from Mother Earth.

Integrated Learning

Through many different writing activities, including the use of modelled writing and independent writing stations, the students developed and demonstrated their understanding of rocks, making rich connections between their inquiry learning and other subject areas. They learned what good transition sentences looked like as they practised independent sequential writing accompanied by pictures of their experiments. Eventually, working in writing journals and using editing processes, they produced a final polished piece of written work.

Cross-curricular Connections: Rocks and Sequential Writing

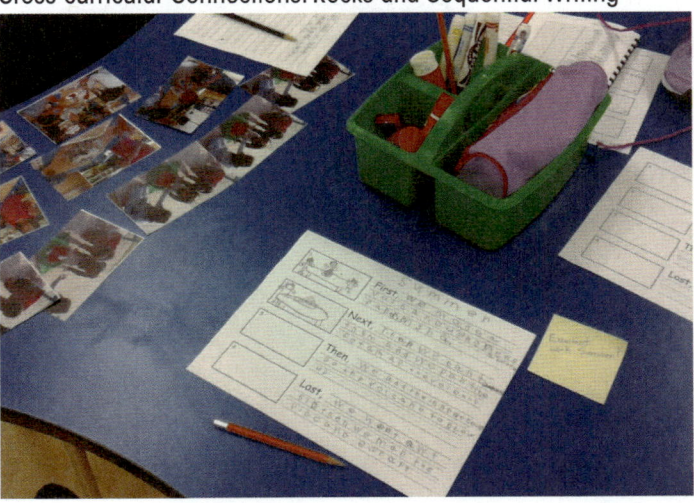

Deeper Connections to the Community: Learning About Mining

Offering Tobacco to the Grandfathers and Spirits in the Teaching Lodge

As we considered the different types of minerals found in the ground, our conversations began to focus on gold, especially in connection with the abandoned gold mine near O'Sullivan Lake. Having heard many stories about this area of Aroland, students assumed it was unsafe and possibly haunted. We planned an afternoon excursion to the mine to hear an Elder, Charlie Megan, speak about his experiences. As a young boy, he had been pushed out of this area by developers looking for gold.

Charlie and Elaine Megan, Aroland Elders, at the O'Sullivan Gold Mine

Charlie explained that in exchange for leaving their homes, families living in this area were offered lard and tea by the mining company. Over time, the operation of the mine caused local lakes and waterways to become contaminated with toxic chemicals and the fish population to be depleted. Since the water was no longer safe to drink, families had to travel great distances to get clean water for cooking. The mine finally closed in the mid-1970s as a result of money mismanagement, leaving the land severely damaged. As we walked through the site with Charlie and his wife, he warned, "We do not take anything from this area. It is not clean. Do not put your aseema down here because it's not good land."

In our KBC the next day, the need for restoration and preservation became the focus of conversation. The students discussed the reasons why their parents had warned them about the area, sharing their concerns about the fish that had been poisoned by chemicals in the lake and talking about the mining company's impact on the area – now and for years to come. They realized that to clean the area was a very different challenge than cleaning their schoolyard.

Water Pollution from Tailings

Waste Rock from Gold Extraction

As a cross-curricular activity, the students wrote narratives about the O'Sullivan Gold Mine. The impact of Charlie's story came through strongly in their writing, noting his memories of hearing the loud noises of the mine and emphasizing his recollections of being forced from the land as a child. All stories referred to the contamination of the fish.

Students then discussed the many types of mines that are still functioning in Ontario. The students worked in small groups to develop charts about the pros and cons of underground versus open-pit mines. Understanding how large an area could be occupied by an open-pit mine, they realized what effect this would have on the natural habitats of animals, the hunting and fishing of the area, and on people's homes.

As a culminating task, each student researched a currently operating Ontario mine. Using online sources, such as the Ontario Mining Association website (2012), books, and their own background knowledge, they reported when their mine became operational, what it produced, its type (e.g. underground or open-pit), and the nearest major city or First Nation.

Students then displayed their findings on a large Ontario map. I wanted them to understand that, just like Aroland, many First Nations communities contain mines with similar adverse effects on their lands and waterways. In our final KBC, the students showed a strong awareness of the impact of mines on the environment. They realized that properly managed mines could potentially benefit neighbouring areas by providing resources to help sustain the surrounding land.

Summary of Student Work on Mining in Ontario

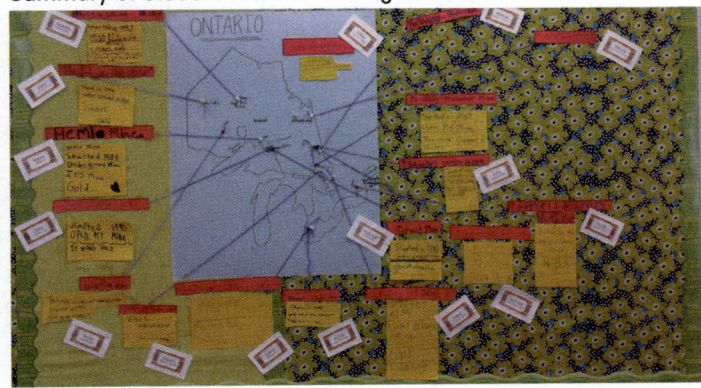

Final Reflections

As we moved forward with our rock inquiry, the classroom continued to evolve with the display of individual scrapbook work and photos and drawings of excursions made outside of the classroom. Throughout, I was active in assessing the children's learning in many ways. Asking them to draw titled, labelled pictures of their ideas about the topic – both at the beginning of the unit and as the lessons evolved – provided me with insight while fostering self-assessment as the children compared their drawings. In our knowledge building discussions, I noted students' preconceptions and assessed the accuracies and inaccuracies of their developing theories. Finally, I videotaped student-teacher conferences and action- or performance-based tasks, and also took photographs and notes, to capture what was happening at a particular moment and allow me to review the development of learning.

Inquiry has allowed me a chance to learn alongside my students. I love the challenge and see many connections between inquiry and traditional ways of learning. Traditionally, Indigenous children would sit and listen to the Elders speak about the teachings. After going into the bush to observe hunting, fishing, and food and hide preparation, they were ready to go out on their own. Similarly, the students in my classroom listen to me explain a process and then have an opportunity to try it themselves. They are always eager to use their hands. Should an experiment not work, they often work as a group to figure out what went wrong and try again. When we are out in the forest or other natural environments, their experience is enhanced by teachings about the area learned from their Elders.

The children have a loving connection to their village and surrounding areas. Through their offerings of tobacco (aseema) to Mother Earth whenever anything is taken, the students make connections, emotionally, physically, mentally, and spiritually. Offerings are also given back to the Grandfathers after listening to an Elder's teaching. We say "thank you" (miigwech) for our good knowledge of how important rocks are to the people. I take great pride in listening to the teachings of the Elders who worked with us on the project. To listen to someone speak about their personal experience and learn from their teachings deepens my own learning about a topic.

I truly believe that the students, in my classroom and in the school as a whole, have changed their perspective about the land on which they live. They connect with the teachings of the Elders who tell them that everything comes from the Earth. They offer tobacco when taking anything for their own personal use and show much more respect for their environment. They have a much deeper connection to Mother Earth and a stronger sense of how to protect her.

Robin's Story
Grade 4
Dr. Eric Jackman Institute of Child Study Laboratory School

> Robin's story is unique among the educators' stories in its unwavering focus on teaching Indigenous content, including the cultures, histories, and perspectives of the Indigenous peoples of Canada. Doug Anderson has added his reflections on this piece in the form of footnotes. As teachers move forward with the important challenge of building both their own and their students' knowledge in this area, it is critical to work with Indigenous educators to address the inevitable misconceptions that will arise and to identify where Eurocentric ways of thinking may obscure full understanding. We hope that making this essential collaboration visible will encourage readers to take their own risks and appreciate such reflections and corrections as crucial aspects of an ongoing journey.

Starting the Environmental Inquiry Process

Making a Change

My childhood experiences as the daughter of two archaeologists who worked each summer in Greece so inspired me that when I became a teacher I was excited to share my enthusiasm for geography and history with my students. Up until 2012 I had incorporated learning about ancient civilizations into our social studies work each year. That summer, as the time for planning a social studies unit for my upcoming Grade 4s approached, I hesitated. As I considered topics, I came to the realization that when Canadian children studied ancient civilizations, Indigenous Canadian cultures were rarely included as an important part of the curriculum or were touched upon in a cursory and Eurocentric manner. Thus, as I reflected on which cultures did predominate in elementary school learning I came to the conclusion that Canadian children were not learning enough about their own country's history, in particular about the Indigenous peoples who have always lived here. The more I reflected on this notion, the more I felt compelled to address this shortcoming. It would be a responsible educational choice, I thought, to teach about the peoples and cultures that were indigenous to our own part of the world. This was how I came to my decision to teach Indigenous Studies in Grade 4.

Stepping Outside My Comfort Zone

I knew that this decision involved stepping outside my comfort zone and embracing a topic I knew little about and did not feel particularly qualified to teach. The more I read, the more concerned I became about how to approach this complex topic. I felt that to address this subject matter appropriately I would have to teach more than just the history. I would also have to provide experiences that would expose the children to contemporary social and political concerns as they related to Indigenous history and help them begin to understand how these challenges have evolved over time and continue to affect Indigenous peoples today.

As I began to plan, I struggled with the discomfort that I would teach material disrespectfully or incorrectly. After all, resources can be fallible and even contradict one another. I also learned that Indigenous people hold a range of opinions on many issues. I wondered how to bring sociopolitical issues into the classroom at this grade level. What were Grade 4s cognitively and emotionally ready to learn? What would be developmentally appropriate? How would I adequately prepare and support the children in learning about difficult topics such as residential schools? Finally, I came to realize that I would also need to avoid portraying Indigenous peoples solely as victims. I would need to carefully develop an approach that would also strongly communicate Indigenous peoples' diversity, strength, and achievements as well as their determination to maintain and pass on elements of traditional culture to younger generations.

In order to avoid being paralyzed by these matters, I decided that in addition to continuing to inform myself through coursework, reading, and media viewing, the most effective way to address my concerns would be to adopt an approach of complete transparency with the children in the class. This meant that I would share my own thinking process and journey. I would express to them why I thought it was important to study this topic, explain the hesitations I had, and reiterate my willingness to acknowledge errors and then modify my knowledge and teaching accordingly. Persevering and pursuing something unfamiliar or uncomfortable despite its challenges also seemed a worthwhile value to model for my students.

Fostering Understanding and Compassion Through Biography Studies

As I began to plan my approach, I thought about how I had introduced sensitive topics in the past. For years I had taught about diversity and social justice issues through Biography Studies.[1] I tended to choose stories that represented life journeys characterized by adversity and challenge closely followed by empowerment and personal triumph. My experience was that when children heard stories of real people's lives, those journeys inspired in them compassion and open-mindedness. I found that through these stories, complex discussions about difference, prejudice, discrimination, strength, pride, and achievement could develop and gradually contribute to building a stronger classroom culture of awareness, acceptance, caring, and personal perseverance. It was my hope that building a community with these values would gradually provide the children with opportunities to connect this learning to their personal lives and to interactions with others. I had already begun incorporating Black History more explicitly into Biography Studies and so it made complete sense to begin including the lives of Indigenous peoples.

I began to seek out and read biographies of and stories by Indigenous individuals, both from the past and the present. These included, but were not limited to, stories of both historical and more contemporary figures such as Sacagawea, Sitting Bull, and Louis Riel, ballerina Maria Tallchief, hockey player Jordan Tootoo, artists Pudlo Pudlat, Kenojuak Ashevak and Jessie Oonark, and finally residential school survivors Larry Loyie and Margaret Pokiak-Fenton.[2] In some cases we read and discussed a specific biography. At other times we explored activities related to the individual about whom we learned. For example, we read about Norval Morrisseau, viewed images of his artwork, and then tried our own hand at his style of painting. We read *The Old Man with the Otter Medicine* (2008), a Dene legend retold by G. Blondin, J. Blondin, and Beaverho, and then listened to the story on CD, each page read in English then in Dogrib. We read *Mwâkwa Talks to the Loon* (2006), considered the teachings offered by this story, and then read about the author and artist Dale Auger and his many achievements.

Building the Foundation

Over the past five years there have been certain elements of teaching this subject that have remained essentially the same. Other aspects have been consciously removed or modified, or have simply fallen aside as other ideas and opportunities have presented themselves. Always, I am cognizant that the conversation within the classroom community is the powerful vehicle through which we process our learning, share our perspectives, and build understanding and empathy. The following is the story of how this area of study evolved in 2015-2016.

It is September and the new children have arrived in my classroom. They are a lively but clearly kind and cohesive group, eager, curious, and thirsty for stimulating conversation. We begin the year's Biography Studies by focusing on individuals from North America. We use Google Earth to look at the shape of North America and where it is situated in relation to the other continents. The children learn about cardinal and intermediate directions and explore orienting and navigating using maps. We remind ourselves that some Indigenous peoples who were first on this land named North America Turtle Island. With each biography we read, we find the geographical home of each individual and relate its location to the origins of other people we have read about. Over time, we travel to different continents through story.

---

[1] While diversity and social justice issues are one very likely entry point to learning about Indigenous peoples and perspectives, it is important to ensure that engaging in such learning does not reduce Indigenous issues to diversity and social justice lenses. Indigenous issues are not equity or diversity issues, if we take diversity as usually considered, i.e., as a way of supporting a kind of "multicultural" Canadian "mosaic." Of course, Indigenous people want (and still await) equity in matters related to funding for health care and education (for example), as a small part of treaty and other nation-to-nation understandings compensating for massive territorial encroachments by Canada; but this is far from equating Indigenous peoples with Canadians who strive for equal representation or participation in Canadian systems, or whose notions of diversity are often limited to wanting their cultures reflected or respected in Canadian contexts. Indigenous polities and other systems have existed for millennia whereas Canada has recently been established, and are the foundation for whole ways of living that can never be adequately reflected in or represented through a Canadian system.

[2] The histories of remarkable and generally unknown Indigenous leaders, people like Payepot, Deskaheh, and many more, need to be built into modern learning contexts. Often such leaders have been neglected in Canadian stories precisely because they were so powerful and principled in ways that deeply reflected their own cultural perspectives and did not fit typically self-congratulatory Canadian narratives.

Some of the biographies we read simply celebrate achievement or tell people's interesting life stories, but many of them either explicitly or more subtly share narratives of difficult experiences, of discrimination of one form or another. The stories also, however, bear witness to perseverance and *resilience*, to struggles overcome. I decide that resilience is such a powerful word that I will use it often this year. Each story provides an opportunity for the children to consider another person's point of view, to try and see life from their perspective, to empathize, to reason about what is just and right. Not surprisingly, the children are uniformly perplexed by the stories of unkind treatment of others and they wonder why people make choices to be cruel. This is, of course, a very complex topic which has no simple answer. Each time we share a biography, we reflect on the themes and concepts that seem to repeat themselves and the class begins to develop a shared vocabulary. We talk about *rights*, *prejudice*, and *discrimination* in its many forms including racism, sexism, homophobia, ableism, ageism, and colonialism. We look at people's actions and try to understand what prevents them from making more thoughtful choices. We then identify the strengths and strategies protagonists show in overcoming obstacles to happiness and success.

Initial Group Brainstorm

We begin our formal Indigenous Studies in February 2016 with a group discussion. I ask the children what they know about Indigenous peoples. Some of their responses are . . .

- *They are people who lived before most people.*
- *They are people who mostly lived off the land.*
- *There are still some people today.*

The students focus on hunting, the respect for animals, and the use of tobacco to give thanks:

- *They would kill animals to make food and clothing.*
- *They used every single part of the animal they killed. Like up North.*
- *If you were a whale hunter, you'd use everything [to make] tools, meat, candles, clothes …*
- *When they hunt, they leave tobacco, it's for the God[3] but also for the animal, saying thank you for giving us your life and they used tobacco because wasn't tobacco special back then?*

The Class's Original Brainstorm

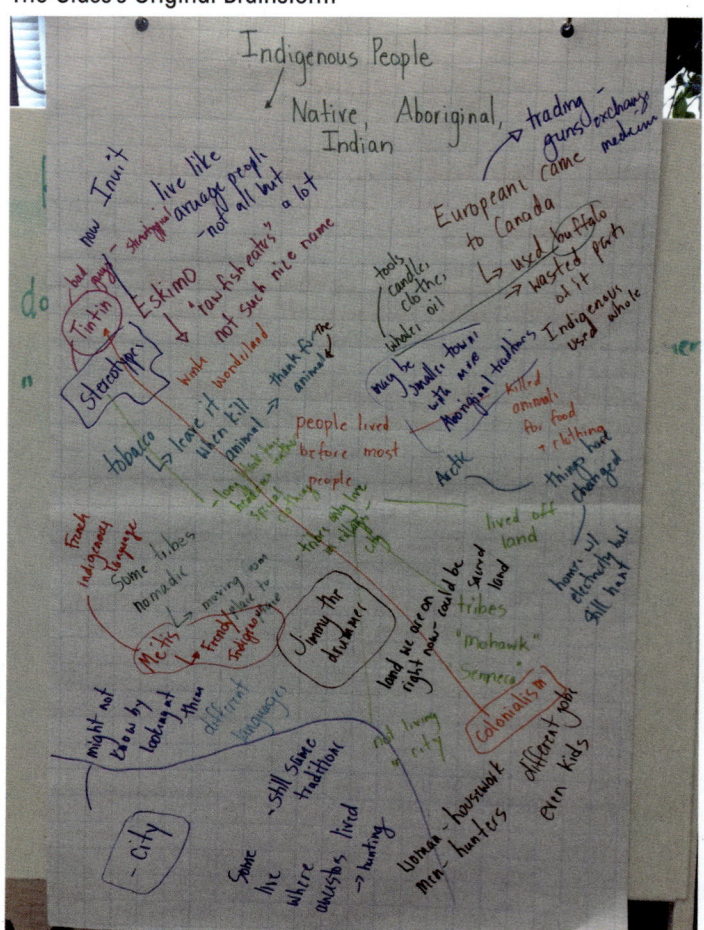

It is interesting to me that in the examples just shared they seem to use both past and present tense to share their knowledge. Their word choices convey this tension between what was and what still is: "they are," "they would," "they used," "they hunt," and "back then." Their ideas show me that they wrestle with the notion that although things are obviously different from the past, that aspects of this way of life have been preserved, although their comments also seem to suggest that they are struggling with understanding how this works.

---

[3] The language in the children's answers unavoidably reflects common misconceptions inherent to Eurocentric thought and language. For example (and recognizing that we do not know what the child was thinking in this specific instance), a term like "the God" reflects a superstitious and problematic way in which many modern people see Indigenous spiritual traditions – as a kind of "paganism," in which diverse "gods" are worshipped in different places as if they were all humanly conceived, apart from any inner, unified source or higher metaphysical reality. Nothing could be further from the truth. Of course, it is a long road to addressing the many misconceptions that arise regarding Indigenous peoples in the thinking and language of children and teachers alike; the point at this stage for most teachers is to maintain an awareness of this fact while not getting too wound up about it! After all, English and French are the unavoidable starting points for most of us, and we should not be paralyzed by the fear of being politically incorrect.

Robin: So far we have mainly been talking about history. What do people know about Indigenous Peoples today?

Student 1: They have the same traditions, but it's not like, the same. I think they still have the same traditions but it's not like as big as it used to be.

Student 2: Some of them still do the traditions but some of them don't.

Student 3: They can't just do it anymore because they're in a city – they're not just able, like the men aren't able to go around shooting a rabbit.

Robin: So, somewhere in your minds you know that Indigenous Peoples still celebrate some of their traditions today, but they also probably don't celebrate exactly like they did in the past. Some said they live in the city. Do all Indigenous Peoples live in the city? What do people know about that?

Student 4: Some still live where their ancestors used to live and still do the same stuff their ancestors used to do instead of going to the store and buying stuff. Not all Indigenous Peoples live in the city. You can't just go around and "see" an Indigenous person. They blend in, you can't really tell.

Robin: Are you saying that Indigenous people are in the city but you might not notice by looking at them?

Student 4: Yeah, that makes sense.

Student 5: They kind of change when they go different places, they might not look the same.

Student 6: In the Arctic they live in homes with electricity but also sometimes go on hunting trips and live in igloos…

Robin: Yes, sometimes they still practice traditions but things also modernize and change.

Student 7: I think they live now like average people, a lot of them, maybe not all of them.

Student 8: I'm building on to [Student 6]. There might be a few small little towns that might have bigger Aboriginal traditions than maybe the city like they might still hunt, but still they might have electricity.

Student 9: So, there's all these cities. What we're standing on could be a hunting area. It doesn't leave that much space. They're basically leaving the worst places to survive to the Indigenous people.

Robin: [Student 9] is bringing something up – the conflict that there is about traditional land and now that land has been taken over and developed.

Student 10: It's also a stereotype to say every single one is an Inuit. It's specifying that exact one group. It's basically stereotyping that every single person is Inuit there and they're all the same and no different there.

This last comment allows me to probe their understanding of stereotypes in relation to Indigenous People. I ask them about what, if any, stereotypes they are aware of:

Student 1: All of them wear a dress, kind of, and have beads, and long hair, long black hair and feathers.

Robin: So some of the stereotypes might be about how they look: For example they all have long black hair, wear headdresses with feathers, wear special clothing … any other stereotypes?

Student 2: All Indians, I mean, Indigenous tribes, only speak an Indigenous language. Because, I actually studied a group called the Métis and they actually speak French, they're half French.

Robin: So let's slow down, who are the Métis again?

Student 2: They're a French group.

Robin: They're part French – from when Europeans came over and intermarried with Indigenous people – their children would be Métis. So you're saying not all people might speak an Indigenous language? I think the key word is SOME. Do you think SOME Indigenous people have long black hair? [**Class:** Yes.] Do you think ALL Indigenous people have long black hair? [**Class:** No.] Not all Aboriginal people look the same. They can be blonde with blue eyes.

Student 3: You know in Tintin. Aboriginal people were the bad guys a lot of the time. Somehow, they're always on the bad guys' team, and they all have black hair, and they all look the same. A lot of the time it's some kind of Indigenous people who are being tricked or being bad.

I bring the discussion to a close by summarizing what the group has shared and what we will be pursuing in our studies.

Robin: I'm so excited by how much this group knows already. We'll learn about history but also the present. We will try to become more knowledgeable about issues in the present day, and also how Indigenous people live today.

Teacher Sharing of Information

At this point, I feel the children need a little more information about Indigenous history to give them a broader context so they can make the most of our shared class experiences as well as their own group research. Through an interactive presentation format, we explore the Bering Land Bridge Theory and consider how it conflicts with Indigenous peoples' belief that they have been on Turtle Island since "Time Immemorial."

We explore other topics during two separate sessions:

- Historical dating (CE and BCE). We play a game where the children each get a card with a date on it and they have to use only gestures to organize themselves chronologically.
- When and from where explorers came to North America.
- Viewing and discussion of two maps – one that shows the approximate distribution of seven main Indigenous cultural groups at the time of first contact and another that shows the many tribes that exist within each of these cultural groups. This is important in order to support conversations we have been having about why we add a letter 's' to the end of Indigenous Peoples. We work towards understanding that Indigenous Peoples have great diversity and that the plural 's' helps us to remember that although groups and tribes may share commonalities, they also have many differences.
- We review the concept of colonization (which has arisen several times since the fall) and then talk about the negative consequences it has had for Indigenous peoples including exposure to disease and loss of connection to language, culture, and traditions.
- Finally we discuss where Aboriginal people live today. We learn that they live in rural or urban settings such as cities, small towns, reserves or a combination. The class does not seem to know anything about reserves so we spend some time talking about what they are and then use the internet to look up the names of all the reserves that exist in Canada and their respective populations.

Major Indigenous Cultural Groups at Time of Contact (Silvey & Mantha, 2005)

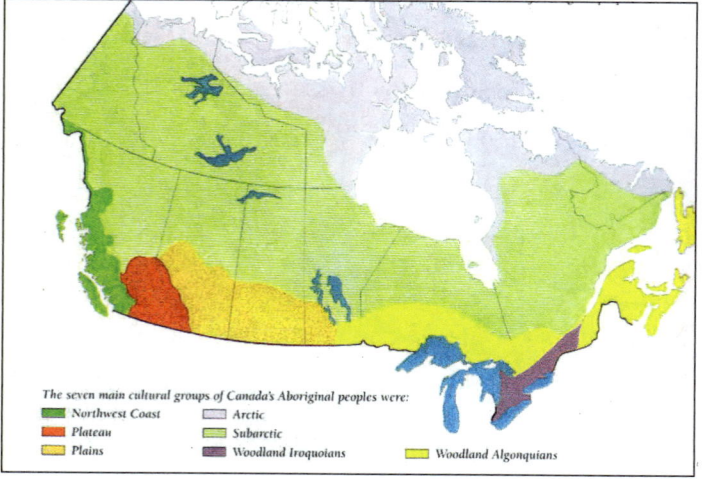

Estimated Distribution of Tribes at Time of Contact (Canadian Broadcasting Corporation [CBC], 2009)

I let the children know that they will be conducting research about different topics related to our Indigenous Studies and eventually creating presentations to share their learning with their classmates. Through this research, the children will practice and hone many skills including working collaboratively, reading for information, taking jot notes (which involves identifying key information and summarizing in one's own words), developing computer skills, and delivering oral presentations.

Analyzing Media Through a Social Justice Lens

During our next Inquiry period I decide to show the class a film available for free viewing through the National Film Board. The film is called *For Angela* (Botkin, MacDonald, & Prouty, 1993) and is a true story written by an Ojibwa woman about an experience she had, with her daughter, of being harassed on their way to school one day. The students' answers to questions I pose, and the conversations that develop, allow us to delve deeply into their understanding of how stereotypes, bullying, and discrimination affect individuals. We also discuss effective consequences and the role of bystanders. Their comments also enable us to explore the origins of our respective ancestors. In the coming weeks, two students will come to school and tell me, with great excitement, that they have discovered they have some Indigenous ancestry.

I introduce the film to the children:

In this film you'll see re-enacted what happened to an Indigenous woman and her daughter. It's about an experience they had on their way to school, and they are harassed by a group of boys. Here are the kinds of things I want you to be looking and listening for: What forms of racism/discrimination do you see/hear in the movie? What role do the bullies and bystanders play? How do the mother and Angela react to the bullying? How does it affect them? What happens in the end? Be looking and listening for the actions, the body language, and dialogue.

After the movie the children share the following observations and I try to guide the conversation, pulling together related threads, introducing terminology, and encouraging connections.

Student 1: The boy put her down just because she was Aboriginal. They made fun of their traditions.
Robin: Can you think of a specific example?
Student 1: I remember he was mean to her because of her braids.
Robin: Do you remember what he called her?
Student 1: Pocahontas.
Student 2: It reminded me of how the Jim Crow laws were made. When they [the bullies] were walking around, they were acting kind of stupid like that's what Indigenous people were like.
Student 3: They made fun of their skin, that's why she [Angela] chose the lighter crayon.
Robin: Right, that moment with the crayon. She [Angela] says the lighter one is a nicer colour.
Student 4: When they look at Angela they're like "Oooooh braids, she's an Indian. That would be like me pointing to [Student 5]. I can't assume he is Indian. It's basically a huge stereotype.
Student 5: Well actually you can because I am Indian. [Student 5 is of East Indian origins.]

At this point we take a moment to clarify the difference between East Indian and North American Indian using the world map for reference. The children have studied a great deal of geography over the course of the school year and have learned about the different continents and their locations. We also remind the class what the Jim Crow laws were which we learned about during Black History studies.

Student 6: Some people try to make fun of you if you're Black or you look like someone. They made fun of her hair, said she looked like Pocahontas, that's why she cut them [her braids] off. When she said the lighter crayon was the nicer colour she didn't want to be the colour she was because she felt bad.
Robin: At the end you probably heard her refer to herself as "Indian." She also used the word Aboriginal. At the time [1993] people still used this term more often. Over time, terminology changes. Also, not all Aboriginal people refer to themselves as Indigenous; some people use different words. My understanding is that there is no one term that everyone prefers and that many Indigenous people actually prefer to be referred to by their specific nation. For example they would say they are "Cree" or "Ojibwa" or "Sioux" and so on. What was Ian [in the film] doing when he did this "Aw Wah Wah Wah" with his mouth? [I pat my hand against my mouth and make this sound.]
Student 7: I'm not so sure about this. If I get it wrong ... I'm pretty sure that Indigenous people used to have a chant, a tribe, and they sing songs and stuff and they make noises and I guess he was making fun of them by pretending [to do that].
Robin: Right, like [Student 1] said, they were making fun of their traditions. Then he said, "Oh boys, we should really act more ..."
Class: "... civilized."
Robin: "And less like ..."
Class: "... savages."
Robin: Remember how we talked about how Europeans wanted to assimilate Indigenous people? They wanted their land, but they also tried to change them to be more like them because they believed they were better, superior. What did you notice about the bystanders in the incident?
Student 9: They were trying to ignore it. Everyone would look ... Even the bus driver.
Robin: Why do you think they didn't intervene?
Student 9: They might have been worried that they would get in the problem too.
Student 10: The bus driver looked at the situation.
Robin: Right they showed his eyes in the rear-view mirror.
Student 10: I don't know the laws on the bus. I don't think you can force someone to get off, but I think in this situation it would be reasonable.
Student 11: You can't force someone to get off their seat but if there's an elder and you're sitting in an elder seat you have to get off.
Student 12: Maybe they didn't want to get involved or maybe they believed, they agreed with what the boys were doing.
Student 13: Maybe they were Aboriginal themselves and they get the feeling that the boys would be relentless and just keep going. Maybe the old couple were some Elders.
Robin: [Student 13] brings up a very important issue. Indigenous people can look as different as anybody. So they *might* have long dark hair or they *might* be blonde and blue-eyed. They could be of mixed heritage. There is no one way that Indigenous people look. And yes, it could be that the old couple were Indigenous and they didn't want to become victims themselves.

Student 13: Well we are all probably descended from some Indigenous person.

Robin: Well, it's something you can go home and ask about. I have had students who have gone home and found out they have Indigenous roots. I know that I myself do not have any Indigenous roots. My ancestors are from Europe. You can ask your parents about your heritage and where your ancestors are from. What do you think about how the principal reacted to the situation?

Student 6: In a lot of stories, there's someone who's in denial of the truth, so they don't get in trouble or arrested or something. So, he [the bully] was denying it but the principal he knew, he understood.

Robin: What did the principal make him [the bully] do?

Student 6: He made him look at her.

Robin: And what happened once Ian [the bully] really looked at her?

Student 6: He had to face the truth.

Robin: One more question: it's really interesting how, at the end, she talks about the *resolution* they chose as a group. Rather than choose suspension or expulsion from school, what did they decide on?

Student 1: They had to spend the day together.

Robin: I am curious what people think about that solution. Often Indigenous communities come together as a healing circle and decide what people have done wrong and it [the solution] often involves giving back to the community in some way. What do you think about this compared to a more typical punishment?

Student 14: I think the reason they did that was to show what it was like to be them.

Student 15: I think it's because, imagine you did something very, very, very hurtful and you think you've totally got away with it, and then you have to spend the whole day with them and you have to basically do what they're doing – walk around with them. It must have been really hard. I think it's a really good punishment – you're with the people you hurt the whole day, but in this one you're not the person who has more power, you're at the same level as them.

Robin: This relates to our role plays. Remember how we talked about how each person has to decide what they feel safe doing in such a situation? It's not always easy to stand up for others. So for her, remember what the first thing was? She asked them to stop, then she tried to walk away. [As part of our studies at the end of Black History Month the children took part in role plays where they acted out scenarios in which they witness or experience some form of discrimination and they have to decide how to respond.]

Student 16: She also held her daughter's hand.

Robin: [Student 17] would you like to share your comment I heard you making during our break?

Student 17: I said if I was Ian [the bully] I'd rather be expelled because you don't want to spend the whole day with the person you hurt.

Robin: Right, but the intensity of your reaction to that possibility ... Do you think it would have been a good punishment?

Student 17: Yeah! [with expression and eyebrows raised high]

Robin: Maybe Rhonda [the mother] didn't even view it as a "punishment," but rather something that could lead to something better. What did she say she learned from the boys?

Student 13: She said that they learned all this stuff about where the boys learned those stereotypes, in the news and the media, and so, since she's a journalist, she kept writing stories to kind of help Aboriginal tribes.

Setting up for Research

For a period of time, we take a break from these heavy topics and the children begin to set up their research folders. Each child is part of a research group and the children are reading and taking jot notes on a variety of topics including different nations and cultural groups, European explorers, the impact of contact with Europeans on Indigenous Peoples, social and political activists and organizations, and contributions of Indigenous Peoples to Canadian culture. Their groups are created with several needs in mind including academic strengths and needs, content knowledge and interest, and also social dynamics. The children are very excited about this process. We begin by reviewing and practicing reading and recording information in jot note form. We also discuss ways to work collaboratively in a group and strategies for avoiding or addressing conflict. Over the next few weeks, the children will gather information and eventually use their findings to create PowerPoint presentations for their classmates. This end goal is extremely motivating for them.

The Children Create Their Research Folders

As they work, the children call me over to share interesting things that they have learned. In some cases, they complain that it is hard to select what to make notes about because everything is interesting.

One child exclaims: "Did you give us the smartest group on purpose? Listen to this" He then reads me the following passage from his text:

They practiced slash-and-burn agriculture in which trees and brush are burned and the soil is fertilized by ash ... The plants were highly compatible, and the farmers wisely took advantage of this by growing them together. The corn stalks provided a natural support for the beans to climb up while the squash plants growing close to the ground smothered the weeds. (Silvey & Mantha, 2005, p. 40)

As the children record their ideas, they ask me on several occasions whether they should use past or present tense to describe what they are learning. This is difficult to answer – and this is what I tell them – because although we are studying history, we also know that in some Indigenous communities some of the same traditions continue to be practiced today.

Considering a Controversy, Different Perspectives, and Taking a Stand

One day, the Grade 5/6 teachers approach me and ask me whether the Grade 4s would like to join in on their classes' homework for the upcoming weekend. They are going to be designing logos and proposing a name for our school's sports teams. I feel this is a great opportunity for the children to get a sense of the homework they will be doing in Grade 5 and so I agree. Over the weekend, I recall that I have an article put aside from the *Canadian Reader* [a children's current events magazine to which I subscribe]. The article is called "What's in a Name?" (LesPlan, 2013) and explores the current controversy over the names and logos of sports teams such as the Washington Redskins and the Cleveland Indians, which are seen as derogatory and offensive by many. This seems like a perfect time to explore this issue with the children. Through the article, we explore new and familiar vocabulary and work to understand the differences between words such as *slur*, *derogatory*, *racism*, *stereotype*, and *discrimination*. At the end of our discussion (and we do consider both sides of the controversy) I ask the children to write a few words sharing their thoughts about the debate.

- *If I was the general manager of one of those teams I would definitely change the name because I think it's extremely racist. Stereotyping teams with goofy logos like the one on the Cleveland Indians is not nice.*
- *I support changing controversial team names because I think it will be offensive to some people and if I was an Aboriginal person I would be really angry and sad because it's making fun of us (or them).*
- *I sort of don't want to change the teams because it will change so much people won't recognize them! On the other side of things, it's racist and discriminatory ... so I can't quite make up my mind.*
- *I support changing controversial team names because they could be offending people and also because in some team names, like the Atlanta Braves, they used something for their name that they did not have permission to use.*

Another child expresses her point of view by creating a cartoon strip and relating the issue to racism in general and her own personal experiences:

Student Reflection on Racism and Personal Experiences

For a time we explore some of the topics the children have specifically shown interest in and asked questions about. We read about the Eagle Feather and its significance. We share stories of the origins of our own names and traditions. The children discuss the meanings of their names and who they were named after. They share stories of baptisms and ceremonies at mosques, synagogues, and churches and they explain the meaning of their names. We then read about Inuit and First Nations naming ceremonies.

Turtle Island at the Time of Contact: Canada Before Confederation

At the front of the room, I have placed a large sheet of plastic laminate over our classroom map of Canada and the children have begun to colour in the approximate areas different Indigenous cultural groups inhabited at the time of contact. I am hoping that the children can come to understand that before Confederation, there were no provinces, no territories, no Canada, and no United States. The following discussion ensues:

Robin: [Student 1] and [Student 2] coloured in approximately where the People of the Plains lived at the time of first contact when Europeans came over. [Student 4] Run your finger along the southern line of that orange part. What do you think about that? Why is it coloured in like that? That's the border between what?

Student 4: Between America and Canada.

Robin: So what do you think about the way we have coloured in the People of the ... [**Class:** Plains] What do you notice right away about where the People of the Plains lived?

Student 5: It's very big.

Student 6: It's not just in one place. It's kind of spread across.

Robin: So when you say it's not just in one place it's not just in one ...

Student 6: Area.

Class: Province.

Robin: [Student 4] said this is the border between Canada and the U.S. So what's happening here? Do you think the People of the Plains, their tribes, stopped exactly here?

Class: No.

Robin: So what's happening here?

Student 7: It's where most people are?

Student 8: This is just Canada!

Robin: Yes! Maybe we can find a map of the U.S. that's about this subject as well. If we did find a map of the U.S. that did show where different cultural groups were living at that time, what do you think we might see?

Student 4: It would go down like this [points south].

Robin: You think it would maybe come down here [gesture south of the Canadian border]?

Class: Yeah.

Robin: Because at that time was there Canada and the United States?

Student 5: No, it was all Turtle Island.

Robin: Did these borders exist?

Class: No

Robin: So it's very unlikely it would just have stopped there. I think you're right and I think what we would see is that it would carry further south.

Over the coming weeks, the mapping process is completed and the children learn that not only do some groups continue south into the U.S. but there are other, different Indigenous groups south of the border.

Over Several Weeks the Children Contribute to the Laminate Overlay

Residential Schools

Some time has passed now and the children have been working on their research. I have decided it is an appropriate time to teach them about residential schools. I have spent a great deal of time thinking about how to share this information with them. I am cognizant that this is an upsetting piece of history for anyone to learn about, but especially for children, whose lives revolve around their families and the security and comfort of their homes. There seems to be no way to teach about this part of Canada's history except to describe it honestly and openly with, of course, sensitivity as well as help them to connect it to issues of power, oppression, and racism.

This is the last heavy topic we will address. In a brief summary I explain to the children what residential schools were, where and when they were established, and when they ceased to exist. The children are shocked, as most people are, to learn that the last residential school closed in 1996. Over a few weeks the children engage in a number of activities:

- They listen to both autobiographical and fictional stories about the residential school experience.
- We study a simplified version of the United Nations Declaration of the Rights of the Child and work in groups to determine which rights were violated when Indigenous children were forced to attend residential schools.
- We view a shortened clip of the Government of Ontario's broadcast apology to Indigenous People for residential schools.

Introduction to Residential Schools

Robin: Remember when we talked about how when Europeans came to North America they had a certain attitude towards Indigenous Peoples? What was that attitude for the most part?[5]

Class:
- They were uncivilized.
- Wild.
- They didn't think they were like them and they wanted them to be like them.
- Savage.
- They wanted to take over.

Robin: Remember that word *assimilation*? It means making other people like you and absorbing them into your culture and when there is cultural assimilation, what happens to the group that's being assimilated? What happens to their culture and their traditions?

Student 1: They can't do it anymore. They can't speak their language, they can't do their culture, and these people are like "Oh they are so lucky we came 'cause now we're going to change what they do because they are just so unorganized." But they actually have their own way.

Robin: So [Student 3] was mentioning that over time when you are not allowed to follow your traditions or speak your language some of that can start to get lost.

Student 2: It's like those stories, when people colonized, all the stories were going to get lost but then you pass them down from each generation so they are not going to be lost. So remember when that speaker came to our school to tell those Anansi stories? Sandra Whiting? Remember Christopher Columbus thought he was going to India and he actually ended up in the Caribbean? And Jamaica's in there so the Anansi stories probably would be lost but then they went down to each generation and that's how Sandra Whiting knew them but they're SO GOOD! They're so good stories!

Robin: Wouldn't it be a shame if they were lost?

Student 2: Yeah!

Robin: So that's the wonderful thing about the oral tradition.

Student 4: And there were probably lots that have been lost!

Class: Yeah.

Student 2: But there's like 20 books but that's probably not all of them.

Robin: So that's the thing about colonization. We talked

---

[5] This is another example of a common misconception, often held by those sympathetic to Indigenous people: that Europeans were generally racist and assimilative from the earliest contact with Indigenous Peoples. While many certainly were racist (not to mention atrociously genocidal), at first these negative tendencies were, at least in some areas, not nearly as prominent as they later became. In fact, many early European immigrants either wholly or partially assimilated into Indigenous societies, for diverse reasons having to do with the very real appeal of Indigenous ways of life. Nor was this reality limited to impoverished refugees from remoter parts of Europe. William Johnson, who was the highest representative of the British Crown in all of "Indian Country" prior to the American revolution, spoke Mohawk, had Mohawk children, attended Mohawk ceremonies, and generally helped frame relatively respectful, nation-to-nation relationships with a vast territory in eastern North America. His own British descendants were sorely disappointed in the rapid and disrespectful devolution of these relationships after the War of 1812.

about the word *resilience* before and so one thing that happens is that people who have been colonized manage somehow to continue doing their traditions, sometimes secretly.

Student 2: Yeah, it's like the slaves figured out special words in their songs. They didn't stop them from singing. Well, they kind of did but when they were singing they didn't suspect that their message was actually in the song.

Robin: We are going to continue learning over time what kinds of traditions Indigenous Peoples from different tribes had and how Europeans created laws preventing those, but one of the things that happened was that, at a point in time, the Europeans decided that it would be best for Aboriginal children to not be educated by their families but to receive a "proper education" – to be sent away to schools called "residential school." So "residential" means "somewhere where you live." You know what boarding schools are, right? Well it's like that but imagine you are five or six years old, sometimes even as young as three years old, and you are taken away from your family and your family is told "If you do not allow us to take your child you will be put in jail." [A child asks whether parents would be killed and I respond no, but that they might be arrested and put in jail.] So many, many Indigenous children were sent away to these schools and for the most part they were not a great place to be. They were not allowed to speak their language, they did not see their parents for many months, sometimes years, and when they came back to their homes they had forgotten how to speak their language. And they felt different from their families. So the reason it's important to know about this is that today, Indigenous people are still feeling the impact of that. It affected a lot of people. Can you imagine how you would feel if that happened to you? Now most people are grown up, but imagine if you didn't grow up with your parents, you didn't experience being parented. So, sometimes when these people grew up and had their own children, they themselves didn't know how to parent or they had other problems because of what they had experienced. We are going to read an article then share some stories about people's experiences.

Learning the Facts

I project the article "Coming to Grips with a Shameful Past" (Grant, 2015). The article refers to the 19th and 20th century so I pause to explain this.

Robin: Let's stop there because that can be confusing. The 19th century is in the 1800s. It is 1801, 1802 and so on up to 1900. The 20th century is anything in the 1900s. That always confused me when I was growing up.

Student 1: But I thought it was like twenty was two thousand

Student 2: It's one behind.

Robin: Right it's always one behind because from 0-100 is a century,

Student 3: It's like your birthday. It's like when I am born I say I'm zero. You know how your parents say when you see someone's kid, "How old are they?" They say they are two months old so that first year is a year. Most kids in this class have been on the earth for ten years.

Robin: The first residential School opened in 1831 and the last one was closed as recently as 1996, not that long ago.

Class: Whoah!

Student 4: That's 20 years ago

Student 5: 18 years?

Student 4: No 20

We do the Math on the board and confirm the correct answer. We read the rest of the article and then I ask the children:

Robin: What do people think of that piece of history? Does it make you think anything, feel anything?

Student 5: It's really sad and it's not even that long ago. It's 1996.

Student 6: Shocking.

Student 1: It's kind of insane how the last residential school was closed 20 years ago because one of my cousins is 23 now and my cousin was alive when one of those schools was still on the Earth. I'm thinking kids would be punished and sent away from their parents is really scary. Imagine that you were on a boat by yourself or a plane or whatever, you have no one to sit with, you're just there by yourself and you can't talk with people because you have no way of speaking with them.

Student 6: Imagine that you were sent away and you knew everything when you got there but you forgot everything when you came back. Like let's say you forgot who your parents were or you forgot English or like a different language.

Robin: It did happen. Sometimes children couldn't communicate with their parents when they went back to their families. Or they couldn't eat the food anymore because they hadn't been eating that food for so long.

Student 7: Sometimes I get nightmares at night then I have to go into the room with my parents and it's so scary overnight and I don't know … if I was them what would I do?

Student 8: It's kind of like the movie Holes. They have to be locked into this place and do whatever they are told and they have to eat the same food from the cafeteria.

Student 9: Aboriginal People were living in what's called America and just imagine a bunch of boats are coming towards the island you live on with all your friends, family, brothers, sisters, cousins, etc., and literally you are shipped away and across the ocean and if your brother or sister was there and you weren't even allowed to say "Are you okay?" or "This is so scary."

Robin: They were often punished at the schools if they spoke their own language. Imagine what a community would be like without children.

Student 10: I think it's really sad how they were sent off and it reminds me of other children who were slaves who were also sent off to other plantations without their parents and they couldn't speak their own language and they had to do everything they were told to do and I think it would be really sad if all the children are taken away.

Student 11: I am just wondering if possibly in some schools there were tons of rebellions. I'm thinking of the word resilience, was there ways the kids fought back?

Robin: I think there were some ways that children fought back. Sometimes they would run away. Sometimes they would find ways to work around some of the things they didn't like, but for the most part who had the power?

Class: The adults.

Robin: Yeah.

Student 12: I have a question. Would the children go with siblings?

Robin: In some cases, yes. In some cases older siblings would go and come back in the summertime, and then once the younger sibling was old enough they would go to the residential school together. It just depended. In some places children were even taken by force. In some cases Indigenous children felt or thought they wanted to go because they were promised an education – learning how to read and all of that, but the reality was that when they got to these schools, they may have learned some things but for the most part they did a lot of labour, farming, and cleaning. So they got some education but they were also forced to do all kinds of chores.

Student 3: 1996! My parents were 25 at the time and it was still [happening]. Most of the world, big things that happened like Martin Luther King [Jr.], WWI, WWII happened all before our parents were born, but these schools went on. 1840, that was more than 150 years that they went on for and in Black History Month everyone thinks of hardships of the African people and slaves. It never comes to mind for Aboriginal Peoples. It never comes to mind. It's not the main thing. But when you hear the crazy things about this, that these kids had to be taken away from their family and put into these schools that really didn't teach them, they were basically slaves in schools, you want to read more and see what happened because many people don't know about this.

Robin: And important for us to know about because it happened in our country. And we learn about things so that hopefully we don't make the same mistakes again.

Student 3: People make these books of issues that countries have done – what are they called? Everyone thinks Canada is a great country ... no one ever thinks of us doing stuff wrong.

Shi-shi-etko: The Story

Next we read the introduction to *Shi-shi-etko* (Campbell & Lafave, 2005), a beautiful story in which a family lovingly guides their daughter in creating powerful memories of her life with her people before she leaves for residential school. In the introduction the author describes how Indigenous children were given European names at the schools.

Student 11: Like Nelson Mandela.

Robin: Like slaves. They were given their masters' names ...

Student 11: Nelson Mandela's real name meant "to pull on a tree branch" and also "trouble maker."

Student 3: My family also had to change their last name. I told a few ... It was because we're a Jewish last name and something with our great grandparents – we were moving into North America and we couldn't keep our Jewish last name and that was an issue in World War II. My last name would have been Bernstein.

The Debrief

After reading the story I ask the children what they think:

Student 13: Really sad.

Robin: What did this story focus on? How is the family reacting?

Student 12: It shows how they react to it before it actually happens. They try to make her feel as good as she can without her knowing what is actually going to happen.

Student 13: I'm not sure, but it sounded like she was excited to go. But then when she got there she probably wasn't.

Student 7: When they said "Shi-shi-etko. It's time to go" I don't like that feeling.

Robin: If you didn't know everything I told you about residential school do you think you would have had a different reaction to the story?

Student 13: Yeah! Because it's the first time you get to go to school and on the first day of JK I was smiling. I was ready to show off my Spider-Man shirt! [Class starts laughing.]

The Government's Apology

As we are viewing the Canadian government's apology to Indigenous People, we pause every few minutes and reflect.

> **Robin:** Stephen Harper identified the main goals of residential school. He didn't say they were to make their lives better or teach them to read. They were to remove children from their cultures … and what else?
>
> **Class:** Their traditions, their families.
>
> **Robin:** Then he used that word we have talked about before …
>
> **Several Students:** Assimilate.
>
> **Robin:** What does assimilate mean?
>
> **Student 1:** To make Aboriginal people more like normal people.
>
> **Robin:** Well, not "normal" but more like …
>
> **Student 1:** Ordinary, average.
>
> **Robin:** Not ordinary or normal … who were they trying to make them like?
>
> **Class:** The Europeans.
>
> **Robin:** Right, like themselves. Normal or average, it just depends who you are, right?
>
> **Student 2:** Nobody's "normal."
>
> **Student 3:** It's like an accent. Like someone from Italy like saying "Oh you have an accent" and then the person they're talking to says "No you have an accent."
>
> **Robin:** So assimilate, means you don't want those people to look like they have their own culture or talk their own way or do their own thing. You want them to be like you and fit into your culture.

In the next clip, Harper apologizes to the many children who never made it home after residential school. The children fixate on this. They ask why some children did not return and even come in the next day with additional theories they want to share with the group.

> **Student 4:** Question: Why didn't they return to their families?
>
> **Robin:** Some never returned because they died. What might be some other reasons they never returned to their families?
>
> **Student 5:** The ice froze every year and they couldn't get back and they died.
>
> **Student 6:** They actually liked it there? Something about being "civilized?"
>
> **Student 4:** Maybe they ran away and they couldn't find them.
>
> **Student 7:** Maybe they weren't allowed to.
>
> **Student 8:** Maybe because they forgot their language.
>
> **Student 3:** They had different food and culture.
>
> **Student 9:** Maybe the parents wouldn't want them.
>
> **Student 3:** Maybe groups of kids were really good at cleaning and they would want to keep them. Maybe they were feeling embarrassed in case they had been forgotten.
>
> **Student 10:** They made promises to their parents. If they had to stay there a long time, they might forget those promises and they might think "They'll be mad at me."
>
> **Student 11:** Maybe they forgot who their parents were or their parents died?
>
> **Student 6:** Sickness?

Creating a Timeline

This year, for the first time, I try keeping a timeline in class to support our learning. Initially, we add items related to a Black History timeline: First African Slaves Brought to America, the Duration of the Underground Railroad, Harriet Tubman's Birth, the Civil Rights Movement, the Civil War, the Emancipation Proclamation, the Civil Rights Act, the Voting Rights Act and several more.

Throughout our Indigenous Studies we gradually add other items: Vikings Arrive in Newfoundland, Christopher Columbus Arrives in the Caribbean, First Residential School Opens, Indian Reserve System Is Created, Confederation, Indian Act Is Passed, Last Residential School Is Closed, Royal Commission on Aboriginal People Begins, Nunavut Is Created, and Canadian Government Issues Formal Apology to Indigenous Peoples for Residential Schools. As we create the timeline, the children express great interest in when different groups of people gained voting rights. We begin to do some research and discover that it is far more complicated than we think. When an opportunity arises, a few of the more interested children help to do some online research and together we put together a series of cards that represent a simplified evolution of federal voting rights in Canada. This includes when white women, Blacks, other minorities, and finally, Indigenous people, gain the vote.

The Timeline

In 1867 Indigenous men were allowed to vote if they denied their Aboriginal heritage. In 1914 enlisted First Nations military men gained the vote while they served but had it revoked when they became veterans after the war. It was not until 1960 that all Indigenous people gained the vote.

One child in the class brings up the internment of the Japanese in Canada during World War II. Other children talk about women being denied the vote. There is a lot of commotion in the discussion: "You shouldn't have to do something to get the right to vote." "Yeah, they were the ones in Residential School." "They're still in Residential Schools!" We conclude as a group that there is one segment of the population that holds the greatest power.

> **Student 1:** It was 56 years ago [that Indigenous people got the vote]. My dad's 50 so it was six years before my father was born. That's just crazy.
>
> **Student 2:** Both my grandfathers would have lived through that and my grandfather on my dad's side. He lives in Quebec and he's Black and he would have probably taken notice of this.
>
> **Student 3:** That's a disgrace [...] White men have been able to vote whenever they want for a long time and that's a tiny bit of the population of the whole world! "Oh I'm sorry you have Asian roots in your family. Sorry you can't vote!" My grandma was born in 1936. That's basically meaning that until the 1960s she wasn't able to vote. It's the same for everyone else. The Indigenous people and Black people weren't able to vote until the 1960s while just white people were allowed to vote from 1921. [**I interject:** "Not *all* white *women* were allowed to vote at that time."] Right. White men. A bunch of people weren't allowed to vote for 30 years even though they were adults.
>
> **Student 4:** It doesn't even make sense because that group of people are actually a really small population of the whole world.
>
> **Student 5:** Not the whole world ... Canada.
>
> **Student 4:** I know but ... I feel like why didn't everyone who was being discriminated and trying to be changed by that small group of people ... it might work if they would all kind of gang up with each other and try to stop this altogether.

This seems like such an obvious solution and I try my best to introduce some of the complexities relevant to this thinking but feel I cannot tackle this issue with a simple response.

> **Robin:** Well, and sometimes that does happen and usually results in some kind of civil war. [**Class:** Yeah.] A war within a country. And it's also not that easy to organize. And sometimes there would even be racism between these groups. One minority group might not get along with another minority group.

As this discussion concludes, we reflect on how far we have come since the 1960s and that although things are not perfect, we live in a very multicultural city and are heading in the right direction.

A Visit to the Royal Ontario Museum (ROM)

In December 2015 I attended a conference at the Metro Toronto Convention Centre entitled "Indigenous Days." At a session on residential schools I met Jacques Lavoie, from the ROM's Learning Department, who specializes in object-based learning. I spoke with him about my plans for my classroom in the new year and through subsequent e-mail exchanges we were able to plan a visit for the Grade 4s. I was delighted that the children would have the opportunity for a hands on experience with Indigenous artifacts.

During the workshop, in addition to being allowed to gently handle the materials, Jacques encourages the children to inspect the objects carefully, to theorize about what they are, and to determine what natural materials they are made from.

A Student Tries Her Hand at the Traditional Game of "Ring and Pin"

The children are so engaged in this experience that we have time for only a brief tour of the Gallery of Canada's First Peoples. Their reactions to the artifacts are not surprising:

- *I thought it was really cool looking at stuff that I hadn't really seen before, like stuff that was dug up. Some stuff was like 10,000 years old like that rock we saw which was really cool 'cause that's really old – the one at Forest Hill. Remember we saw on the map?*
- *I really liked how we got to feel materials they had and it just really showed me how when they make their tools it's all out of natural things that they can find and animals. Now they can just make a pickaxe out of metal but they made it out of stone, strong and a big piece of wood.*
- *It was really cool when we were feeling the different tools and things we got to guess what they were used for and it was cool how some of the things resemble things that we use today.*
- *I learned that sometimes people will look at an object like a stick […] and they think of it as boring, but when Indigenous People looked at that stick [they could see] that something wonderful [could be made] out of it!*

Many of the children also share that they are deeply affected by the images presented in Jane Ash Poitras' piece "Potato Peeling 101" in the Gallery of Canada's First Peoples at the ROM. They are particularly focused on the two side-by-side images which show a young Indigenous boy of unknown identity before and after his residential school experience. One child comments that he cannot believe they are the same person. This conversation leads us to a discussion of life on reserves for children and the sometimes poor conditions they experience including a lack of proper education. We speak briefly about Attawapiskat, Shannen Koostachin and her legacy of "Shannen's Dream," the youth-driven movement which advocates for equitable education funding for on-reserve First Nations children. Two of the children have heard about this in the news and one from a family member who works in the North. Both refer to suicides on the reserves. I feel that learning about some of the mental health challenges on some reserves is a topic more appropriately addressed at a slightly older age and while honouring these children's contributions we gently move away from this discussion.

"Potato Peeling 101" by Jane Ash Poitras

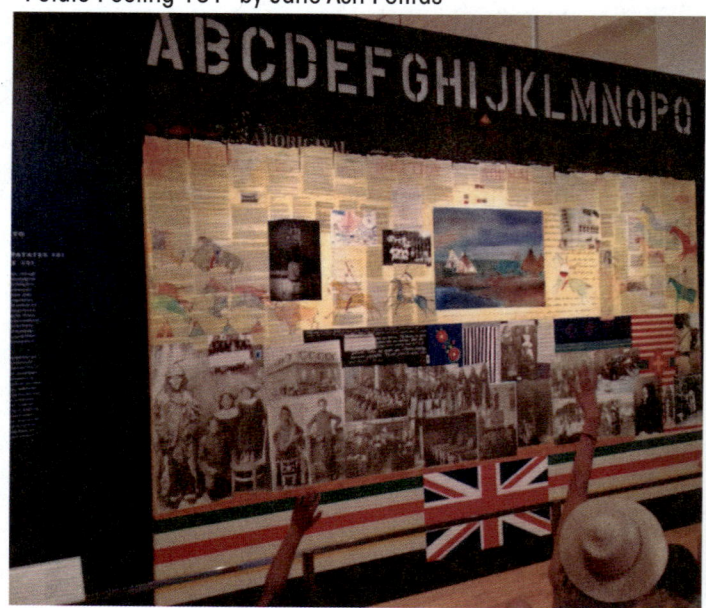

Concluding with PowerPoint Presentations

In the last week and a half of school we set up the classroom with a stage and audience chairs. Each presentation is recorded and the children are asked to listen actively and save questions and comments for the end of each presentation. The children demonstrate a range of levels in their presentation skills, their enthusiasm, the depth of knowledge of their material, and their ability to answer questions from the audience.

I am pleased by their presentations and the sense that this has been a good way, for now, to bring closure to their learning.

Students Introduce the Class to the Music of Buffy Sainte-Marie

On the very last day of school I ask the children to write to me about their experiences – what they learned, what they enjoyed the most, and what they felt was important about this unit of study.

What they learned and what they enjoyed:

- *I think that one thing that really helped my learning was the PowerPoints [...] everybody got to learn about something and not just try and learn about a lot of different subjects [...] and we got to share them with the rest of the class.*
- *I liked when we learned about the government's apology. I really liked that you showed us that because it showed that there were some good things that happened.*
- *I feel that I learned about how Canada was formed, Canada's First Peoples and some of the U.S.*
- *One of my favourite parts was learning about the different types of resilience.*
- *The residential schools were meant to assimilate the First Nations, erase their future, and make sure the whites were in power.*
- *My favourite part of this study was probably reading books, writing the presentation, and presenting.*
- *My favourite part about this study was learning where all the tribes were and all the things they used in a normal day.*
- *My favourite art is Potato Peeling 101 and my favourite part of the painting is it has a boy with his tribe's clothes and him after residential school and his new clothes.*
- *One of my favourite things was learning about the Métis. [This child came to school to tell me she had learned she was Métis]*
- *I enjoyed the PowerPoints and drawing the map of Indigenous Peoples' groups in Canada.*
- *I loved reading the books and making the PowerPoints. The artwork that I saw was so powerful.*
- *Seeing the short movie about Angela [the mom and daughter who were verbally harassed] was just so sad and powerful and to see their resilience while those boys just wouldn't give up on teasing them.*

Why they thought it was important:

- *It was important because we got to learn the history of where we live [...] It was important because we got to learn what happened here before we came here.*
- *I found out about things I never ever heard or thought of before. I thought it was important because it's nice to know how some other people live and how their life can be so different from some others.*
- *I think this was a very important area of study because when we are all older we will know these things and we can talk about them.*
- *My experience was amazing this year learning about Indigenous Peoples. I think it is very important for people to know about what has happened to Indigenous Peoples and the great people that have been Indigenous. People may not pay much attention to this certain topic. Personally I never really thought about this before.*
- *Now I know how important it is to learn about struggles [...] and what they were feeling when it happened [...] Every day I came home with a new piece of information. It was not just struggle though ... people had resilience. It was amazing. Whenever we gathered to talk*

about residential schools I thought hard ...

- *I thought this was a very important part of our learning because it taught us about the people before us on our land. It provoked very interesting conversations. We did not only learn about information in the past, we learned about Indigenous tribes today. We learned about their lives on reserves and how their conditions of living are now.*

Final Thoughts on the Journey

As I reflect on this year's journey, I note that, as individuals, the children have each identified strongly with specific learning experiences, both in terms of input and output. This is evident both in the comments shared above but also through ongoing, in-class observation of each child's level of engagement and contribution to discussions and activities. While some children loved hearing stories, others were drawn to the research process, the chance to present, the group conversations, the mapping explorations, or other hands-on opportunities. Some children took pride in sharing their historical knowledge, others enjoyed articulating their awareness of social injustices, while still others created meaning through the analogies or personal experiences as ways to help make sense of events or socio-political dynamics. Some students excelled in class discussions; others discovered they were relied on for their technological prowess when developing their PowerPoints. Some children presented as strong leaders in organizing and delivering group presentations. Allowing for many ways to both take in information and express one's learning maximizes the chances that each child will find an effective connection to the learning.

It is my hope that the children can take this learning forward and deepen their understanding as they grow and mature. But most of all, I hope they use what they have learned across the year about struggle and resilience to perceive themselves as people who are aware, who care, and who can make a difference both in their own lives and in the lives of others.

I end with one child's thoughts about his learning experiences:

I think it was an important topic to study because you learned what has happened and how you could make it better.

Mike's Story
Grade 5
Dr. Eric Jackman Institute of Child Study Laboratory School

Starting the Environmental Inquiry Process

Going into my second full year of teaching the Grade 5 students at Jackman ICS, the thought of tackling a topic as immense as climate change seemed incredibly intimidating. As I began to do my own personal research over the summer months, I realized how much material there was for learning about the causes and effects of climate change, but also how easily misconceptions could arise in the learning process. As my research raised more and more questions, it brought to mind the timeless quote, "An answer only changes the nature of the question."

The question that remained as we began the first day of school was, of course, where do we begin? The answer came through the weather and climate itself. September 2016 arrived on the heels of one of the warmest summer seasons on record in Toronto, a fitting provocation for our Grade 5 class as they reflected on their personal experiences of this environment, thinking deeply about how phenomena impact them directly.

Following our first afternoon recess on an uncharacteristically hot and sunny day at Jackman ICS, the students came in to the class sweaty and feeling relieved to be back in an air-conditioned space. We delved into a reflection on the students' immediate experiences by asking, **"Why is everyone sweating so much?"** Among other explanations, the overwhelming response was, "Because it's hot." This led to a further question, **"Why is it hot outside?"** While some students admitted that they did not know, most responses essentially fell into one of two categories: due to the season, and due to "global warming."

> **"Why is it hot outside?"**
>
> **Student 1:** There are no clouds in the sky and the sun is shining.
> **Student 2:** The sun is right above us.
> **Student 3:** The Earth is closer to the sun in the summer.
> **Student 4:** The tilt of the Earth makes the sun's light waves stronger.
> **Student 5:** It depends on the country. Heat could be good for crops but bad because of drought.
> **Student 6:** The Earth is becoming warmer because people are driving more.
> **Student 7:** My mom said the melting ice caps are bad. Polar bears get hot and can't survive. If it happens over the next few years, it's our fault because we use too much electricity and cars.
> **Student 8:** The planet is getting hotter and the glaciers are melting in the arctic because people are driving so much.
> **Student 9:** Climate change is all because of humans. I feel annoyed because the world is changing because of adults.
> **Student 10:** Scientists are saying the melting ice is causing waves and tsunamis.

During this brief conversation, students touched upon a few of the big ideas we might encounter in our studies, such as weather, properties and states of matter, energy sources, habitats, and light. In the following days, the weather turned and we experienced some cool, cloudy days, more typical for that time of year. Venturing outside to sit in a local park, we picked up on the threads of our previous conversation, thinking a little more deeply about the responses already shared and reflecting on the difference in conditions.

> **"Why was it so hot last week and so cool today? How can such a change be explained?"**
>
> **Student 1:** It has been cloudier so it is cooler.
> **Student 2:** It is cooler because it is getting darker earlier. Winter is coming.
> **Student 3:** Nothing dramatic has happened. It's just that the breeze is a little cooler.
> **Student 4:** Raining may have helped over the past few days because of a cooler breeze.
> **Student 5:** We are close to the lake so waves create some wind and breeze.
> **Student 6:** Maybe people have not been driving as many cars so it cooled down.
> **Student 7:** The sun is farther from the north side of the Earth's position. It is moving away from the northern hemisphere.

Knowledge Building in a Local Park

Beginning with an open-ended question that could have a few different answers allows for students to enter into the discussion at a level that suits their comfort and understanding. Also, holding back from offering my feedback on their ideas allows students to more openly share thoughts and reveal their understanding, exposing possibilities for further exploration.

Connecting with the Land

Gaining an appreciation for the land by seeing ourselves as part of nature is a crucial aspect of our environmental learning. Using our connections with the outside world as a framework for the essential learning goals of our year ahead, our Grades 5 and 6 classes traveled to Sandbanks Provincial Park for their annual overnight camping trip. Over three days and two nights, students engaged in a variety of activities meant not only to cultivate social skills and relationships among classmates, but also to give students the chance to experience nature from a slightly different perspective than what they are accustomed to. Situating ourselves in an outdoor space (where digital devices were forbidden!) provided the conditions for the students to develop empathy with nature, enabling them to see their place in it as part of a larger whole. This sense of empathy is critical to our learning process.

During one activity, students travelled to a nearby marsh where they independently explored and observed its many characteristics. It was a reminder of how intrinsically motivating a natural setting can be. This became especially clear when we later debriefed the experience. Students first listed the different species they had observed, and then offered theories regarding the possible relationships between them.

Exploring a Marsh

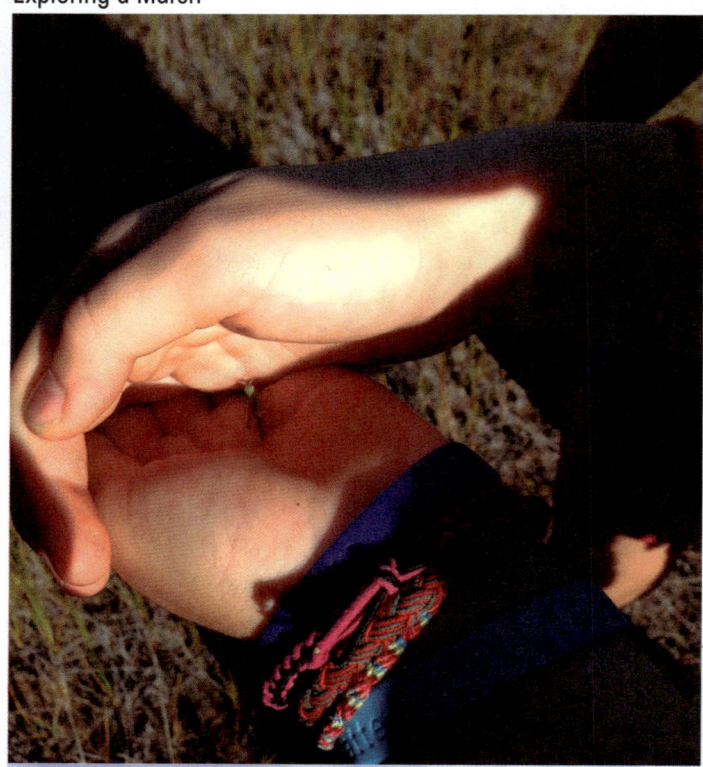

As this was the second visit to Sandbanks for the Grade 6 class, they were able to contribute observations that allowed us to identify differences in conditions, such as how the marsh was much drier this year as compared to last. Benefitting from this input, the Grade 5 students returned to earlier discussions about why conditions may change from one day, week, month, or year to the next.

Another opportunity to facilitate our connection with nature came during a poetry unit the Grade 5s studied later that winter on the haiku form. Expressing their appreciation of the environment through haiku allowed the students to take a breath and connect with nature in a reflective way. Working with the haiku expert, Makoto Nakanishi, students began the process by brainstorming a large set of "season words," which could be from their immediate surroundings or evoked by memories of the winter season. The class then spent some time outside, capturing their observations in the urban neighbourhood with short, simple, two-line phrases. Notes of what they heard, saw, felt, and smelled contributed to descriptions that captured a moment in their world.

Capturing Observations of Our Urban Environment

Combining these two-line observations with a "season word" or "season phrase" completed the haiku and created a very personal picture, yet one that any reader could analyze and interpret in unique ways. The children saw how just a few simple words can so powerfully capture a moment in their world, and that by further changing just a single word, the meaning and overall experience of the world, in the eyes of both the writer and reader, can be altered.

"Snow drifting white, Big Bear, Sleeping"

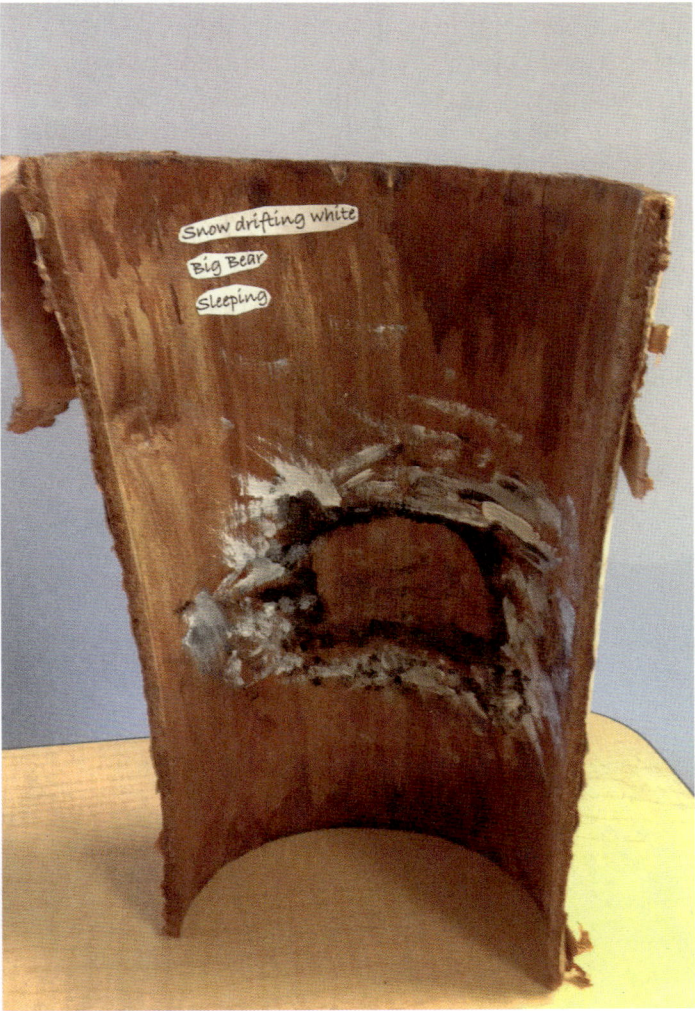

"Cold rushing water, Pushes jumping salmon back, Autumn spawning home"

Unpacking (Mis)conceptions

It seemed obvious to the students that global warming and climate change were things to be avoided. It was mentioned time and again how driving cars can lead to melting glaciers. They were also keen on offering suggestions about how to stop global warming and, inevitably, save the planet. However, I thought it important to refrain from leaping into this stewardship role without providing some opportunities for students to deepen their background knowledge of the subject. Having observed the cyclical nature of their theories, I was aware that the students needed to unpack their ideas in ways that they could better understand them.

To better understand why driving cars and factories are leading to melting polar ice caps, the students embarked upon a diagnostic assessment of their ideas, which aided them in conceptualizing the cause and effect relationship between behaviours and resultant environmental issues. Many students felt that cars and factories are lead causes of polar bears dying due to melting glaciers. They were prompted to stretch this relationship into a five-panel comic, with the sketch of a factory, car, or other cause of pollution in the first panel, and a sketch of melting glaciers in the last. They were tasked with filling in the middle three panels, illustrating their theory of how and why pollution created in a single place in the world (such as our local neighbourhood) ultimately leads to melting ice caps in the Arctic.

Diagnostic Assessment – Cause and Effect of Environmental Issues

Part 2 – Environmental Inquiry in Action: The Educators' Stories

While dealing with such a large, complex topic, each conversation that provides an opportunity to share knowledge and shed light on concepts also leads to more questions and, quite often, the discovery of further misconceptions. One student captured this difficulty while sharing thoughts about climate change in a way that many of us can relate to: "Some people may be confused about it. It's hard to get their head around all the information." Another student who had extensively researched the ozone layer and engaged with different media, peers, and resources, while providing an impressive amalgamation of the information, made very little progress in her development of ideas a month later. When asked to fill in a second, five-panel comic strip, the designs she created were very similar to those she had sketched just over a month before.

There are many points to take from this, including (but not limited to) just how sticky and pervasive misconceptions are regarding the science around climate change. Further, it points to the very limits of the assessment task, highlighting why it is important to assess students in multiple ways. Although some students were able to integrate new information and produce a very different "post" assessment, others were not able to demonstrate any change in thinking on this specific task. And yet these students were able to show the many new ideas they had taken from their experiences during our inquiry into climate change through other methods – conversations, notes, written materials, and projects.

Post Assessment – Cause and Effect of Environmental Issues

Deciding on Directions

To maximize the students' learning opportunities, I felt it was important to make the students part of the process, involving them in decisions regarding big ideas and the directions of our learning. This led to the creation of the learning community we had aimed to achieve.

Sharing their comics led to rich knowledge building discussions and revealed more conceptions, theories, and questions. The students collected and subsequently sorted the questions they generated into categories as a class, working together to sort through ideas and, eventually arrive at main points for discussion. Once the categories were established, the students began to share their working definitions of vocabulary, and more clearly identify recurring topics and big ideas they wanted to develop. Participating in different focus groups allowed students to sign up to investigate a question or topic of deep interest to them across a wide range, including weather, climate change, melting ice, manufacturing and fossil fuels, heat and humidity, and animals and their effects.

Working Together to Sort Our Topic Ideas

After having been immersed in their chosen question and having spent some time positing theories specifically associated with their topic, the class was ready to bring new information from authoritative sources into our conversations. Students first engaged in guided reading of pre-selected informational texts, which would support their research. Discussing the material in small groups allowed for voices to be heard in a different way and gave students the chance to start debating new ideas and think about how they would integrate new information with currently held conceptions.

Following this further research and some discussion about findings, the students came together to re-address the earlier set categories and identify the big questions as a class. Some new topics emerged alongside other recurring themes:

- climate change and weather
- ozone layer
- sun and greenhouse effect
- fossil fuels and heat
- effects of climate change (species)

As the class became more independent in their research, a wider variety of suggested websites, books, media, and materials were made available. The students took this opportunity to work on certain research and literacy skills by reading expository texts, re-reading for comprehension, note-taking, identifying important ideas, summarizing main points, and making connections.

Deciding on Questions to Investigate

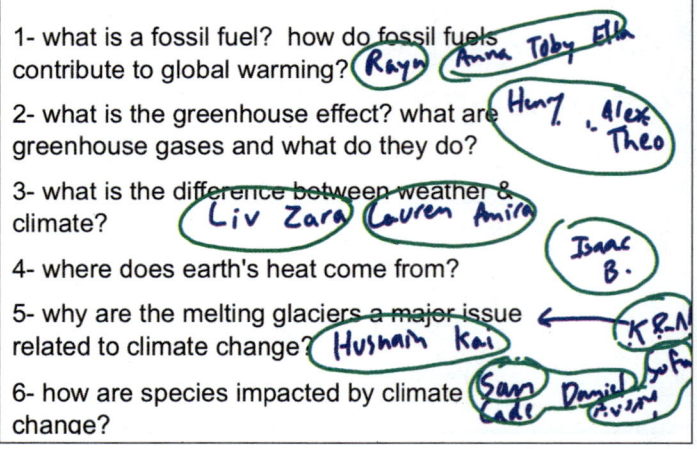

Student Research and Note Taking

Sharing Knowledge

In addition to voicing their opinions about the direction of their learning, the students were given a choice of topics from the established list decided upon by the class, creating a truly meaningful learning community in which they could disseminate their ideas with purpose. In smaller focus groups, students become more accountable for researching ideas and sharing information with the class, taking responsibility for bringing clarity to a chosen topic and reporting it to the rest of the class, much like putting together a jigsaw puzzle.

One method that enabled students to consistently share ideas with the classroom community was with Knowledge Forum, a digital knowledge space created as a means of facilitating knowledge building communities (Branch I, p. 20). Knowledge Forum would be used for students to ask questions, share theories and ideas, build on to one another's theories, and introduce new information. Furthermore, the class used this space to look over ideas and "notes" they had created in Grade 4 related to their learning about light. Collaborating with a research study from the University of Albany, New York (Zhang, 2014), students had the chance to share their ideas on Knowledge Forum and connect new thoughts to ideas from their previous year's work. As students engaged in their research, new notes were published on a class-wide "view," and peers could read one another's notes and comment or build onto ideas as a way to further develop the community's understanding of the topics. Furthermore, after some time researching and documenting ideas, students were prompted to co-author summarizing notes reflecting on their journey thus far, and what new questions or themes still required more research.

Student Research and Note Taking

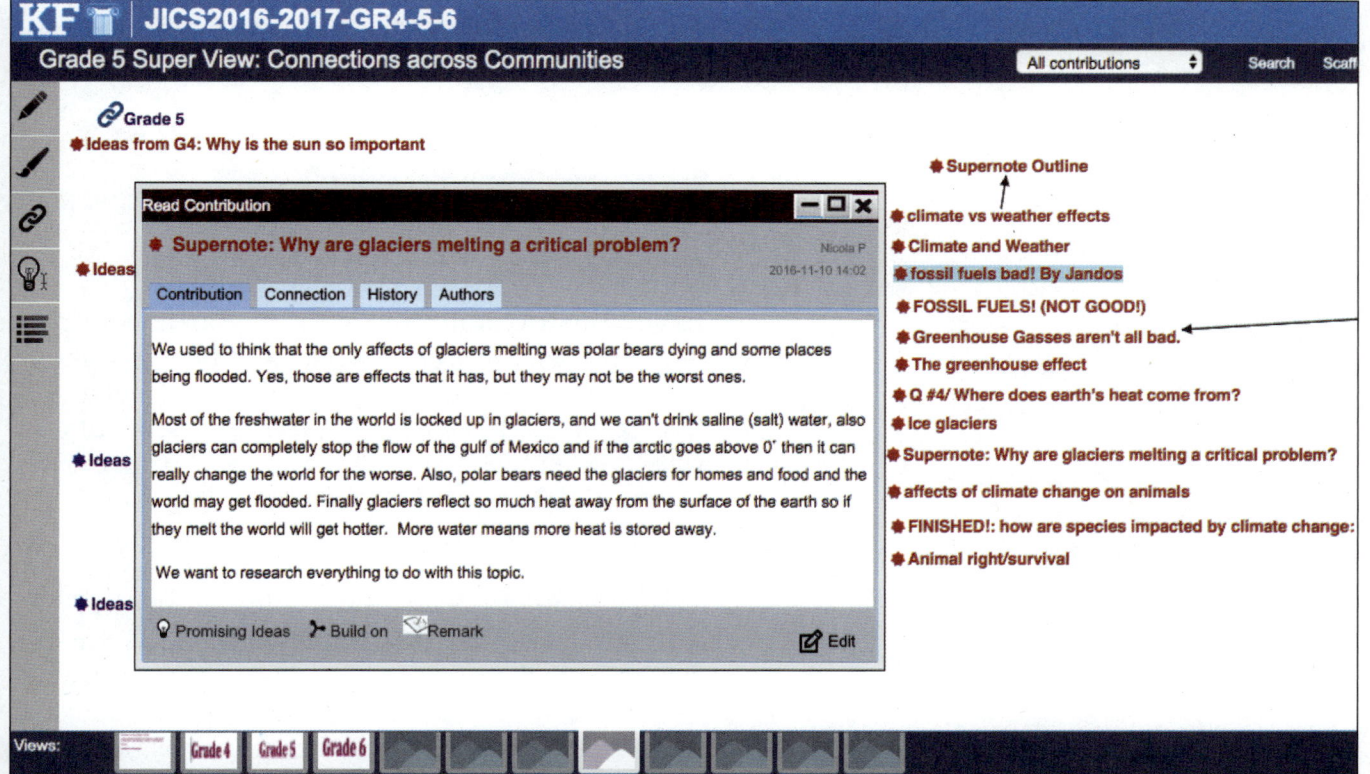

Continuing conversations based on student interests and topics of focus provided energy for our learning. Students were allowed to constantly check-in through knowledge building discussions to help perpetuate their learning and ask new questions for further clarification of ideas. In one such instance, the students took a special interest in the sun and its role in climate change.

Alternative Energy Sources Research

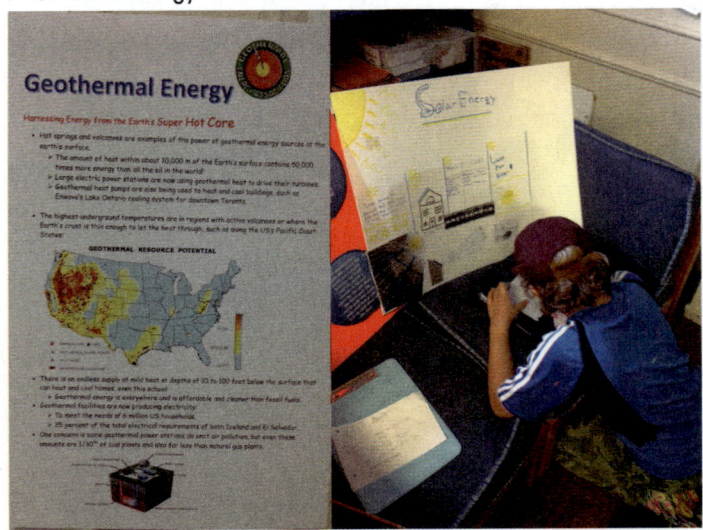

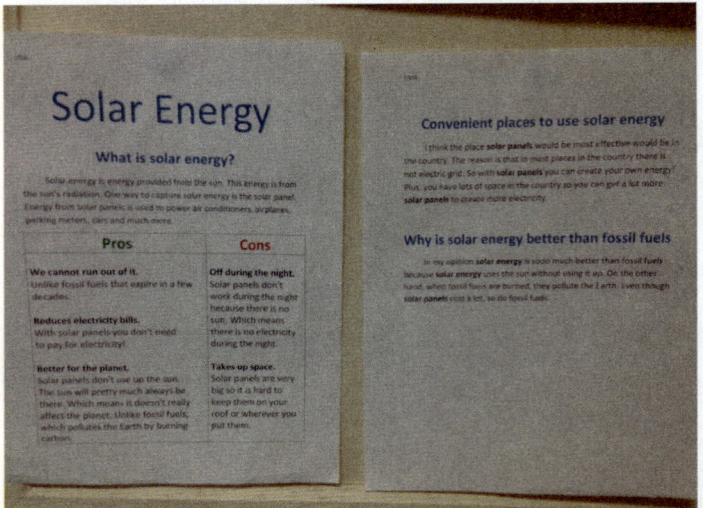

> **"What is the role of the sun? Is it important? Why or why not?"**
>
> **Student 1:** Back in history it would have been harder to live without the sun. Now we have electricity and other things.
>
> **Student 2:** The sun helps us see things because of its light.
>
> **Student 3:** We need the sun or else the Earth would be floating through the universe. Also, plants need sunlight to live.
>
> **Student 4:** If there were no sun, water would freeze. This means no heat, resources, plants, food, etc.
>
> **Student 5:** The sun provides us with heat and vitamins. If there was no sun, there'd be no heat. The sun also helps us to fight off diseases.
>
> **Student 6:** Maybe we could still survive for a little while if there were no sun, because we could get some heat from the Earth's core.
>
> **Student 7:** The heat and light from the sun reaches the Earth and gets trapped in the atmosphere.
>
> **Student 8:** The Earth is slightly tilted, which gives us the seasons. If there were no sun, we would not have any seasons.

The discussion carved a path towards looking into energy sources. At this point, students researched and presented posters on alternative energy sources and the pros and cons associated with each. Students then shared these posters with one another in a gallery-walk format where students could browse one another's work independently. Embedded in the gallery walk was an opportunity for students to write down specific feedback on their peers' work. The content of this mini-project helped lay some foundational knowledge of energy sources alternative to fossil fuels for students to grasp.

Integration

In addition to connecting with the Earth through haiku poetry, the students explored photographs. Attending an exhibition at the Ryerson Image Centre entitled *The Edge of the Earth*, students were offered the chance to engage with timely photos of different aspects of climate change and its far-reaching impacts. To prepare for the experience, the class took a look at the climate change photography website, "Climate Visuals" (Climate Outreach, 2004), and engaged in some preliminary discussion about what photos are able to capture, what motivates photographers, and what messages are conveyed through photos. This set the stage for taking a live tour of the incredible photographic works at Ryerson. The experience provided students an opportunity to view some of the causes and impacts of climate change, as well as recognize both the beauty and the despair that is prevalent in the world when faced with this topic. Giving students license to ask questions and share their feelings and thoughts made for an incredible educational experience and ignited a renewed passion to make a difference.

Learning at the Ryerson Image Centre

There are many opportunities to integrate mathematics with the topic of climate change. Looking at patterns in graphs, using measurement units, and considering the spatial and causal nature of cycles, the students engaged in mathematical thinking without even realizing it! Also, during a brief investigation of carbon emissions, the students used the website, "Breathing Earth" (Bleja, 2015), to better understand through basic geography how much carbon is being released around the world. Additionally, the class had a chance to play with numbers, read graphical information, and explore rates relating to carbon dioxide emissions.

Exploring *Breathing Earth*

To encourage more thought about climate change and global warming in discussions extending beyond the classroom, the students read, as part of their weekly News program, recently published news articles on these topics. During these News periods, students are assigned once a week to research, read, summarize, and present one recently published news article for the class to discuss. Topics such as global warming, habitat loss, pollution, and species extinction were shared. Many had been written on the topic of the record-breaking high temperatures of the year 2016, and although students are afforded an extremely wide range of topics from which to choose, many brought in articles about the environment, relating deeply to the learning that had been happening in the class. A few students brought in articles related to projects happening around the world that were combating climate change. These articles served as a springboard to jump from researching content related to global warming into students positing solutions. That students could independently choose these topics to present to the class spoke to how deeply invested they were in the process, and added momentum to the continuing learning in the class.

During early readings, the point about differing opinions among scientists on the nature of global warming and climate changed was raised. It was important to me that we revisited this idea later in the term. After watching some clips from Al Gore's *An Inconvenient Truth* (2006), an excerpt from the book *The Deniers* (2008) by Lawrence Solomon was read. The excerpt critiqued Al Gore and many scientists who have supported the notion of global warming and climate change wholeheartedly. Pointing to the reality that there are people who do not share the same view of global warming and climate change as that which is most widely accepted, students reflected on the dissention of views, and why some people support ideas about the severity of climate change while others do not.

- "Some people may not know much about the topic. Some people said it was a hoax and others start to believe. I don't get it because they probably see on TV and newspapers and yet they still don't believe it is happening. I don't know why."
- "People don't believe because they are scared. They fear something will happen and the Earth will end. So, they deny it and say it does not exist because they are scared."
- "Sometimes people don't go on media or hear anything about it. It may be a lack of information."
- "People are scared because they don't want the Earth to be destroyed by all the pollution. If they think it's not true, it won't happen."
- "People are too scared to believe it. People may be stubborn to not listen and consider what others are saying. Others have ideas that can help and fix the problem. It may get worse and worse if we don't work to fix it."
- "What about the natural signs in the world? People have to find out some way. Everyone has noticed it's getting hotter. Why wouldn't they do research? Maybe they don't know ways to prevent it. But if you do some research, maybe you can find a way."
- "Another reason people don't want to believe is because they do a lot of things in their lives that produce pollution. We are so accustomed to using things that aren't very good for the planet, so if some people just don't want to change … they don't like change. And don't want to change what they do."
- "Some people may be confused about it. It's hard to get their head around all the information."
- "Some people are obstinate and it's hard to change our ways. Future generations are in some trouble because adults are handing over the Earth that is not in good shape."

Stewardship

While student learning progressed dramatically as the class discussed and researched topics related to climate change such as global warming, fossil fuels, the ozone layer, the greenhouse effect, impacts on animals, and more, our learning was far from complete. It felt like an appropriate time to shift gears. Students had time and again made suggestions about taking action to build onto the learning they had been doing. To support our shift toward building a sustainable relationship with the Earth, the students first listed all of the issues we had encountered in our investigations. Next, the students identified one problem they wished to address through proposing potential short-term and long-term solutions. The short-term solution was meant to aid students in thinking about things we can be doing every day in our immediate community to make a difference. The long-term proposal allowed students to dream a little bigger and plan projects they could continue or come back to in months or years. Using organizers to aid them in shaping their projects, each student identified a specific issue, proposed a solution, listed materials or steps in their plan to action, and explained the rationale behind why their solution could work. As students engaged in creating their proposals, some groups identified the need for more research on certain topics, which kept the strings of our journey taut.

Student Stewardship Project Proposals

Video/Documentary

FACTS

61 species that only extinct in the wild
4,749 species that are critically in danger
7,050 species that are in danger
10,694 that are vulnerable
5,028 that are near threatened
790 that are extinct
That's only out of about 82,900 species. That is not very many compared to species that we haven't assessed.

HABITATS/reasons why animals are endangered

Habitat destruction and pollution
Exotic species can wreck habitats
Illegal hunting
Legal exploitation
Animal endangerment also has natural causes
Three major kinds of habitat loss habitat destruction, habitat fragmentation and habitat deration
The main drivers of habitat loss in the US agriculture, land conversion for development, water development, pollution, and global warming.

Small skit ideas

We want it to be informative, something that is joyful when people watch it, serious.
There is a company owner and they want to cut down all these trees and build a big factory. An activist try's to stop him and she does so. Then we show what could've happened if there was no activist

---

Issue: Plastic Oceans!
Proposed Solution: Art from Recycling!

Method/Materials to be used:
1. Approval from the Chriss + Richard
2. Form Admin Team!
3. Get people to join the "Blue Bin Club"
4. Form routine
5. Figure out how to teach Grade 4's
6. Plan further
7. Have fun and teach younger kids about the environment

I do believe that the environment is dying from fossil fuels and toxins and garbage. It is very important that we all recognize that we need to help the Earth, and not destroy it. One of the things destroying the Earth is poor education. When kids and adults don't know about climate change, and why it's happening, they inadvertently do things that destroy the Earth, but with destruction just around the corner, we can't afford to let it happen.

When recycling is thrown out, fish and other animals eat it, and poison themselves. Also, fish breathe through water, so polluted water is like polluted air for them. Recycling is also burned, releasing carbon dioxide and other poisons that block the Sun, and heat up our Earth by not letting heat out. But heat is in the form of smaller areas, meaning other areas do not get sun (or heat), therefore they are colder, meaning that eventually they will not be able to support life, human or not.

So, I propose a club. I call it the "Blue Bin Club", And I have decided to put it into action with a green light, of course, to teach younger children about the environment through creating art from recycled materials. My plan is to collect recycling in the lobby from visitors and parents, so at the end of the week we have enough to create sculptures from recycled things. *It is not stopping at paper!* We can sell the sculptures and put them on display, and the proceeds will go to the David Suzuki foundation, and make the school eco-friendly! YOLO right?

Mike is holding a Blue Bin for us, so we can move on first notice. Also Alex will be helping me form the club, and keep it moving! Also, I'm involving the grade 4s so that they can take over later. I will be teaching grade 2 and 3. The point is to teach each other, younger kids about climate change, so that they don't make mistakes!

When I began writing this story, I had anticipated that this inquiry would be a one-term unit. It has since grown into an ongoing project that has contributed so much to the learning in the classroom, and which we anticipate will continue through to the remainder of the school year. Many of the students have devised plans to educate others and create awareness around environmental issues through posters, blogs, art projects, videos, documentaries, and plays. Some have thought deeply about theorizing and creating technologies to help combat water pollution, use renewable energy sources, or address the planet's need for fresh water. Others have planned to create campaigns to raise money for more accessible and environmentally friendly options for waste disposal around the school. Still others have collaborated to formulate a "challenge" they plan to open to the JICS community where families are encouraged to walk, bike, or take public transit to school during the week leading up to Earth Day. As well, many students in the Grade 5 class have volunteered to take on the role of environmental ambassadors for the school community. These students will visit certified environmentally focused schools to learn about new and effective initiatives to bring back to JICS. They will then disseminate this knowledge by sharing these ideas with other schools.

Concluding Thoughts

The unit has gone further than I had thought it would. Many concepts have been addressed, and many more remain to be tackled in future learning. By having students take control of their learning, they have been able to use their creativity and the freedom they have been given to dream big. It has been an encouraging experience to see students take the reins and want to make a difference. Climate change is one of the largest issues facing contemporary society. It is pervasive, terribly complex, and its impact on our everyday lives is serious. This is what makes climate change such an important and necessary area of inquiry to explore with students. The learning from this inquiry into climate change will not, and cannot, stop.

Murray's Story
Grade 6
Rideau Heights Public School, Limestone District School Board (LDSB)

Starting the Environmental Inquiry Process

I have been teaching at an urban school in what is now called the Limestone District School Board since 1995, starting off as a supply teacher for a number of years before settling in as a Primary teacher. Four years ago I was given the opportunity to become a Junior teacher and welcomed the change, excited to learn alongside my students as we dug more deeply into questions. Unfortunately, I soon learned that this was not the reality; I found myself just skimming the surface in order to "cover" the curriculum. I had heard about inquiry and did a little research, but decided it was something my students would not be able to handle. Perhaps more accurately, I didn't think I could handle the challenge of coming up with an integrated plan for inquiry work that would help me predict where all of the curriculum connections were going to come from.

One evening, I responded to a researcher who was looking for a teacher to participate in a project that was focused on climate change and technology. It sounded interesting, but as I had never worked with a researcher before, I had no idea what to expect. The project's pedagogical approach centred on a form of inquiry called Knowledge Building, a collaborative digital environment that allows students to share what they are thinking about and working on. It involves the constructing of knowledge by students as they navigate their learning on a shared platform called Knowledge Forum (Branch I, p. 20). I was suddenly faced with a completely new way of teaching, as well as the task of introducing my class to an entirely new way of operating.

Over the course of the project, my students and I experienced many struggles and high levels of frustration. However, by the end of the project there was a definite transformation, which significantly involved my own shift away from being a teacher, and toward being an educator. I stopped trying to be the knowledge keeper and became more of a guide who met his students where they were in their learning, not where they "should" be. My students shifted from passive consumers of knowledge who just wanted to be told what to do, to empowered participants who were internally compelled to find answers.

What is climate change and what are the causes? This was one of the initial questions I asked. Of my entire class, three students had a vague idea. They knew climate change was not a good thing and thought that pollution had some connection to the problem. One presupposition involved the change of weather patterns: "You know when you are outside playing with your buds and the sun is shining and then it starts to rain? That's climate change." Needless to say, there was a lot of room for growth. To make the point that climate change was a real issue being tackled by countries all over the world, I shared with the students that our new prime minister was on his way to France to attend a climate change summit. This appeared to catch their attention and they wanted to know more, so in an attempt to get a baseline sense of their understanding of the topic, I asked them to describe their relationship with nature. The inquiry process was underway.

Describing Our Relationship with Nature

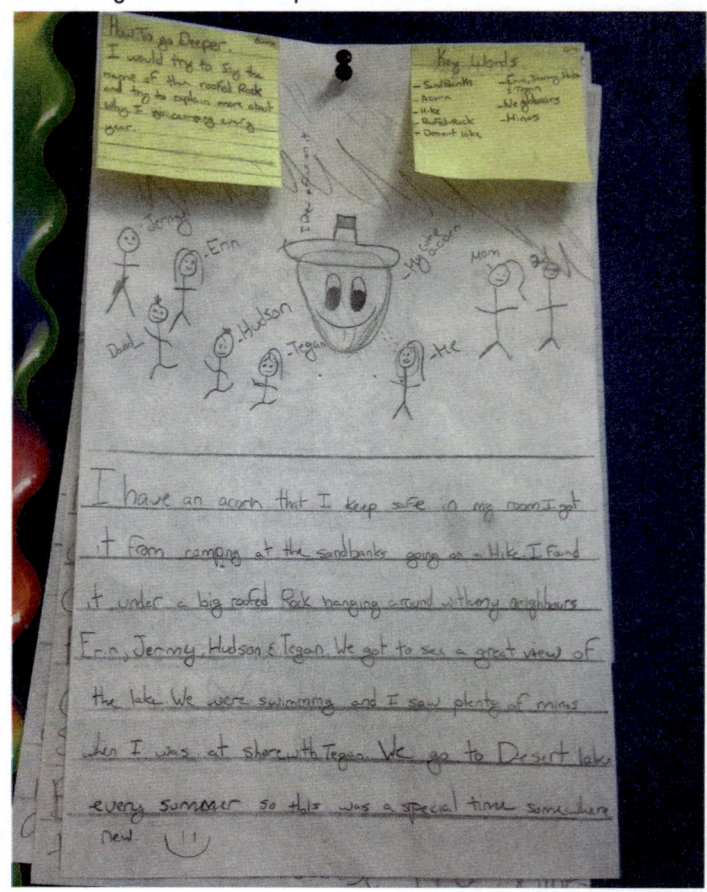

We organized the students' descriptions of their relationship to nature – animals on one side, plants on the other, and places in the middle. When it became clear to the students that this task was related to work we would do on climate change, they waited for me to be the expert and start handing out worksheets or writing notes on the board. This was how they were accustomed to functioning in the world/classroom. I informed them that the class was going to operate very differently during our Knowledge Building block. Our mission would be guided by the question **"How can we improve our relationship with nature by building our knowledge as a community?"** It was going to be up to the students to work under that umbrella. Where to start? They began by providing answers to the first question: **"What do we not get about climate change?"**

Our Beginning Ideas on Climate Change

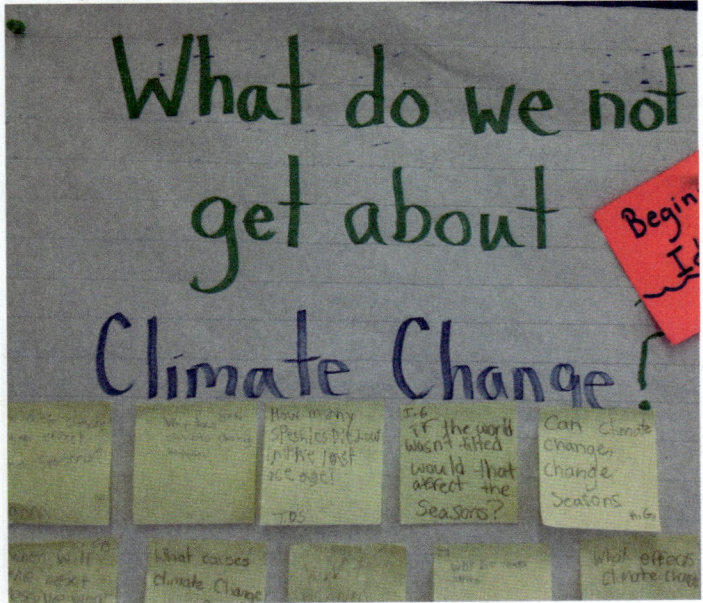

"How many species died out in the last ice age?"

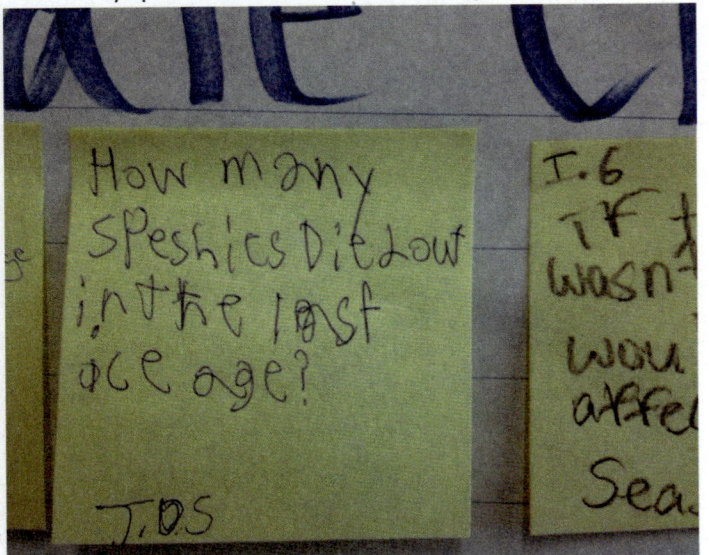

I began to observe the students' awareness of what they needed to learn in order to answer our question. The majority of the students wanted to know what caused climate change, while others were focused on the Earth's relationship with the sun. They were provided with resources and leads on information (Chromebooks in the classroom, texts from the library, readings that I had found, etc.) so that they could conduct their own research, answer their questions, and record their findings in their journals.

Initial questions at the beginning of our discussions introduced some important and relevant concepts into our inquiry: **"What is climate change?" "What causes climate change?" "What is the greenhouse effect?" "Why do we have seasons?"** In the past I would have written out the explanation on the SMART board for the students to copy down and then moved on. This time, however, I wanted them (and myself) to go deeper. At first I was not sure how to do this. Asking them to explain in their own words their theories on the greenhouse effect or why we have seasons began to yield answers that made it clear to me that they had a very limited understanding of these topics, and many misconceptions. To address this, I decided that the students needed to explore ways of demonstrating their knowledge in ways that departed from the traditional way of my calling a few volunteers to come up in front of the classroom. Instead, the students were to decide how they would demonstrate their learning and develop a way to share it with the class. Initially, this created a fair bit of confusion, since they had never had this type of freedom before, and I had never given up so much control. I still offered some guidance and suggestions, but the results were pretty incredible and set the tone for the rest of the inquiry.

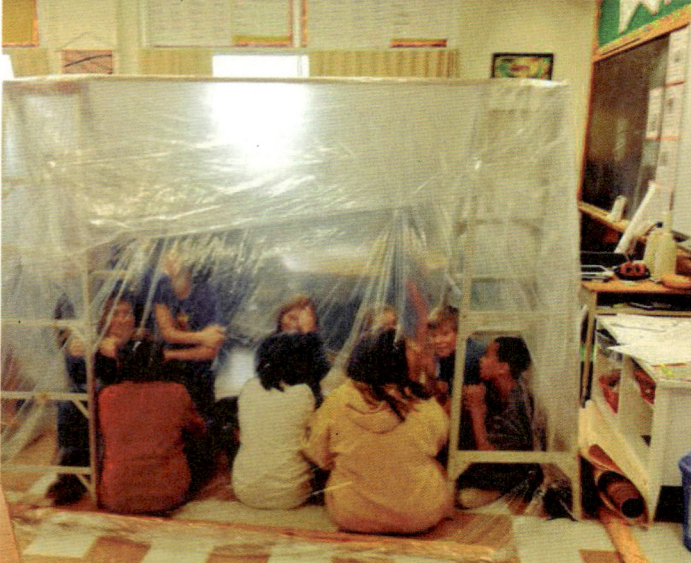
Students Teaching Peers About the Greenhouse Effect

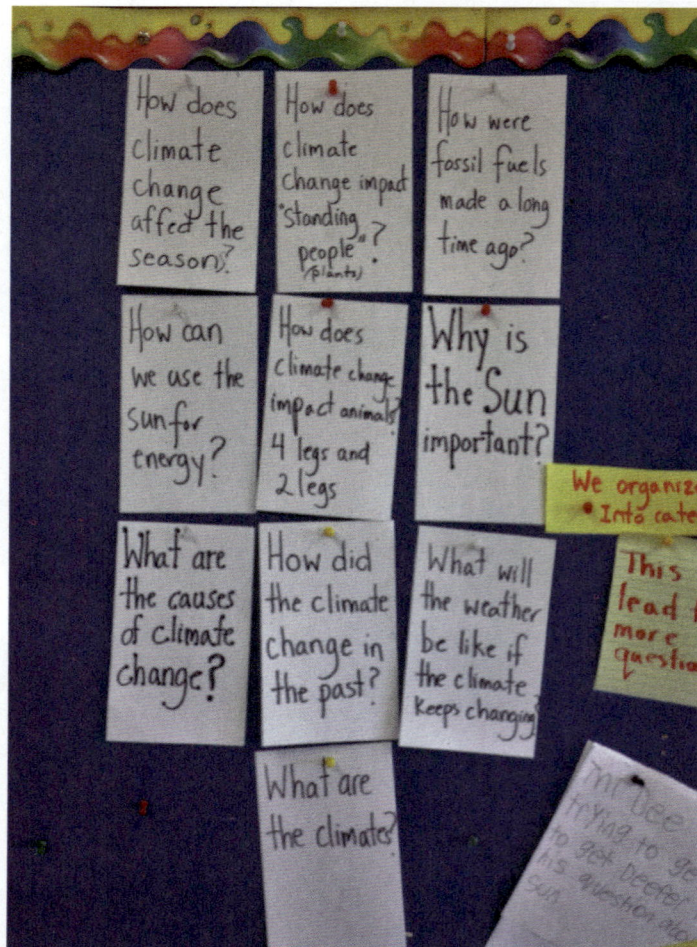
Students Organize Their Individual Questions into Larger Categories

Modelling the Reason for Seasons as the Earth Orbits the Sun

Building Knowledge as a Community

Questions started to become more refined and there was clear evidence of idea improvement. To share their findings or problems of understanding, the students would go into the Knowledge Forum database and make a post based on the notes from their journal. This new element of building knowledge online, a key design feature of inquiry-based learning, replaced the old method involving students taking notes in their binders, making a diagram, and then placing their work in their desk. It would not have been shared. The students really took to posting their ideas and some began to build on to the comments. One problem we faced was the sheer number of posts and the lack of organization. Mentioning this issue to the class, and reminding them that the database was a representation of their work, a student proposed organizing the database. We decided to print off a hard copy of each post and spread them out on the floor so that the students could read the posts and highlight important words. The posts were then organized by keywords, titles, and content. It was messy, loud, and a little chaotic but eventually they came up with the categories on their own: Causes, Seasons, Animals, Weather, Fossil Fuels, the Sun. These became the main themes of the database and represented the first step in the students' taking control of their learning.

Climate Change Knowledge Building on Knowledge Forum

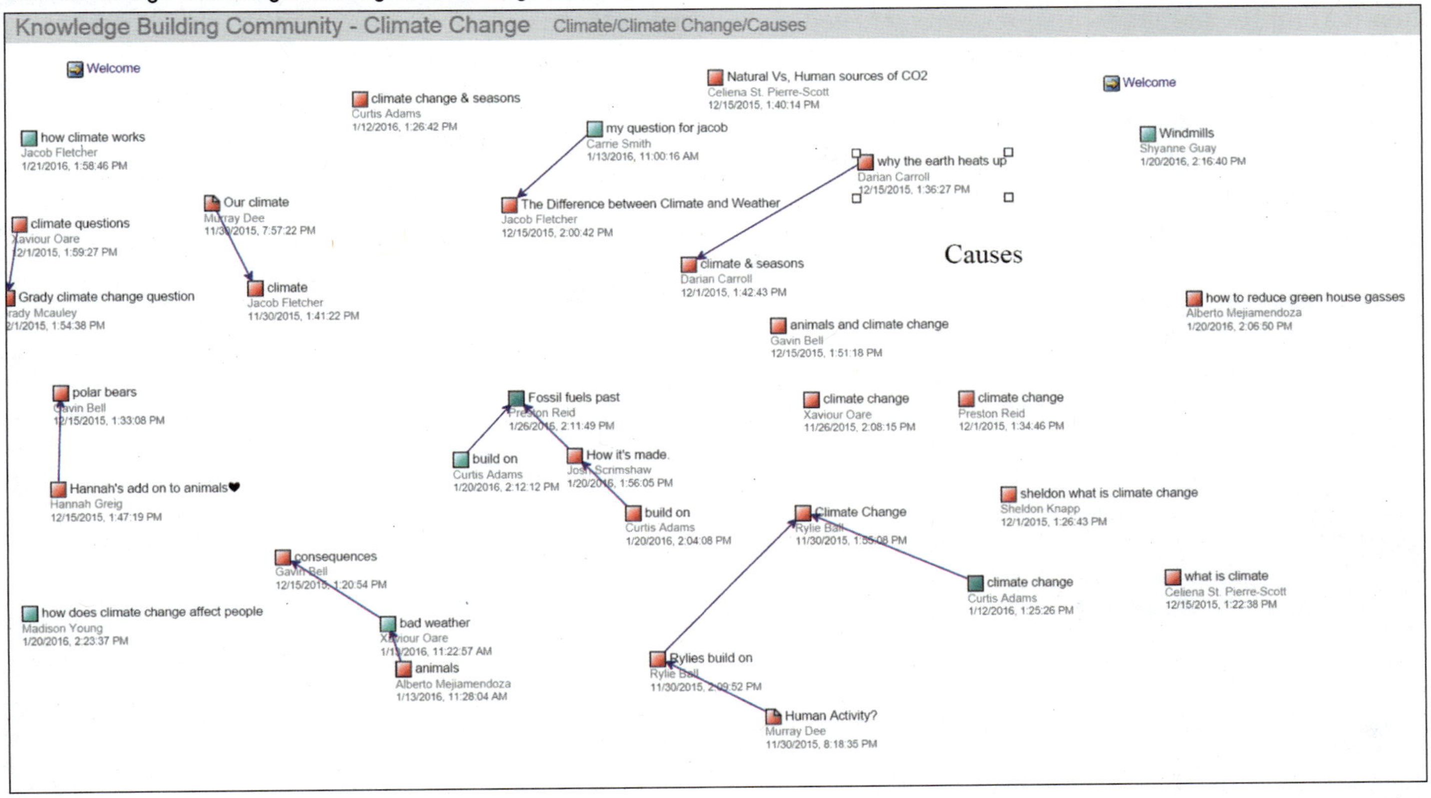

Knowledge Building Community - Climate Change — Climate/Climate Change/Causes

- Welcome
- how climate works — Jacob Fletcher, 1/21/2016, 1:58:46 PM
- climate change & seasons — Curtis Adams, 1/12/2016, 1:26:42 PM
- Natural Vs. Human sources of CO2 — Celiena St. Pierre-Scott, 12/15/2015, 1:40:14 PM
- Welcome
- climate questions — Xaviour Oare, 12/1/2015, 1:59:27 PM
- Our climate — Murray Dee, 11/30/2015, 7:57:22 PM
- my question for jacob — Carrie Smith, 1/13/2016, 11:00:16 AM
- why the earth heats up — Darian Carroll, 12/15/2015, 1:36:27 PM
- Windmills — Shyanne Guay, 1/20/2016, 2:16:40 PM
- Grady climate change question — Grady Mcauley, 2/1/2015, 1:54:38 PM
- climate — Jacob Fletcher, 11/30/2015, 1:41:22 PM
- The Difference between Climate and Weather — Jacob Fletcher, 12/15/2015, 2:00:42 PM
- climate & seasons — Darian Carroll, 12/1/2015, 1:42:43 PM
- **Causes**
- animals and climate change — Gavin Bell, 12/15/2015, 1:51:18 PM
- how to reduce green house gasses — Alberto Mejiamendoza, 1/20/2016, 2:06:50 PM
- polar bears — Gavin Bell, 12/15/2015, 1:33:08 PM
- Fossil fuels past — Preston Reid, 1/26/2016, 2:11:49 PM
- climate change — Xaviour Oare, 11/26/2015, 2:08:15 PM
- climate change — Preston Reid, 12/1/2015, 1:34:46 PM
- build on — Curtis Adams, 1/20/2016, 2:12:12 PM
- How it's made. — Josh Scrimshaw, 1/20/2016, 1:56:05 PM
- sheldon what is climate change — Sheldon Knapp, 12/1/2015, 1:26:43 PM
- Hannah's add on to animals ♥ — Hannah Greig, 12/15/2015, 1:47:19 PM
- build on — Curtis Adams, 1/20/2016, 2:04:08 PM
- Climate Change — Rylie Ball, 11/30/2015, 1:55:08 PM
- consequences — Gavin Bell, 12/15/2015, 1:20:54 PM
- climate change — Curtis Adams, 1/12/2016, 1:25:26 PM
- what is climate — Celiena St. Pierre-Scott, 12/15/2015, 1:22:38 PM
- how does climate change affect people — Madison Young, 1/20/2016, 2:23:37 PM
- bad weather — Xaviour Oare, 1/13/2016, 11:22:57 AM
- animals — Alberto Mejiamendoza, 1/13/2016, 11:28:04 AM
- Rylies build on — Rylie Ball, 11/30/2015, 2:09:52 PM
- Human Activity? — Murray Dee, 11/30/2015, 8:18:35 PM

Knowledge Forum After Students Had Organized Their Research into Larger Themes

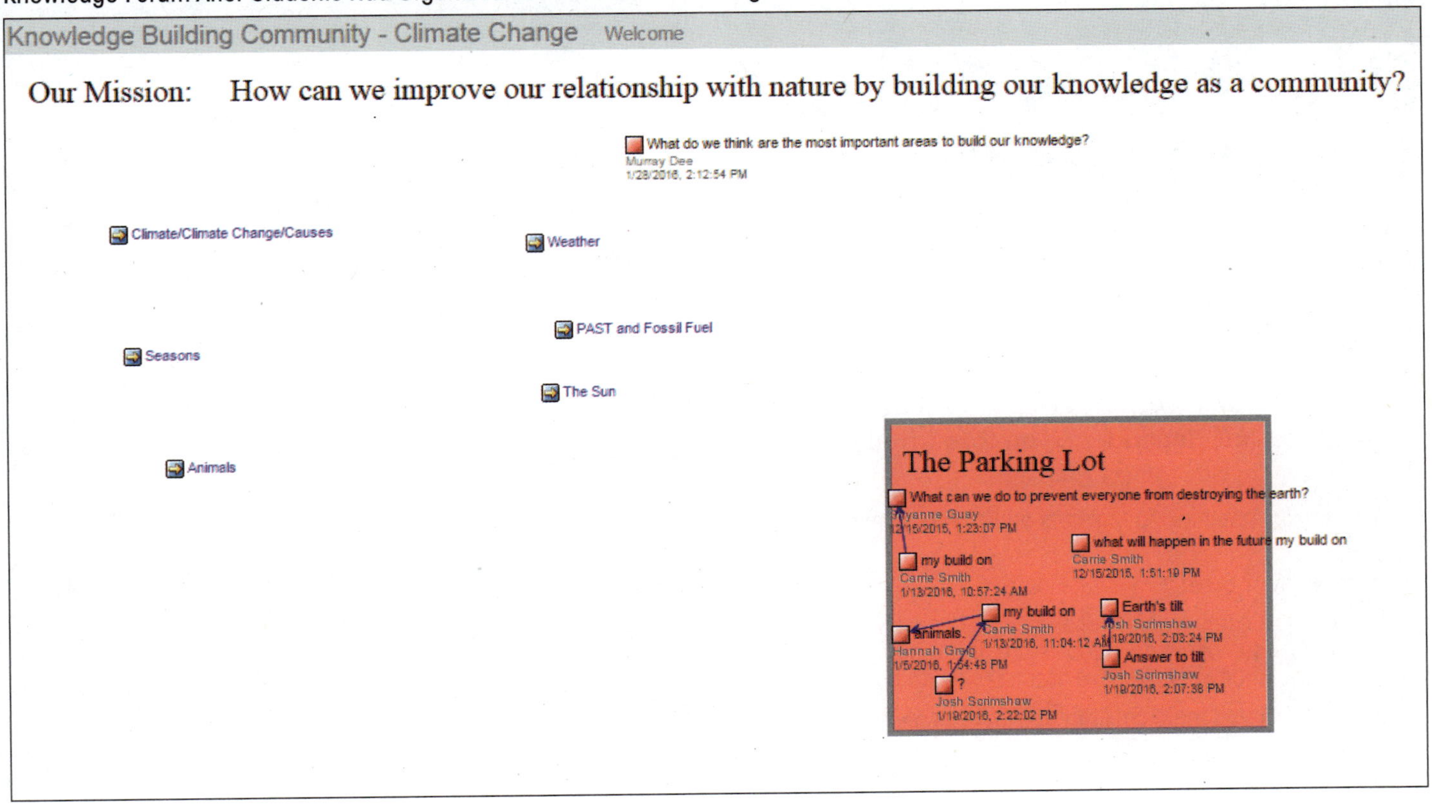

Knowledge Building Community - Climate Change — Welcome

Our Mission: How can we improve our relationship with nature by building our knowledge as a community?

- What do we think are the most important areas to build our knowledge? — Murray Dee, 1/28/2016, 2:12:54 PM
- Climate/Climate Change/Causes
- Weather
- Seasons
- PAST and Fossil Fuel
- The Sun
- Animals

The Parking Lot
- What can we do to prevent everyone from destroying the earth? — Shyanne Guay, 12/15/2015, 1:23:07 PM
- what will happen in the future my build on — Carrie Smith, 12/15/2015, 1:51:19 PM
- my build on — Carrie Smith, 1/13/2016, 10:57:24 AM
- my build on — Carrie Smith, 1/13/2016, 11:04:12 AM
- Earth's tilt — Josh Scrimshaw, 1/19/2016, 2:03:24 PM
- animals — Hannah Greig, 1/5/2016, 1:54:48 PM
- Answer to tilt — Josh Scrimshaw, 1/19/2016, 2:07:38 PM
- ? — Josh Scrimshaw, 1/19/2016, 2:22:02 PM

Murray's Story: Grade 6

While the students focused on their knowledge about climate change, a big question emerged: "Shouldn't we be trying to do something about climate change? It seems like a big deal." This prompted the creation of a new category – "Actions" – and an exciting momentum began to build in the class. I have to admit it was a bit of a struggle to not force my students to begin to look at actions right away. I now doubt that doing so would have had the same impact. By giving them time to understand the mission, letting them pursue their own areas of inquiry, the "action" part came naturally from them and it was much more impactful.

Actions to Address Climate Change

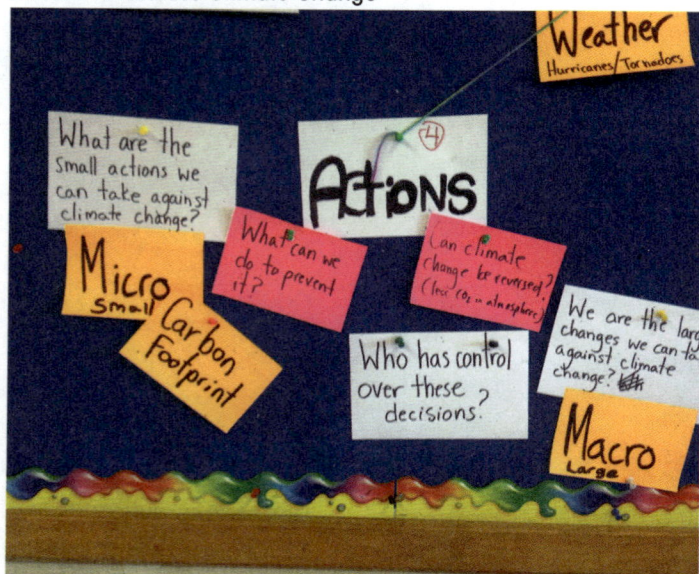

A turning point occurred during a knowledge building circle in which the students were discussing the different types of actions – micro, or small changes people could make (such as reducing our carbon footprint by turning off the lights), and macro, or large-scale changes (such as eliminating our dependence on fossil fuels).

> **Student 1:** I am thinking that cars could be both macro and micro.
> **Murray:** Why? Explain your thinking.
> **Student 1:** A car is a personal choice, so it is a small thing that one person could do. But cars are also a big problem because so many people drive them. So it's kind of both.
> **Student 2:** Aren't there cars that are just electric?
> **Murray:** Yes, but not that many. I have seen a Tesla in Kingston.
> **Student 2:** (jokingly) Do you know the owner? We should get that person to come into our class?

A student commented that the type of car a person chose to drive could be both: "It's a small, personal choice, but it could lead to a massive change if everybody switched to electric cars." Having told the students that a local resident, Rob Baker, owned an electric car, a student suggested that we ask him to bring it by the school. My instinct was to laugh about this, but thinking a bit more about it, I realized the moment represented a major shift in control for our class. The first opportunity for the students to invite a guest to our classroom would be someone who shared a common interest in climate change; someone who also wanted to take action. I really believe that this event was the moment the class moved away from being engaged to being empowered. It left the students with a sense that anything was possible.

Rob Baker, of the Tragically Hip, Visits the Class to Talk About Electric Cars

After learning more about Teslas and other electric cars, another big question arose during a frank discussion about how much of a difference we, as a class, could make.

> **Student 1:** This has been fun, but it's not going to do anything. I mean the problem is too big for us to solve. We can do lots of little things, but we have no control over the big stuff.
>
> **Student 2:** I don't get why there isn't a rule that makes everybody drive an electric car. If cars are so bad why aren't they against the law?
>
> **Student 3:** Who gets to make those big decisions? Like, who is in control of this stuff?
>
> **Student 4:** I think it's the government.
>
> **Student 2:** Why can't the government just make a law?

"Who is in charge of making BIG decisions?" That was the question that got students motivated to find out about the government. The class quickly began writing to different levels of government – our local councillor, mayor, MPP, and MP. The students seemed to understand they were writing to a very specific audience, and set the bar high for this exercise, wanting to do a really good job so that they would be taken seriously. One student felt there was no reason why they shouldn't write the prime minister. While some were doubtful, the student was supported by many others who believed that, given the importance of the issue, anything was possible. We were fortunate to have our MPP visit our classroom, who explained how decisions are made and the difficulty given the many "stakeholders" involved. At the end of our inquiry, the class received an unsolicited letter from our local MP, acknowledging the impressive work of the students, which had been shared on social media and in the local newspaper. In his letter, he promised that he would personally speak to the prime minister about the work the students were doing. This was such a validating experience for the students, who strongly believed they were tackling a "real" issue and were being taken seriously.

A Visit from Our MPP

A Letter from Our MP

In a later discussion about the different forms of alternative energy, some of the students asked about the possibility of taking a field trip to see a wind farm and a recycling plant our MPP had mentioned previously. Standing at the bottom of a wind turbine gave the students a true sense of the sheer massiveness of these objects, and they learned how the turbines operate and the process of distributing electricity. A tour of the recycling plant allowed the students to make connections to their own experiences, bringing more meaning to their inquiry. They learned that the production of a single can of coke requires the same amount of energy to operate a television for three hours, and that food waste that ends up in the landfill releases methane, a harmful greenhouse gas. We concluded our trip with a walk along our waterfront, and as the students talked of cars, buses, hybrid vehicles, solar panels, garbage and recycling, and wind farms, I realized how incredible it was to watch them making observations about their environment, which they had become so aware of during our inquiry. The highlight came at the end, when a student asked, "Did you like our field trip Mr. Dee?"

Observing a Wind Turbine Up Close

Students Visit a Recycling Plant

Exploring the Waterfront

Putting It All Together

It was very clear that our mission was not something that could be assessed by testing the students. During the process of inquiry, a wealth of information had been entered into the database, and I had recorded the details of our group discussions, observing the development of the students' thinking along the way. Rather than work toward a final product or performance, this had been about the students' thinking, and they now wanted to take their knowledge out of the classroom and share it with others. We decided to share our journey with other classes in the school by holding a Climate Expo, inviting students from grades three to eight to come to our library and become part of our community. The expo gave the students the opportunity to display the "actions" they were interested in exploring. Taking time to reflect, our class proudly reported the outcome of their expo and their learning with this inquiry with the following statements:

- The school has made a commitment to becoming an Eco School.
- We inspired other classes to explore the problem of climate change.
- Our custodian has made it a priority for the school to switch to energy efficient lights.
- We are going to try and implement "lightless" lunches, where each class turns off their lights during the lunch hour.
- We are going to monitor our waste.
- We shared our mission with thousands of people on social media.
- We inspired other teachers to try a different pedagogical approach.

Sharing Our Learning with Our School Community

The Transformative Power of Inquiry: Moving from Compliance to Engagement to Empowerment

Realizing the freedom they had during this inquiry, the students became much more engaged in the process. They eagerly sought answers to their questions, and felt free to ask more. It also became very apparent to the students that with freedom comes responsibility, and they took on this responsibility by being accountable to each other and to the inquiry process. They realized how important their mission was, and with that realization, our classroom environment changed: it looked, felt, and sounded different as we made the shift from engagement to empowerment. No longer were the students researching or working because "Mr. Dee told us to," they were doing it because they felt compelled to find answers to their questions. They knew and talked about the importance of this empowerment, and its impact on their ability to make decisions in the future. If students feel like they are in control of their lives, even at a young age, it will grow with them. I believe that a student who has a sense of empowerment will be unstoppable.

The inquiry process was also transformative for me. I could see the effects of slowing down to give students the time to dig deeper. I had become much more attentive to their thought processes, learning to embrace their misconceptions and problems of understanding as opportunities to help them develop their thinking. I learned about the importance of an authentic classroom, and I felt that I had become an educator.

Evidence of the extent of the students' work in this inquiry came months later in the form of a tree planting. I had forgotten that a student had written a letter asking a local landscaping company if they would donate a tree to the school. Much to my surprise and delight, at the beginning of the next school year, my former students approached me demanding to know when the tree was going to be planted! They remembered and they cared. The company came to deliver the tree for planting as I prepared to teach a new group of students. And on November 17th, my former students planted five more new trees on our school grounds. The trees will represent the difference a single class can make, and will provide shade, capture carbon, produce oxygen, and offer enjoyment for future students at Rideau Heights Public School for years to come.

Planting Trees at Rideau Heights

Janice's Story
Grades 5 and 6
Belfountain Public School, Peel District School Board (PDSB)

Starting the Environmental Inquiry Process

Several years ago, I was approached by representatives of the Caledon Bruce Trail Association and the Gosling Foundation; concerned about the diminishing interest of young people in hiking and the stewardship of the Bruce Trail, they had begun visiting elementary schools in the area to offer guided hikes to classes of students. They felt that getting kids outside to take part in positive hiking experiences could help them connect more meaningfully to nature and, if students were excited, engaged, and motivated by the experience, they might introduce their families to hiking on the Bruce Trail, thus becoming an integral part of the association in the future. Led by learning innovator Pamela Gibson, teachers would discover ways of integrating curriculum into the hiking experience so that getting outdoors would be valued on an ongoing basis.

The process of what would become a yearlong inquiry with my students began when two members of the Bruce Trail Association came to my Grade 5/6 classroom at Belfountain Public School to share the history of the Bruce Trail. As part of the presentation, the members described an initiative organized by hiking clubs within the association that involved motivating hikers by offering them badges upon the completion of certain sections of the trail. A defining moment for this inquiry came when one of the students asked, "Are there any badges for kids?"

I immediately jumped at the opportunity to get the students involved and have them take on leadership roles. I knew from past experiences that giving students ownership over their learning would enhance their motivation and organically give rise to numerous curriculum connections. I also knew that these students had the necessary skills, flexibility, and independence to pursue learning in this way.

We decided that a badge system could be used by the Bruce Trail Association as a new tool to attract young people to hiking. The students were excited about the possibility that the badges that they created could be used to support this initiative. Knowing that their learning had purpose and impact in their local community contributed to their motivation and dedication to the project.

We conducted a Knowledge Building Circle (KBC) and shared ideas about what sorts of badges the students themselves would be interested in earning. The KBC allowed students to listen to and build on one another's ideas respectfully, and resulted in dozens of ideas. Because of the students' understanding of the Bruce Trail Association, they realized that they needed to consider the realities of the organization: was there a reasonable number of badges that the Bruce Trail might offer that would be within their means? This led to a discussion around the value of each badge and which ones were the most reasonable and attainable for a variety of ages. In the end, we reduced the total number of badge types to 12, and the students self-selected the badge they wished to work on.

Research

"Now what?" I asked. The students decided that it was important to find out what the Bruce Trail Association's existing badges looked like, and what criteria might be required to earn each badge. The students researched current adult badges on the Bruce Trail website, as well as those of other organizations. They shared some existing knowledge of merit badges such as those used within the Boy Scout and Girl Guide clubs. Noticing that shape typically didn't matter but that size and simplicity did, the students concluded that their badges should all be similar in format and appearance, and decided that a set of three criteria seemed optimal for earning each badge. The students' next question was "How will we know if kids actually completed the criteria to get the badge?" The students had to come up with ideas for a simple system of evaluation that would provide proof that hikers had earned their badge. The system had to be easy for the Bruce Trail Association to track.

The Fun Begins

At this point, the learning became very student-directed. In groups, they applied math, art, and language skills to come up with rough copies of their badge ideas. They broadened their thinking to include science, social studies, physical education, and health criteria in the development of their badges, according to their interests. The Nature Hunter Badge needed to incorporate aspects of what students should learn about nature while on the trail. The Gar-Badge considered sustainability. Citizenship and safety on the trail was important for the Volunteer Badge. Testing their criteria, they wondered about such things as "Is it feasible for a five- or six-year-old to earn the 5km Badge on the Bruce Trail?"

It's Party Time Badge

Assessment

During this process, the students were constantly questioning and revising all aspects of their work until they were satisfied with their rough copies, using co-constructed success criteria to evaluate their final product. An important part of this self-assessment stage was the sharing of their work with peers and thoughtful consideration of the resulting comments. This, in addition to the feedback I was giving to each group, resulted in a solid plan to be presented to the Bruce Trail Association.

Learning Together on a Partner Hike

While our badge project was being developed, the Bruce Trail members set up a partner hike that we would embark upon with another school. Before the hike took place, each class set out to determine the intrinsic value of the hike in relation to how it might help meet curriculum expectations. For inspiration, we looked at a local magazine that covered outdoor activities and experiences in the Caledon area. This helped us to integrate more subject areas and develop assessment criteria for our journals.

These journals would be where students documented their learning on the hike. Knowing that their journals would be their own gave students ownership over what they experienced and widened their lens, inspiring them to be more observant and attuned to the environment while we hiked.

On the Trail

The students were excited to meet the other class. Learning outside was a regular occurrence for Belfountain students, so they made exceptional leaders and mentors for the students we were partnered with who were still developing a comfort level with exploring the outdoors. It is interesting to note that one student from the other school had remarked, "I hate bugs but it's okay because in the future, we will be able to make a virtual forest experience without the bugs." Some Belfountain students felt that this was shocking because they knew that everything is connected and removing one part of the web would have dire consequences. This kind of understanding is at the heart of environmentally conscious citizens and why these outdoor experiences are critical.

Making Observations on Our Hike

At this point, the Bruce Trail had met their initial goal of exposing the kids to hiking on the Bruce Trail in Caledon, yet the question remained whether or not this experience would connect them to the trail and draw them back there with their families.

Back at School

While reflecting on the hike, the students identified what interested them and began to create their journal page. Having the Bruce Trail Association as an attentive adult audience was exciting and motivated them to do their best work. They consulted with each other, shared ideas, researched further, and collaborated with one another, engaging in a process of deep critical analysis before attempting to define their final badges. We had a deadline to meet, which galvanized the focus of the class and infused a positive and energetic feeling into the classroom atmosphere. I was truly the "guide on the side."

The "Pitch"!

A meeting had been arranged with members of the Bruce Trail Association, at which all of the students' journal pages and badge designs would be presented. Students were given the choice to attend or be represented by other students; in the end, a few students attended on behalf of the entire class. The journal pages the students had created showed evidence of their learning and newly acquired awareness of the importance of the Bruce Trail. The badge designs were a surprise to most of the Bruce Trail members and they were very impressed with the students' initiative and maturity. They were also amazed at their ability to speak in front of a group of adults, advocating for something they believed could help with the goal of attracting more young people and families to the Caledon Bruce Trail. The evening was a great success.

In the words of a Bruce Trail executive member who attended that evening, "The students, on their own initiative, came to the meeting and very professionally presented their ideas. We thought their presentation was wonderful and what they worked on was very comprehensive. We were happy with the results and other people who have seen it are really impressed with it. We have written it up in our newsletter and have had inquiries about the badges."

A Grade 6 student expressed this perspective on the evening: "We felt nervous and a little excited to present. Once we entered the room and saw all of the people there, we were less nervous because they seemed very friendly. The presentation went very well. They thought that our idea was really great!"

The outcome was now in the hands of the Bruce Trail Association members. Back at school, we reflected on the inquiry process, and students talked about all the positive unanticipated outcomes: relationships developed with students from other schools, better understanding of alternative perspectives, graphic designing and marketing badges, successfully interacting with an organization of adults, influencing a local community organization, and the realization that they had a voice in the local community which could lead to change.

Change Takes Time

Summer came and went. The students moved on to Grades 6 and 7 and still we waited. They began to understand that things take time. The next spring, I received an email from the Bruce Trail executive, letting us know that they had chosen one of the student badges, had a company produce it, and were now offering the first ever children's badge to Caledon hikers.

Nature Hunter Badge

From the Caledon Hills Bruce Trail Club website (2017):

Criteria for earning the badge:

1. *Take a photo of 3 different types of flowers and 3 different types of trees.*
2. *Identify each of the above.*
3. *Tell us about the life cycle of one of the plants.*

Bonus: In addition to the above requirements, if you find and take a photo of a fossil on the trail, then you can receive the badge for $3.

The students were wowed! All of their work had become a reality, making it clear to them that they had made a difference. The students decided to share their success with the entire school community. They wanted to motivate other students to go hiking and earn the badge. Some students took up the challenge. They were all very proud of themselves, especially when the first student went out and earned the badge.

In the words of that first badge achiever, a Grade 3 student, "It was really fun earning the badge, especially finding the fossil. The badge is sewed on my backpack."

Closing Thoughts

I have come to recognize the value in community partnerships and how schools and classrooms can work locally to learn and collaborate on projects that fall within the mandates of the organizations and the school curriculum.

During this inquiry, we all realized that real life experiences have the potential to produce lasting learning that builds citizenship and shifts focus from the classroom to the community. Moreover, kids can make a difference if we give them the opportunity.

References

Aboriginal Education Directorate of Manitoba Education and Advanced Learning. (2014). *Smudging protocol and guidelines for school divisions.* Retrieved from http://www.edu.gov.mb.ca/aed/publications/pdf/smudging_guidelines.pdf

Aikenhead, G., & Michell, H. (2011). *Bridging cultures: Indigenous and scientific ways of knowing nature.* Toronto, Canada: Pearson Education Canada.

Alliance for Childhood. (2012). *The benefits of risk in children's play.* Retrieved from http://www.allianceforchildhood.org/node/96

Auger, D. (2006). *Mwâkwa talks to the loon.* Surrey, Canada: Heritage House.

Armstrong, J. (2013, October 1). My body is the land: An Okanagan worldview of society. *Sacred Fire Magazine, 2*(7), 32–36.

Bamberg, S., & Moser, G. (2007). Twenty years after Hines, Hungerford, and Tomera: A new meta-analysis of psycho-social determinants of pro-environmental behavior. *Journal of Environmental Psychology, 27*(1), 14–25.

Bang, M., & Medin, D. (2013). Culture in the classroom. *Phi Delta Kappan, 95*(4), 64–67.

Baylor, B., & Parnall, P. (Illustrator). (1985). *Everybody needs a rock.* New York, NY: Aladdin Paperbacks.

Bell, N., Wheatley, K., & Johnson, B. (2012). *The ways of knowing guide: Earth's teachings.* Retrieved from http://www.torontozoo.com/pdfs/tic/ways-of-knowing.pdf

Bereiter, C., & Scardamalia, M. (2012). Theory building and the pursuit of understanding in history, social studies, and literature. In J. Kirby & M. Lawson (Eds.), *Enhancing the quality of learning* (pp. 160–177). New York, NY: Cambridge University Press.

Bird Studies Canada. (2017). *Great backyard bird count.* Retrieved from http://gbbc.birdcount.org

Blatz, W. E., Bott, E. A., & Bott, H. (2010). The expanding world of the child. In R. Volpe (Ed.), *The secure child: Timeless lessons in parenting and childhood education* (pp. 115–221). Charlotte, NC: Information Age Publishing.

Bleja, D. (2015). *Breathing earth.* Retrieved from http://breathingearth.net

Blondin, G., Blondin, J., & Beaverho, A. (Illustrator). (2008). *The old man with the otter medicine.* Penticton, Canada: Theytus Books.

Botkin, N., & MacDonald, J. (Producers), Botkin, N., & Prouty, D. (Directors). (1993). *For Angela* [Motion picture]. Canada: National Film Board.

Brazee, E.N., & Capelluti, J. (1995). *Dissolving boundaries: Toward an integrative curriculum.* Columbus, OH: National Middle School Association.

Bruner, J. (1996). *The culture of education.* Cambridge, MA: Harvard University Press.

Caduto, M. J., & Bruchac, J. (1997). *Keepers of life: Discovering plants through Native American stories and Earth activities for children.* Golden, CO: Fulcrum Publishing.

Cajete, G. A. (1994). *Look to the mountain: An ecology of Indigenous education.* Durango, CO: Kivaki Press.

Cajete, G. A. (2000). *Native science: Natural laws of interdependence.* Sante Fe, NM: Clear Light Publishers.

Cajete, G.A. (2015). *Indigenous community: Rekindling the teachings of the seventh fire.* St. Paul, MN: Living Justice Press.

Caledon Hills Bruce Trail Club. (2017). *Club badges.* Retrieved from http://caledonbrucetrail.ca/hiking/club-badges/

Campbell, N. I., & Lafave, K. (Illustrator). (2005). *Shi-shi-etko.* Toronto, Canada: Groundwood Books.

Canadian Broadcasting Corporation. (2009). *Estimated distribution of tribes at time of contact.* Retrieved from http://www.cbc.ca/8thfire/map.html

Canadian Broadcasting Corporation. (2012). *8th fire: It's time* [Video file]. Retrieved from http://watch.cbc.ca/doc-zone/season-6/episode-14/38e815a-009e5b91e8

Canadian Council on Learning. (2007). *Lessons in learning: The cultural divide in science education for Aboriginal learners.* Retrieved from http://s3.amazonaws.com/static.pseupdate.mior.ca/media/links/Feb-01-07-The-cultural-divide-in-science.pdf

Canizares, S., & Chanko, P. (1997). *Who lives in the arctic?* Toronto, Canada: Scholastic.

Carle, E. (1990). *The tiny seed.* New York, NY: Simon & Schuster.

Carson, R. (1998). *The sense of wonder.* New York, NY: HarperCollins.

Caswell, B. (2017). *Raising awareness of drinking water advisories in First Nation communities.* Retrieved from https://wordpress.oise.utoronto.ca/robertson/2017/02/21/raising-awareness-to-drinking-water-advisories-in-first-nation-communities/

CBC News. (2012). *Water calculator.* Retrieved from http://www.cbc.ca/pei/features/watercalculator/index.html

Charles, C., Louv, R., Bodner, L., Guns, B., & Stahl, D. (2009). *Children and nature: A Report on the movement to reconnect children to the natural world.* Santa Fe: Children & Nature Network.

Chawla, L. (2006). Learning to love the natural world enough to protect it. *Barn, 2,* 57–78.

Chawla, L. (2007). Childhood experiences associated with care for the natural world: A theoretical framework for empirical results. *Children, Youth and Environments, 17*(4), 144–170.

Chawla, L. (2009). Growing up green: Becoming an agent of care for the natural world. *Journal of Developmental Processes, 4*(1), 6–23.

Chiarotto, L., & Dr. Eric Jackman Institute for Child Study Laboratory School. (2011). *Natural curiosity: A resource for teachers – building children's understanding of the world through environmental inquiry.* Oshawa, Canada: Maracle Press Ltd.

City of Toronto. (2016). *Trees, shrubs, & vines of Toronto.* Retrieved from https://www1.toronto.ca/City%20Of%20Toronto/City%20Planning/Environment/Files/pdf/B/Trees,%20Shrubs%20&%20Vines%20of%20Toronto.pdf

City of Toronto. (2017). *Parks & trails: A city within a park.* Retrieved from https://www1.toronto.ca/wps/portal/contentonly?vgnextoid=5c98dada600f0410VgnVCM10000071d60f89RCRD

Climate Outreach. (2004). *Climate visuals.* Retrieved from http://climateoutreach.org/climatevisuals/

Cole, A. G. (2007). Expanding the field: Revisiting environmental education principles through multidisciplinary frameworks. *The Journal of Environmental Education, 38*(2), 35–44.

Conroy, E., Wheatley, K., & Johnson, B. (2010). *Walking with miskwaadesi.* Retrieved from http://www.torontozoo.com/pdfs/tic/Walking_with_Miskwaadesi_full.pdf

Csikszentmihalyi, M. (1975). *Beyond boredom and anxiety: Experiencing flow in work and play.* San Francisco, CA: Jossey-Bass.

Curtis, D., & Carter, M. (2008). *Learning together with young children: A curriculum framework for reflective teachers.* St Paul, MN: Redleaf Press.

David, L., Lawrence, B., Burns, S. Z. (Producers), & Guggenheim, D. (Director). (2006). *An inconvenient truth* [Motion picture]. United States: Paramount Pictures Corporation.

Derman-Sparks, L., & Edwards, J. O. (2010). *Anti-bias education for young children and ourselves.* Washington, DC: National Association for the Education of Young Children.

Dewey, J. (1915). *The school and society.* Chicago, IL: The University of Chicago Press.

Dewey, J. (1938). *Experience and education.* New York, NY: Kappa Delta Pi.

DiCaprio, L., Peterson, L. C., Castleberry, C., Gerber, B. (Producers), Conners, N., & Petersen, L. C. (Directors). (2007). *The 11th hour* [Motion picture]. United States: Warner Independent Pictures.

Drake, S., & Reid, J. (2010, September). Integrated curriculum: Increasing relevance while maintaining accountability. *What Works?: Research into Practice.* Retrieved from http://www.edu.gov.on.ca/eng/literacynumeracy/inspire/research/WW_Integrated_Curriculum.pdf

Earl, L. M. (2004). Classroom assessment for deep understanding. In K. Leithwood, P. McAdie, N. Bascia, & A. Rodrigue (Eds.), *Teaching for deep understanding: Towards the Ontario curriculum that we need* (pp. 94–99). Toronto, Canada: Elementary Teachers' Federation of Ontario (ETFO) and the Ontario Institute for Studies in Education of the University of Toronto (OISE/UT).

Etna Elementary School. [SmithsFifths]. (2014, December 9). *Real world science: Ecosystems and biomes* [Video file]. Retrieved from https://www.schooltube.com/video/781e7f93115d474785d8/Real%20World%20Science:%20Ecosystems%20and%20Biomes

Expeditionary Learning. (2012). *Austin's butterfly: Building excellence in student work* [Video file]. Retrieved from https://vimeo.com/38247060

Engel, S. (2015). *The hungry mind: The origins of curiosity in childhood.* Cambridge, MA: Harvard University Press.

Erdrich, L. (2016, December 22). Holy rage: Lessons from Standing Rock. *The New Yorker.* Retrieved from http://www.newyorker.com/news/news-desk/holy-rage-lessons-from-standing-rock

Finger, M. (1993). Politics of the UNCED process. In W. Sachs (Ed.), *Global Ecology: A New Arena of Political Conflict* (pp. 36–48). London, United Kingdom: Zed Books.

Fogarty, R. (1991). Ten ways to integrate curriculum. *Educational Leadership, 49*(2), 61–65.

Fostaty-Young, S., & Wilson, R. J. (2000). *Assessment and learning: The ICE approach.* Winnipeg, Canada: Portage & Main Press.

Galanaki E. (2005). Solitude in the school: A neglected facet of children's development and education. *Childhood Education, 81*(3), 128–132.

Galanaki, E. (2004). Teachers and loneliness: The children's perspective. *School Psychology International, 25*(1), 92–105.

Ganeri, A. (2006). *From seed to apple.* Chicago, IL: Heinemann Educational Books.

Gardner, H. (1991). *The unschooled mind: How children think and how schools should teach.* New York, NY: Basic Books.

Garnett, J. I. (2005). *Newgrange speaks for itself: Forty carved motifs.* Victoria, Canada: Trafford Publishing.

Ghafouri, F. (2014). Close encounters with nature in an urban kindergarten: A study of learners' inquiry and experience. *Education 3–13: International Journal of Primary, Elementary and Early Years Education, 42*(1), 54–76.

Gelman, R., & Lucariello, J. (2002). Role of learning in cognitive development. In H. Pashler (Series Ed.) & C. R. Gallistel (Vol. Ed.), *Stevens' handbook of experimental psychology: Vol. 3. learning, motivation, and emotion* (3rd ed., pp. 395–443). New York, NY: Wiley.

Geniusz, W.M. (2009). *Our knowledge is not primitive: decolonizing botanical Anishinaabe teachings.* Syracuse, NY: Syracuse University Press.

Global Alliance for the Rights of Nature. (2017). *Learn about rights of nature.* Retrieved from http://therightsofnature.org

Goulais, B., & Curry, D. (2005). *Debwewin: Three-city anti racism initiative.* Retrieved from: http://www.debwewin.ca/intro.htm

Grant, J. (2015, June 7). Coming to grips with a shameful past. *Teaching Kids News.* Retrieved from http://teachingkidsnews.com/2015/06/07/coming-to-grips-with-a-shameful-past/

Green Thumbs. (2017). [Home page]. Retrieved from http://greenthumbsto.org

Gruenewald, D. A. (2003). The best of both worlds: A critical pedagogy of place. *Educational Researcher, 32*(4), 3–12.

Halewood, C. (2014). *Twenty minute field trips.* Retrieved from http://www.naturalcuriosity.ca/pdf/Twenty_Minute_Field_Trips.pdf

Hampton, E. (1993). Toward a redefinition of American Indian/Alaska Native Education. *Canadian Journal of Native Education, 20*(2), 261–310.

Hayes, B.K., Goodhew, A., Heit, E., & Gillan, J. (2003). The role of diverse instruction in conceptual change. *Journal of Experimental Child Psychology, 86*(4), 253–276.

Hidi, S. (1990). Interest and its contribution as a mental resource for learning. *Review of Educational Research, 60*(4), 549–571.

Hungerford, H.R., & Volk, T.L. (1990). Changing learner behavior through environmental education. *The Journal of Environmental Education, 21*(3), 8–21.

Ignas, V. (2004). Opening doors to the future: Applying local knowledge in curriculum development. *Canadian Journal of Native Education, 28*(1/2), 49–60.

Invert Media. (2012). *Four directions teachings.* Retrieved from http://www.fourdirectionsteachings.com

Jensen, D. (2002, March). Thinking outside the classroom: An interview with Zenobia Barlow. *The Sun.* Retrieved from https://www.thesunmagazine.org/issues/315/thinking-outside-the-classroom

Kagan, J. (2002). Childhood predictors of states of anxiety. *Dialogues in clinical neuroscience, 4*(3), 287–293.

Kairos Canada. (2017). *What is the blanket exercise?* Retrieved from https://www.kairosblanketexercise.org/

Katz, J. T., & Khoshbin, S. (2014). Can visual arts training improve physician performance? *Transactions of the American Clinical and Climatological Association, 125*, 331–342.

Kids Do Ecology. (2004). *Biomes.* Retrieved from http://kids.nceas.ucsb.edu/biomes/

Kellert, S. (2009). Reflections on children's experience of nature. *Children and Nature Network Leadership Writing Series, 1*(2). Retrieved from https://www.childrenandnature.org/wp-content/uploads/2015/04/LWS_Vol1_02.pdf

Kolb, D. (1984). *Experiential learning: Experience as a source of learning and development.* Upper Saddle River, NJ: Prentice Hall.

Kostecki-Shaw, J. S. (2011). *Same, same but different.* New York, NY: Henry Holt and Co.

Kozak, S., & Elliot, S. (2014). *Connecting the dots: Key strategies that transform learning for environmental education, citizenship and sustainability.* D. Israelson (Ed.). Oshawa, Canada: Maracle Press.

Kuhn, D., Cheney, R., & Weinstock, M. (2000). The development of epistemological understanding. *Cognitive Development, 15*(3), 309–328.

Kuhn, D. (2010). Teaching and learning science as argument. *Science Education, 94*(5), 810–824.

Latta, S. L. (2006). *What happens in winter?* Berkeley Heights, NJ: Enslow Publishers.

LesPlan Educational Services. (2013, December). What's in a name? *The Canadian Reader, 4*. Victoria, Canada: Author.

Long, C. R., Seburn, M., Averill, J. R., & More, T. A. (2003). Solitude experiences: Varieties, settings, and individual differences. *Personality and Social Bulletin, 29*(5), 578–583.

Louv, R. (2007). *Last child in the woods: Saving our children from nature-deficit disorder.* Chapel Hill, NC: Algonquin Books of Chapel Hill.

Lucariello, J., & Naff, D. (n.d.). *How do I get my students over their alternative conceptions (misconceptions) for learning? Removing barriers to aid in the development of the student.* Retrieved from: http://www.apa.org/education/k12/misconceptions.aspx

MacKenzie, J. (2009). *Nelson literacy 3.* Toronto, Canada: Nelson Education.

Macy, J. (1995). Working through environmental despair. In T. Roszak, M. E. Gomes, & A. D. Kanner (Eds.), *Ecopsychology: Restoring the earth, healing the mind* (pp. 240–259). San Francisco, CA: Sierra Club Books.

Malone, K. (2016). Reconsidering children's encounters with nature and place using posthumanism. *Australian Journal of Environmental Education, 32*(1), 42–56.

Matthews, J. R. (1992). Adult amateur experiences in entomology. In J. Adams (Ed.), *Insect potpourri: Adventures in entomology* (pp. 321–328). Gainesville, FL: Sandhill Crane Press.

McGregor, D. (2014). Lessons for collaboration involving traditional knowledge and environmental governance in Ontario, Canada. *AlterNative: An International Journal of Indigenous Peoples, 10*(4), 340–353.

Martin, H. [HopiMartin]. (2013a, April 14). *A kindergarten tribute to Andy Goldsworthy* [Video file]. Retrieved from https://www.youtube.com/watch?v=UIT5nWmTh-s

Martin, H. [HopiMartin]. (2013b, April 27). *A kindergarten tribute to Andy Goldsworthy part 2* [Video file]. Retrieved from https://www.youtube.com/watch?v=kw0UG_VRUPM

Messina, R. (2001, April 12). *Intentional learners, cooperative knowledge building, and classroom inventions*. Paper Presented at the
Annual Meeting of the American Educational Research Association, Seattle, WA.

Metallic, J., & Seiler, G. (2009). Animating Indigenous knowledges in science education. *Canadian Journal of Native Education*, *32*(1), 115–128.

Meyer, M. (2013). Holographic epistemology: Native common sense. *China Media Research, 9*(2), 94–101.

Mojang AB. (2009). *Minecraft* [Computer software]. Retrieved from https://minecraft.net

Morgan, H. (2009). Picture book biographies for young children: A way to teach multiple perspectives. *Early Childhood Education Journal, 37*(3), 219–227.

National Association for the Education of Young Children. (n.d.). *The four core goals of anti-bias education*. Retrieved from https://www.naeyc.org/content/four-core-goals-anti-bias-education

Nazir, J., & Pedretti, E. (2016). Educators' perceptions of bringing students to environmental consciousness through engaging outdoor experiences. *Environmental Education Research, 22*(2), 288–304.

Oatley, K. (2011). *Such stuff as dreams: The psychology of fiction*. Malden, MA: Wiley-Blackwell.

Ogu, U., & Schmidt, S. (2009). Investigating rocks and sand: Addressing multiple learning styles through an inquiry-based approach. *YC Young Children, 64*(2), 12–18.

Ontario Federation of Anglers and Hunters. (2017). [Home page]. Retrieved from https://www.ofah.org

Ontario Literacy and Numeracy Secretariat. (2010, September). Integrated learning in the classroom. *Capacity Building Series*. Retrieved from http://www.edu.gov.on.ca/eng/literacynumeracy/inspire/research/CBS_integrated_learning.pdf

Ontario Mining Association. (2012). [Home page]. Retrieved from http://www.oma.on.ca

Ontario Ministry of Education. (2005a). *Many roots many voices: Supporting English language learners in every classroom – A practical guide for Ontario educators*. Retrieved from http://www.edu.gov.on.ca/eng/document/manyroots/manyroots.pdf

Ontario Ministry of Education. (2005b). *The Ontario curriculum grades 1–8: Mathematics*. Retrieved from http://www.edu.gov.on.ca/eng/curriculum/elementary/math18curr.pdf

Ontario Ministry of Education. (2007). *The Ontario curriculum grades 1–8: Science and technology*. Retrieved from http://www.edu.gov.on.ca/eng/curriculum/elementary/scientec18currb.pdf

Ontario Ministry of Education. (2009). *Acting today, shaping tomorrow: A policy framework for environmental education in Ontario schools*. Retrieved from http://www.edu.gov.on.ca/curriculumcouncil/ShapeTomorrow.pdf

Ontario Ministry of Education (2010). *Growing success: Assessment, evaluations and reporting in Ontario schools*. Retrieved from http://www.edu.gov.on.ca/eng/policyfunding/growSuccess.pdf

Ontario Ministry of Education. (2013). *The Ontario curriculum social studies grades 1–6; History and geography grades 7–8*. Retrieved from http://www.edu.gov.on.ca/eng/curriculum/elementary/sshg18curr2013.pdf

Ontario Ministry of Education. (Winter 2016 - Draft for Consultation). *Community-Connected Experiential Learning: A Policy Framework for Ontario Schools, Kindergarten to Grade 12*. Retrieved from http://www.edu.gov.on.ca/eng/general/elemsec/job/passport/CommunityConnected_ExperientialLearningEng.pdf

Ontario Ministry of Education. (2016). *The kindergarten program*. Retrieved from http://www.edu.gov.on.ca/eng/curriculum/elementary/kindergarten.html

Orr, D. W. (2004). *Earth in mind: On education, environment, and the human prospect*. Washington, DC: Island Press.

Paradise, R., & Rogoff, B. (2009). Side by side: Learning by observing and pitching in. *Journal of the Society for Psychological Anthropology, 37*(1), 102–138.

Partnership of 21st Century Learning. (n.d.). [Home page]. Retrieved from http://www.p21.org

Pine, K., Messer, D., & St. John, K.(2001). Children's misconceptions in primary science: A survey of teachers' views. *Research in Science & Technological Education, 19*(1), 79–96.

Pyle, R. (2002). Eden in a vacant lot: Special places, species and kids in community of life. In P. H. Kahn & S. R. Kellert (Eds.), *Children and nature: Psychological, sociocultural and evolutionary investigations* (pp. 305–327). Cambridge, MA: MIT Press.

Richards, J., & Hariton, A. (Illustrator). (2002). *A fruit is a suitcase for seeds*. Minneapolis, MN: Millbrook Press.

The Robertson Program. (2016). *Liz Osawamick shares her water song with the Robertson program*. Retrieved from https://wordpress.oise.utoronto.ca/robertson/2016/05/06/liz-osamawick-shares-her-water-song-with-the-robertson-program

The Robertson Program for Inquiry-Based Teaching in Mathematics and Science. (2017). [Home page]. Retrieved from http://www.therobertsonprogram.com

Rogoff, B., Paradise, R., Mejía Arauz, R., Correa-Chávez, M., & Angelillo, C. (2003). Firsthand learning through intent participation. *Annual Review of Psychology, 54,* 175–203.

Root, P., & Krommes, B. (Illustrator). (2004). *Grandmother winter*. New York, NY: Houghton Mifflin Harcourt.

Ryder, J., & Gorbaty, N. (Illustrator). (1996). *Earthdance*. New York, NY: Henry Holt & Co.

Scardamalia, M. (2000). Can schools enter a knowledge society? In M. Selinger & J. Wynn (Eds.), *Educational technology and the impact on teaching and learning* (pp. 5–10). Abingdon, United Kingdom: Research Machines.

Scardamalia, M. (2002). Collective cognitive responsibility for the advancement of knowledge. In B. Smith (Ed.), *Liberal Education in a Knowledge Society* (pp. 67–98). Chicago, IL: Open Court.

Shapiro, J., Rucker, L., & Beck, J. (2006). Training the clinical eye and mind: using the arts to develop medical students' observational and pattern recognition skills. *Medical Education, 40*(3), 263–268.

Sidman, J., & Zagarenski, P. (Illustrator). (2009). *Red sings from treetops: A year in colors*. New York, NY: Houghton Mifflin Harcourt.

Silvey, D., & Mantha, J. (Illustrator). (2005). *The kids book of Aboriginal Peoples in Canada.* Toronto, Canada: Kids Can Press.

Simard, S. (2016). Notes from a forest scientist. In *The hidden life of trees: What they feel, how they communicate* (pp. 247–250). Vancouver, Canada: Greystone Books.

Simard, S.W., Perry, D.A., Jones, M.D., Myrold, D.M., Durall, D.M., & Molina, R. (1997). Net transfer of carbon between tree species with shared ectomycorrhizal fungi. *Nature 388*(6642), 579–82.

Simpson, L. B. (2011). *Dancing on our turtle's back: Stories of Nishnaabeg re-creation, resurgence and a new emergence.* Winnipeg, Canada: Arbeiter Ring Publishing.

Simpson, L. B. (2014). Land as pedagogy: Nishnaabeg intelligence and rebellious transformation. *Decolonization: Indigeneity, Education and Society, 3*(3), 1–25.

Sobel, D. (1998, November 2). Beyond echophobia. *Yes! Magazine.* Retrieved from http://www.yesmagazine.org/issues/education-for-life/803

Sobel, D. (2008). *Childhood and nature: Design principles for educators.* Portland, ME: Stenhouse Publishers.

Sobel, D. (2013). *Beyond ecophobia: Reclaiming the heart in nature education.* Great Barrington, MA: Orion Society.

Solomon, A. (1990). *Songs for the people: Teaching on the natural way.* M. Posluns (Ed.). Toronto, Canada: NC Press.

Solomon, L. (2008). *The deniers.* Minneapolis, MN: Richard Vigilante Books.

Strife, S. (2010). Reflecting on environmental education: Where is our place in the green movement? *The Journal of Environmental Education, 41*(3), 179–191.

Suzuki, D. (2008). *David Suzuki's green guide.* D. R. Boyd (Ed.). Vancouver, Canada: Greystone Books.

Suzuki, D. (2016, January 21). Environmental rights are human rights [Blog post]. Retrieved from http://www.davidsuzuki.org/blogs/science-matters/2016/01/my-grandparents-came-here-from/

Tanner, T. (1980). Significant life experiences: A new research area in environmental education. *Journal of Environmental Education, 11*(4), 20–24.

TeachEngineering. (n.d.). *Teach engineering: Curriculum for k–12 educators.* Retrieved from https://www.teachengineering.org

Teckentrup, B. (2014). *The memory tree.* London, United Kingdom: Orchard Books.

Thomson, G., & Hoffman, J. (2004). *Measuring the success of environmental education programs.* Ottawa, Canada: Canadian Parks and Wilderness Society and Sierra Club of Canada, BC Chapter.

Thornhill, J., & Bisaillon, J. (Illustrator). (2014). *Winter's coming: A story of seasonal change.* Toronto, Canada: Owlkids.

Thornton, L., & Brunton, P. (2015). *Understanding the Reggio approach: Early years education in practice* (3rd ed.). London, United Kingdom: Routledge, Taylor & Francis Group.

Tierney, J. (2011, July 18). Can a playground be too safe? *The New York Times.* Retrieved from http://www.nytimes.com/2011/07/19/science/19tierney.html

Tizard, B., & Hughes, M. (1984). *Young children learning.* Cambridge, MA: Harvard University Press.

Toronto District School Board. (2016). *Treaty acknowledgement.* Retrieved from http://www.tdsb.on.ca/Community/AboriginalEducation/Resources.aspx

Truth and Reconciliation Commission of Canada. (2015). *Honouring the truth, reconciling for the future: Summary of the final report of the Truth and Reconciliation Commission of Canada.* Winnipeg, Canada: Author.

Tuck, E., & Yang, K.W. (2012). Decolonization is not a metaphor. *Decolonization: Indigeneity, Education & Society, 1*(1), 1–40.

UK Metric Association. (n.d.) *Volume.* Retrieved from http://thinkmetric.org.uk/volume.html

United Nations Educational, Scientific, and Cultural Organization. (2010). *Understanding sustainable development.* Retrieved from http://www.unesco.org/education/tlsf/mods/theme_a/mod02.html?panel=2#top

United Nations Educational, Scientific, and Cultural Organization. (2017). *Education for sustainable development: Learning objectives.* Retrieved from http://unesdoc.unesco.org/images/0024/002474/247444e.pdf

University of Colorado Boulder. (2004). *Hands-on activity: Biodomes engineering design project.* Retrieved from https://www.teachengineering.org/activities/view/cub_bio_lesson02_activity1

University of Toronto. (2016). *Statement of acknowledgement of traditional land.* Retrieved from https://memos.provost.utoronto.ca/statement-of-acknowledgement-of-traditional-land-pdadc-72/

Valberg, M. (2012). *Ben and Nuki discover polar bears.* Ottawa, Canada: MV Photo Productions.

Waters, J., & Maynard, T. (2010). What's so interesting outside? A study of child-initiated interaction with teachers in the natural outdoor environment. *European Early Childhood Education Research Journal, 18*(4), 473–483.

Watetch, A. (2007). *Payepot and his people.* Regina, Canada: Canadian Plains Research Centre, University of Regina.

Wellman, H. (1990). *The child's theory of mind.* Cambridge, MA: MIT Press.

Wells, N. M., & Lekies, K. S. (2006). Nature and the life course: Pathways from childhood nature experiences to adult environmentalism. *Children, Youth and Environments, 16*(1), 1–24.

Wemigwans, J. (2016). *A digital bundle: Exploring the impact of Indigenous knowledge online through fourdirectionsteachings.com* (Doctoral dissertation). Retrieved from ProQuest Dissertations and Theses database. (UMI No. 10140876)

West Tisbury School. (2010). *World biomes.* Retrieved from http://www.blueplanetbiomes.org/world_biomes.htm

Western New South Wales Regional Aboriginal Education Team. (2014). *8 ways: Aboriginal pedagogy from Western New South Wales.* Dubbo, Australia: New South Wales Department of Education and Communities.

Wilson, E. O. (1984). *Biophilia: The human bond with other species.* Cambridge, MA: Harvard University Press.

Winship, M. (2016, February 3). Naomi Klein: Climate change "not just about things getting hotter… it's about things getting meaner". *Moyers & Company.* Retrieved from http://billmoyers.com/story/naomiklein-climate-change-not-just-about-things-getting-hotter-its-about-things-getting-meaner/

Whitecloud, T. B. (2015, September 21). FAQ on being an Indigenous ally. *Red Rising Magazine.* Retrieved from http://redrisingmagazine.ca/faq-on-being-an-indigenous-ally

Whyte, K.P., Brewer, J.P., & Johnson, J.T. (2016). Weaving Indigenous science, protocols, and sustainability science. *Sustainability Science, 11*(1), 25–32.

Wohllenben, P. (2016). *The hidden life of trees: What they feel, how they communicate.* Vancouver, Canada: Greystone Books.

Worth, K. (2001). The power of children's thinking. In *Foundations, A monograph for professionals in science, mathematics, and technology education* (Vol. 2, pp. 25–32). Washington, DC: National Science Foundation.

World Commission on Environment and Development. (1987). *Report of the world commission on environment and development: Our common future.* Oxford, United Kingdom: Oxford University Press.

Yokota, J., & Kolar, J. (2008). Advocating for peace and social justice through children's literature. *Social Studies and the Young Learner, 20*(3), 22–26.

Young, J., Haas, E., & McGown, E. (2010). *Coyote's guide to connecting with nature.* Santa Cruz, CA: OWLink Media.

Zhang, J. (2017). *Connecting idea threads across innovative classrooms (CITIC): A NSF cyberlearning DIP Project (2014–2018).* Retrieved from http://tccl.rit.albany.edu/wpsite/?page_id=694

Zilio, M., & Stueck, W. (2017, September 20). Trudeau addresses Canada's relationship with Indigenous peoples in UN speech. *The Globe and Mail.* Retrieved from https://beta.theglobeandmail.com/news/politics/trudeau-to-use-un-speech-to-recognize-canadas-relationship-with-indigenous-peoples/article36338926/?ref=http://www.theglobeandmail.com&

Zinn, H. (2002). *You can't be neutral on a moving train: A personal history of our times.* Boston, MA: Beacon Press.

The Authors

Doug Anderson is Métis (Bungee). His family is originally from Reedy Creek and Kinesota, Manitoba, and BC, and he grew up in Ontario. He has been the Creative and Strategic Director at Invert Media since 2003 and has consulted on Indigenous education and program development across Canada for over 25 years. Since 2001, he has been devoted to research and writing on Indigenous histories and cultures, translating them to contemporary education systems and media. Since 2010, his focus has been on learning in the land, mostly in the city. He enjoys designing new ethical platforms for Indigenous knowledge, and is committed to supporting the preservation of these forms of knowledge as models for thinking and problem solving in the 21st century. Doug worked at both the government and community levels for many years in the development, delivery and evaluation of learning programs, and has many years of front line experience in building learning and training opportunities for community members of all ages and levels of learning.

Julie Comay was a classroom teacher at the Lab School and in Toronto public schools for over 20 years and currently works with graduate education students at the Dr. Eric Jackman Institute for Child Study. In 2009, she received a PhD from OISE/UT for research focused on the growth of narrative skill and social understanding in young children. As a researcher and practitioner with a strong interest in children's play, Julie has collaborated with teachers, academic researchers, and community members to design and implement engaging literacy and math programs in Ontario elementary schools. The opportunity to work in First Nation communities in northwest Ontario with the Robertson Program for Inquiry-Based Teaching in Mathematics and Science kindled her interest in Indigenous education. She is honoured to participate in writing this new edition of *Natural Curiosity*.

Lorraine Chiarotto is an Ontario Certified Teacher, lover of nature, and author of the first edition of *Natural Curiosity* (2011). Lorraine earned her MA in Child Study and Education at the Institute of Child Study where she discovered and fell in love with inquiry-based learning. From there, she began her career as a member of the teaching staff at the Dr. Eric Jackman Institute of Child Study Laboratory School (JICS). Lorraine was appointed with the task of creating *Natural Curiosity* by researching, documenting, and sharing the Lab School's environmental inquiry approach with all educators. Lorraine currently teaches at Centennial Infant and Child Centre, a preschool for children with special needs. A proud young mother, her favourite pastime is spending entire days outdoors with her two little boys … enjoying nature.

Notes

Notes

Notes

Notes